D1448633

BLOODY BULLECOURT

BLOODY BULLECOURT

DAVID COOMBES

Pen & Sword
MILITARY

First published in Australia as *A Greater Sum of Sorrow: The Battles of Bullecourt*,
in 2016 by Big Sky Publishing Pty Ltd
PO Box 303, Newport, NSW 2106, Australia

Reprinted in hardback format in 2017 in Great Britain by
Pen & Sword MILITARY
An imprint of
Pen & Sword Books Ltd
47 Church Street, Barnsley
South Yorkshire
S70 2AS

ISBN 978 1 52671 343 8

The right of David Coombes to be identified as Author
of this work has been asserted by him in accordance with
the Copyright, Designs and Patents Act 1988.

A CIP catalogue record for this book is
available from the British Library

Printed and bound in England
by TJ International Ltd, Padstow, PL28 8RW

Pen & Sword Books Ltd incorporates the Imprints of Pen & Sword Aviation,
Pen & Sword Family History, Pen & Sword Maritime, Pen & Sword Military,
Pen & Sword Discovery, Pen & Sword Politics, Pen & Sword Atlas,
Pen & Sword Archaeology, Wharncliffe Local History, Leo Cooper,
Wharncliffe True Crime, Wharncliffe Transport, Pen & Sword Select,
Pen & Sword Military Classics, The Praetorian Press, Claymore Press,
Remember When, Seaforth Publishing and Frontline Publishing

For a complete list of Pen & Sword titles please contact
PEN & SWORD BOOKS LIMITED
47 Church Street, Barnsley, South Yorkshire, S70 2AS, England
E-mail: enquiries@pen-and-sword.co.uk
Website: www.pen-and-sword.co.uk

Bullecourt represents for Australians a greater sum of sorrow and honour than any other place in the world.

Sergeant Walter Downing
57th Battalion AIF

For dear Tally who offered me the greatest encouragement of all: unconditional love.

Legend of symbols used in This Book

▬ ▬ ▬ ▬ ▬	Australian Front Line
▬ ▬ ▬ ▬	Final/Intended Objectives Line
─·─·─·─·─	Division Boundary Lines
··············	Artillery Protection Lines
⌐⌐⌐⌐⌐	Trenches
✕─✕─	Barbed Wire
～～～	Rivers
冊冊	Cuttings/Sunken Roads
➤	Australian Attacks/Counterattacks
➤	German Attacks/Counterattacks
➤	British Attacks/Counterattacks

	Urban Areas
↙	Machine Gun
⚡	Tanks
⤢	Batteries
♪	Battalion Headquarters
⸮	Brigade Headquarters
⌐	Pits intended for Concrete Dugouts
═══	Roads/Tracks
┼┼┼┼┼	Railways/Trams
├ + ─┤─	Dismantled Railways/Trams
⊞⊞⊞⊞	Raised Railways

CONTENTS

ACKNOWLEDGEMENTS

I offer my foremost appreciation to the Australian Army History Unit — particularly Dr Roger Lee and Dr Andrew Richardson — for helping to fund this project in Australia, the United Kingdom and France and also for offering valuable advice. My special thanks to Andrew for the way he coped with my continual requests and, in particular, for providing the additional maps and photographs I requested.

I would also like to thank Catherine McCulloch, designer at the Defence Publishing Service, for her meticulous drawing of the image of the Mark I tank, Number 586.

My grateful thanks to the staff at the Australian War Memorial in Canberra, in particular the historical section and the research centre, for extending their typically valuable service, for always being willing to help and answer any question — even the most mundane — and for their first-rate counsel. My gratitude extends also to the staff at the Imperial War Museum, London, the National Library of Scotland, Edinburgh, the National Archives, London and the Liddell Hart Centre for Military History, Kings College London. In Australia, I would like to thank the staff at the J.S. Battye Library of West Australian History, Perth and the Mitchell Library in Sydney. I am also indebted to the School of Humanities, University of Tasmania, for allowing me access to the Chalk collection. These valuable sources provided crucial assistance, particularly in relation to the First Battle of Bullecourt. My thanks also to the Army Museum of Western Australia for permission to use the portrait of Lieutenant General Sir Joseph Talbot Hobbs.

I would like to thank the academic and administrative staff at the School of Historical and Philosophical Inquiry at the University of Queensland (where I am an Honorary Research Fellow), particularly

Associate Professor Martin Crotty and Ms Lucy O'Brien, for their kind assistance.

I am also very grateful for the help and advice offered by Professor Peter Stanley (Australian Defence Force Academy) particularly in providing guidance on how to walk and gain a feel for the ground over which Australian and British soldiers fought and died. Likewise, I could not forget the people of Bullecourt for their wonderful hospitality during my visit there. My thanks also to Peter for his generosity hospitality and his willingness to offer and talk over new ideas.

To those many kind folk who wrote to me, offering me use of their personal papers and anecdotes relating to the battle and its aftermath, I say a heartfelt thank you. To name any one in particular would be unfair, so I offer a collective thanks to all.

At Big Sky Publishing I would like to thank Denny Neave, particularly for his help in organising the maps and his push to get the manuscript completed, Sharon Evans for her marketing expertise, Eric Olason for drawing the maps so precisely and Pat Kan for his careful typesetting and innovative design. My thanks also to Sarah Plant for her meticulous work in indexing what is quite a complex book.

Last, but by no means least, I would like to record my gratitude to Cathy McCullagh, not only for her wonderful and careful editing but also for picking up numerous factual errors and providing me with a few helpful snippets to add to the text.

INTRODUCTION

Bullecourt is a tiny, sleepy village in Le Nord, the northernmost region of France, not far from the border with Belgium. Indeed, the village is so small that, even now, it is mentioned in very few travel guides. In 1914 it was a picturesque hamlet with a population of just 396, located in a river valley among the great coal fields of France. As was the custom in that part of the country, almost all the small but well-kept houses had red roofs while the *Grande Rue*, which ran through the centre of the village, soon gave way to winding and circuitous lane ways. These wound into rolling green farmland with large trees at the base of small hills which, in turn, gave way to extended horizons and vast skies.

But by early 1917 all this had changed — World War I had seen to that. Although not completely levelled, as were Thiepval, Combles and other villages of the Somme Valley after the great battles of 1916, Bullecourt bore little resemblance to the pretty little hamlet of just a few years earlier. Most — if not all — the inhabitants had left. Then came April and May 1917 and the two tragic battles that practically flattened the entire village.

Australian soldiers were involved in both battles. Oddly enough, little has been written on their contribution to the final outcome. And, perhaps even more peculiarly considering the myth that has evolved around the Australian soldier in World War I, both battles figure little in the national consciousness. Only one account told from the Australian perspective comes to mind, first published as long ago as 1933. Charles Bean has written five lengthy chapters (245 pages of text or approximately 55,000 words) on both battles in Volume IV of the *Official History of Australia in the War of 1914-1918* which have been critically mauled by the Australian historian Professor Eric Andrews.[1]

Despite the presence of some simple factual errors — including that the second battle 'dragged on till 10 May' when it actually concluded on 17 May — some of Andrews' criticism is indeed warranted. Bean certainly failed to address the less than adequate staff work by senior Australian officers, particularly the commander of I ANZAC Corps, Lieutenant General Sir William Birdwood, and I ANZAC's Chief of Staff, Major General Cyril Brudenell White — a man with whom Bean had developed a great friendship and who, according to Andrews (who argues somewhat convincingly) Bean 'worshipped'. Other parts of Andrews' critique are less persuasive, including such details as the distance the 5th Australian Infantry Brigade had to cover in the advance of 3 May.

***

The two battles of Bullecourt occupy a unique place in Australian military history. The first, fought over a time span of not much more than nine hours, marked the first occasion on which Australian troops had fought alongside that new cumbersome advance in technological warfare, the tank. The performance of the tanks was to eventually turn the battle into something akin to a Greek tragedy. However, despite massive casualties and the loss of over 1200 men captured, two brigades of infantry from the 4th Australian Division came close to achieving the impossible. They not only captured parts of the extremely well protected Hindenburg Line without artillery or tank support, but held their ground against numerous German counter-attacks until finally weight of numbers told and they were forced back to their jumping-off point. The 4th Division was so severely mauled in the attack that it took many months to restore its units to anywhere near full strength.

In the second attack — on this occasion assisted by the more common preliminary artillery barrages — which continued for almost two weeks, three of the other four Australian divisions (Major General John Monash's 3rd Australian Division only missed out because the men were still in training) were forced into the meat grinder that was Bullecourt. Casualties amounted to another 7482 men. Yet again Australian officers and their men overcame enormous odds and not only succeeded in capturing parts of the German OG1 and OG2 trenches but held them — assisted at times by the British — against countless large (or 'general') and smaller counter-attacks.

Bullecourt became a charnel house for Australian soldiers. Many who had been through the relentless and severe enemy artillery bombardments the previous year at Pozieres considered Bullecourt far worse. Second Bullecourt was certainly little more than slaughter. And for what? While Field Marshal Sir Douglas Haig considered the capture of Bullecourt 'among the great achievements of the war', almost 14,000 Australian and British soldiers were killed or wounded for a village which, even at the time of the second attack, held no strategic or tactical value whatsoever.

***

Apart from the account by Charles Bean, very little has been written on the two battles, at least from the Australian point of view. Some of the battalion histories which remain available (many more are out of print) provide a reasonable to good account of Bullecourt. Craig Deayton, for instance, has used more recent scholarship to research and write a history of the 47th Battalion, *Battle Scarred*, which provides a better than average account of the first battle — at least from the perspective of that battalion. Other battalion histories barely mention the battles or, if they do, only in an exiguous and less than useful fashion. There are also a few brief articles, including Eric Andrews and Bede Jordan's 'Second Bullecourt Revisited', written in 1989, and Peter Burness' 'The Battles for Bullecourt' (*Wartime*, Issue 18) as well as chapters in general books on the First World War. Certainly one of the better examples is the relevant part of Peter Pedersen's lengthy tome *The ANZACS*.

Accounts of the battles from the British perspective are more inclusive. Apart from the usual chapters in general histories and General Sir Hubert Gough's account in his autobiography, as well as the numerous biographies of Gough, two recent additions stand out. Jonathon Walker's *The Blood Tub*, first published in 1998, critically examines both battles. Chiefly focusing on the British contribution, Walker's book leans more towards an analysis of Gough's style of command and scrutinises his role, particularly his planning and conduct of the battles. By contrast, Paul Kendall is essentially concerned with the part of the 'ordinary soldiers', specifically 'the poor bloody infantry', in *Bullecourt 1917*, which was first published in 2010. Neither British author has overlooked the significant involvement of the Australians.

In *A Greater Sum of Sorrow*, I have endeavoured to provide a fresh account of the contribution of those Australian soldiers in these two battles. The book will explore how the AIF came to fight at Bullecourt, and how British and Australian officers planned and executed these battles. It aims to place the Australians' experience at Bullecourt more firmly in the context of recent research, including changes to British and German military doctrine, as well as shedding fresh light on several controversies surrounding the battle such as the employment of tanks in the first attack, and the contentious issue of poor Australian staff work in the second battle, particularly in failing to target German machine-gun positions around Queant. And, while Australian battalion war diaries are usually rather vague and add little useful information, they describe quite clearly the panic and ineffective leadership of a few junior field officers at platoon and even company level, particularly when confronted by the murderous machine-gun fire.

The book is based for the most part on recent scholarship and unpublished archival material, specifically that of the Australian War Memorial in Canberra. Other archives that feature prominently are those of the Imperial War Museum, Liddell Hart Centre for Military

Archives, Kings College and the National Archives, all located in London. Main sources include unit war diaries, operation orders and draft plans, all of which contribute operational and tactical details of the attacks. The personal papers of senior officers (those responsible for planning the battles), more junior field officers (those leading the attacks) and 'ordinary soldiers' have been used freely throughout the book. Indeed, I have included many lengthy quotes in an endeavour to provide a 'feel' for the conditions before, during and after the battles. I have also frequently consulted personal diaries, letters and interviews with some 40 men who took part in the first battle, all from the Chalk Collection at the University of Tasmania.

Occasionally in the course of my research I uncovered some information that I decided not to include, either because it appeared too anecdotal, because there were finer points that had been missed and I was unable to complete the pieces of the puzzle or, indeed, because I found the soldier's account problematic. Sometimes, too, there were several contradictory versions of the same incident. I have attempted to use only those narratives which are supported by those of other soldiers or which accord with what is included in war diaries or operational orders, although they too are at times contradictory and conflicting.

***

Charles Bean's observation that 'Bullecourt, more than any other battle, shook the confidence of Australian soldiers in the capacity of the British command' certainly rings true. Bean also wrote that Australian troops braved the odds in numerous battles, but that 'Bullecourt was the most brilliant of these achievements, impressing enemy and friends alike; it was in some ways, the stoutest achievement of the Australian soldier in France, carried through against the stubbornest enemy that ever faced him there.'[2] We need to remember, however, that the two battles took the lives of many thousands of decent, courageous soldiers — Australian, British and German alike. A large number of those men, including 2249 Australians, have no known grave. They are listed simply as missing in action. This book is, in some small way, an acknowledgement of the achievements of all those soldiers — men who made the supreme sacrifice.

CHAPTER 1

'A great deal of work to do.'

THE WESTERN FRONT, 1917

By the beginning of 1917 Lieutenant General Sir William Birdwood, the British officer who commanded I ANZAC Corps, was growing increasingly uncomfortable with the role his Australians were expected to play in battles on the Western Front. In addition to the large numbers of Australian casualties incurred in seemingly fruitless and poorly planned battles such as Fromelles and Pozieres, there was also the more intangible problem of command structure to consider.[1]

At Gallipoli, Birdwood had exercised a somewhat independent command, usually with little interference from General Sir Ian Hamilton, the commander of the Mediterranean Expeditionary Force. Hamilton, unwisely as it transpired, had directed the expedition from his headquarters aboard the battleship HMS *Queen Elizabeth*, where his primary concern lay with the progress of the main landing party of British troops further south at Cape Helles.

Arriving in France Birdwood discovered that his corps was just one of 18, comprising 44 infantry and five cavalry divisions, dispersed throughout five British armies. Despite this, the benefits quickly became evident. Australian officers and soldiers soon learnt the art of so-called technological warfare from their British counterparts — as well as all its horrors. At schools established by the British, the Australians were instructed in the finer points of advancing across no man's land, supposedly under the protection of their own artillery barrage. There were also lessons in the proper use of machine-guns and trench mortars; how to respond to a gas attack; the pitfalls of failing to throw 'bombs' (hand grenades) correctly; methods to avoid detection by snipers and, for competent marksmen, the opportunity to learn the most efficient way to kill exposed enemy troops.

The disadvantages of the AIF's command structure were also clear to Birdwood and to most other senior Australian officers. I ANZAC Corps generally comprised troops whose primary purpose was to fight the enemy while others belonged to 'combat support units'. But, as Jeffrey Grey points out, 'for logistic and much higher administrative support the Australians, like the Canadians, relied upon the British.' Probably more significantly, Australian soldiers were combined with 'British formations, and in keeping with British doctrine, the ANZAC Corps were also supplied with tanks and heavy artillery from British resources, and British staff officers filled some of the technical and specialist posts on their headquarters which the Australians lacked the resources to supply themselves.'[2] At first the arrangement worked well. But — particularly following the increased casualties in subsequent fighting around the Somme — some Australian junior officers and their men began to lose confidence in British staff officers and to question the wisdom of having the British plan *their* battles. It was also not lost on Australian survivors of the Gallipoli campaign that they were now pitted against a more competent and lethal enemy. Good soldier the Turk may have been, but he did not have the training, skills and weaponry of his German counterpart.

By January 1917 all five Australian divisions were on the Western Front. The most recent addition, Major General (later General Sir) John Monash's 3rd, had only moved into the line in November 1916 and, while probably the most comprehensively trained, was not as battle hardened as the others. Yet even the most battle-hardened men suffered in the bitter European winter — the worst for almost 40 years — with freezing rain and relentless snow which turned the terrain to an endless quagmire of sticky mud. Even in the early weeks of winter large numbers of frostbite and trench-foot cases were reported, with each Australian division losing around 200 men a week with trench foot. Birdwood intervened, reminding all junior officers that their 'thoughts and efforts should always be to look after [their] men first.' While some platoon and company commanders may have been offended at what appeared to be needless 'mothering', most nonetheless 'began checking that their men regularly aired their feet and rubbed them with whale oil, that they wore dry socks, that their boots were unlaced at the top, that they discarded puttees, that they loosely wrapped sandbags around their ankles.'[3]

The Western Front 1914–1918 with details of trench lines. Note the position of Bullecourt and the small area of north-eastern France — approximately 75 by 45 miles — which was under the control of the BEF.

As a consequence, cases of trench foot diminished. However many troops froze to death and there were others who simply could not cope with the extreme cold. And, if early January was bad, worse was to come. In late January, according to one Australian soldier, 'it froze hard … Even by day, the bitter winds cut through greatcoats and sheepskins … One awoke at evening to another night of Herculean labours, of peril and misery, as the silent quest rose to a silent heaven, "How long, O Lord?" from thousands of souls which had lost faith for a little in both their God and their country, from neither of which came aid.'[4]

Largely through the efforts of I ANZAC Corps' Chief of Staff, Major General Cyril Brudenell White, Australian soldiers at the front gradually received some assistance in coping with the bitter weather. Roads were repaired and duckboard tracks laid near the line to enable iron and timber, used in dugouts and revetting, to be transported to the front. Warm woollen clothing and waterproof coats became more freely available. Almost 65,000 sheepskin jackets were hastily despatched from Australia. The length of time battalions were forced to spend in the line was reduced. All Australian units occupying a front-line position were rotated every six days or so, which meant 'at the worst a single man seldom does more than forty-eight hours continuous front trench duty in every twelve days.'[5]

Hot food and canteen consumables were also on hand when in the line. Behind the front, men returned to warmish Nissen hutments while sporting and recreational facilities had not been forgotten. Subsequent frosts caused the sticky mud to harden, giving the troops more cause for joy. However most Australians found the absence of what they regarded as 'proper' light difficult. 'We all wish we could see the sun,' noted a sergeant from the 27th Battalion in February 1917, adding ruefully, 'that we have not seen since October last.'[6] As if the freezing conditions were not sufficient, squads of Australian soldiers were expected to participate in the much-despised trench raids which brought further casualties for little or no gain. Little wonder that, for many Australians, the winter of 1917 'was the hardest of the war ... Several shot themselves, more malingered, and one or two deserted to the enemy, an offence usually unheard of in the AIF.'[7]

Through it all, Monash remained undaunted, emphasising that raids increased 'morale' and acted as a 'powerful stimulant for all ranks'. He also observed that his divisional sector covered only five of the more than 90 miles of British front-line trenches, and was

> ... held defensively by only one platoon of each of four companies, of each of four battalions, while all the other nine battalions, all the artillery and engineers [remained out of the line] ... The front line is not really a line at all, but a very complex and elaborate system of field works, extending back several thousand yards, and bristling with fire trenches, support and communication trenches, redoubts, strong points, machinegun emplacements, and an elaborate system of dugouts, cabins, posts, and observation cells.'

This meant very little to Australian soldiers who, even in late February, were still suffering from the extreme weather conditions. Most undoubtedly would have agreed with Monash's sentiments that 'life in the front [line] ... is very arduous and uncomfortable.'[8]

Alongside this was the constant danger of being killed by a German sniper and some of the inexperienced newcomers were soon found dead. 'It was not wise to put his head over the parapet in daylight,' wrote one veteran. 'Fritz's snipers are pretty keen, and anyhow it gives the position of the post away.'[9]

In March 1917 however, the drab life of the trenches was to come to an end. Earlier, before the snow had begun to thaw, the German High Command had developed an innovative new strategy which would indirectly bring Australian troops into another great battle close to an obscure French village. What then had brought the Australians to this part of France, and why were so many to fight and die around Bullecourt?

***

Field Marshal Sir Douglas Haig, Commander-in-Chief of British and Commonwealth Forces on the Western Front from late 1915 to 1919 (AWM A03713).

Despite over 30 months of fighting in France and Flanders, the Western Front had changed very little since December 1914. Stretching from the English Channel coast to the border with Switzerland, the terrain had borne witness to some fearful and costly battles, particularly in 1916. The first day of the Somme campaign (Saturday 1 July), for example, has been universally labelled the greatest calamity in the British army's noble history. At 7.30 am approximately 100,000 troops attempted the dash across no man's land. By the end of the day, of the 57,470 casualties, 19,240 men had been killed, all for the gain of a little over one mile. Australian troops were soon ordered into the battle. All the while conditions on the Somme battlefields continued to worsen. Heavy rain and almost non-stop artillery fire had turned the ground to a virtual swamp. By mid-October the British front line had advanced very little. With the onset of winter and the mounting toll of casualties all but destroying his 'New Armies', General (later Field Marshal) Sir Douglas Haig finally recognised the folly of continuing the attack, and ordered its cessation.[10]

***

The coming of New Year 1917 saw the strategic situation in France and Flanders alter dramatically. While the Somme battles may have marked the beginning of the end for the British 'New Armies', the Germans had fared little better. Poor tactics, including unnecessary counter-attacks, had also drained their divisions of men and equipment; given that the Germans were fighting on two fronts, these were resources that they could ill afford to lose. By early 1917 however, the Russian armies on the Eastern Front were close to defeat and revolution erupted in Petrograd (St Petersburg) which soon spread to Moscow. With little resistance from the once powerful Russian army, more German divisions could be redeployed to the Western Front.

Prior to this redeployment, the German High Command has already recognised that the Allies would, in all likelihood, launch another major attack in the spring to take advantage of the German shortfall in men, and that they would probably break through. To best utilise those troops and weapons that remained, the High Command ordered a general withdrawal to a shorter front which could be better defended, sited well behind the former German line. At first the withdrawal was gradual. Step by cautious step, enemy soldiers pulled back to previously constructed temporary defensive positions, all the while covered by a rearguard of elite infantry units.[11] German strategy on the Western Front for the coming year was all but dictated by the construction of those stronger positions behind the old front line.

The British named the new defences the 'Hindenburg Line', a collective name for the various *stellungs* already divided into codenames by the Germans. The strongest and most elaborate was the *Siegfriedstellung* which ran south from Arras to St Quentin then down to Laon and the Aisne. Straightening this bulge (or salient) released more German troops to defend a shortened line around the Somme. In some places along the Hindenburg Line the withdrawal saw the Germans surrender as much as 45 miles of territory. More significantly however, the shorter front released the equivalent of 13 infantry divisions.

At the same time the Germans were implementing a new defensive doctrine of flexible (or 'elastic') defence in depth. The Hindenburg Line provided a region of defensive zones rather than the former single continuous line of well-defended strongpoints. A network of two or three deep trenches, usually following the lie of the land, was protected by mile after mile of up to nine deep belts of barbed wire, in most places many feet thick. Every part of the line had a forward 'outpost zone' covering around 2700 yards which comprised the first and second principal trenches (or strongpoint line) while an expertly sited system of machine-gun emplacements (sometimes thick concrete pillboxes), located in the best tactical positions, provided an overlapping arc of ceaseless fire criss-crossing no man's land. Attacking infantry stood little chance of surviving this maelstrom.

German artillery pits were well camouflaged and sited to provide the highest possible firepower for mobile guns and anti-tank weapons. Strengthened underground bunkers ensured enemy troops were relatively comfortable in even the worst weather conditions while keeping them safe from all but the heaviest artillery bombardments. A labyrinth of communication ('switch') trenches connected the rear and forward trenches. If attacking troops managed to break through, reinforcements could move forward quickly, thereby catching hapless survivors in something akin to a salient. Further behind the forward trenches were more dugouts and concrete bunkers for headquarters staffs, medical officers and, most importantly, the counter-attack infantry units or *eingreif*. Described as 'an iron wall that no human power can overcome', the German High Command not surprisingly was convinced that the Hindenburg Line was all but impregnable.[12]

***

However late 1916 also heralded the development of a more dangerous long-term strategy for Germany. On 22 December the Chief of the Admiralty Staff, Admiral Henning von Holtzrendorff, prophesised to the German Chancellor (Theobald von Bethmann-Hollweg) that the 'war demands a decision by autumn 1917 if it is not to end with a general exhaustion of all parties and thus disastrously for us.'[13] Senior German officers and politicians were aware that Germany had little chance of winning a war that continued beyond 1917. The answer, Holtzrendorff was informed by his civilian advisers, lay in unrestricted submarine warfare. If German 'U-boats' operating out of Belgian ports were to sink up to 600,000 tons of Allied merchant shipping each month for six months, Britain would be deprived of some 39% of her necessary imports. However risks were plentiful. The most likely scenario was the United States of America entering the war on the side of the Allies.

For the moment this did not overly concern the Germans who were convinced that, without necessary food and equipment, the Allies would be suing for peace within six months. Moreover, there was no possibility that American troops could be mobilised within such a short time frame. Admiral Eduard von Capelle, the Secretary of State for the Imperial Navy, went so far as to claim that the United States posed 'zero' threat. This optimistic assertion was supported by German general Paul von Hindenburg who informed the Reichstag that American military assistance would be 'minimal, in any way not decisive'.[14]

Bethmann-Hollweg was less certain. Aware that this could well be Germany's last chance to secure victory or a negotiated peace with favourable conditions, he remained apprehensive over the rash predictions of those few senior officers. Before committing his government, the Chancellor decided to throw one last olive branch to Petrograd, Paris and London. Only once the offer was rejected by all three Allied governments (it was regarded as too demanding) did Bethmann-Hollweg accept the strategy. He could now claim some moral ground, protesting that Germany had been compelled to escalate to unrestricted U-boat warfare. On 1 February 1917 attacks on merchant shipping in the North Atlantic commenced.[15]

***

On 4 February, with its strategy of unrestricted attacks at sea in place, the German High Command issued orders to commanders in the field to consolidate and hold their positions behind the Hindenburg Line. The British garnered some information from German prisoners of war which, along with aerial reconnaissance reports, revealed the boldness of the enemy's flight. However it took Anglo-French intelligence experts over a week to recognise the significance of the movement and by then it was far too late to retaliate. Smaller groups of German soldiers began pulling back from early to mid-February, with the main withdrawal (Operation *Alberich*) completed in four days from 16 to 20 March 1917.[16]

While information may have been passed to army commanders, by mid-February the Australians apparently remained unaware of any significant enemy activity. One divisional diarist noted that, as late as 22 February, Australian troops began to suspect 'that momentous developments were afoot on the other side of No Man's Land.' Regardless of expectations, the front appeared normal as German 'machine-guns swept our forward zones with intermittent bursts of fire.' Enemy 'snipers were quick to resent undue curiosity.' German artillery continued to fire 'on our dumps, and duck-walks, and trenches'. And, more significantly, enemy 'lines remained as we had known them, sinister, inscrutable, pregnant with death.' The following day harboured 'growing tension, of fleeting rumour, of deepening conviction.'[17] However on 24 February an Australian patrol confirmed that parts of the old German front-line trenches were unoccupied, as enemy troops pulled back towards the village of Bapaume.[18] Now it would be up to the Australians to give chase.

Since their arrival in April 1916, Australian troops had already contributed a great deal to the British army's efforts on the Western Front. With the Somme battles now well and truly behind them, those Australians could finally see the dreadful winter come to an end. However, any thought of further rest rapidly diminished as the Germans covered their withdrawal by occupying and fortifying a line of French villages directly in front of the Hindenburg Line. Before the British could have a crack at the Hindenburg Line itself, those outpost villages had to be captured. And Haig had no time to waste. Australian units were ordered to pursue the fleeing enemy. How they performed would determine the timetable for the next major British operation — the attack around Arras.

**

Meanwhile the Germans continued their systematic withdrawal, devastating everything that stood in their path. Bridges were demolished and roads mined. Ancient churches were destroyed to prevent the towers being used as observation platforms. Farmhouses and out-buildings were burnt or booby-trapped to prevent their use as billets. Livestock were killed. Water reservoirs and wells were poisoned — some booby-trapped — killing or maiming many unsuspecting soldiers. All this destruction was completed with the sole purpose of delaying chasing troops and providing the main body of Germans and their artillery batteries valuable time to reach their key defensive positions.

At the same time German engineers continued to labour industriously all along the Hindenburg Line to meet the High Command's expectations. The engineers concentrated on providing maximum fortification for troop safety and comfort. Multiple lines of deep, heavily strengthened trenches, assisted by specifically selected strongpoints of concrete shelters and machine-gun emplacements, all protected by belts of barbed wire, ensured a deep, extensive and formidable rear defensive zone. The chief priority — the massacre of advancing Allied infantry — seemed a mere formality.

General Sir Hubert Gough, General Officer Commanding (GOC) Fifth Army, had ordered a systematic advance. Heading his priorities were 'Strong patrols, backed up by the advanced guards, [which were] to be pushed forward as far as possible.'[19] Whatever Gough's other errors of judgement, he retained a strong sense of history. Clearly remembering the disaster that followed the detaching of his brigades at the Aisne in 1914, he decided that his advance guards should be 'mixed' and comprise infantry, cavalry, artillery and engineers. Two Australian divisions — the 5th and 2nd — were to lead the advance. The British 7th Division on the left was to coordinate the advanced guard movement as closely as possible with the Australians, while continuing to despatch patrols of its own. The British units began well — in a little over a day they had moved their line almost two miles while capturing the villages of Warlencourt, Pys, Irles, Miraumont and Serle.

The Australian units met with similar success. By the end of February they had secured the village of Gommecourt and were around one and a half miles from the outskirts of Bapaume, some eight miles behind the old German front line.[20] Gough wrote, 'The enemy's rear guards ... now stood firm for some time.' Confronted by 'two powerfully-constructed and quite undamaged hostile lines of entrenchments facing us, the first known as the Grevillers line, stretching roughly from the village of Bucquoy on the north by Achiet-le-petit, Loupart Wood and the village of Thilloy; the other line, from 2000 to 3000 yards behind it, stretched across by the villages of Ablainzeville, Bihucourt, and the western outskirts of Bapaume,' the British advance became bogged down.[21]

Gough became further agitated on 14 March following a British assault on Bucquoy which was easily 'repulsed'. Harbouring little doubt that the attack 'was not sufficiently prepared', Gough noted that he 'had reconnoitred the front the previous morning and had thought that the defences of this village still appeared in too good a state to warrant an assault, and I suggested to the corps that the attack should be delayed for further preparations, but the commander was confident of success.' However, when his corps commander pressed ahead with the attack, Gough did not intervene, reasoning that he should allow his 'subordinates to act on their own initiative'.[22]

The Australians had encountered problems of their own as they fought their way to within striking distance of Bapaume. They were ordered to prepare for an attack on the village and were confident of success. One young lieutenant, George McDowell — described as energetic, buoyant and 'dedicated to the awful business of war' — wrote that the German retirement was leading to 'a headlong fight which is being hurried all along the line [and] when we catch up with the old dog we will trounce him soundly.'[23]

**

Haig had always insisted that Bapaume must be taken. His rationale may have been questionable — after all, this was a village that had obsessed him since the first day of the Somme. This was the same village, in fact, that he had expected the British cavalry to capture on that first day. Then, as now, he claimed that the village's significance lay in the tactical position it occupied. Haig reasoned that, following its capture, Australian units could fan out in an easterly direction and move against other scattered outpost villages that stood between Bapaume and the Hindenburg Line. Gough eagerly supported Haig's rationale. After all, an Australian success might provide some compensation for recent defeats in the Fifth Army's British sector. Considering what had happened at Bucquoy, on this occasion Gough was guilty of ordering an attack without sufficient time for adequate preparation.

On 16 March Australian 'artillery fire was directed against enemy's trenches and wire [around Bapaume] ... up till 9p.m.' At around 5.00 am the following day, infantry from the 8th Brigade (5th Australian Division) moved forward. A little over two hours later, a report from the 30th Battalion confirmed that the village was occupied and the Australians 'had established ... [a line] on the main Beaulencourt Road through Bapaume.'[24] At midday the division's commander (Major General Talbot Hobbs) told I ANZAC headquarters, 'Mopping up of Bapaume complete.'[25]

Withdrawing enemy troops had, however, left the village in ruins, in the process destroying anything useful and leaving behind numerous well-concealed booby traps and time-bombs, which caused many casualties. One British officer wrote that:

> From a captured German [operation] order it appears that our patrols entered the hostile trenches only one hour after they had been vacated; pretty sharp work ... The German trenches we have taken over are deep, well constructed and surprisingly dry ... Masses of beer bottles (unfortunately empty) are strewn about, and guncotton, attached to shell cases and grenades, has been left ready to explode when picked up or accidentally kicked. We have had five casualties in this way.[26]

Two days later, on 19 March, those remaining Australian soldiers demonstrated that their spirits remained high when the 5th Australian Brigade's band marched through the ruins into the old town square, *Place Faidherbe*.

***

In the British sector, Gough recorded that the advance 'was now stayed for a while, to allow the roads, railways and bridges – which had been thoroughly destroyed by the enemy – to be repaired and reconstructed to serve as our communications.'[27] However, Australian advance guard units moved on. Brigadier General Harold 'Pompey' Elliott's 15th Brigade (5th Australian Division) was given arguably the more difficult task, operating to the north of John Gellibrand's 6th Brigade (2nd Australian Division). Elliott was an enigmatic, if somewhat difficult leader. On 17 March he divided his formation into two parts — one 'to swing half right' as far as Fremicourt while the other remained 'in the old line as a reserve'.[28] British intelligence had already ascertained 'the strength and disposition of the rearguards before the 5th Division.' But the same intelligence could not determine the number of troops Gellibrand's formation faced and only 'assumed' that it would meet a 'similar sized' force. Probably as a safeguard should he encounter larger enemy units, Gellibrand was provided an additional 'troop of light horse, a battery of field artillery, and engineer, machine-gun, and medical detachments.'[29]

The ruins of Bapaume, 17 March 1917. View of a ruined street in Bapaume taken on the same day that the Australians captured the village (AWM E00348).

Now that Bapaume was in Australian hands and effectively a base for both 'advance guard' brigades, Gellibrand's formation moved against outpost villages including Sapignies, Favreuil, Vaulx-Vraucourt, Vraucourt, Lagnicourt, Noreuil and Longatte. Elliott's objectives included Fremicourt, Beugny, Lebucquiere, Velu, Beaumetz, Hermies,

Doignies, Morchies, Louverval, Demicourt and Boursies. The advance through open countryside was a totally new experience for those Australians involved. There were no trenches or bomb craters scarring the landscape and without massive strands of barbed wire (except some covering a few of the outpost villages) they were guaranteed broad freedom of movement.

Brigadier General Harold 'Pompey' Elliott, GOC 15th Australian Infantry Brigade (AWM H15596).

Lieutenant George McDowell wrote that his unit's recent plentiful amount of 'open warfare tactical exercises' was put to good use as they chased retiring German infantry 'over comparatively open country'.[30] If German troops were cornered, however, they usually offered stout resistance and fighting in open fields or in the villages was sometimes savage and bloody. Those same Australian soldiers soon understood that the enemy was not retreating, rather biding their time as the main body of troops and their artillery pushed further back towards the Hindenburg Line.

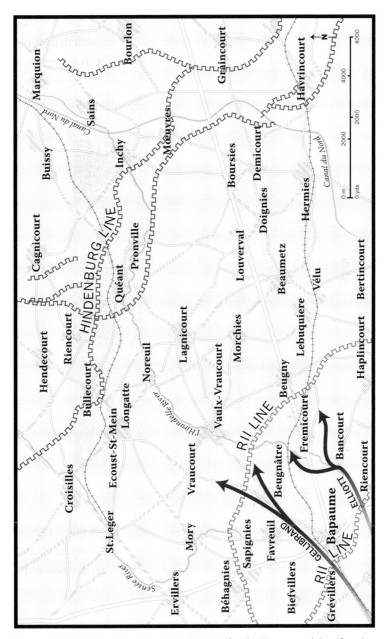

The advance to the Hindenburg Line, March–April 1917. After the Germans withdrew from Bapaume in mid-March, the 2nd and 5th Australian divisions formed advanced guards units to chase the fleeing Germans to the Hindenburg Line.

In Elliott's sector Haplincourt, Beugny, Le Bucguiere, Velu, Velu Wood and Morchies were taken in rapid succession. Beaumetz, however, was a tougher nut to crack. A unit of select German troops initially offered stubborn resistance. But by 21 March Elliott's men had forced the enemy to withdraw and he recorded that 'at 7a.m. our Light Horse patrols supported by infantry patrols found Beaumetz unoccupied and at once consolidated in the village which was incorporated in our outpost line.' The Germans nonetheless refused to relinquish the village. At around 4.30 am on 23 March enemy artillery pounded Australian positions in and around Beaumetz. Half an hour later some 200 infantry counter-attacked. A report noted later that, after almost 30 minutes of intense fighting, the Australian 'garrison in Beaumetz was driven out.'[31] However by 7.30 am the Australians had attacked again and retaken what was left of the village. A body count revealed around 100 dead enemy soldiers and nine wounded prisoners.

Gellibrand experienced much the same success. Yet both commanders would be 'carpeted' by Birdwood. Advancing well ahead of the British columns, they were ordered to slow down. Gellibrand ignored the order, instead instructing his exhausted formation to move against Noreuil. Without proper reconnaissance the night attack stood little chance of success. When Birdwood and White heard of the attack, they were reportedly livid. For his part, Elliott effectively disobeyed an order, issued by his divisional commander and sanctioned by Birdwood, not to move against Bertincourt, located in the neighbouring British sector. Elliott — yet again the charismatic but unorthodox commander — decided to deal 'with the situation itself' by attacking the village, only to be subsequently admonished by Birdwood.[32] In retrospect, Elliott should have considered himself fortunate not to have forfeited his command — more so as, on 20 March, Gough had ordered 'that the outpost villages would only be attacked when heavy guns had been brought up and after thorough preparations.' Gough's order effectively directed the Australian columns to press on and play a waiting game while the British formations took time to prepare and consolidate against each village they faced. But neither Australian brigade commander would countenance this. Just a few days later their troops were deemed ill suited 'for this second phase of the advance' and 'the columns were dispensed with'.[33]

Meanwhile, on 24 March Brigadier General E.A. Wisdom was told that his 7th Brigade (2nd Australian Division), supported by part of Elliott's brigade, must prepare for an attack on Lagnicourt which was 'garrisoned' by around 260 Germans. In what has been described as a 'classic envelopment', Wisdom's plan involved A Company, 26th Battalion, moving against the village 'from cross-roads ... "C" company 26 Btn will attack the village the frontage being from Junction Road ... to Eastern side of village ... Vickers Machine Guns will advance after village has been taken.' The two companies were to link up at the rear of the village while a third swept through Lagnicourt. Another company was to 'mop up' any 'isolated' groups of enemy troops offering 'resistance'.[34]

Studio portrait of Captain Percy Herbert Cherry, VC, MC, 26th Battalion, c. 1916. Note that his VC and MC have been painted onto the photograph some time after it was taken (AWM P02939.012).

On 26 March Wisdom put his plans into action. Captain Percy Cherry's courage, which won him a Victoria Cross, was indicative of the Australians' fighting spirit. The citation read:

> After all the officers of his company had become casualties, he carried on with care and determination in the face of fierce opposition and cleared the village of the enemy. He sent frequent reports of progress made and when held up by an enemy strongpoint, he organised machine-gun and bomb parties and captured the position. His leadership, coolness and bravery set a wonderful example to his men.
>
> Having cleared the village, he took charge of the situation and beat off the most resolute and heavy counter-attacks made by the enemy. Wounded about 6.30a.m., he refused to leave his post and there remained, encouraging all to hold out at all costs, until, about 4.30p.m., this very gallant officer was killed by an enemy shell.

The 7th Brigade suffered 377 casualties, considered a low price to pay by British GHQ.[35]

As Australian and British troops moved closer to the Hindenburg Line enemy resistance strengthened. Elite German units had established themselves in villages and the surrounding countryside with expertly positioned machine-gun posts and other elaborate fortifications. The exhausted Australians suffered further casualties. Finally the 7th Brigade was relieved by Brigadier General Thomas Glasgow's 13th (4th Australian Division) while, further south, the 1st Australian Division took over from Hobbs' 5th Division. On 2 April Doignies fell.[36]

The following morning Australian guns fired a 'thin' barrage against enemy positions around Noreuil. German artillery responded, although few casualties were reported among the gathering troops. At 5.15 am the 50th and 51st battalions (13th Infantry Brigade) moved forward. However the Australian artillery had failed to silence all the machine-gun posts and the infantry was forced to advance through a wall of fire. They countered with rifle grenades and bombs, killing most of the German machine-gun crews who fought gamely to the end. In some places, however, particularly on the right of the village, uncut wire hindered the Australians' progress.

As the infantry moved through the village, hidden machine-gun nests on the right flank accounted for more Australian casualties. However, as the battalion report noted, 'the line pushed forward and secured themselves within 100 yards of their objective, having advanced over 1,700 yards.' By late afternoon Australian officers reported the capture and consolidation of Noreuil, albeit not without heavy casualties, particularly among the officers. Ten were listed as dead or wounded, as were 350 men. The report also noted the capture of 'between 70-80 prisoners including 8 officers' as well as 'two trench mortars and two machine guns'.[37]

Only Demicourt, Boursies and Hermies remained. The Australian artillery had already commenced laying down softening-up barrages against those villages, preventing enemy troops from adding to their forward defensive positions, several patrols having established that machine-gun nests were sited as far forward as Havrincourt Wood. Senior Australian officers and their staff decided that the main 'attack will be launched without artillery support. Normal artillery activity against enemy villages will be carried on until 0400. At Zero Hour batteries will open on Demicourt ... and eastern approaches to Hermies.' If, however, during the attack, rifle or machine-gun fire erupted from the direction of Demicourt (located on a ridge between the other two villages), 'heavy artillery will shell that village and the exits towards Boursies and Hermies.' Cautious Australian officers who had learnt from their men's insistence on looting booby-trapped souvenirs or being caught by well-placed time-bombs, arranged 'for Engineers to examine the villages for mines and traps immediately after they are occupied'.[38]

The ruins of Hermies, 8–9 April 1917. Many of the buildings have been reduced to rubble while parts of the walls of others are still in place. Hermies was one of the last of the several outpost villages captured in April 1917 (AWM C00440).

Zero Hour was set for dawn on 9 April. The 1st Australian Infantry Brigade was to assault Hermies and Demicourt while the 3rd conducted a diversionary attack on Boursies. Divisional officers knew that the Germans 'would be expecting some form of attack on these villages and it was hoped that we might be able to divert his attention almost entirely to Boursies.' As late as the night before the attack, 'it was determined to push out on the ridge north of Boursies to lead the enemy to the obvious conclusion that early operations against Boursies would be undertaken.' The same planners subsequently decided that Hermies and Boursies — the two outer villages — were to be attacked 'simultaneously and by surprise' trusting that Demicourt, approximately two miles to the right of Hermies, would then be isolated and 'soon become untenable to the enemy'.

At 4.15 am the 2nd and 3rd battalions (1st Brigade) moved against Hermies. As the infantry closed in on the enemy front line, opposition stiffened. The two forward companies fixed bayonets and charged the first German trench. Ferocious hand-to-hand fighting followed. A large number of German troops were killed while others chose to surrender. The Australians pushed on. In another almost perfect example of 'envelopment', one company attacked from the left and swung around, catching enemy troops between crossfire from the company on the other flank. By 6.00 am Hermies was in Australian hands. Exuberant troops counted 264 Germans killed. Another 173 were taken prisoner.

Looking towards the French village of Hermies and old German wire entanglements. Hermies was captured on the morning of 9 April by the 2nd and 3rd battalions in a surprise attack from the flanks. Some of the German defences can be seen in the foreground (AWM E01382).

Demicourt proved far from 'untenable to the enemy', and was attacked at 7.30 am. Held up by accurate machine-gun fire coming from the village, those Australian officers leading the advance were soon forced to request artillery support. When it arrived, the Germans lost no time responding with artillery fire of their own, accurately directed onto Australian troops attempting to outflank enemy positions close to the village. As the surviving Australians closed on the German front line, more vicious hand-to-hand fighting ensued. Only at 11.00 am could Australian officers report that Demicourt was secure and that they had established a line east of the village.

Meanwhile, at Boursies, intelligence reports should have alerted senior officers and those planning the attack to the danger of enfilading fire from well-positioned German machine-guns on the high ground to the north and north-east of the village. Somehow the same reports also seriously underestimated the strength of German units in and around Boursies. The 12th Battalion (3rd Brigade) was subsequently presented with the unenviable task of silencing these machine-guns before moving against the village. Early in the evening of 8 April Australian infantry began moving cautiously towards their starting line at a sunken road.

Not all went according to plan. A later report described how German attacks on the same night 'seriously interfered with the preparations for the operation ... timed for 4.15a.m., the 9th.' Still the attack went ahead. Leaving the cover of the sunken road near Louverval, Captain J.E. Newland's A Company, supported by a platoon from B Company under the command of Lieutenant R.E. Newitt, advanced the 900 or so yards across no man's land against Boursies. The troops had covered a little over 500 yards and were about to attack a ruined mill in front of the village when they were spotted by the enemy, who opened up heavy machine-gun and rifle fire. Newitt's men, all of whom had been skilfully positioned on the right flank of the advance, lent support, allowing the second wave of Newland's platoon to overpower what was left of the enemy's forward positions.[39]

A view of front-line trenches following the German withdrawal, March 1917. Note the soldier lying dead and the roll of barbed wire between his legs (AWM E04714).

Major General Harold Walker (GOC 1st Australian Division) later commended both Newland's and Newitt's grasp of the situation. 'Two platoons skilfully led', Walker noted, 'attacked the enemy trenches ... and captured them taking two enemy machine-guns with little loss themselves. The captured machine-guns were at once turned on the retiring enemy.' By 2.00 pm what was left of the German garrison was 'driven out', fleeing back towards their 'main line'.[40] In a daringly executed — and somewhat lucky — attack, the last of the network of defended outpost villages in the Australian sector had been taken.

Adequate planning had contributed to the success at Boursies, as had the resolve of junior officers (and their men) and, rather surprisingly, the poor deployment of machine-guns by German officers. Planning for Hermies was far better. Charles Bean wrote that, of all the 'important operations, the attack upon Hermies was the first, within the experience of Australian infantry, to develop from start to finish almost precisely in accordance with plans.'[41]

Major General Walker received a laudatory message from Gough: 'Best congratulations on operations for the capture of Boursies, Hermies, Demicourt. They were skilfully planned and gallantly carried out ... Throughout the advance since the end of February the enterprise, tactical skill and gallantry of the whole ANZAC Corps has been remarkable and is deserving of the highest commendation.'[42] The cost of taking the three villages was 649 Australian soldiers.[43] Little did the survivors realise that those attributes Gough had praised so lavishly would very shortly be called on again, at another small French village not too far from where they had just fought.

***

The capture of the last of the outpost villages effectively brought the war of movement to a close. Australian officers and men had learnt that there were different ways to fight a war than the nerve-racking anticipation of waiting in a trench to attack — or be attacked — across no man's land. Being mobile and not confined to an underground catacomb was a tonic for Australian troops. Yet those units engaged in the chase still suffered large numbers of casualties.

On the same day that the Australians were celebrating their victories, a little further to the north the British Third Army commenced the much-anticipated spring campaign, its objective a breakthrough around Arras. The stage had been set for an attack on Bullecourt by the 4th Australian Division which, following the capture of Noreuil on 2 April, had established its divisional front along a line running north of Lagnicourt and Noreuil.

CHAPTER 2

'The value of preparation.'

THE ARRAS OFFENSIVE

The German army's strategy for 1917 had been clearly defined. Senior Allied officers and politicians understood that, by withdrawing to the Hindenburg Line, the enemy intended to fight a defensive war on the Western Front while the bulk of its forces would be used to pursue a more successful outcome in the east. Haig had other ideas. He wanted nothing less than to continue his strategy of wearing down the enemy in France and Flanders, aware that allowing the Germans to gain the impetus in the west risked losing the war. However politics intervened. The new British Prime Minister, David Lloyd George (who came to power in December 1916), was never a great admirer of his commander-in-chief's strategy, particularly in the wake of the appalling casualties on the Somme. Lloyd George decided he needed a 'knockout blow', although not necessarily in the west. Almost immediately on taking office he created a smaller executive War Cabinet, designed to provide greater input into prosecuting strategy and military operations.

The French government had similar ideas concerning its army commander's strategy. In December 1916 the government had replaced its commander-in-chief, the bumbling Marshal Joseph Joffre, with the more audacious General Robert Nivelle. At the Calais Conference from 26 to 27 February 1917, the British Prime Minister went so far as to suggest to his French counterpart that the British Expeditionary Force (BEF) and, by necessity, the Australian Imperial Force (AIF), be placed under French military command, with Nivelle as supreme commander. Haig was livid, writing later that 'it would be madness to place the British under the French, and … I [do] not believe our troops would fight under French leadership.' The British commander-in-chief was even prepared to 'be tried by Court Martial [rather] than betray the Army by agreeing to its being placed under the French.'[1] A crisis threatened, particularly after news reached the politicians that Haig had informed King George V of his threat to resign. With little option, the notion that the BEF be subordinated indefinitely to French leadership was shelved. However Nivelle and Lloyd George agreed to implement earlier plans (first discussed in December 1916) for the Allies' first great spring offensive of 1917 which would see British GHQ answerable to French command. Haig was reluctantly forced to accede.

***

Nivelle's initial plan involved a breakthrough by the French army along a ridge between the Aisne and Ailette rivers around the Chemin des Dames in Champagne. He was convinced that this offensive could win the war for France as early as mid to late 1917. During the early planning stages this part of the enemy front was weakly defended, although the Germans held the high ground and enjoyed uninterrupted observation of French troop and artillery movement. With the German withdrawal to the Hindenburg Line, Nivelle's plans should have been put on hold.

British and French politicians, still alarmed at the casualty bill of 1916, sought to shift the war from a series of relentless battles of attrition. While the German withdrawal surprised Nivelle — as it did other senior British and French officers and politicians — he continued to argue that his strategy of pursuing a rapid and convincing breakthrough along a broad front with overwhelming artillery support would provide the means to bring the war to an end. General Franchet d'Esperay, commander of the French Northern Group of Armies, was less certain. He called on Nivelle to launch an immediate attack to catch the unsuspecting withdrawing German divisions off guard. Nivelle rejected this out of hand as too 'audacious' a request. The headstrong Nivelle was not prepared to diverge from his plan to accommodate d'Esperay, or anyone else for that matter, refusing 'even to acknowledge the shift in German deployments'. Nivelle further pressed for two diversionary attacks — one by the British in the north between Arras and the River Scarpe and the other by d'Esperay's French Northern Group of Armies near the River Oise — to draw German troops away from Chemin des Dames and conceal French preparations for the main offensive. Neville's stubbornness was to 'cost him and the French dear in the months to come'.[2]

The French commander-in-chief was a strong believer in set-piece offensives — infantry attacking limited objectives with the support of massed artillery. He assumed that what had worked well for him at Verdun, albeit in dissimilar conditions on a limited front, would work in much the same way along a far larger front. He refused, however, to sanction the use of tanks, and indeed was critical of a British suggestion that the 'best way of disturbing the enemy would be to carry out an attack in which tanks would play a part.'[3]

Nivelle remained undaunted by the task facing him and his troops, describing his offensive as inflicting a blow with a 'mass of manoeuvre'. With 27 divisions ready to take advantage of a break in the enemy line, he confidently predicted that his men would take the city of 'Laon in 24 hours and then break out.' While he subsequently accepted that this main breakout would be more likely within 48 hours, he asserted confidently that 'the ground [would then] be open to go where one wants, to the Belgian coast or to the capital, on the Meuse or on the Rhine.'[4] Nivelle's self-belief and 'certainty' concerning the Champagne offensive was repeated by his close confidante General Charles Mangin (who had served alongside him during the last part of Verdun): 'We know the method and we have the Chief [Nivelle]. Success is certain.'[5] Haig remained unconvinced, continuing to argue for an attack in his favoured area around the Ypres salient. Again, he was overruled.

Planning went ahead for the main offensive at Chemin des Dames and diversionary attacks around Arras. On 18 March it appeared that

Nivelle's ambitions would be thwarted when a socialist member of the French Chamber of Deputies, Paul Painleve, was named new Minister of War with far-reaching powers. Painleve was less than impressed by Nivelle's charisma or, for that matter, by his strategy. Called to Painleve's parliamentary office, Nivelle changed the rationale for the attack, which initially was to be part of a three-pronged offensive with the Russians advancing in the east and the Italians in the south. But neither the Russian nor Italian army was in any position to attack, a situation Brigadier General John Charteris, GHQ's intelligence chief, had already communicated to Haig and presumably Nivelle.[6] Nivelle now advanced an alternative. The French offensive, he reasoned, would assist the Allies' precarious position on the Russian and Italian fronts. Much-needed German divisions would be moved from those fronts to bolster enemy troops at Chemin des Dames who, he persisted, would be soundly mauled by his French troops.

Following Haig's example of the previous month, Nivelle threatened to resign if he failed to gain approval for his plan. He told Painleve that the 'only thing I fear is that the enemy will evacuate. The more Germans there are, the greater the victory will be.' Painleve eventually acceded, but with the proviso that Nivelle 'agree to halt the offensive if no breakthrough occurred at the Chemin des Dames within 48 hours.' Giving his solemn agreement, Nivelle added, 'I do not intend to restart the Battle of the Somme.'[7]

***

At the Calais Conference Haig had been forced to accept Nivelle's strategy. He committed the British First, Third (whose troops would be the principal striking force) and Fifth armies to support the French offensive by launching an attack at and around Arras. The British offensive, it was reliably believed, would pull German reserves away from Chemin des Dames. On 5 February Haig issued a secret memorandum to his army commanders in which he noted that he expected them 'to make ... preparations on the probability that the

Third Army operations will commence shortly after the 15th March.'[8] The German withdrawal to the Hindenburg Line should have put paid to any further expectations concerning those dates. But, if Haig thought that Nivelle would cancel, or at least postpone the French attack, he was to be sadly mistaken. The Frenchman insisted that both advances proceed.

Nivelle still had high hopes of a rapid Allied victory and of concluding the war by year's end. On 26 March Haig's Chief of Staff, Lieutenant General Sir Lancelot Kiggell, told the British army commanders that 'Nivelle's opinion was that the enemy would not leave the Hindenburg Line until he was attacked and driven off.' But, of more significance were Haig's own plans. From the beginning, Arras was conceived as essentially a 'bite-and-hold' operation. 'The Third Army will attack', Haig emphasised, 'with the object of breaking through east of Arras and advancing in the direction of Cambrai.' He went on to point out 'the importance of the Divisions on the right [south] of the Third Army attack getting within assaulting distance of the Hindenburg Line *at the earliest possible date*.'[9] Two divisions from General Sir Hubert Gough's Fifth Army would provide that assistance, attacking along a front in a suitable location around Bullecourt between Croisilles and Queant.

Haig also told General Sir Henry Horne (GOC First Army) that his main objective was the capture of Vimy Ridge and that he should then move 'in the direction of Douai with the object of covering the left of the Third Army.' Horne had a reputation as a careful and professional officer who understood the plight of the 'ordinary soldier' and recognised the human cost of war. Yet he was also reputedly a less than outstanding leader. His Chief of Staff (Major General Sir Hastings Anderson) described him 'as stern, reticent and impatient of slackness, indiscipline and eyewash ... [He] was calm and confident in the exercise of his duties ... his decisions were generally sound, crisp and reasoned and ... he was usually happy to leave the detailed execution of orders to his staff.'[10]

When the army commanders were provided an opportunity to present their case, Horne argued that he 'had not yet considered the problem of combining an operation north-eastward with the advance on Douai after he had captured the Vimy Ridge.' However, when informed by Haig that General Sir Edmund Allenby [Third] army should have 'sufficient ground north of the Scarpe to enable it to turn the villages in the valley from the north', Horne modified his stance, asserting that he was 'satisfied ... [and] was quite clear as to the dividing line between himself and the Third Army.' Allenby then outlined the status of his own planning. Noting the existence of caves located to the east of Arras, he told Haig that they would be used 'for the assembly of troops' prior to the attack. There was consensus that the offensive should commence 'very early in the morning ... [because] the enemy had such good observation.' For his part, Gough reported that his Fifth Army would be ready to assist Allenby by attacking enemy positions along the Hindenburg Line near Bullecourt on 8 April.[11]

***

At the same time, more detailed preparations for the Arras offensive were continuing. The Somme experience had taught British GHQ a number of logistics lessons concerning the rapid movement of large numbers of men and quantities of equipment to the front. At first, Nivelle accepted most of Haig's ideas; however he had some misgivings over attacking the high ground around Vimy Ridge. Haig was not to be dissuaded. He warned his French ally that, 'for tactical reasons', with his army 'left on the Vimy Ridge ... [the British] had a secure flank and my attack would bring me *in rear* of the Hindenburg Line.' Haig later explained that he was trying his 'utmost to comply with the strategical requirements of Nivelle's plan, but in the matter of tactics I alone could decide. That is to say, Nivelle having stated that his plan required the British to break the enemy's front north of the Somme and march on Cambrai, I decided *where* and *how* I would dispose of my troops for that purpose.'[12]

Haig was well aware that the capture of Vimy would come at a heavy cost. Already, given its strategic value, the ridge had been the subject of three separate battles during 1915 and 1916. In a poorly planned (and even more poorly executed) attempt in 1915, the French had suffered around 150,000 casualties. Early the following year the British took over the Arras sector and successfully assaulted the ridge. A few months later, in May, German infantry attacked and recaptured Vimy Ridge.

Portrait of Field Marshal Sir Julian Byng, GCB, KCB, KCMG, MVO, CB, signed 'Byng of Vimy'. Byng received plaudits for his expertise in commanding the Canadian Corps at Vimy Ridge and was arguably the finest British and Commonwealth general of World War I (AWM P03717.001).

Horne chose the elite Canadian Corps — comprising the 1st, 2nd, 3rd and 4th Canadian divisions and the 24th British Division — to lead the attack on Vimy. The corps commander, Lieutenant General Sir Julian Byng (undoubtedly one of the better performing senior British officers of the war) was already acknowledged as a no-

nonsense, 'inspiring, tough competent and sympathetic' leader.[13] Fortunately, Horne gave Byng more latitude than usual when planning the operation, as Byng was a shrewd tactician who left little to chance and cared about the lives of his men. Byng, too, was buoyant given Horne's encouragement, writing later that his army commander was 'more than helpful and backed me up in everything'.[14]

A section of Vimy Ridge taken from the basket of a kite balloon stationed over the battlefield, April 1917 (AWM H06972).

The Canadian Corps had also learnt valuable lessons from the Somme. On 15 March Byng began preparing plans for the attack on Vimy. Horne had told him that there were to be two separate attacks — the 'Southern Operation' against 'the main crest with the exception of "The Pimple"', a 200-yard-high hill at its northern end. Horne anticipated that 'The Pimple', together with the Bois-en-Hache across the Souchez, would be taken later in the Northern Operation by the British I Corps. Byng was also warned that he 'would need all his Canadian divisions in the initial assault'. The careful Horne promised that the 5th British Division would act as a reserve, and that there would be 'massive artillery support'. Possibly more meaningfully, Byng was able to secure a large number of machine-guns — 80 for each brigade, including one Lewis light machine-gun for every platoon.[15]

Still not satisfied, Byng intensified his men's training. More extensive preparations included the construction of several underground compartments and tunnels designed to reduce the troops' exposure to enemy artillery and machine-gun fire. Byng also made sure that his sector was provided with adequate electricity, reinforced communication bunkers, command headquarters and dressing stations as well as water pipelines and a light railway and tram system. Attacks were rehearsed and officers and men fully briefed. Byng utilised what he had learnt from other failed attacks, taking particular care to ensure his troops would not advance in waves along an extended straight line. Instead, training at platoon level focused on rapid movement in open formation and, if need be, in a zigzag pattern. Platoon commanders were given more freedom. Their orders were uncomplicated. Not required to adhere to rigid battalion orders, they were able to move their men to where they were needed — and the troops were encouraged not to needlessly expose themselves but rather to look for suitable cover as they crossed no man's land.[16]

***

The main attack, along a front measuring almost 20,000 yards, was finally scheduled for 5.30 am on 8 April. Nivelle's preferred date had been 1 April, and the revised date now meant that the French would have only one week, not the desired two, before they launched their offensive. Allenby had hoped for surprise, although this was virtually impossible to achieve given the enemy's ability to observe Allied troop movements and the consequent intelligence reports which would describe the huge build-up of men and equipment along the entire front. Planning became more intense at Allenby's Third Army headquarters as his men would bear the main brunt of the attack at Arras. The first day's objective was defined as the German trench system fronting the villages of Guemappe and Monchy-le-Preux. The villages were the next objective. Capturing Monchy would be a daunting task. Located on the highest hill, it commanded views of the open fields below — which the British infantry would need to cross. Allenby and his staff were aware of the enormous toll of casualties that the enemy machine-guns and artillery would potentially inflict.

Like Byng, Allenby and his co-planners had learnt a great deal from the flawed British tactics of the previous year. He too ordered his engineers to dig over 12 miles of underground tunnels to complement the caves and which would allow some 24,000 troops to move safely to an attacking position not far from the enemy trenches. Explosives had been laid in disused mines just yards from the German line, ready to be detonated minutes before the infantry attack. Those same infantry had conducted extensive rehearsals and now knew precisely what was required of them.

The assaulting troops were to move in 'open formation' enabling units to 'leapfrog' one another so that the men had time to 'consolidate and regroup'. The engineers had also constructed light railways, enabling ammunition and other necessary supplies to be rushed to the front. However, it has been suggested that there were major flaws in Allenby's preparations, if for no other reason than he allowed technicians who knew their craft — such as tank and Royal Flying Corps (RFC) senior officers — little input into planning. It has even been suggested that Arras 'like the large battles of 1916, was basically another infantry affair in which the big guns, aeroplanes and tanks were assigned supporting parts.'[17]

Supporting parts they may have had, yet all subsidiary arms contributed in one way or another — at least initially. Certainly the artillery planning was time-consuming and comprehensive, albeit with no thanks to Allenby who argued for a brief barrage lasting just 48 hours. Haig, on the other hand, insisted on a lengthier bombardment lasting five days. Despite hostile skies around Arras and the bad weather, which made flying all the more difficult, RFC pilots and observers made a significant contribution, considerably improving the barrage's accuracy. Reports from observers in their flimsy biplanes kept gunnery officers updated with reliable information on the location of mobile German artillery and damage to major gun emplacements. And the artillery observers' role was also improved by recent innovations such as sound ranging and flash spotting. Artillery techniques — which had also proved indecisive on the Somme — had improved markedly. By April 1917 the creeping barrage, which had become more sophisticated since the Somme due to better synchronisation and the enhanced calibration of each gun, was now an essential part of the BEF's doctrine of attack.[18]

Compared to the Somme, where one British heavy gun had to fire on targets every 55 yards of the German front, at Arras one gun covered almost every 20 yards. Better quality ammunition (with fewer 'duds') was also on hand. Barbed wire and other obstacles could now be cut by shells making use of the '106' instantaneous fuse.[19] Eighteen infantry divisions were to be supported by 2818 artillery pieces (almost three times more than the number used on the first day of the Somme) and 2340 Livens Projectors (usually camouflaged tubes arranged for simultaneous electrical firing of Thermite or, in some instances, gas) and, more significantly, a number of tanks.

In fact, a smaller preliminary bombardment had been scheduled to last around three weeks before building up to those final five days — referred to as 'the greatest barrage ever seen'.[20] When the men left their trenches, 'massed machine guns' were to fire 'a barrage' over their heads, while the 'creeping barrage' prevented enemy machine-gun crews leaving their dugouts to fire on British infantry moving across no man's land. Forty tanks were to 'rumble into action alongside' the infantry.[21] Almost at the last minute — and for no apparent reason as the inclement weather was not expected to improve, but rather to worsen — Haig agreed to a request from the French to push back the attack to 5.30 am on 9 April. Regardless of the changes to the plans — and most seemed beneficial, including making available another eight tanks (which now totalled 48) — Haig was still 'confident that the attack has a very good chance.'[22]

***

The British army's first major offensive of 1917 commenced precisely on time. Although the weather had deteriorated as anticipated — turning into a snowstorm — conditions initially offered some assistance to the attacking troops, catching the 10 German divisions unprepared. Despite the movement of thousands upon thousands of British soldiers and equipment to the front, and the interception of uncoded French wireless signals, the German High Command was sure that no attack would take place over that Easter weekend. Intelligence reports had already alerted the enemy to the time and place of the French attack further south. The same reports indicated that the British would launch their offensive at around the same time. Instead, 15 minutes before assaulting troops were to go 'over the top', known German artillery emplacements were shelled with poisonous gas while, almost simultaneously, the carefully prepared mines were exploded with devastating effect.

At Zero Hour the first wave of infantry left their trenches. Facing the British advance was the German *Sixth Army*, commanded by *General-Oberst* von Falkenhausen. If, as suggested, the German general's 'grasp of the concept of the new "elastic defence in depth" was not as firm as that of commanders of other German armies on the Western Front', it was little wonder that 'the Sixth Army was rather caught "in transition" between positional and flexible

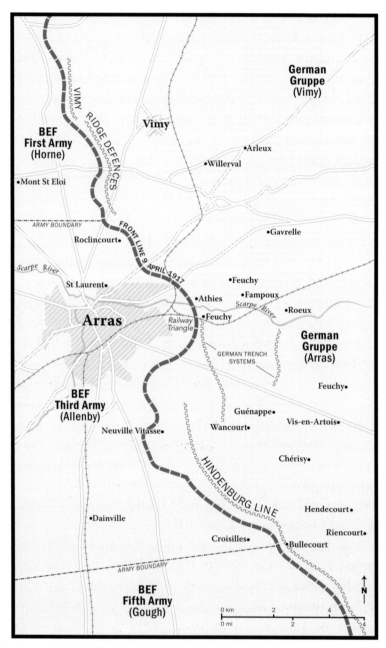

Battle of Arras showing the front on 9 April 1915, River Scarpe and location of the main system of German defensive positions along the Hindenburg Line. Note the location of Bullecourt in relation to Arras.

defensive methods. The main problem on the ground were [sic] that the forward zones remained crammed with troops, instead of lightly manned, and the important *eingrief* (counter-attack) divisions were kept too far to the rear to provide any rapid reaction forces against the British penetration of the German positions.'[23] While some of the planning by senior British officers proved effective, flawed enemy tactics nevertheless partially explain why British troops were able to make such impressive gains on the first day.

Following the initial onslaught, however, the relentless blizzard presented unexpected problems for the attacking troops. In some parts of the line the advance faltered as they discovered that the barbed-wire entanglements remained uncut. In other sections that had somehow escaped the creeping barrage, German troops were able to win the 'race to the parapet' and fire their machine-guns and rifles into lines of attacking infantry. Soon after midday the advance slowed. The tanks, in which British officers had probably placed too much faith, proved almost useless, following not in front, but rather behind the infantry. Others developed mechanical trouble. Some became bogged in the mud. The second and third wave of infantry could not maintain the momentum as the first German reinforcements began reaching the front.

Despite varying reports from different parts of the advance, senior British officers were generally satisfied with the news they received. For instance, in the XVII Corps sector, the 4th and 9th (Scottish) divisions covered over four miles in the most substantial advance since the advent of trench warfare. Along the VI Corps front an advance of some two miles was recorded — including the capture of the tactically important Battery Valley by the 12th and 15th (Scottish) divisions which also seized enemy field guns and their crews along the way. However in the northern sector VII Corps could only move its front forward some 1800 yards. Yet troops were still able to secure the well-defended village of Neuville Vitasse and sections of the enemy's forward trenches.

German troops in trenches not far from Arras watching shell bursts. Note the supply of 'stick-grenades' on right and the equipment each German infantryman carries (AWM H12392).

By nightfall the Third Army was laying claim to another notable achievement — the capture of 5600 prisoners and a large quantity of equipment, including machine-guns and artillery pieces. At 10.25 pm Allenby called a halt, ordering 'all units to consolidate ... in readiness for a renewed push at eight the following morning towards ... Monchy-le-Preux an objective that should have been gained by late afternoon on the first day.'[24] Dusk came as a blessed relief to von Falkenhausen and his regiments. More artillery and *eingrief* units, too far to the rear to offer any relief during the day's fighting, could now move forward under cover of darkness to assist those of his stricken troops still manning front-line trenches. Senior officers remained confident that German courage and discipline would prevent any further breakthrough.

***

Meanwhile, further to the north, at almost the same time on 9 April, the Canadian Corps had attacked Vimy Ridge. An already extensive artillery bombardment (which had commenced on

20 March) intensified as Zero Hour approached. Later reports confirmed that the heavy artillery had silenced a large number of enemy artillery emplacements in the Vimy sector. According to the official Canadian historian (G.W. Nicholson), Byng's careful planning was rewarded as 'This great volume of fire neutralized a large proportion of the enemy's guns.'

Canadian artillery bombardment of German trenches prior to the Canadian attack on Vimy Ridge, April 1917 (AWM H07008).

Protected by a creeping barrage that fired three rounds a minute for three minutes, Canadian infantry moved forward. The carefully calibrated guns 'lifted 100 yards every three minutes, slowing their rate of fire to two rounds per minute.' The field artillery's 18-pounders and a series of machine-guns also contributed to 'a bullet-swept zone 400 yards ahead'. A Canadian soldier recalled that the response of the few remaining enemy guns which had not been destroyed 'to the frantic S.O.S. rocket signals from German front lines was weak and ineffective, the ill-directed counter barrage falling well behind the attacking troops.'[25]

Canadian units advanced purposefully, cleverly utilising their generous allocation of machine-guns. Nicholson adds that 'this employment of machine guns [358 Vickers were assigned to the Canadian Corps] for barrage and supporting fire was on a scale

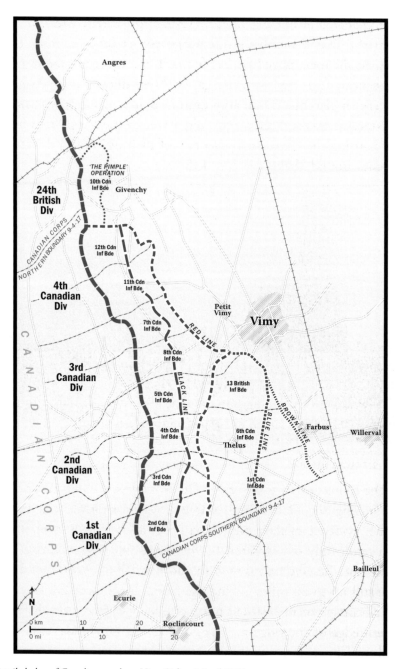

Detailed plan of Canadian attack on Vimy Ridge, 9 April 1917.

unprecedented in military history.' Canadian infantry battalions also received a 'liberal' number of the purpose-built Lewis light machine-guns. As the men moved further forward, mortars and other artillery began firing high explosive and gas shells on the remaining German artillery emplacements and ammunition dumps. Trench mortars laid an extensive smokescreen successfully covering the troops' movement and assisting the Canadians onto two of their objectives, the enemy trenches around Thelus and Hill 135.[26]

Canadian trench mortar shells smash German barbed-wire barriers during the battle for Vimy Ridge, April 1917 (AWM H06981).

The conviction of some senior German officers that their position overlooking the Douai plain was almost impregnable was simply further evidence of their misguided belief in their own invincibility. As a result only one division (*79th Reserve Infantry*) held that part of the line. Reserve troops who should have been rushed into battle were still up to 20 miles behind the front. The Canadians also took full advantage of the narrow band of enemy defences on the steep eastern edge of the ridge and many Germans were trapped in their bunkers. The majority of those in the front-line trenches were either killed or taken prisoner as the Canadian infantry steamrolled forward.

In one of the war's greatest feats, by day's end most of Vimy Ridge had been captured. The *Sixth Army Group* commander (Crown Prince Rupprecht of Bavaria) was in shock — so much so that he decided his troops had little chance of retaking the ridge. He ordered a withdrawal to *III Stellung* (known to the British as the Oppy-Mericourt Line) almost five miles to the east. 'Is it of any use to pursue the war further under such conditions?' he wrote in his diary.[27] The last remaining vestige of German defence on the ridge — around 'The Pimple' — was finally taken by the Canadians on 12 April.

Major General John Monash and his 3rd Australian Division were within 'easy earshot' of the battle. He wrote: 'I went down to see the early stages of it. At night, for many nights past, the southern sky is lit up as by a bushfire, and the roar of the guns has been continuous for days.' However, Monash was disappointed that his division was not drawn into the fight as he believed that 'all is ready'. All that was needed was 'the word from the Chief [Haig]'. Yet, with the Canadians' success, Monash was forced to accept that 'policy in this part of the line is not to move forward, at least *not yet*.'[28]

Byng's biographer wrote that, without question,

Vimy was a great and striking victory for Byng and his Canadians. On a four-mile [seven-kilometre] frontage they had taken what the Germans regarded as an impregnable position, over-running it from its front-line trenches to its supporting artillery positions in a single day. They had then gone on to advance for almost a further five miles [eight kilometres]. The Corps had inflicted heavy casualties on the Germans [the dead numbered almost 2400] including 4,000 prisoners and had seized large quantities of stores and equipment, including 54 guns, 104 trench mortars and 124 machine guns.

Success, however, came at a cost: of the 10,602 Canadian casualties, 3598 were listed as killed.[29]

***

On 10 April Haig confided to his diary, '[considering] the 3rd Army is held up on the West of Monchy-le-Preux I urged Allenby to push forward on the H[eights] of the Scarpe and then move SE in rear of Monchy so as to turn the enemy's flank. He is to do this if circumstances require it.'[30] On the same day British troops attempted to follow up their impressive first day's results, attacking Monchy-le-Preux at around 8.00 am. While the assaults around Arras may have been planned as a 'diversionary' for the larger French offensive, Haig and Allenby now also believed that the 'decisive breakthrough', of which they could only previously dream, was a possibility. Allenby was reportedly 'in a state of high excitement' at the prospect. In less than two days' fighting the line had moved forward almost five miles, 'an unprecedented distance by the standards of the time, and units freed from their trenches were now fighting a battle of manoeuvre in open country.'[31] The following day parts of Monchy were captured. But German defenders in the western part of the village held out, allowing the main body of reinforcements, artillery and *eingreif* units to reach the front.

Intelligence reports describing how *eingreif* divisions, supported by artillery batteries, had moved into position along the Drocourt-Queant line should have alerted Allenby and indeed Gough to the obvious. With more German troops and artillery in and around the sector, Gough certainly needed to revise his plans for the attack on Bullecourt. The optimistic Allenby also maintained pressure on his exhausted troops, telling officers that 'risks must be freely taken in pressuring a defeated enemy'.[32] Allenby was presumably unaware that *Oberst* Fritz von Lossberg, the acknowledged expert on the elastic defence concept and mastermind of the Hindenburg Line had been named *Sixth Army*'s Chief of Staff, his appointment to take effect immediately.

For the British generals worse was to follow. By mid-morning on 11 April their advance had all but run out of steam. Troops moving forward were now encountering uncut German wire. And, having outpaced their horse-drawn 18-pounder field artillery, the infantry were facing difficulties of their own from the mobile German artillery, while British gunners attempted to move their artillery within range of the enemy front line. The Germans may have suffered terrible losses (two days of bitter fighting cost their *Sixth Army* more than 15,000 casualties and 7000 prisoners, while 112 artillery pieces and 350 machine-guns had been lost) but, with plentiful reinforcements in place and the British overextending their lines of communication, the German infantry were soon able to mount a counter-attack.

By the next day Haig's dream of a breakthrough was in tatters. At Third Army headquarters he told Allenby's Chief of Staff (Major General Louis Bols) that,

> ... the Enemy had now been given time to put the Drocourt-Queant line into a state of defence and to organise positions also in our immediate front. He has also brought up a large amount of guns. Our advance must therefore be more methodical than was permissible ... after the Enemy had been surprised and had no reserves on the Spot! Now we must try and substitute shells as far as possible for infantry.[33]

But the following day Haig's hopes for a breakthrough appear to have been rekindled. He wrote to his wife in London telling her that the 'effect of our Victory will be great. Already the Enemy has begun to fall back from north of Vimy.' Later the same day, while visiting the front, he remained buoyant. 'The battlefields had already been well cleaned up,' he noted. However, while motoring to Blairville, he became aware of the difficulties his gunners were encountering and again became disheartened, noting the

> ... heavy artillery which were all ready to leave their emplacements ... on the edge of the Bapaume road and advance to new positions further forward. It is fairly easy work moving these great heavy guns nowadays by means of tractors. The real difficulty is getting the large amount of shells forward. Luckily our railways are following our advance well.

Perhaps Haig was now more concerned at Nivelle's request to 'postpone [French] operations for another day'. For his part, the Frenchman was adamant that he would not go ahead with the postponement unless it suited Haig. Haig 'concurred', adding 'that since the French had been given the main decisive attack to carry out we must do all in our power to help them make their operations a success.'[34]

The Arras sector had, by now, become yet another battle of attrition with both sides suffering enormous casualties. Allenby, however, was not to be dissuaded. On 14 April he again sought to continue the advance. But three of his divisional commanders had had enough. When their argument was overruled by Allenby, they disregarded British army convention and went directly to GHQ, telling Haig that Allenby's 'attempt to narrow advances left vulnerably exposed flanks'. Haig immediately overruled Allenby and 'ordered a suspension of operations'.[35] British losses in five days of battle amounted to almost 80,000 men. However the senior British officers appeared to have learnt little, as Arras 'was not the last time that the limitations of the bite-and-hold approach were to be revealed in the year 1917.'[36] Yet some purpose had been achieved. The German High Command had been forced to rush badly needed men and equipment from the Aisne sector.

**

Despite opposition from the newly elected French government of Prime Minister Alexandre Ribot — which even considered cancelling the entire operation as late as 6 April — Nivelle finally launched his great offensive. After a prolonged 14-day artillery bombardment, on 16 April, *poilus* of the French Fifth and Sixth armies attacked along a 25-mile front. The attacks were intended to bring the German army to its knees; however, following limited success the offensive turned to yet another disaster for the Allies. Exhausted and short of troops, the French army could do little more than hold its section of the line. On

30 April large numbers of French *poilus* mutinied, refusing to enter the battle.[37] A further French offensive was out of the question, at least until the arrival of large numbers of American troops. The United States had declared war on Germany on 6 April and Haig recognised that it would take at least 12 months for sufficiently suitably trained men and supplies to be on hand to assist the French. In the meantime the BEF would need to assume the role of principal fighting force in France.

***

Further south, Gough had been putting the finishing touches to his plans for the Fifth Army's diversionary attack on the Hindenburg Line. Troops from the 4th Australian Division, fresh from resting behind the lines, were said to be hungry for another strike at the enemy. At the small, sleepy French hamlet of Bullecourt, that appetite was to be sated.

CHAPTER 3

'It was an anxious time.'

THE OFFENSIVE SPIRIT

On 9 April, while British and Canadian troops were fighting for the heights around Arras and Vimy Ridge, further south, the 1st Australian Division captured the last of the outpost villages. Now Gough, commander of the Fifth Army, could focus his efforts on attacking German positions along his sector of the Hindenburg Line. Bullecourt had already been chosen as the centre of the attack for two of Gough's divisions — the 62nd British and 4th Australian.

***

General Sir Hubert de la Poer Gough — to whom responsibility for planning the attack on Bullecourt fell — epitomised the best and worst qualities of the typical British cavalry officer. Gough's initial success as a commander was due to his energy, drive and ruthlessness — characteristics that subsequently ensured his unpopularity with many in the army. He could be utterly charming to those he needed — such as his friend, supporter and fellow cavalryman, General Sir Douglas Haig — and dismissive and rude to others, particularly subordinates. Certainly Haig had a great deal of time for his army commander and continued to support him even when it was clear to almost everyone else that Gough was 'not up to the job'. Possibly, as has been suggested, he supported Gough for no other reason than he fitted the idyll as 'the typical cavalryman of popular imagination, who would hurl himself, his horse or his men at any obstacle, where Haig was much more dour, a pounder ... Perhaps Haig saw in Gough some facet that was missing in his own personality and which he therefore admired.'[1]

Temperamentally, Gough was a 'thruster', inclined towards hasty, ill-prepared attacks without proper reconnaissance, frequently on a narrow front — although, to be fair, this was not always the case. For instance, in April 1915, when he was a major general commanding the 7th Division, Gough made a 'personal reconnaissance' prior to an attack at Aubers Ridge which convinced him of its 'uselessness' and 'the certainty of any further attempt being a failure'.[2] Stubborn and impulsive by nature, he seldom listened to subordinates, instead 'bullying' them and demanding that they display the 'offensive spirit'. Staff work throughout the Fifth Army was reportedly 'deficient'. Despite having been commended for his leadership during the Boer War as a regimental commander on the South African veldt, Gough remained aloof, remote from the needs of his front-line troops.

General Sir Hubert Gough (right) inspecting the entrance to a former German dugout with the King of the Belgians, 16 May 1917 (AWM H12215).

Gough's poor standing with Australian officers and men was apparent as far back as 18 July 1916 when, as commander of the Reserve Army (renamed the Fifth Army in October 1916), he ordered

Major General H.B. 'Hooky' Walker, GOC 1st Australian Division, 'to go into the line and attack Pozieres tomorrow night'. Walker could not believe what he was hearing. How, in little over a day, could he be expected to prepare and issue orders for an attack on a 'heavily defended, strategically vital village which had already been the target of a number of unsuccessful assaults'? Walker confided to his diary that these were 'Scrappy & unsatisfactory orders from Reserve Army ... Hope shall not be rushed into an ill prepared ... operation but fear I shall.' Walker also recognised the need for more artillery. His plan was to launch the attack from the south-east, ignoring Gough's preference for the south-west — the area from which previous unsuccessful British attempts had been launched. Only with the intervention of the I ANZAC Corps Chief of Staff (Major General Brudenell White) and following strenuous protest from Walker, did Gough agree to postpone the attack until 23 July. But the damage to Gough's reputation with Australian troops had already been done. His standing was further tarnished by Walker's subsequent assessment: 'the very worst exhibition of Army commandship [sic] that occurred during the whole campaign, though God knows the 5th army was a tragedy throughout.'[3]

Gough had acquired similar notoriety for his style of command throughout the BEF, which 'grew so vocal that even Haig came to hear of it'.[4] This was compounded by his poor choice of Major General Neill Malcolm as the Fifth Army's Chief of Staff. Disliked by most commanders for 'exceed[ing] his powers' Malcolm was, like Gough, a 'bully' who usually overstepped the Chief of Staff's role. More than one senior officer reportedly harboured an 'instinctive feeling of mistrust for Malcolm as an Army chief of staff.' Another confidante of Haig, Brigadier General Philip Howell, when transferred to the Fifth Army, wrote of the malaise he encountered. He considered Gough 'really quite a child & can be managed like one if treated as such & humoured. M[alcolm] is at the bottom of half the mischievous ideas & mischief making.'[5]

For his part, Gough subsequently wrote that 'commanding an Army was not much different from commanding a battalion', and laid the blame for his failures squarely on the shoulders of his staff. He believed Neill Malcolm to be 'too impatient with those who are slow'. This was mild criticism compared to Gough's dismissal of Malcolm's predecessor, Herbert Lawrence, whom he labelled 'useless as a Chief of Staff'.[6] What Gough failed to explain, however, was why it took so long for him to reach these conclusions, and why he did not attempt to replace these 'useless' and 'impatient' men.

Many fellow officers believed that Gough had been over-promoted.[7] Even taking into account how speedily the BEF in France and Flanders had expanded throughout 1915 and 1916, his rise had been rapid. In August 1914 Gough was a brigadier general commanding the 3rd Cavalry Brigade, part of Allenby's division. The following month he was promoted to major general and given command of the 2nd Cavalry Division. At just 44 years of age Gough was the youngest British divisional commander on the Western Front. In April 1915 he was named GOC 7th Division — his first infantry command. Soon after, in the summer of 1915, Gough was promoted lieutenant general and appointed commander of I Corps, attached to General Haig's First Army. Finally, in late May 1916, he was named commander of the Reserve Army, which had been specifically formed for the Somme offensive.

Gough was certainly indebted to Haig for his rapid promotion to Reserve Army commander.[8] Yet Gough was at his best — and happiest — when 'commanding, sometimes by remote control, low level formations' at divisional, even brigade level. Unfortunately, he did not take the time to confer with his divisional or corps commanders and allowed them little input when planning battles, probably best reflected in his insistence on using corps to pass to divisions the detailed plans and other orders drawn up at Fifth Army headquarters. Quite simply, Gough chose to 'bypass' the corps level, favouring a rather 'hands-on style of command' at division and brigade level.

Gough has since been lauded as a general 'who could be trusted to approach the problem with ambition, optimism and drive'.[9] However by March 1917 very few British officers and men shared this opinion — and even fewer Australians. Birdwood certainly had little confidence in Gough's ability to approach any problem methodically. He and most fellow officers on his staff at I ANZAC headquarters were concerned about Gough's intellectual capacity, particularly his planning of major battles. In late January 1917 Birdwood was said to be livid and 'very sick at going to the V Army'. The Australians were not alone in harbouring scant regard for Gough's ability. By April 1917 he had acquired an even more unenviable reputation among his own officers and men. Richard Haldane, for instance, wrote that Gough 'terrorises those under him to the extent that they are afraid to express their opinions for fear of being degomme [sacked].' Some of the more junior officers now accepted that 'heavy losses & complete failure [were] very typical [of] General Gough who apparently does not care a button about the lives of his men.'[10]

British military historian J.M. Bourne, who conducted a detailed study of British command during World War I, identified further flaws in Gough's style of leadership: 'There was a particularly unattractive streak of arrogance and contemptuousness in Gough, which was a weakness in a commander. All great commanders are formidable, but those who are also unapproachable run a real risk of isolating themselves from unpleasant truths.'[11]

Bean, too, had strong opinions on Gough's method of command. While admitting that he did not 'really know enough about Gough to be sure of the nature of his intellect', Bean was not backward in airing his critique. Gough 'had no grasp of the principles which were necessary for the control of great offensives,' he wrote, before adding that the British general

> ... was a cavalry officer and would have been an excellent dashing patrol-leader, but he made many gross mistakes with his army. His worst fault, we used to think, was his

tendency to undertake partial and disjointed attacks on narrow sectors. His chief of staff [Malcolm] cannot I think have been an officer of sufficient grasp, or he would probably have prevailed on his general to prevent some of these attacks. I wouldn't say, however, that his staff was extremely inefficient. I personally think that Gough was a very bad general, impulsive and thoughtless, and he probably made great difficulties for his staff.[12]

Gough's philosophy for the attack was simple. 'Whenever we had enough troops per yard we would always beat the Boche', he wrote. 'It was only when he was allowed to concentrate a crushing superiority that he was able to drive us back.'[13] His inclination towards 'impetuosity and attacking without adequate preparation' was on show again during the early stages of the German withdrawal in February 1917. While visiting the 91st Brigade headquarters Gough was informed of the situation at the front. His initial reaction was to order an 'immediate pursuit'. Brigadier General H.R. Cummings, the brigade commander, felt compelled to advise Gough that 'such a move was impossible before daylight on account of the nature of the ground.' There was also the troops' exhaustion to consider. Following an extensive and animated discussion, Gough relented. Cummings wrote that Gough finally left 'with many injunctions to press on as early and as fast as possible', adding that, only then, could he and the brigade staff plan the 'thousand and one details essential to the morrow's operations.'[14] Yet again, Gough ignored the requirement for detailed planning, particularly that associated with the coordination of artillery and infantry.

Countering these negative assessments were some positive critiques. Duff Cooper, for instance, believed that, while 'he gathered from soldiers that Gough was not fit for anything higher than Divisional Commander ... he had more flair than the other Army commanders but needed the conditions that suited him.'[15] Liddell Hart believed that,

> ... one of the most likeable things about Gough is that unlike so many senior soldiers he has no pomposity – perhaps adversity helped to prevent him developing it ... Even under the extraordinary cramping conditions of the Western Front ... his performance was a lot better than was generally recognised. He received the blame for other people's failures ... and was much less at fault himself than some who preserved their commands and reputations.[16]

While these assessments lend some weight to Gough's more positive character traits, they do not explain why, no more than a few months later, in his hasty plans for attacking Bullecourt, and in conditions that certainly did not suit him, Gough yet again was to demonstrate his tendency towards impetuosity and lack of preparation.

***

After taking part in what some senior British officers referred to as 'minor operations' around Gueudecourt including, in early February, the fight for 'Stormy Trench', the 4th Australian Division was taken out of the line for some well-deserved rest. Reinforcements arrived while the division was being refitted with weapons and equipment at Albert, on the old Somme battlefield, well behind the front. Lieutenant William Shirtley believed that nothing had changed. He wrote that 'this country is still the same. Mud deeper if anything. All's quiet on the Western Front.'[17]

Another soldier expressed a different view, noting that 'We seemed to be in a new land, out of the war area altogether. Here new green could be seen shooting smoothly up, and flowers. Aye, one could hear singing birds too – larks and nightingales. The ... [entire division] from one end to the other, was whistling and singing.'[18] Percy Toft also later recalled that this was a 'somewhat agreeable' period, with football a popular pastime. Four states 'played the Australian Rules code', the other two (New South Wales and Queensland) took part in games of rugby. The matches were sometimes 'brutal. Goudecourt memory was still rankling. Both sides played the man, though all were fair to good footballers. One or two of the men had represented Australia and there were some Interstate representatives.'

But alongside the fun and games was some intensive training. Toft added that the troops 'practiced open warfare. It was very pleasant riding spirited horses across a big plain in which there were no shell holes.' By mid-March recently arrived reinforcements from Australia had boosted the complement of all battalions to something approaching full strength. Toft now believed that the 4th 'Brigade had reached its zenith, its maximum power. Never again was it so good or so strong. Since the landing on Gallipoli and the first attack at Poziers [sic] battalions had fought at an average of 600 men. We were now to fight beyond full strength and as experienced soldiers. How proud all commanders, high and low, were of their men. Pride and a fall – how often that is true.'[19] By early April the men were reportedly 'in splendid fettle' and spoiling for battle.[20]

***

The 4th Division had been raised as recently as early 1916. Following the tragic eight-month Gallipoli campaign, the AIF was reorganised and expanded. In late 1915 the depleted Australian units from Gallipoli returned to Egypt to be reorganised and receive reinforcements. The 1st Division, which had endured the worst of the fighting, and the 4th Infantry Brigade were to be broken up, which meant the complement of each infantry battalion was approximately halved. The new battalions were then boosted to almost full strength by reinforcements arriving from Australia. From the outset the 4th (and 5th) divisions were characterised by an ideal blending of troops: those with combat experience from the peninsula, commanded by energetic, youthful officers who had earned their commissions through their ability to lead men in the heat of battle, supplemented by men who had little idea of what to expect when exposed to unnerving combat. Yet, what was to come in fighting on the Western Front was far worse than anything they could have imagined.

Portrait of Major General William Holmes, GOC 4th Australian Division (AWM 133440).

The unattached 4th Infantry Brigade combined with the newly formed 12th and 13th infantry brigades as the 4th Division. Men destined for specialist formations — such as artillery, engineers, machine-gun companies and 'supply' units — were all carefully chosen, as were the division, brigade and battalion commanders. Divisional commanders were the first appointed. Birdwood, to whom this task fell, considered that 'there was no officer of the AIF whom he could suitably recommend for the new commands. There were, however, in Egypt several British generals already recognised as men of outstanding capacity.' Considering the mettle displayed by Australian brigade commanders at Gallipoli, the Australian government was justifiably disappointed that Birdwood could not find suitable officers from the AIF. The Minister, Senator Pearce, informed Birdwood that 'the appointments of these [British] officers can only have a heart breaking effect on Australian officers in being debarred from attaining the high distinction.'[21] But Birdwood prevailed. The Sandhurst-educated Indian army officer Major General H. Vaughan Cox was named commander of the 4th Australian Division. He commanded the division throughout 1916 until replaced in January 1917 by an Australian, Major General William Holmes.

Born on 12 September 1862, Holmes' credentials were solid. He came from a military family and had been a citizen soldier since the age of 10. He left school to join the New South Wales Public Service, where he became Secretary and Chief Clerk of the Metropolitan Board of Water Supply and Sewerage. As a young man he had served as a bugler with the 1st Infantry Regiment of the New South Wales Colonial Forces before being commissioned in 1886. Holmes served with distinction during the Boer War, where he was awarded the Distinguished Service Order (DSO), Mentioned in Despatches and promoted to brevet lieutenant colonel for his exploits at Colesberg, Pretoria and Diamond Hill. Wounded at Diamond Hill, he returned to Sydney in August 1900. In 1903 he was appointed commander of the 1st New South Wales Infantry Regiment. His next promotion was far less rapid — Holmes had to wait until 1912 for promotion to colonel and command of the 6th Infantry Brigade.

When war was declared Holmes was handed the rather unflattering appointment of commander of the Australian Naval and Military Expeditionary Force, tasked with the capture of German New Guinea. After acting as administrator of the seized colony until January 1915, Holmes was finally given a more substantial appointment. In March 1915 he took command of the

5th Infantry Brigade, which he led at Gallipoli from August until the evacuation. Holmes then took the brigade to France, where he received accolades for his leadership throughout the dreadful Somme campaign, from mid to late 1916. He was rewarded with command of the 4th Division.

Brigadier General Charles Henry Brand, GOC 4th Australian Infantry Brigade (AWM ART03181).

Holmes' brigadiers were all proven and fearless leaders. Brigadier General Charles Henry Brand commanded the 4th Brigade. Brand commenced his career as a schoolteacher in Queensland, but retained a strong interest in the military. In 1898, at the age of 25, Brand received his commission in the Queensland Volunteer Infantry and twice volunteered for service in the Boer War. In 1905 he decided to pursue a permanent Army career, joining the Administrative and Instructional Staff, where he remained until the declaration of war in 1914. Appointed brigade major of the 3rd Brigade, he saw action at Gallipoli — indeed he was one of the 'original' Anzacs, having landed on the first morning, afterwards assisting to establish the beachhead. Wounded in mid-May during a Turkish counter-attack, he was subsequently evacuated. By July his wounds had healed sufficiently for him to return to the fighting and he was immediately appointed commanding officer of the 8th Battalion. From August until the evacuation in December, Brand fearlessly led his men at Steele's Post, one of the most exposed positions on the peninsula. In France he was named commander of the 6th Brigade and, in June 1916, when John Monash was promoted major general and given command of the recently raised 3rd Australian Division, Brand took over as commander of the 4th Brigade.

Brigadier General James Campbell Robertson, GOC 12th Australian Infantry Brigade (AWM ART02991).

At the outbreak of war the 36-year-old James Campbell Robertson was a well-known Queensland stockbroker who took part-time soldiering seriously. In 1903 he was commissioned a lieutenant in the 14th Light Horse Regiment, transferring to the infantry soon after. By 1913 Robertson had reached the rank of major. On 20 August 1914 he enlisted in the AIF and was immediately appointed second-in-command of the 9th Battalion. Wounded at the Gallipoli landing, he was evacuated to Egypt, returning to the peninsula on 3 June to be appointed commanding officer of the 9th Battalion. Following the evacuation Robertson took the battalion to Egypt to absorb and train new recruits before moving to the Western Front. He commanded the unit through some of the heaviest and bloodiest fighting experienced on the Somme. His outstanding leadership did not go unnoticed — on 8 March 1917 he was recommended for the DSO. Earlier, on 18 November 1916, Robertson had been promoted temporary brigadier general and given command of the 12th Brigade.

Brigadier General Thomas Glasgow, GOC 13th Australian Infantry Brigade (AWM ART03341).

The 13th Brigade was commanded by another Queenslander, Thomas William Glasgow. At the age of just 19 he joined the Wide Bay Regiment, part of the Queensland Colonial Forces, but was forced to wait another six years before being granted a commission in the Queensland Mounted Infantry. Shortly afterwards, Glasgow left for South Africa in one of the Queensland contingents. Distinguishing himself in action at the relief of Kimberley and the occupation of Bloemfontein, he was Mentioned in Despatches and awarded the DSO. At the outbreak of war in 1914, he was a major in the 13th Light Horse Regiment, stationed around Gympie. After volunteering for the AIF, Glasgow was named second-in-command of the 2nd Light Horse Regiment. He, too, saw action at Gallipoli. After coming ashore on 15 May Glasgow took command of Australian troops on Pope's Hill. He then went on to lead one of the assaults in the unsuccessful August offensives in which 154 of the 200 men who took part were either killed or wounded. Glasgow yet again demonstrated that his own courage was beyond doubt, endearing himself to his troops when, without regard for his personal safety, he carried out a badly wounded Australian soldier. In late August he was appointed commanding officer of the unit. His next promotion was swift — while assisting in the reorganisation of the AIF in Egypt, he was appointed commander of the recently raised 13th Infantry Brigade. In France he led the unit throughout the appalling Somme campaign.

Unsurprisingly, the battalion commanding officers of the 4th Australian Division could not claim the same experience or expertise. Yet, as Bean points out, the appointments were usually given to 'picked men either those who had performed outstanding service – such as [Raymond] Leane of the 48th ... or young officers of an especially fine character who had come to the front in hard fighting at Anzac ... Such selections were in every case justified; with Australian material a commander of the right character quickly created a magnificent battalion.' And, while there may have been a few questionable appointments among some of the 'older' junior officers whose main claim to promotion was their age and seniority, those men had been weeded out and replaced by the end of the Somme campaign.[22] By April 1917 all the battalions belonging to the 4th Division could be confident that they were commanded by officers with the right mettle and well-credentialled leadership skills.

Portrait of five of the six Leane brothers. L to R standing: Major Benjamin Bennett Leane (1889–1917), 48th Battalion; Lieutenant Colonel Raymond Lionel Leane, MC (1878–1962), 11th Battalion; Warrant Officer Class 1 Ernest Albert Leane (1869–?), 27th Battalion. Seated: Major Edwin Thomas Leane (1867–1928), AIF Ordnance Service and Major Allan William Leane (1872–1917) 28th Battalion (AWM P02136_001).

***

Following their well-earned break of several months, most men from the 4th Australian Division were excited at the prospect of being sent into the line once again to face the enemy. Yet, despite the advent of more mobile warfare and the ease with which most of the outpost villages had been taken, the Australians knew that a formidable task lay ahead. From their vantage points they observed the extensive and unbroken coils of barbed wire stretched across no man's land close to the village of Bullecourt. The troops could only guess the strength of the German trenches that lay beyond. Yet most felt confident that, with good planning and leadership, they could break and hold this sector of the Hindenburg Line. They were blissfully unaware of the difficulties and uncertainties that plagued Gough's Fifth Army headquarters which were to permeate through to division, brigade and even battalion plans for the advance.

CHAPTER 4

'As formidable a blow as possible.'
PLANNING THE ATTACK

While the outpost villages were being captured, Birdwood had become well acquainted with the fact that Haig and Gough had a far larger task in store for his Australian troops. Indeed, the Fifth Army commander had become animated by the rapid capture of those villages and the efficiency with which the so-called 'war of movement' was progressing. With the major Arras offensive fast approaching, he wanted nothing less than a significant involvement for his Fifth Army. The concept of a combined Australian and British attack in the Bullecourt sector of the Hindenburg Line was already part of Haig's planning for Arras although, originally, it had been scheduled to commence prior to the main offensive. When I ANZAC Corps (comprising the 1st, 2nd, 4th and 5th Australian divisions) was again attached to the Fifth Army, Haig had told Gough that this 'may enable you to undertake more than [what] is contemplated ... the preliminary operations to be based on the general idea of enabling you to launch as formidable a blow as possible *shortly before* the Third Army opens its attack.'[1]

Haig's plan to launch an offensive of one kind or another in the Fifth Army sector was apparent as early as January 1917. His initial plan called for Gough to support the Third Army with a 'north-easterly thrust into the Bapaume salient'.[2] On 30 January Haig advanced further concepts for another diversionary attack with 'the objective of Achiet-le-Grand'. A few days later he had yet another change of mind. On 5 February the Chief of the General Staff, Lieutenant General Sir Launcelot Edward Kiggell, informed Gough that his chief wanted more, and that the Fifth Army should:

> ... strike the enemy as strong and vigorous a blow as possible on
> the front between Gueudecourt and Beaumont Hamel ... with

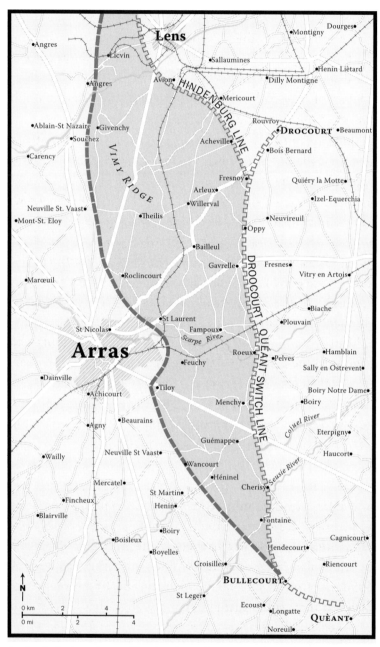

Map showing the furthest advance of British and Canadian troops at the Battle of Arras. Also shown are the positions of Bullecourt and surrounding villages, which General Gough planned to attack in early April.

the object of breaking the enemy's front and attracting as many of his reserves as possible in order to facilitate the operations of the Third Army ... The C-in-C recognises that, with the forces at your disposal, it will probably be necessary to operate in 'bites' and that, of course, the extent of each 'bite' must depend on the number of divisions and guns allotted to the Fifth Army.

Kiggell pointed out yet again that the main reason for the attack was no more than a feint (or diversion) to take some pressure off the major thrust further north.[3]

Haig and his co-planners anticipated that the Germans would react by sending badly needed troops from the Arras front to the areas under attack around Bullecourt. But, once again, Haig also had other ideas. Just a couple of weeks later he informed Gough that the plan needed further amendment, and that he should devise 'the largest and most vigorous attack ... and to retain sufficient fresh troops ... to continue the struggle energetically for a week or more.'[4] But when news that the Germans were pulling back to the Hindenburg Line reached GHQ, the original purpose of the Fifth Army's assault seemed no longer relevant because, as Kiggell pointed out, 'to attract German reserves so close to the point of the main attack would be worse than useless.'[5]

***

The German withdrawal had not altered Haig's approach. Gough was now instructed to continue pursuing German rearguard units to the Hindenburg Line and to develop further plans for a joint British-Australian attack in the area between Bullecourt and Queant. Most of the other plans were placed on hold, including any thought of attacks on the front between Gueudecourt and Beaumont Hamel. It was believed that, should Allenby's army achieve the much sought-after breakthrough, enemy troops would probably fall back to the Drocourt-Queant switch, a well-constructed switch line with strong fortifications, including concrete bunkers with cleverly sited machine-gun nests providing the maximum field of fire, and another two lines of defensive trenches which ran between the villages of Drocourt and Queant.

Gough and Haig were presumably aware that any attack around Bullecourt-Queant would be very challenging for at least three reasons. First, considering the poor state of the roads and the destroyed railway tracks, which already overstretched the lines of communication, the massing of suitable quantities of artillery within striking distance on that part of the front would be slow and labour intensive. And, for the same reason, supplying those guns with sufficient wire-cutting ammunition as well as high explosive shells would prove a formidable task, if not nigh on impossible. Second, due to the priority of artillery and ammunition for the Arras offensive, the First and Third armies were provided the greater part of the available heavy guns, howitzers and ammunition, which meant that there was a limited number for the Fifth Army — even if the roads and railway line were improved. And third, the Hindenburg Line around Bullecourt and especially Queant, with its far more formidable defences, presented a daunting obstacle. From its inception, Haig's scheme represented an extremely difficult task for Gough and his staff.

By this time Gough had drafted another plan for an attack along the main road linking Ecoust to Hendecourt, which led to other smaller roads and tracks behind the German lines. Gough believed that Australian and British infantry, assisted by an Indian cavalry regiment, could fan out to push the advance even further north. Haig, however, could not be persuaded. Instead, he again changed his mind. For the moment at least, he wanted nothing more than an artillery barrage along the Fifth Army's sector of the Hindenburg Line. Gough was not content. He wanted more. He told Haig that two divisions from the Fifth Army were already prepared to assist British and Canadian divisions around Arras by attacking those German positions around Bullecourt and Queant, an action which Haig had sought as early as 8 April.[6]

Haig, however, now apparently understood that Gough had insufficient troops to succeed in such an undertaking, particularly without an adequate softening-up artillery barrage. And someone on Haig's staff agreed, recording that the 'Fifth Army may be [too] weak' for such an operation. Allenby, too, had similar thoughts. Previously, on 11 March, he had acknowledged that there was nowhere near enough artillery in the Fifth Army's arsenal, and that the formation was 'not in a condition to assume a vigorous offensive … [although] we may expect help on our right flank as we advance with our right on the Hindenburg Line.'[7]

Gough's stubbornness now came to the fore. Basically agreeing with Allenby's thoughts, he added that:

… a breach of the Hindenburg Line at Bullecourt, on the immediate flank of the main offensive, would be tactically of great assistance to General Allenby. The Third Army was to operate south-eastward, with Cambrai as general objective, and the axis of its advance would be the main Arras-Cambrai road. Bullecourt was only three and a half miles distant from this road at Vis en Artois, less than two miles from Fontaine les Croisilles; and these two places were on the first objective of the Cavalry Corps, which was to pass through the infantry of the Third Army.

Perhaps, too, there were other reasons at play. Along with Allenby, Gough was a leading contender to command the major British offensive later in the year at Ypres in Flanders. Gough could not allow his rival general to gain an advantage by commanding a major offensive while he was sitting idly by. Thus he was 'eager to do all in his power to aid the Third.'

By now Haig had become more optimistic over prospects for success in the Arras offensive. He decided that any breakthrough must be immediately exploited. He informed Gough that a success at Arras would, most likely, force the Germans to pull back through Monchy to the Drocourt-Queant switch, where they could be trapped. Now

Haig could realistically sanction an attack against the Hindenburg Line around Bullecourt and asked Gough to revisit his original plans.

Gough had become even more conscious of the tactical boost he could provide Allenby whose army was primed to move south-east, the axis of its advance the principal Arras-Cambrai road. The village of Bullecourt was a short three and a half miles from where Vis en Artois joined the road and only some two miles from Fontaine lez Croisilles — the two villages that were part of the Cavalry Corps' first objective as they passed through the Third Army.[8] Grandiose plans these may have been, yet to Gough they were quite achievable.

***

On 20 March Gough met with his two corps commanders and their chiefs of staff. He told them that a prerequisite to the Bullecourt attack was the capture of the remainder of the 'rearguard' villages. Gough was now of the opinion that the best place to attack the Hindenburg Line was around the village of Queant, approximately 500 yards forward of the Hindenburg Line where it joined the Drocourt-Queant switch. He was presumably unaware of the numerous well-sited German machine-gun positions already in place around the village. He was now also considering initially bypassing Bullecourt, instead moving against both exposed flanks and only attacking the village later, once the flanks had been consolidated. But, as Gough went on to explain, 'it was still too early to determine the point of attack, this being dependent rather upon Allenby's desire.'[9] However, he decided that the major attack against the Hindenburg Line and the frontage to the left (western edge) of Bullecourt should be launched by Major General Walter Braithwaite's 62nd (West Riding) British Division. The more difficult right sector (on the eastern side) around Queant was to be attacked by two brigades from the 4th Australian Division.

Yet again (and not for the last time) Gough was attracted to his earlier idea of including a direct assault on Queant. He wrote that the village was tactically crucial due to its position at the junction of the Drocourt-Queant Switch with the Hindenburg Line. By now Gough was receiving intelligence reports which should have alerted him to the much stronger defences around Queant and the ongoing construction of more machine-gun emplacements. South of Queant there was another obstacle where his infantry would have to break through not two but rather four lines of trenches — a front and a support line in each structure of the 'switch' — instead of only two to the west of the village. Queant was, in fact, the focal point of that almost impenetrable line of trenches, having also been recognised by the German High Command as the key to its vital tactical and strategic position.

Haig did not need to be told of the opportunities that a breakthrough around Queant presented. Not only would the Australian-British attack close to this part of the Hindenburg Line succeed in releasing pressure on the main attack further north but, if successful, it could be the start of an encircling movement which could trap withdrawing German troops and expose their flanks, a result Haig had sought from the outset. Indeed Haig was now beginning to form an even more grandiose picture. Further successful attacks could drive the German army from as far as Cambrai to the North Sea. However, following discussions with senior staff, he reappraised the idea. The original plan — a major attack at Arras along with a minor offensive in the Bullecourt sector — was regarded as achievable. Only later, when conditions had become more favourable, would British and Australian troops move against the Drocourt-Queant switch in a 'lateral thrust'.[10]

However — as Haig and Gough were well aware — the already tricky advance at Bullecourt and Queant was made all the more difficult by the fact that this part of the German line formed a re-entrant. As Australian and British troops moved closer to their objective, not only would they encounter heavy fire from both sides (Bullecourt on the left and Queant on the right), but also from the line of enemy trenches directly in front. There were also other well-placed machine-gun posts at the Six Cross Roads. The only means of crossing in the face of this murderous fire was through the employment of an intense preliminary artillery barrage and 'neutralising fire' designed to persuade enemy infantry and machine-gunners 'to cower in the bottom of its trenches and stay there for the duration of the attack', followed by a creeping barrage to provide cover for advancing infantry crossing no man's land.[11]

The effective combination of all these ideas into one unambiguous plan was becoming an administrative nightmare at Fifth Army headquarters, particularly given the ongoing shortage of guns and suitable ammunition. This was a challenge that Gough and his staff were simply unable to meet. As if this was not sufficient, Gough had another rush of blood, deciding that the Australians should go on to capture the village of Riencourt, another 800 yards or so beyond the Hindenburg Line and then, alongside the British division, attack the village of Hendecourt.

***

By 22 March Gough and his staff had become highly optimistic at their prospects for success. Possibly buoyed by the ease with which the Australians had advanced against Bapaume, Gough was of the opinion that the Hindenburg Line, while notionally better defended, could be taken in a similar manner. He subsequently advanced an imprudent suggestion, based on the unlikely scenario that the Hindenburg Line was being held only as a rearguard position and, like the outpost villages, simply represented a delaying tactic. Gough would later change his mind, writing that, by early April 'the Germans were safely and strongly installed in their new Hindenburg Line, and they had been able to effect very considerable economies in their reserves, which were ready.'[12]

Haig, too, had complete faith in his army commander, trusting that he would develop the best possible plans for the operation. On the same day that he ordered the attack to be launched on 8 April, he was still acknowledging 'the difficulties of bringing forward heavy and siege batteries'.[13] Gough, too, was now concerned about the continuing shortage of suitable artillery and ammunition for the preliminary barrage, particularly for cutting the thick strands of barbed wire which appeared to be increasing by the day, and which protected the enemy's trench system. On 24 March Gough instructed his corps commanders to commence moving all the heavy guns that they could lay their hands on to the front 'as soon as the state of the roads permit'.[14]

Gough acknowledged that it would be a long and arduous task moving sufficient guns into place, let alone in time for the attack. The condition of the muddy and snow-covered roads had certainly not improved. Indeed, more recent rain and snow had turned what was left of the roads to a quagmire. Engineers were called in, but they were only able to repair a narrow strip of the road. Motor lorries towing guns inevitably became stuck. Tractors brought in to pull the trucks and guns out of the mud also became stuck. Horse-drawn artillery had little or no hope of getting through. Officers commented on the length of time it took 'getting the traffic gradually along'.[15] Adding to their woes was the state of the railway line. Gough now accepted that it would take too long before the destroyed line between Achiet-le-Grand and Bapaume could be reopened.[16]

On the same day Gough received another message outlining further changes to GHQ's objectives. 'The role of the Fifth Army at the outset,' it read,

> … in co-operation with the attack of the Third Army, will be to capture the Hindenburg Line on as large a front as possible between CROISILLE and QUEANT, but to undertake no serious operation further to the north except in so far as might be advantageous to assist the Third Army's advance and turn to account a favourable tactical situation. As the Third Army progresses the Fifth Army should be prepared to develop

subsequent attacks against the Hindenburg Line from Queant to the East, thus turning the Queant-Drocourt and Douaf-Marquion lines.

More meaningfully, Haig yet again accepted Gough's proposal to include an attack on the village of Queant in his plans.[17]

Despite the problems with his artillery, Gough was unable to delay the date for the attack. Instead, later on 24 March, he inexplicably told GHQ that, by 8 April (the time of the planned Arras offensive), his two divisions would be ready to attack. Satisfied that Gough could achieve his objectives and still convinced that a breakthrough was possible, Haig once more reminded Gough that the '4th Cavalry Division was to be passed through the breach, if effected, and to join hands with the Cavalry Corps advancing from Arras.'[18] More significantly as it transpired, Haig ordered his staff to consider the idea of allocating 'a few tanks' to the Fifth Army. Gough asked for just four. He initially received eight, then 12.[19]

During the evening of 24 March Gough discussed the revised plans with his two corps commanders. He told them that the attack was still scheduled for 4.30 am on 8 April, adding that success 'might be a great embarrassment to the German defence, and, in any case it would draw troops from the front of the 3rd Army.' He reiterated his instructions for the way they were to use their divisions — one on each side of Bullecourt. Instead of attacking the village head on, he was confident that, despite the risks, their men could still 'squeeze it out'. In later years Gough acknowledged that 'it was only possible to concentrate sufficient troops to attack this formidable line of entrenchments on a very narrow front, and an attack on a narrow front always leads to difficulties.' Attempting to justify the expected large number of casualties, Gough added that 'in this case, if the Third Army troops had advanced [as planned] they would very soon have joined hands with ours.'[20]

On 31 March at I ANZAC headquarters Birdwood and his staff acknowledged the difficulties the Australian infantry were likely to experience in their advance. Unlike Gough they understood that breaching the Hindenburg Line would pose a far greater challenge to their troops than their advance against the outpost villages. Certainly White knew the difficulties. He wrote that, 'Between Queant and Bullecourt the enemy's line forms a re-entrant some 1,500 yards deep.' He added that any thought of advancing 'here would be unwise unless Queant were also attacked.'[21] Yet, like Gough, White should have been aware of intelligence reports describing the numerous machine-gun nests in and around the village, making any attack virtual suicide for those concerned. Earlier, Gough had supported Haig's idea of an assault on Queant. But, partly due to the shortage of artillery pieces and reports of heavy enemy activity and the significant troop and machine-gun presence around the village, he was now less certain. By way of silencing the heavy machine-gun fire expected from Queant he ordered that a smokescreen be laid.

In early April Gough told Birdwood that the capture of Bullecourt was central to the attack's success. And, while Birdwood 'agreed with the general plan', he told Gough that both the 4th Australian and 62nd British divisions had little time to make proper preparations for the attack. He also pointed out that there was no suitable trench system in place from which the men could begin their advance. Instead, they would need to move up from a sunken road and be prepared to attack in the open and at dawn. This was far from an ideal scenario as the troops would need to assemble in the dark and move off shortly before first light. As they crossed the snow-covered terrain, they could become perfect targets for German machine-guns and artillery. Considering the unlikelihood of a suitable preliminary barrage, the infantry faced an extremely difficult task.[22] Little wonder that many Australian officers still harboured grave doubts over Gough's plans.

***

On 2 April, the day that Gough received final orders from Haig to proceed with the attack, the 4th Australian 'Divisional front was established on a line running North of Lagnicourt and Noreuil.'[23] Gough now ordered further changes to the artillery preparation, all the while desperately hoping to receive more large-calibre guns to send to the front. He informed both corps commanders that 'Every available heavy gun was to be pushed forward and no thought of risk was to be allowed to cause delay.' Even in the unlikely event that this proved possible, Gough should have recognised that there was insufficient time to put down anything resembling a suitable barrage. Still, by 5 April, Gough was reportedly more confident of success than ever.

On the same day, following fierce fighting, the 49th Battalion captured the railway embankment south of Bullecourt. Heavy casualties, inflicted by well-sited German machine-gun nests, provided some insight into what to expect in any attack against the Hindenburg Line. Yet Gough remained firmly convinced that the 'second objective … Riencourt and the third Hendecourt' could be captured and again emphasised that 'the village of Bullecourt formed the centre' of the front and was the primary objective.[24] He seemed unconcerned, or at the very least unaware, that the three villages formed a rough V-shape, with Hendecourt and Riencourt enabling the Germans to provide more covering fire on Bullecourt, mostly from heavy Maxim machine-guns. When added to the heavy machine-gun fire expected from Queant, Gough's reasoning was all the more peculiar. Coupled with his bizarre assumption that German troops were only temporarily holding the Hindenburg Line, Gough's revised plans ensured that the attack could only end in tragedy for the Australian and British infantry. The capture of Bullecourt alone was a formidable undertaking — when combined with the other objectives and Gough's constant demands and changes, the attack's prospects of success had become close to minimal.

Gough was presumably aware of other intelligence reports indicating that the Germans had developed more novel and deadly battle tactics and strategy, including recent changes to their defence-in-depth doctrine. The Hindenburg Line's two lines of trenches were far more formidable than anything Allied troops had previously encountered. The forward and support trenches around Bullecourt were some seven feet deep and separated by distances of anywhere between 150 and 200 yards. Both lines of trenches had been cleverly dug around a 'gentle semi-circular ridge', edging closer to Bullecourt at the crest's western perimeter, then snaking past Riencourt, which guarded their junction with the newly dug Wotan Line (the Drocourt-Queant switch). Another trench, 'Balcony', was 'extended from it to enclose Queant, near the eastern end of the crest two and a half miles from Bullecourt.'[25]

The forward trenches were, in fact, protected by three belts of barbed wire, all between 10 and 15 yards wide, some five yards apart, set in a zigzag pattern, backed by numerous well-sited heavy machine-gun nests manned by the *Schasfschutzen* (sharpshooter) battalions. Further complicating the task of the attacking infantry was the layout of the communication trenches, set at an angle which allowed the machine-guns to fire continuously along the boundaries. Infantry who managed to get through the first line would then face another single barbed-wire entanglement before they reached the enemy support trenches.[26]

Birdwood was becoming increasingly anxious about the attack. He was well aware of the quality of German troops garrisoning that part of the front. Crack infantry from the *27th*, an elite and fresh *Wurttemberg* division attached to General Otto von Moser *XIVth Reserve Korps* (*Gruppe Queant*), part of General Falkenhausen's *Sixth Army*, were considered 'among the German Army's best'.[27] Without sufficient artillery support and high explosive shells, Birdwood, if not Gough, was more aware than ever of the difficulty of the task confronting his infantry.[28]

***

Given the strength of the Hindenburg position, most senior officers, including Gough, knew that they could not dispense with a strong artillery barrage. If attacking infantry were to stand any chance, the German wire had to be cut and deadly machine-gunners forced to remain in their dugouts. Success or otherwise would depend on the artillery's preliminary barrage. However, regrettably, like a few other senior British officers, Gough had learnt very little from that disastrous first day of the Somme when similar planning had resulted in an ineffective 'softening up' bombardment which had seen the British 'New Army' cut to pieces.

The Somme offensive had posed countless difficulties in coordinating an artillery barrage with an infantry advance, not least the inaccuracy attributed to gun crews. Better training was considered a priority. The Somme had also reinforced that a preliminary bombardment would almost certainly surrender any surprise surrounding an infantry attack. Moreover, there was lack of certainty that the barrage would cut the wire in front of the German trenches, let alone kill or wound enemy troops or force them to flee their positions. Other quandaries included worn and over-used gun barrels which were liable to explode, killing or seriously maiming the crew, and poorly manufactured ammunition which contributed to its inaccuracy. Those shells that did explode were usually shrapnel (which when detonated threw out steel balls that were deadly against troops in unprotected positions, but virtually useless for cutting the barbed wire or killing those troops protected underground in their trenches) and not high explosive shells which, at the very least, should have cut large chunks of the wire.[29]

On the Somme, artillery spotters had been provided outdated maps that proved almost useless, as were some of the methods they had used to aim and range their artillery. The outcome was inevitable. Inaccurate fire had dire consequences for attacking troops. Lieutenant Colonel Frank Maxwell, VC (commanding officer of the 12th Middlesex), best described the crisis his battalion faced after a failed advance on 29 June when he revealed that 'Much too often … something goes wrong, and guns or infantry get tangled up in their plans, with the result that our infantry run into the fire of our guns, and have to come back for fear of being killed.' He observed that, ideally, during an attack there should be no artillery barrages at all.[30] After Bullecourt, Australian troops would certainly argue with Maxwell's hypothesis.

By April 1917 the British had made inroads into mastering what was referred to as the 'creeping barrage'. Paddy Griffith has described this as characterising 'a decisive shift from "destructive" fire to "neutralizing" fire'.[31] The doctrine was developed primarily to prevent enemy machine-gun crews setting up their posts at the end of a barrage and then firing on attacking troops at will.

The 'creeping barrage' also afforded the infantry additional protection as they moved across no man's land, the area that separated the British from the German trenches. The 'creep' continued, 'lifting' by between 50 and 100 yards at regular intervals, usually around 100 yards in three minutes. Communication for the 'lifting' barrage was the responsibility of wireless operators or spotters. As would be expected, if the infantry advance was to proceed smoothly, almost perfect communication was required between infantry and artillery officers. Anything less could only have devastating consequences. If the barrage was to lift prematurely shells would fall on attacking infantry. If it was to lift too quickly, they would be at the mercy of enemy machine-guns and riflemen, safe and secure in their trenches.

***

German counter-attacks were inevitable. Once a trench had been captured, successful communication had to be maintained. However, in practice, this proved far more difficult due to the rapid descent of battles into chaos and confusion — the 'fog of war'. Communication, whether by telephone, runner or even carrier pigeon, usually broke down, preventing the artillery providing assistance to those troops who occupied captured enemy trenches. Prior to Bullecourt, Australian soldiers were generally aware of what could go wrong while officers took steps to coordinate the artillery and the advance as best they could. Regardless of the evolution of British artillery throughout the latter half of 1916 and into early 1917, including modifications to the creeping barrage, there were still difficulties in moving the optimum number of guns and ammunition as close to the front as possible to provide that necessary support. Regrettably, this proved to be the case at Bullecourt.

***

On 20 March a few 18-pounders belonging to the British field artillery had commenced firing on German positions around Bullecourt. Birdwood remained unconvinced, even when Gough reminded him of the eight days of solid preparatory artillery bombardment commencing on 1 April, designed to soften up the enemy defences. Gough added that he expected to have 'sufficient guns and howitzers to bombard 4,000 yards of front', but that the 'guns must fire hard'.[32]

By early April Birdwood, still concerned at the lack of suitable heavy guns and ammunition, was growing weary of Gough's reasoning. He told Gough that he was unhappy with an untried formula developed by seasoned staff officers which required at least 136 artillery pieces. Gough believed that he could secure another 26 guns, producing a total of 126 field guns and 36 howitzers, adding that this was the minimum number required to put down a reasonable preparatory barrage. Gough also demanded that, as soon as the last outpost villages were captured, the smaller calibre batteries be moved forward as quickly as humanly possible.

On the same day Gough informed Birdwood of Haig's instruction that the roads not be further damaged by 'hurrying up guns and ammunition'.[33] With barely a murmur, Birdwood accepted this, also agreeing to Gough's decision to temporarily halt the movement of ammunition to the front. While the railway line had recently opened as far as Achiet-le-Grand, Gough further instructed that it should be used to move stone for road construction and equipment to restore the railway line to Bapaume. Yet there was no mention of transporting essential guns or ammunition.

While ammunition may have been in short supply and field artillery stuck behind the front, heavy artillery was providing additional problems of its own. On 29 March the princely total of just eight heavy guns was available. The labour of sappers and gun crews ensured that, four days later (on 2 April), more heavy artillery had been moved closer to the front. I ANZAC Corps headquarters could now call on 30 howitzers and 18 sixty-pounders to support the Australian attack. However, inexplicably, Gough's headquarters devised a formula in which only 22 of the howitzers were to fire on the wire and enemy trenches, while another eight, supported by all of the 60-pounders, were to be used in counter-battery work engaging German artillery behind Bullecourt. Birdwood was promised that, on 9 April, another battery of heavy howitzers, belonging to the 194th Siege Battery, would be moved up to Beugny and be available for the final preliminary barrage. The reality would prove somewhat different.

***

While the two field artillery brigades of the 4th Australian Division had been temporarily expanded with the addition of some 18-pounders from other Australian divisions, unsurprisingly, they were now hampered by the need to transport the guns to the front. A few motor lorries were found which could pull an 18-pounder and limber while transporting its crew of 10, its necessary equipment and as many as 176 rounds of ammunition. Horses were also brought in to help. The roads — muddy tracks full of potholes — ensured that moving the equipment would be a slow process. Gough was informed that the earliest all the guns belonging to the field artillery could be in place was 8 April.[34]

On 31 March the 4th Australian Divisional Artillery began taking over positions close to Noreuil from the 2nd Division. Confusion ensued. On the same day, battery commanders were told that the 'relief has been postponed by … 48 hours'. Two days later, they were informed that the '2nd Australian Divisional Brigades will not be relieved. The 4th Australian Divisional Artillery Brigades will after reconnaissance, go into positions from which the enemy's line … W[est] of Bullecourt … can be engaged. These brigades will go into action on a date to be settled later.'[35] Gough's appeal for an eight-day preliminary softening-up barrage was fast becoming a distant memory.

***

As the day of the attack drew closer, Birdwood and White became increasingly cautious about the prospect of success, particularly without the necessary artillery support. Further delays, however, meant that even fewer 18-pounder field artillery batteries would be in place prior to the attack. Gough was told that enormous effort was being invested in the movement of the remainder of the 4th Division's field artillery which was still hampered by the condition of the roads and lack of transport to move the guns. It was now doubtful that all seven field artillery brigades could be in position by 8 April. Any hope of an effective creeping barrage was now all but out of the question. Cutting the wire would depend almost entirely on the heavy artillery and howitzers, some of which were now using the recently developed instantaneous '106' percussion fuse, designed to burst the shell immediately it came into contact with a solid surface and strew shrapnel for up to 650 metres. This was not the ideal method to create gaps in the enemy wire.

Later on 31 March Gough told Birdwood that the preliminary barrage must 'begin this day'. However, due 'to the transportation difficulties in the supply of ammunition, the commencement of the bombardment of the Hindenburg Line will be light, but it will gradually become heavier day by day. It will be intense from April 7th onwards till the day of the attack.'[36] While the early bombardment may have caught the enemy by surprise (they did not expect the railway line, which had been destroyed with typical German diligence, to be rebuilt so quickly), it also alerted their officers to the fact that an attack was on the cards, most likely in the vicinity of Bullecourt. When it eventuated, their troops would be well prepared.

On 2 April Gough was still of the opinion that more had to be done and 'ordered the most energetic preparations for the attack', urging that 'every available heavy gun … be pushed forward, and no thought of risk was to be allowed to cause delay.'[37] Sourcing sufficient suitable ammunition for the heavy guns was still a problem. On 3 April Gough finally relented. Ignoring Haig's earlier directive to avoid further damage to the roads by ammunition supply vehicles, he directed some of the motor trucks belonging to I ANZAC Corps to bring forward ammunition, albeit for just one day. At the same time the V Corps trucks were inexplicably told to carry 'half-loads' of ammunition. All in all, it was not a very satisfactory outcome for the artillery and, more significantly, for the infantry relying on the gunners' support.

On the same day I ANZAC Corps heavy artillery fired 1100 rounds of ammunition. The following day it fired another 1695 rounds — barely sufficient to do any real damage to enemy positions, let alone make serious inroads into cutting the wire. However, by 5 April, Australian and British heavy artillery were able to considerably increase their rate of fire. Over the next three days 12,346 shells — mostly from 6-inch, 8-inch and 9.2-inch howitzers — were fired by 26 batteries belonging to V Corps and I ANZAC Corps, although only a small number of high explosive shells were armed with instantaneous fuses designed to cut the wire. Another two counter-battery groups fired a further 11,235 shells.

On the afternoon of 8 April aerial reconnaissance over Bullecourt and its surrounds showed that the wire had only been partially cut. Patrols also indicated little or no damage. At a conference held at Gough's headquarters later on the same day, Major General White told Gough that Australian troops would most likely be cut to pieces if the attack — now scheduled for 10 April — proceeded. White believed that at least another eight days of solid bombardment would be required to satisfactorily cut the wire. But, not for the first, nor indeed the last time, the Australian's protest fell on deaf ears.

As late as the night of 9 April Australian and British patrols confirmed that, in some places, the barbed wire was up to 33 yards thick and 'still uncut along practically the whole front'.[38] On the same evening an order originating from I ANZAC artillery directed that, from 9.00 pm until Zero Hour at 4.30 am, the heavy artillery would fire '60 rounds per hour' at Bullecourt and Riencourt 'in order to destroy all possible buildings'. Then, between 4.30 and 5.30 am, 'siege batteries' would lay down a heavy barrage on and around Queant and the enemy forward and support trenches.[39] But, instead of relying on a further preliminary barrage — which may still not have completed the task — Gough now turned to a recent innovation of technological warfare on the Western Front.

***

Prior to World War I a number of politicians and more progressive senior British officers had shown interest in armoured vehicles, speculating over their role in future combat. An Australian, L.E. de Mole, had in fact presented his concept of an armoured tractor which used a continuous metal track to the War Office in 1912. Although subsequently hailed as 'a very brilliant invention', it gained few plaudits among those who mattered at the ministry.

By late 1914, with defensive trench systems firmly established (which made a breakthrough by attacking troops all but out of the question), the need for some sort of armoured vehicle able to break the stalemate had become apparent. The Secretary of the British Committee for Imperial Defence, Maurice Hankey, advocated the use of:

> Numbers of large, heavy rollers, themselves bullet proof, propelled from behind by motor engines, geared very low, the driving wheels fitted with 'caterpillar' driving gear to grip the ground, the driver's seat armoured, and with a Maxim gun fitted. The object of this device would be to roll down the barbed wire by sheer weight, to give some cover to men creeping up behind, and to support the advance with machine gun fire.

At first the army considered developing any weapon of this kind extremely foolish. Instead, the genesis for a prototype tank, known as 'Little Willie', can be credited to the Royal Naval Air Service.[40]

Built in 1915, 'Little Willie' was extremely primitive, even when compared to tanks developed later in the war. Mounted on conventional caterpillar tracks with a high body, it resembled something from a science fiction comic. However, by now, the army was showing some interest. It was left to a Royal Engineers officer, Lieutenant Colonel E.D. Swinton, to churn out some ideas on how a modified version could overcome the tactical stalemate prevailing in France and Flanders. And, while the War Office was coming to terms with his ideas, Swinton produced an 'outline tactical doctrine for his own design' which, with a little modification, also found favour.

Assisted by Lieutenant W.G. Wilson and Mr William Tritton (from Foster's, a company in Leicestershire which had already been contracted by the army to manufacture tracked motor vehicles), the trio settled on a tank with a somewhat lower profile, which was christened 'Mother'. The height was reduced by a rhomboid profile, while the tracks completely encompassed the rhombus. Swinton was satisfied that this gigantic, ugly vehicle — powered by an unreliable engine of barely 105 horsepower and weighing 28 tons which could move at only half a mile per hour while consuming one gallon of fuel

— might well crush the enemy wire before crossing their trenches and, in the process, deal with shell holes and other obstacles in no man's land. On 8 September 1915 these 'experimental armoured vehicles moved under their own power for the first time.'[41]

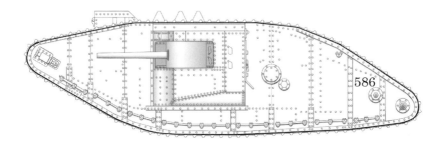

Sketch of Mark I Tank (Male) Number 586 (drawn by Catherine McCulloch).

A British Mark I 'female' tank ready to go into action. The visible crew member is wearing a British-style tank helmet. The netting over the top of the tank provided minimal protection against bomb and grenade attack, proved highly impractical, and had been discarded by the time of the Bullecourt attack. The wheel at the rear was for steering and was operated by the driver through a primitive form of remote control. Not surprisingly, the steering system was soon deemed unsatisfactory and quickly abandoned (AWM H08749).

Not long after, similar vehicles with fewer modifications entered larger scale production. Somewhat unimaginatively named 'Mark I', they were also rhomboid or lozenge-shaped with all-round tracks. The 'Mark I' came in two versions. The 'male' was armed with two 6-pounder ex-naval guns (located in the side sponsons) complemented by four Hotchkiss machine-guns. The 'female' version had no 6-pounders, carrying instead two additional machine-guns. Due to its sheer size and design, each tank needed a crew of nine — a commander, one driver, two 'gearsmen' (responsible for the transmission) and another five to operate and fire the weapons.

In an effort to compensate for the low-powered engine, the armour plating was light. While adequate to protect the tank against small arms fire, it was nonetheless effortlessly pierced by artillery fire. Tests also revealed that, when machine-gun shells came in contact with the armour, small flakes peeled off inside the crew's compartment, causing metal fragments — or 'splash' — to orbit about. Tank men were consequently provided with ridiculous leather helmets, goggles and chain-mail visors for protection, reminiscent of the armour of medieval knights. However a large number of crew members refused to wear this ungainly and constrictive protection. As if this was not enough, crews were also subjected to deafening noise from the engine and fumes that filled their compartment.

Steering and navigation of the cumbersome vehicle was challenging, with, initially, two 'brakemen' managing one track each. The officer commanding each tank had to use a complicated system of compass bearings and time lapse to try to calculate his position. Poor vision also hindered the commander and crew and occasionally tanks would fire on their own infantry. And, because radio communication was only developed towards the end of the war, tank officers had to relay messages by runner, telephone system or even carrier pigeon — somewhat similar to the system employed by the infantry. Making life still more difficult for tank commanders, telephone wires were frequently cut by the vehicle's own tracks

Despite all the limitations and deficiencies, the novel weapon's tactical value soon became apparent. Given the ease with which tanks were able to flatten barbed wire and cross trenches, they appeared to have triumphed over one of the foremost difficulties of attack over defence which, as the war continued, produced increasing numbers of casualties. Now, in theory, tanks not only provided the necessary firepower for infantry but, more significantly, gave them more flexibility in what they could attack.

This armed 'land battleship' now (at least in theory) made it possible for advancing troops to deal with enemy strongpoints previously left untouched by artillery fire. Senior British officers further understood that tanks could provide accurate tactical fire, allowing their infantry the opportunity to exploit the damage caused by the massive preliminary barrages that usually preceded an attack. Yet it was left to individual tank commanders to determine how best to employ the machines under their command. If the attack was to stand any chance of success, tank officers needed not only to decide on the most appropriate method of tactically deploying the vehicles, but the best way to coordinate the tanks with their own artillery fire and the movement of the infantry.

Tanks were first used in combat by the British army on the Somme (at the Battle of Flers) on 15 September 1916. In spite of high expectations for their impact on the battlefield, tanks proved unreliable, under-gunned, under-powered and, most significantly, under-armoured. During the latter stages of planning, corps and divisional commanders — most of whom were totally unfamiliar with this recent innovation and new arm of the British army — were frequently allowed to overrule the more junior tank officers in decisions on the way their vehicles could best be tactically employed. Of even greater consequence, given the devastating toll of casualties (without any appreciable gain) and Haig's desire to employ tanks to boost his infantry's flagging morale, tanks were used in too small numbers and before crews were adequately trained. The compressed time scale meant that tank crews and infantry had not been afforded the opportunity to train alongside one another.

One critic, the future British Prime Minister Winston Churchill, was subsequently unapologetic in his condemnation of Haig and his staff. 'I was so shocked at the proposal,' he wrote, 'to expose this tremendous secret to the enemy [on 15 September] upon such a petty scale and as a mere makeweight to what I was sure could be only an indecisive operation.'[42] During the battle, crews discovered that, due to the noise of the engine, it was extremely difficult for them to communicate inside the tank, and near impossible to communicate with anyone outside the vehicle. Not unexpectedly, the thin armour plating proved a costly mistake. Those early tanks may have been somewhat shielded against small arms fire, and could smash through barbed wire and cross trenches, but their vulnerability to all kinds of artillery and even machine-gun fire soon became all too evident.

At first enemy troops, apparently secure in their trenches, were shocked and frightened at the sight of these mechanical monsters. Some fled. However, the Germans quickly adapted. Anti-tank measures, particularly the skilful use of artillery, were devised. If anything this should have served to remind British officers of the extent to which rapidly improving artillery employment (combined with better shells) was a matter of tactics as well as technology and numbers. Many, including Gough, failed to recognise any of these incremental changes.

Throughout the winter of 1916–17, the expansion of the Heavy Branch Machine Gun Corps (the official name of the tank arm) began in earnest. By the time of the Arras offensive on 9 April, tanks had been produced in sufficient numbers to be used somewhat more effectively, although many still became bogged in the shell-cratered mud. However, those that were able to press on generally provided some valuable support to the infantry.

Certainly British officers were buoyed by the achievements of tanks in the early stages of the offensive. Others, including Haig, were initially cautious. Yet Haig would later claim 'that a division of Tanks was worth 10 divisions of infantry'. According to one mid-ranking British staff officer (Colonel Stern), 'some brigadiers did not want Tanks for fear of drawing fire on their troops [but] all begged for them afterwards.' And, although five became 'bogged going into action' (which should have served as a warning), Stern was convinced that tanks were responsible for the capture of seven enemy strongholds including Thelus and Vimy village.[43]

Further south, encouraged by another tank officer, Lieutenant Colonel J. Hardress Lloyd (commanding officer, 1st Battalion Heavy Branch, Machine Gun Corps), Gough agreed to a scheme not unlike that used at Arras. The 12 tanks that Haig had allocated to the Fifth Army were to assume the role of the artillery and, indeed, expand it. While providing cover to advancing Australian infantry, the tanks were also expected to move forward and smash gaps in the enemy wire.

Initially it was considered best to use 'the tanks in pairs, distributed along the two mile front'. However, this tactic was soon dismissed as 'contrary to the tactical theories of the tank officers'. Experience had taught them that tanks 'so dispersed were easy targets and were unlikely to make satisfactory breaches for the infantry; if concentrated they would, on the other hand, have a good opportunity to roll up the wire on their whole frontage, creating one wide gap instead of a series of narrow ones.'[44]

This initiative, in fact, was not the brainchild of Hardress Lloyd but rather Major William Watson, commander of No. 11 Company, D Battalion, Heavy Branch, Machine Gun Corps. Hardress Lloyd jumped at the idea, essentially making it his own. When Gough was told, he immediately directed the tank commander to prepare detailed plans for his tanks to attack at daybreak the following day (10 April).

Staggered at Gough's recklessness in using the tanks (presently situated in a quarry at Mory Copse, a little over four miles from the front) so hastily — without any prior training of tanks advancing alongside Australian infantry, or any proper reconnaissance of the front by tank commanders — Hardress Lloyd nevertheless agreed. After all, this was an opportunity for which he had been waiting: to use his tanks *en masse* in front of the infantry rather than advancing alongside. In consultation with Watson, he decided that the 12 tanks would launch a 'surprise' attack along a front of around 1200 to 1500 yards, crushing the wire before the infantry moved forward to capture the enemy trenches. The artillery would recommence firing only after the tanks had passed through the wire.[45]

But Hardress Lloyd failed to point out precisely how that 'surprise' could be achieved. As these lumbering monsters made their way to the front the deafening noise would almost certainly be heard by enemy troops. And, because the RFC was unable to provide adequate air cover during daylight hours, there also was the tricky night approach to the Australian lines to take into account. Hardress Lloyd gave this important issue little thought. Given his reputation as 'very good in the field, but inclined to be lazy so far as training and organisation were concerned behind the front', Hardress Lloyd's oversights were less than surprising.[46]

Gough's last minute revised plans called for a 'surprise' attack by two brigades of the 4th Australian Division with minimal or no artillery support, along a narrow front against the re-entrant in the Hindenburg Line between Bullecourt and Queant. The 12 tanks — four in front of each brigade — were expected to lead the infantry advance and smash through the wire, while the other four moved along the shallow valley that separated the brigades by some 500 yards. That gap — in reality a depression running at right angles to the Hindenburg Line — was expected to be hammered by machine-gun fire, the machine-guns to be put out of action by the tanks. Once the Australians had taken the enemy trenches, four of the tanks would redeploy westward into Bullecourt. An Australian battalion from the 12th Brigade would follow, clearing the village of German troops. And Gough still had not abandoned his other hare-brained idea. Only then would the 62nd British Division move through, capture Bullecourt, and then advance against Hendecourt. At the same time, the 4th Brigade on the right, assisted by four of the tanks, would attack and secure Riencourt.[47]

Without taking into account the obvious flaws — the most obvious how all the tanks would survive the attack against the strong Hindenburg Line unscathed — Gough ordered both divisions to capture their objectives as quickly as possible. Both Gough and Hardress Lloyd deserve condemnation for their planning. Not only was too much expected of the infantry — and tank crews — but neither seem to have taken into account the strong probability that some (if not all) of the tanks would be put out of action by German artillery fire.

When informed of the plan for the attack, Birdwood and White could not believe what they were hearing. Gough attempted to assuage their concerns by emphasising that the tanks could flatten the wire — something the artillery still had not achieved — before the infantry arrived. The Australians, nevertheless, remained concerned at the difficulties of launching an attack on this part of the German line without significant artillery preparation, pointing out — not once, but numerous times — that the Hindenburg Line formed a re-entrant with the village on one side and a gentle rise on the other, around which the Germans had dug deep, almost impenetrable trenches, emphasising also the presence of numerous well-sited machine-gun nests around the village of Queant. However neither Gough nor, for that matter, Hardress Lloyd, could be dissuaded. Birdwood and his Chief of Staff had little option but to accept the plan or resign in futile protest.

***

Haig's directive to Gough appeared simple enough — capture a section of the Hindenburg Line sufficient to allow a squadron of cavalry to pass through to meet other cavalry divisions that would break through the gap made by the Third Army attack on the front around Arras. Gough's idea to break into the rear of the enemy was strategically sound. However, in his usual impulsive style, the British general had overlooked the tactical obstacles. His plan to launch an attack at the re-entrant was extremely unwise and virtually impossible to achieve as it would allow those expertly sited German machine-gun nests an unimpeded field of fire on advancing Australian infantry. Other flanking machine-guns were located in the adjoining villages. Moreover, the attack front was too narrow. The enemy also had good artillery observation posts on the ridge behind the villages. Tank commanders had advised that the best way to employ the new weapon was 'en masse'. Considering a total of 12 tanks 'en masse' is fanciful at best. Yet, with this in mind, Gough sanctioned their use and final preparations for the assault on Bullecourt proceeded.

CHAPTER 5

'Never acted with tanks before.'
FINAL PREPARATIONS

Planning for the attack on the Hindenburg Line around Bullecourt had been flawed from the beginning. As the day of the assault approached, Gough's ongoing changes continued to confuse the Australians. German defensive positions all along this part of the Hindenburg Line were very strong. Massive belts of wire protected the two lines of trenches while oblique communication (or 'switch') trenches allowed German reinforcements to move rapidly to the site of a potential breakthrough. If the attack went ahead as planned, the most likely scenario would find Australian infantry trapped in a lethal salient with little chance of escape. The almost non-existent preliminary artillery barrage and use of tanks untested in difficult terrain only added new and problematic dimensions.

The inadequate number of artillery pieces that could be assembled for the preparatory barrage, along with ineffective planning, meant that the attack was doomed to fail. Even without taking into account the biggest flaw of all — attacking a re-entrant covered by the massive German machine-gun nests in and around Queant — there were far too many other errors. Why, for instance, did the artillery plan of attack ignore a number of other well-sited enemy machine-guns located at the junction of the Six Cross Roads? And how were the tanks expected to deal with those machine-gun nests without coming under fire themselves? The final plan of attack afforded senior Australian officers and their staff limited input. Even on the few occasions when Birdwood and White voiced their objections and mentioned perceived flaws in the planning, they were usually ignored or overruled. Perhaps more significantly, Gough had allowed himself to become convinced that the enemy lacked strength and that his defences were weak.[1]

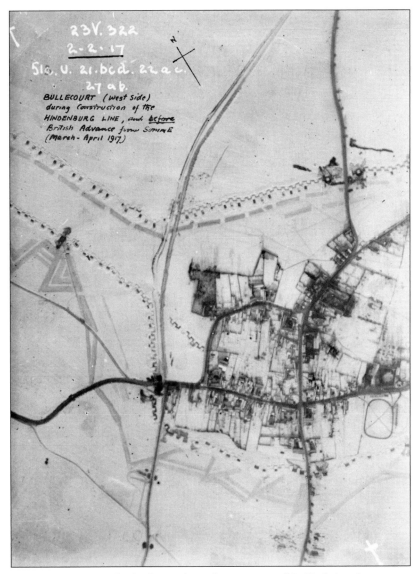

An aerial view of the west side of Bullecourt during the construction of the Hindenburg Line, February–March 1917, prior to the British–Australian advance (AWM A02477).

By the first week of April almost all the German soldiers had pulled back to the Hindenburg Line taking their equipment and weapons. On 9 April — the same day that the British commenced their thrust towards

Arras — troops from the 1st Australian Division occupied the last of the outpost villages. Scanning some two miles into the distance, they could now see the hazy outline of the enemy positions. What they saw must have disturbed them. Thick strands of rusty barbed wire defended the first line of trenches while, further to the rear, other defensives lines, also covered by wire, were vaguely visible.

View of trenches close to Bullecourt village, 1917 (AWM H12360).

At the same time final measures were being put in place for the combined Australian-British operation. On 2 April Gough had informed the two corps commanders that:

> Preparations for the attack on the Hindenburg Line must now be taken in hand with the greatest energy. Every available heavy gun must be pushed up without further delay and got into action at suitable range. All risks must be accepted. Infantry must work forward to assaulting positions and any necessary trenches must be prepared.[2]

The next day Major General Holmes was told to make preparations 'to attack the Hindenburg Line in the neighbourhood of Bullecourt at an early date.'[3]

***

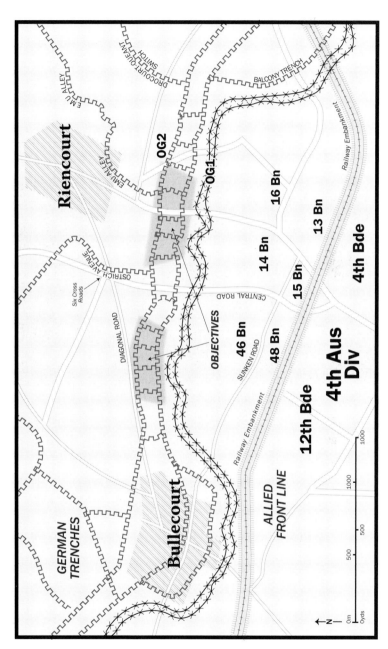

Map of Bullecourt and Riencourt showing planned objectives for the 4th and 12th Australian Infantry Brigades.

On 4 April Holmes 'carried out a thorough reconnaissance of the front, and decided that the best plan was to send one complete Brigade against Bullecourt, whilst another Brigade attacked the line immediately east of that point.'[4] Because the two lines of German trenches slightly resembled those encountered the previous year at Pozieres, Holmes and his headquarters staff decided to call the first line OG1 and the support trench OG2.[5]

The front along which his infantry were expected to attack troubled Holmes. The terrain has been described as:

> ... without strongly marked features, a succession of shallow valleys and low spurs running roughly from north-east to south-west. Bullecourt itself stood partly in a valley, partly on the eastern slope of a spur, so that the west side was thirty or forty feet higher than the east. The railway, partly embanked and partly in a cutting, provided good cover but limited the movement of the tanks.[6]

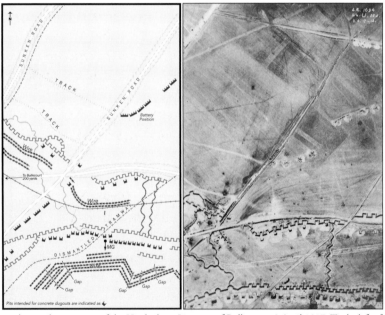

An aerial view, showing part of the Hindenburg Line east of Bullecourt, 3 April 1917. To the left of the trenches are two lines of heavy artillery batteries (AWM A01097). Alongside is a map of the same part of the Hindenburg Line based on the photograph taken from the air. Captured by a British airman, these intelligence photographs proved extremely useful for British cartographers in drawing their maps. Unfortunately once passed to senior and staff officers completing the plans, the maps were not always used wisely as demonstrated by Gough and his co-planners at Bullecourt.

Holmes saw for himself that the men would be faced with the most daunting challenge — the re-entrant — from which they could be fired on from three sides. Holmes feared the worst. Plans had to be changed.

The following day Brigadier General Charles Brand (GOC 4th Australian Brigade) and Brigadier General James Robertson (GOC 12th Australian Brigade) were told that 'Preliminary reconnaissances will be begun at once by officers … so as to get thoroughly acquainted with their front and approaches to it.'[7] On the same day, Brand accompanied his battalion commanding officers in a personal inspection of what their men would face. Scrutinising the front around Bullecourt and Riencourt through binoculars, they too understood the almost impossible task facing their infantry as they attempted to cross no man's land.

On 5 April Gough circulated more detailed plans for the attack. The 4th Cavalry Division was now expected to move into open country and link up with the Cavalry Corps which should be 'on the line of the [River] Sensee'. For this reason, Gough told Birdwood that it was imperative that the second objective, Riencourt, and the third, Hendecourt, be captured without delay.[8]

Numerous conferences followed. Over the next couple of days battalion leaders guided their company commanders as close as possible to the Hindenburg Line, where they too could examine the defences more closely. While the 14th Battalion's intelligence officer, Captain Albert Jacka, was surveying no man's land he came across a sunken road which he considered would make an ideal 'jumping-off point' for troops leading the attack.

Some Australian officers became more pessimistic over their prospects of success with each passing day, while others remained cautiously optimistic. Captain David Dunworth (15th Battalion) wrote that:

> … general pleasure was felt that for the first time in France we were to do the stunt as a Brigade – not piecemeal – that we would be supported by and supporting each other … Easter Sunday and the days preceding the attack officers and N.C.O.'s

had gone and examined our objectives to the best of our ability. No efforts had been spared to make every man thoroughly acquainted with his individual job. A general feeling of optimism prevailed in all ranks.[9]

Lieutenant George McDowell had few doubts that the attack would succeed 'in spite of all preparation which he [the enemy] may have made on the line to which he is retiring. Another thing which will worry him ... is the morale of his troops ... after this retirement it will be absolutely zero.'[10] British soldier Private Walter King (2nd London Regiment) echoed McDowell's thoughts. On 5 April he wrote that he was optimistic that the Hindenburg Line would be broken and that 'the war won't last long'.[11] Others were less sure. The respected commander of the 15th Infantry Brigade, Brigadier General Harold 'Pompey' Elliott, instinctively recognised the obstacles. In a letter to his wife, he reflected that 'we will be checked for quite a while by the Hindenburg Line ... The wire there is from 400 to 600 yards thick.'[12]

An oblique aerial view of Bullecourt showing a section of the Hindenburg Line with wire entanglements in the centre, 5 April 1917 (AWM A02474).

On 6 April Holmes received 'further instructions which laid down that Bullecourt was not to be assaulted, but was to be bombarded during the attack and subsequently squeezed out.' Just where that artillery was to come from was never spelt out to Holmes. Still he proceeded with his final preparations. During the next day or so the 4th and 12th Australian infantry brigades took over parts of the line 'so as to be ready to deliver the attack, when required, at short notice.'[13] Setting up his brigade headquarters in a dugout near Noreuil, Brand ordered the 14th and 16th battalions into the forward trenches, no more than 800 yards from the German front line.[14]

The following day, the commanding officer of the 13th Battalion, Lieutenant Colonel J. Durrant, decided to take another look at the front. He wrote of 'impregnable positions', particularly those flanking well-sited machine-guns located around Queant which, in all likelihood, would bring murderous fire onto his attacking infantry. Durrant added that all

Machine gun emplacements in each company sector (150 yards) have been constructed to give a perfect enfilade from one or other of these points along almost the entire of the outer edge of the wire … [which] in front of the Fire trench consists of from two to four belts arranged in strictly parallel lines about 5 yards apart. The width of a belt varies from about 10 to 15 yards. There are numerous angles but no curves. The wire is supported on corkscrew stakes varying in height from 2 1/2 to 6 feet. There are six rows of stakes in each belt. The support line is also wired, but the belts are fewer, less continuous and   straighter.

He could not have known how prophetic his final observation would be: 'No traces have been discovered of trench gun positions for dealing with tanks. Little is known, however, of this class of emplacement, and it might possibly pass unrecognised.'[15]

As if those enemy defences were not sufficiently formidable, intelligence reports (taken mostly from German prisoners of war) described other obstacles the Australians would encounter:

Fire trench and Support trench – concrete used in trenches. Open communication trenches, two in each battalion sector underground leading from support to fire trench from rear usual open type.

Dug outs in fire trench shallow concrete shelter under the parapet for each group of 1 NCO and 8 men. Below each shelter is a deep dug out connected by a passage running the whole length of the front line, into which the covered communication trenches lead. In parts of the Support trench [there are] similar shelters and dug-outs … [There are] NO CONCRETE Machine Gun Emplacements. Sentry Posts [consist of] observation post with reinforced head cover and a periscope protected by steel plates constructed at intervals.

In some places 'sunk wire' … [and] three zig-zag belts in front of Fire trench. Support Line protected by straight belts of wire. Loose coils of plain wire 12 to 15 inches in height have been laid diagonally between the barbed wire belts.

Considering all the other difficulties attacking infantry were to face, the report's conclusion that German 'trenches [were] sited entirely on the reverse slope' was even more alarming, and provided good reason to revisit the plans already in place.[16]

***

The Germans were well aware of what was happening. On 8 April Australian troops preparing for the attack 'were amazed to see an enemy "plane", flying at a low altitude'. Shooting down and destroying British observation balloons not far from the front, the German pilot flew over the Australian lines before he 'shot off at full speed for home. Straight as a rocket he flew, with every gun or rifle upon the front pouring lead at him … A number of us felt a trifle serious over the German airman's visit, for he, no doubt, upon his return to his own lines, reported the presence of cavalry, and such report would lead the Germans to suspect an attack.'[17]

The cavalry observed by the German airman was none other than the 13th Australian Light Horse Regiment. Patrols from that same regiment had already collected vital information on enemy defensive positions and supported reports from other Australian patrols of the still largely uncut wire in front of the German trenches. Previous reports passed to I ANZAC Corps headquarters described other threats —including a large number of German guns massed behind the villages — which would hamper the Australian attack and cause increased casualties. Headquarters staff had even decided to use some light horse troops in the advance. On 8 April the commander of C Squadron received an unwelcome surprise when told to prepare his men for action. His troop was 'to move as advance guard' for the planned attack.[18] Instructions were also distributed describing how Australian machine-guns, firing from positions along the sunken road, were to cover the advance, firing over the heads of the infantry as they moved forward.[19]

Later the same day, another intelligence report alerted Holmes to the larger than expected number of underground passages — catacombs in Riencourt — where enemy soldiers could be rushed from one threatened position to another. Brigade commanders were instructed to keep on hand 'Mopping up parties [which] must be large and although dug-outs may apparently have been emptied, guards must be left on all the entrances as it is possible that … fresh parties of the enemy may find their way into dug-outs through tunnels which have not been noticed.'[20]

On 9 April there was some relief and anticipation when rumours reached 4th Division headquarters that the attack might be cancelled. German troops had apparently pulled back from parts of the Hindenburg Line near Bullecourt. Speculation soon spread among the waiting Australian infantry and fighting patrols were ordered to find out whether the information was genuine. Holmes instructed that if the line was 'vacated, it was to be occupied. In the event of it being still held … the attack was to be carried out at dawn … on the 10th.'[21]

Reports from Australian patrols told the real story. Enemy troops had stayed put. More alarming was the patrols' discovery that, in many places — particularly east of Bullecourt — there was still little or no damage to the wire which remained largely uncut. In other places where the wire had been cut, German sappers had already made repairs. One patrol established that, in its part of the attack front, the wire was up to 33 yards thick.[22] Another patrol, led by Captain Albert Jacka, came across a German officer and one of his men doing their own reconnaissance close to the Australian 'jumping-off' tape at the sunken road. Jacka captured both Germans who subsequently yielded information on enemy troop strengths. If those figures were not alarming enough, then what they revealed about machine-gun numbers and emplacements surely was.

***

Gough's final plan called for a surprise attack at dawn by the 4th Australian Division, assisted by 12 tanks. Providing the first part of the advance proceeded as planned, three tanks were to move through Bullecourt and subsequently smash through the German wire in front of the 62nd British Division's area of attack. Only then was the 62nd to launch a daylight attack through gaps made in the wire. Gough continued to maintain unswerving faith in the ability of his tanks to complete the task. The reality was somewhat different. Holmes, for one, was staggered. After all, as he noted later, his Australian troops had never trained alongside those mechanical monsters, let alone taken part in an advance against a re-entrant protected by largely uncut enemy wire.

Birdwood and White also continued to harbour doubts over the likelihood of the tanks performing as required. Confronting Gough for what they hoped was the last time, they were unceremoniously told that the offensive must go ahead prior to dawn the following day. Undaunted, Birdwood again pointed out the near impossibility of successfully advancing against 'where the Hindenburg Line formed a deep gulf or re-entrant, with Bullecourt standing on one side, and a gentle rise (on which a loop of the German line ran round Queant) on the other.' Gough reminded his corps commander yet again that it was Haig's expectation that the attack proceed as planned.[23] Yet, due to his insistence that it was the army commander's role to devise plans without interference from GHQ, it is unlikely that Haig was even vaguely aware of the weakness of Gough's revised tactics.

Without taking into account the likelihood of some tanks being put out of action, Gough again pointed out that:

As soon as the Hindenburg Line had been taken four tanks were to swing westward into Bullecourt followed by an Australian battalion, and to clear the village. The 62nd Division was then to push through to its original objective of Hendecourt, while the Australian right, assisted by four tanks, advanced on Riencourt.

Little wonder that some senior Australian officers were confused by Gough's constantly changing plans. Gough, quite simply, expected too much from Australian and British troops. With no time whatsoever to practise even the most basic cooperation for such a complex operation, tank crews and their officers were as much in the dark as their infantry counterparts. Even the plan's 'authors' were said to be 'somewhat startled' by Gough's recklessness and impropriety. Daring to confront Gough, Watson protested about his tanks being used 'over a wide front rather than a narrow one'.[24]

Late in the afternoon of 9 April, Holmes was again issued a series of last-minute changes to orders. Four tanks were now to advance ahead of each brigade, moving along the front on either side of 'Central Road', which led through the re-entrant to Riencourt. The other four tanks were expected to somehow drive through the gap between the two Australian brigades. Holmes considered the idea senseless, particularly as he had less than 12 hours to devise a new plan of attack for the infantry. As late afternoon turned to evening he became even more pessimistic over what the tanks could achieve. During the afternoon of 9 April, Australian infantry began moving 'to the jumping off tape, laid just forward of the front line. Good spirits predominated.'[25]

Holmes' main concern had become the point 'between the objectives of the two brigades [where] there was a gap of some 500 yards, across a depression running at right angles to the Hindenburg Line which would probably be swept by machine gun fire.' It seems that Gough was also aware of the damage that those machine-guns could inflict on the infantry. But, not unexpectedly, he had faith in the way 'the tanks would deal with the defences here, and that the brigades would afterwards be able to close the gap by extending their inner flanks.'[26]

Meanwhile, on 8 April, Major General W.P. Braithwaite, commander of the 62nd British Division, was also puzzling over the conflicting orders he was receiving, particularly that 'Bullecourt will not be attacked in the first instance, but will be pinched out.'[27] On 9 April Braithwaite was instructed to make arrangements for an advance by pushing out 'strong patrols at 4.30 a.m.' on 10 April, 'under an artillery barrage, and occupy the enemy's front line and support trenches if he had vacated them.' Braithwaite was assured that troops from the 2/7th West Yorks would be supported by tanks and by the Australians on their right.[28]

Later that same day, I ANZAC Heavy Artillery headquarters issued a final operation order. At 8.00 pm guns from the 2nd Heavy Artillery Group (HAG) were to fire '60 rounds per hour into Bullecourt, in order to destroy all possible buildings', while those from the 14th HAG shelled Riencourt. Firing was to cease shortly before 4.30 am, the scheduled time for the tanks to lead off the advance. Between 4.30 am and 5.30 am the batteries of the Australian Siege Artillery were to lay down a barrage along the flank of the attack in the 'Queant salient'. Each battery was instructed to fire only '60 rounds per hour'.[29] How such a modest number of shells was expected to smash enemy positions, let alone inflict much damage, was never spelt out.

***

At 12.30 am on 9 April Holmes received what was assumed to be his final order from Fifth Army headquarters reiterating once more the importance Gough placed on the tanks leading the advance. Artillery, however, was now instructed to keep firing separate flank barrages. The order's last few sentences must have been of more concern to Holmes:

> If action successful tanks and infantry will clear Bullecourt and advance will be made to Riencourt. V Corps are to take their objectives if we succeed and are to move on Hendecourt. 4th Cavalry Division are to follow 4th Australian Division and operate in direction Vis-en-Artois. Keep 4th Cavalry Division informed of progress.[30]

Holmes faced the distasteful task of calling together his brigade commanders and informing them of their revised tasking. Robertson was told that the 12th Brigade would advance on the left with 'only the two battalions which had been holding the Boisleux-Marquion railway since the 7th … [and] follow the tanks into Bullecourt.' Brand was informed that his 4th Brigade must do more. Advancing on the right, his troops 'had the further objective of Riencourt, and therefore required all four of its battalions, the two which were resting having to march some seven miles from Favreuil during the night.'[31] By now all knew that any chance of success was less than slim.

The final plan basically called for the leading wave of troops to capture OG1 — the first line of enemy trenches. Supporting units were to pass through, take OG2 — the second line — anywhere from around 100 to 200 yards further back. Brand chose to follow the British order of battle, requiring four of his battalions from the 4th Brigade to advance in artillery formation — two in the first wave and two in the second. The 16th and 13th battalions were to move forward on the right flank. The 14th Battalion, supported by the 15th, was to advance opposite Riencourt. Robertson employed similar tactics with his 12th Brigade, but stated definitively that 'the infantry will not advance until tanks have reached the trenches'.[32] All of this would have to occur without the support of even an acceptable preliminary artillery bombardment to assist the flank barrage. Instead, the tanks would effectively assume the role of the artillery. Perhaps even more fanciful was the role of the cavalry troop, waiting to exploit the gains made by the infantry.

On paper the 4th Division's final objectives appeared straightforward, albeit implausible, as did those of the British. After the capture of Riencourt came the clearing of enemy troops near Bullecourt. A battalion from the 185th Infantry Brigade (62nd British Division) was then to move through Bullecourt from the south-west. Once Bullecourt had been taken, the infantry would turn their attention to clearing and occupying the remainder of the Hindenburg Line, supported by whatever number of tanks had not been put out of action. They were then to advance against enemy troops in and around Hendecourt. Officers were told that, only once the village had been taken, were their men to 'move forward in the general direction of Villers-les-Cagnicourt … (joining, in the north) with the Cavalry Corps and covering the left of the ANZAC Corps, who will be advancing against Cagnicourt.'[33]

As late as 10.00 am on 9 April, Durrant received Brigade Order Number 74 advising him that the attack was to go ahead 'with artillery'. A little over 12 hours later, at 10.20 pm, he received another message from divisional headquarters reaffirming 'Attack with artillery support.' It was not until 11.59 pm that Durrant was informed that the advance, still scheduled to commence at 4.30 am, was to proceed, but 'with tanks' and only a minimal barrage and flanking artillery support.[34]

Holmes was just as much in the dark. With barely a moment to consider the revised orders he was receiving from army and corps headquarters, he sent last-minute instructions to his brigade commanders, shortly after midnight on 10 April:

1. All troops will form up in rear of the jumping off trenches already marked out, under cover of the railway embankment and cutting.

2. At 4.30 a.m. the Artillery will put down a flank barrage on Queant and Bullecourt, and the Tanks will move forward.

3. On reaching the trenches, and as soon as they have occupied them the Tanks will display a green disc, meaning "come on" or make some other prearranged signal.

4. The Infantry will then advance and occupy the trenches.

5. The Artillery flank barrage will be kept on until ordered to stop.

6. The heavy artillery are shelling Bullecourt, Riencourt and the Queant Salient Trenches until 4.30 a.m.

7. As soon as the trenches have been made good the 4th Australian Infantry Brigade will move forward … This subsequent operation will be supported by Tanks which will go to Riencourt and Bullecourt.

Almost as an afterthought, Holmes added: 're paragraph 1. Stow the men away somehow.' Perhaps optimistically there was still some hope that the attack might be called off. Holmes wrote that there 'is no certainty that the attack will take place – all depends on Third Army – The Tanks will crumble down the wire.'[35]

Not long before the scheduled 'jumping-off' time, the brigade commanders met their battalion commanding officers who were to pass on orders to company and platoon commanders. Captain Dunworth recalled his feelings at the time as they

… found Brig-Gen Brand apparently despondent. Then and only then we learned that the orders had been altered. The barrage had been dispensed with and Tanks substituted. This news came as a thunderclap. Every officer and man knew his job by heart. Now we had to cancel all their instructions and rush out fresh ones. No chance to get the men together the best we could hope for would be to get the officers and NCOs to know the new plan as well as we could.

The 4th [Brigade] had every confidence in its ability to follow a Barrage. It had been said of the 4th Brig. 'They lean up against the barrage and when it lifts they just fall in on top of the enemy.' But tanks we knew nothing of – we had never seen one in action. At my suggestion Lt-Col McSharry [commanding officer of the 15th Battalion] asked couldn't we have the barrage as well but met with the answer that 'the tanks could not co-operate with artillery'.[36]

Junior officers were also advised that the tanks would move ahead of their infantry, cutting through the 'German wire by rolling over it, and would then provide close support within the enemy's trench system.'[37]

Dunworth added that with 'vile humours we rejoined our unit and got into position deployed along the Railway Line about 1600 yards east of Noreuil. That was our only shelter, a permanent way three feet (about) high. We had to use ground sheets to blanket our torch lights whilst we endeavoured to explain the new instructions to our Officers and NCOs.'[38] Holmes worked hard to ensure success. However he was informed that the morale of the enemy troops facing the Australians (particularly the crack *Wurttemberg Division*) was first-rate, as they had been 'rested after Somme' and they were 'stubborn fighters'. Countering this was the consistent 'high' morale of most of the Australian troops.[39] But the issue of orders to brigade and battalion headquarters was becoming increasingly poorly managed. Some orders from the 4th and 12th Brigade headquarters were simply confusing. Little wonder that many junior officers remained uncertain of what exactly they should do at the time set for the advance.

There were also setbacks with supplies and equipment. In one instance it was revealed that 36,000 bombs (or hand grenades) already in the forward area had no detonators. When Holmes was notified he was furious, ordering six trucks forward and 600 troops from behind the line to rush the detonators to the forward positions. Not unexpectedly, troops waiting in the snow ready to move forward were unsettled by the fraught last-minute preparations and constant changes.

The 62nd British Division fared little better. Final orders spelling out the method of attack were only received at 12.45 am on 10 April. With less than four hours to Zero Hour (4.30 am) British officers did a sterling job preparing their men. Three patrols from the 2/7th and 2/8th West Yorkshire regiments were instructed to move forward and 'occupy the front and support trenches' until 'reinforced and the position secured'. In the 'unlikely' event that British troops became stuck in enemy trenches, tanks supporting the Australians were expected to mop up the Germans in those trenches before turning their attention to the remaining enemy positions in Bullecourt, then move west along the enemy front line, 'across the front of attack of the 185th Infantry Brigade'. The flawed planning assumed that any undamaged tanks could then support other unscathed British infantry, 'killing' any surviving German troops before occupying Bullecourt.[40]

Another operation order, issued to the British division at 3.00 am on 10 April (little over one and a half hours before the attack was due to commence), had British infantry moving against the village of Villers-le-Cagnicourt. As if this was not farcical enough, the order went on to require the operational commander to 'push out Cavalry Patrols well to the front and also pay particular attention to the high ground on left flank and will endeavour to gain touch with the 2nd Cavalry Division operating in the neighbourhood of Fontaine lez Croissilles, and 12th Australian Brigade in the neighbourhood of Riencourt-lez-Cagnicourt.'[41] If nothing else, this order, coming at the time it did, gave both officers and men little opportunity to make proper preparations, and further highlights the unrealistic world that many of the staff officers inhabited, safely ensconced in their chateaux remote from the harsh conditions of the front.

***

At around 10.00 pm on 9 April the two Australian infantry brigades began moving into position. Despite having little time to prepare a suitable line, they gained some assistance from several features of the terrain, which Durrant described as shaped roughly like an 'amphitheatre'.[42] Prior to their move, the Australian infantry had been camped around Noreuil, a little over a mile back from the front. As the men approached the front, they took advantage of several sunken roads close to the villages. Moving even closer to the front, they found some shelter in a railway cutting which ran parallel to and was some 800 yards from the German forward trench. Not far from the railway was the useful sunken road that Jacka had found where the troops were now forming up for the advance.

At 1.00 am British guns commenced firing phosgene gas from 4-inch Stokes mortars and Livens Projectors against known enemy positions around Riencourt and Bullecourt. During this time the tanks should have been moving towards the front so that they could be in position forward of the Australian infantry by 4.30 am to lead off the attack. By 4.15 am all the Australian infantry were in position some 600 yards from the first enemy trench and approximately 500 yards from those massive wire entanglements, waiting on freezing, snow-covered ground, not far from the barrels of German machine-guns. Anticipating the tanks' arrival, a few of the men displayed a confident air of expectation over what this novel weapon could accomplish.

At precisely 4.30 am the artillery commenced firing a barrage on the flanks around Bullecourt. But the tanks were still nowhere to be seen. It was vital that the advance commence before daylight to afford the infantry maximum protection from enemy machine-guns, particularly those positioned around Queant and the Six Cross Roads. However, as the first light of the new day broke (it was timed to start at around 5.30, with sunrise due at 6.18), the infantry began to panic at the absence of the tanks. By first light they would make easy targets for enemy artillery and machine-guns.

Holmes refused to commit his men to battle without proper support. At around 4.15 am a tank officer reported that his cumbersome vehicle could not possibly arrive before dawn. More alarmingly, and somewhat comically, as first light approached another 'exhausted tank officer stumbled into a telephone office in Noreuil valley, a mile behind the railway embankment and told the 4th Division's headquarters that his machines had met blizzard weather and could not be [there] in time.'[43]

Numerous excuses were subsequently made by other officers from the Heavy Machine Gun Branch — for example there were mechanical problems or the tanks had lost their way — for their non-arrival. A later account noted:

> The explanation of the delay was telephoned to Major Watson at divisional headquarters. The tanks were still two miles short of Noreuil; they had been caught in a blizzard on the downs, and though never actually lost had had to feel their way yard by yard; it would take them another hour and a half to reach their starting point … Major General Holmes took it without referring to higher authority. "We must postpone the show. I think there is just time [before dawn] to get the boys back," was his verdict.[44]

Orders to withdraw were quickly passed to the battalion commanding officers.

However word of the postponement failed to reach the 62nd British Division. Ordered to advance, strong patrols penetrated the wire and reached enemy trenches before realising that the Australians were not alongside them. When German machine-guns and artillery opened up, the troops of the three West Yorkshire battalions were massacred before they had time to withdraw. Only at 4.55 am, precisely the same time that British troops were being massacred, did word of the postponement reach British divisional headquarters. Much of the blame was attributed to staff at Australian divisional headquarters as they certainly had time to notify the 62nd Division of the delay. Yet, for some unknown reason — perhaps incompetence or even sheer laziness — they failed to do so.

The famed British military theorist Cyril Falls had no doubt where the blame for the 162 casualties lay. 'Not being informed by the 4th Australian Division that the tanks had not appeared,' he wrote, 'the 62nd Division sent forward strong patrols from three battalions of the 185th Brigade.'[45] One Australian, Private Lewis Sharp (13th Battalion), had other ideas, however. Probably confused, he incorrectly claimed that the 'Pommies were running. They were running like hell they were, and we were going forward [like] at Passchendaele.'[46] Regrettably, over time, unsubstantiated claims such as those of Sharp, have become part of Australian mythology concerning the actions of British soldiers, not only at Bullecourt, but in many other engagements.

**

Lieutenant Colonel Ray Leane, (commanding officer of the 48th Battalion) recalled that 'it was about 5.30a.m. on 10th April before I received any instruction from Brigade that the attack upon Bullecourt was postponed.' Brand's simple message summarised the folly of the night and morning: 'The stunt is off. Dispositions as yesterday. Move.'[47] The men needed little encouragement. Fully aware that they could be spotted, they rushed back, resembling 'the departure of a crowd from a Test match'.[48]

Donald Fraser (13th Battalion) later wrote that 'the weather favoured us, as it started to snow. In fact it was a light blizzard. I feel that the enemy did not see us, as there was no barrage or artillery shells pumped at us, only a few shells, which was normal.'[49] Company Sergeant Major C.S. Emerson (C Company, 15th Battalion) recollected that 'there was no system or organisation about this retirement. Each section of men went back as best it might.'[50]

German observers noticed the last of the men hurrying back to their line. When the artillery finally opened up, a number of Australians were killed or wounded. Leane wrote that his men 'retired in full view and under shell fire to the sunken road left of Noreuil.'[51] Another Australian soldier, Victor Groutsch (13th Battalion) summarised the foolhardiness of the operation and its aftermath:

The tanks were supposed to come up and take – there was no artillery at all. In other words, the wire was intact. The theory was that the tanks were going to knock the wire down so the troops could get in, but they never turned up. Then just before it got daylight, they decided they'd have to go back ... And going back through the snow was like telling the Germans what we were going to do tomorrow ... They'd see us going back over the snow! See the khaki uniforms on a snow background ... [M]orale was pretty low, pretty bloody low.[52]

A divisional report was careful to state explicitly that 'All the troops concerned were considerably exhausted as the result of being under arms most of the night.'[53]

The example of the 13th Battalion was mirrored throughout both brigades. All the men of the 13th were said to be 'dog-tired, disappointed and more pessimistic than at any other period in their history concerning the higher authorities.'[54] During the last week these men had not only performed hard physical labour, including constructing roads and carting equipment and supplies, but also endured a demanding night march to move into position. They were then subject to the stress of waiting for combat and the prospect of death or being maimed prior to being told the attack was postponed.

After reaching the sunken road, the exhausted infantry were forced to march back to Noreuil. Following a brief respite, they trudged their way another few miles to Favreuil. Some Australians, in a show of black humour, were already referring to this as the 'Dummy Stunt' or the 'Buckshee Battle'. Others believed that they had lost a golden opportunity — Dunworth subsequently wrote, 'had we attacked the first night with an efficient barrage we had an excellent chance of success that would have enabled us to turn the flank of the German forces.'[55]

For his part, Birdwood recorded that he was 'very glad it had to be postponed. I don't like it at all. The people on our left are not [far] enough up – when they get up a good deal further it will be different, but I don't like the affair at all.'[56] Despite Birdwood's reluctance, he was instructed that the attack would go ahead — again, with the assistance of tanks. The tired and dispirited soldiers, their confidence at its lowest ebb, and fully aware that the Germans had been forewarned, were permitted a short rest before being told to be ready to attempt the same stunt the following morning.

***

Taking into account the foolhardiness and lack of foresight displayed by Gough and his co-planners, and the confusing orders that originated from Australian headquarters — from corps through to battalion — officers were provided the opportunity to revise their tactics and plans for the next attack. Minimal changes were made. Little wonder that Australian troops were beginning to lose confidence, not only in British, but also in some areas of Australian command.

CHAPTER 6

'It is useless to talk about gallantry.'
THE FIRST ATTACK

Following the postponement of the first assault and the hasty return to Noreuil, most of the men were frustrated and exhausted. More significantly, as one Australian soldier recalled, they were 'intensely soured and disgusted. The bungling that had resulted in this grotesque fiasco was evident to everyone, and confidence in the higher leadership was badly shaken. It was due more to good luck than to good management that the retirement had not ended in Australian shambles.'[1]

The irony of the delay was not lost. Over the past few days Australian soldiers had endured challenging physical preparations followed by an overnight march into no man's land, all combined with the stress of imminent combat. They were then forced to march back to Noreuil before completing a further lengthy trek to their camp near Favreuil, fully aware that they would soon have to complete the same journey again. Another soldier wrote that they were all 'dog tired, disappointed and more pessimistic than at any other period in their history concerning the higher authorities.'[2]

While the troops were making their way back, Gough, in the comfort of his headquarters, was assembling his staff to formulate a few fresh ideas for the new attack. On this occasion, however, Birdwood and White refused to be silenced. Confronting the British general, they told him of their persistent doubts. Not only was the men's fatigue a major consideration, but they were also concerned at the unreliability of the tanks, their confidence in those mechanical monsters well and truly shaken. Not unsurprisingly, Gough refused to listen, having already set his sights on repeating the same attack the following morning.

The failed attack also had more immediate consequences. Enemy officers now realised that another assault was imminent. A German lieutenant colonel commanding a brigade of *Wurtemburgers* recalled that the Australian 'attack on April 11th had been anticipated … the first and second lines had been only thinly held [on 10 April] whilst large reinforcements had been brought into reserve including large numbers of machine guns.' Another German officer later revealed that he and his fellow officers, along with their men, were better prepared and 'knew we would return to the attack … they had rushed up strong reinforcements and they had seen our troops falling back and the cavalry riding away, hence they knew a serious attack had for some reason failed.'[3] A trainload of German troops, preparing to move north to the Arras front, was instead instructed to remain behind and man the forward trenches around Bullecourt.[4] Adding to the Australian woes was their new-found knowledge that the German *27th Infantry Division*, which was defending the Bullecourt sector, was known to be 'one of the finest ground-holding divisions in the entire German army'. Moreover, the commander, *Generalmajor* Heinrich Maur, was 'an outstanding career gunner' who not only ordered his men to be 'on full alert', but ensured that his officers placed greater emphasis on 'careful control and use of artillery fire and infantry-artillery cooperation'.[5]

Australian soldiers were well aware that the Germans would be prepared for a new attack. Sergeant A.L. Guppy feelings were all too familiar. 'All [the men] are in good spirits,' he confided to his diary, 'though we feel that this morning's mess up will do us a lot of harm.'[6] Likewise, Sergeant D. Blackburn (14th Battalion) was convinced that it 'put Fritz wise to our little game.'[7] Another Australian, Victor Groutsch, pictured the disaster that would enfold his brigade. 'Going back through the snow,' he remembered later, 'was like telling the Germans what we were going to do tomorrow … [They would] see the khaki uniforms on a snow background.' More significantly, he believed that, in his unit, 'morale was pretty low, pretty bloody low,' — and for good reason.[8]

Toft later recalled that 'the big majority of those fresh German troops were machine-gun companies ... [who] helped to make the next day a sad one for Australians.'[9]

The village of Bullecourt in ruins, April 1917 (RMC Blamey album).

***

However Gough maintained his unswerving faith in the tanks to complete their task, athough Birdwood and many other senior Australian officers did not share his conviction. Birdwood and White again tried to reason with Gough, telling him that another attack would be foolhardy. Gough refused to countenance any thought of cancelling the attack. At midday on 10 April he assembled his two corps commanders, their chiefs of staff and the senior artillery and tank officers. Assured that the tanks could achieve what they had failed to do the previous morning, Gough demanded that the 4th Australian Division replicate the attack and scheduled it for dawn the following morning. Birdwood made one more desperate attempt to have it called off. Expressing his reservations about the plan, he told Gough that he considered it 'fraught with danger'.[10] Once again, Gough took no notice. However he did make one concession: instead of being expected to go as far as Villers-le-Cagnicourt, the final objective of the British was now Hendecourt. The Australians would take Riencourt.[11]

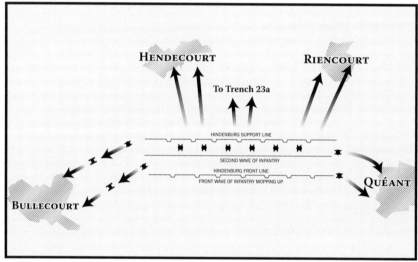

Sketch of proposed tank positions for attack on Bullecourt, highlighting the direction the tanks were supposed to take (source: 1st Tank Brigade headquarters, April 1917, UK National Archives, WO95/97).

Not long afterwards Birdwood received written instructions from army headquarters with an annotation that 'as verbally arranged tanks will precede advance. Heavy artillery will co-operate under orders of 4th Australian Division. Special bombardments will be arranged to protect flanks.'[12] Senior Australian officers remained dumbfounded by the foolhardiness of the order. Yet, after what he had heard from Gough earlier in the day, Birdwood knew that any further confrontation with his army commander would be pointless.

Birdwood had little option but to send an urgent message to Holmes. 'The 4th Australian Division will accordingly attack the enemy on the line ... on the 11th instant and seize Riencourt,' Birdwood wrote, before adding, somewhat optimistically:

Troops will be held ready to exploit any success gained. Twelve tanks are placed at the disposal of the 4th Australian Division for co-operation and wire cutting. Four tanks will after the seizure of the first objective, move on and clear Bullecourt. The GOC 4th Australian Division will detail at least one battalion to accompany these tanks for the purpose of clearing   Bullecourt. Two other tanks will be directed on the factory [at the western end of the village] ... These six tanks will subsequently pass under the orders of [Major General W.P. Braithwaite's] 62nd Division.

When the tanks have reached Bullecourt and our troops have entered the village, the 62nd Division will be informed at once. Special arrangements have been made for the communication of this information.

He also told Holmes that he would again be responsible for drawing up plans for the flanking artillery barrage.[13]

Holmes assembled his brigade commanders and his staff for an urgent afternoon conference. During the conference Holmes was told that, in many places, the wire was still only partly cut at best. He decided to make a series of small changes to the plan, including instructing the infantry to move forward 15 minutes after the tanks, 'independently of their progress', without relying on signals from tank officers in tanks 'that had passed through [the wire].'[14] However these changes represented too little, too late. In fact, in flawed planning and tactics, the attack now resembled that most horrific first day of the Somme. Perhaps surprisingly, the tank attack at Bullecourt to this point has been described as 'imaginative'. A subsequent suggestion that it was 'poorly planned' is much closer to the truth.[15] One Australian soldier preparing to go into the line put it more bluntly. 'This is a messed up show,' he wrote, 'damn the law of averages ... [of being] "knocked." It's not that that matters; but the rotten arrangements – no artillery!'[16]

At approximately 3.00 pm Major General Braithwaite received further instructions, informing him of the precise role of the 62nd

Division — the same British division that had been badly mauled less than 12 hours previously. He was told that the Australians would initially clear Bullecourt as far as its western end. Only then would six of the tanks come under Braithwaite's command. The 2/6th West Yorks, commanded by Lieutenant Colonel J. Hastings, supported by Lieutenant Colonel A. James' 2/8th Battalion, was to move against the village from the south-west, occupy it and, assisted by the tanks, 'clear and occupy' that part of the Hindenburg Line, before moving against Hendecourt.[17]

Later in the day, I ANZAC Heavy Artillery headquarters issued its final operation orders. Still wildly fanciful and optimistic, the orders instructed the 2nd HAG to fire just 60 rounds each hour into Bullecourt with the expectation of razing to the ground 'all buildings which are now standing'. The 14th HAG was to shell Riencourt. The batteries were also provided with other targets, most noticeably, new front line and support trenches, revealed in recent aerial reconnaissance. The gunners were to direct all possible fire against those trenches from 4.30 am until 5.12 am, when their guns would put down a 'lifting' flanking barrage in support of advancing infantry. At 5.45 am all artillery fire was to cease.[18]

***

Perhaps Gough's realisation that the Third Army was gaining little ground around Monchy-le-Preux further encouraged him to proceed with the attack. Another message from Haig's headquarters pointing out 'that the assistance of the Fifth Army would be precious to the Third on the 11th April, when a great effort was to be made to reach the Green Line on the whole front and pass the Cavalry Corps through', increased Gough's determination.[19] The hopelessness of expecting the cavalry to pass through seems to have been lost on Gough. Ever the cavalrymen, Gough — and Haig, for that matter (even after numerous previous disastrous cavalry charges) — still held high hopes of a breakthrough by their beloved arm.

Faulty aerial reconnaissance reports also encouraged Gough. One report showed the opposite of what infantry patrols were reporting. 'Enemy Defences [around] the Hindenburg Line South East and East of Bullecourt', it noted, 'appear to have suffered from our shelling, as has also the wire.'[20] Buoyed by these reports and Haig's message, Gough was now able to add extra rationale for what was about to take place. Calling Birdwood to his headquarters, Gough told the Australian corps commander 'that the Anzac attack, which had been essential the day before to support the success of Third Army, was essential today to prevent a Third Army failure.' Birdwood remained unconvinced. Given the opportunity to make one final bid to cancel the attack, he told Gough 'that the Germans had now been alerted all along the Hindenburg Line.' Gough again took little notice. Remaining adamant that the advance would proceed, he added that Haig 'considered the attack to be urgently required.' Birdwood said nothing.[21]

Final detailed preparations for the attack were yet to be put in place. In fact, even as the troops were making their way to the jumping-off line, plans were being updated and changed. Finishing touches were only conveyed to battalion commanders shortly before midnight — a little more than four and a half hours before the tanks were to lead the advance.[22]

***

At 6.00 pm on 10 April Durrant was at battalion headquarters when he took delivery of another order confirming 'attack on 11th with tanks'. He waited another four and a quarter hours for further information. Only then did 'The Continuation Order of 10/4/'17' arrive, followed later by 'The Tank barrage maps'. Durrant had already decided that 'too much [was] expected of the tanks – very slow – could not cut that wire – poor at turning.' Perhaps more significantly, he predicted confidently that there would be 'Mechanical break downs' and too few tanks to support his infantry.[23]

Horatio Ganson (16th Battalion) also recalled that the troops were given little detail on how the attack was to proceed. In an attempt to calm their men, the 'officers told us it was going to be a surprise attack' and 'that there would be no barrage. But they wouldn't tell you much. They told us what time we would be going over. They told us the tanks were going to come up.'[24] What else could young officers tell their men, without further dampening their spirits? Most senior and middle-ranking officers like Durrant were well aware that, without proper artillery support, another attack was sheer madness. And for this they were already laying the blame squarely on the bloody-mindedness of Gough and his staff.[25]

Brigadier General Charles Brand was not one to sit idly by. He continued to press for more artillery support, right to the end. 'Brand appeared to have a premonition of failure', Toft wrote. 'He was not confident and was visibly unhappy. All through he had fought the higher authorities for a big supporting fire from the artillery. "I have no faith in the tanks, as they haven't been proved," he told Colonel Barnard.'[26] Brand, however, was a man who knew his duty. He had been given a job to do. He would do it to the best of his ability and he expected the same from his officers and men. As brigade commander his philosophy was simple. He needed

… to take the same risks as … [his] men. It was the taking of those risks which gave a leader experience and secured the confidence that won battles. They [officers] who never saw "No man's land" lived in another world, they were in the A.I.F. but knew not its soul. Nothing bucked up front line units so much as to see their Brigade and Battalion Commanders moving around the foremost trenches at least once every 24 hours gaining first hand knowledge of the position, appreciating their difficulties, sinking ankle deep into the mud and slush, sheltering temporarily in a shell hole till a strafe was over. That was not empty bravado. A word of encouragement to nerve racked diggers [soldiers] was worth pages of eulogy afterwards.[27]

As his troops were preparing for battle, Brand was applying the same standards, moving among them, offering encouragement and hope.

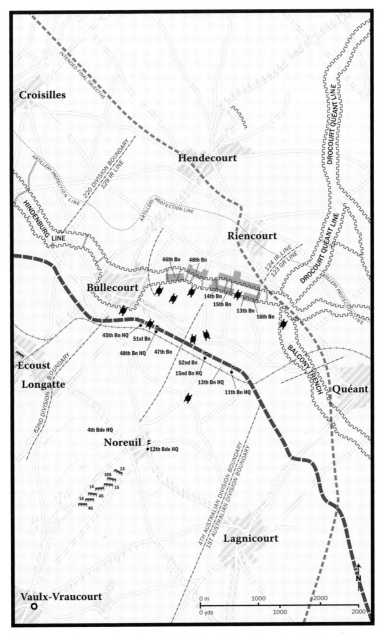

Map of Bullecourt and surrounding villages showing disposition of Australian-British and German units as well as the intended final objective. Note position of Queant from where German machine-gun positions inflicted heavy Australian casualties.

At 12th Brigade headquarters there was similar last-minute frenzied activity. As a brigade commander's capacity to affect operational and tactical planning was severely limited, Brigadier General Robertson, like Brand, had to follow orders that came from higher authority. Based on what he had received from divisional headquarters, Robertson summarised what he expected from battalion commanding officers and outlined the task of the 12 tanks. 'As soon as the second objective has been made good,' he instructed, 'the 4th Australian Infantry Brigade on our right will move forward supported by Tanks and occupy Riencourt. Simultaneously the 48th Battalion will push Lewis Guns forward and establish Strong Points … along the line of the sunken road … in order to protect the left flank of the 4th … Brigade.' Machine-gun companies were to fire on German positions around Bullecourt and parts of Queant known to be enemy strongpoints.[28] While brigade staff were reviewing last-minute changes, intelligence officers were patrolling the area in front of the sunken road and the 'jumping off place. Tapes were then attached to the small pegs fixed two nights previously, to indicate flanks of Battalions and Companies.'[29]

***

Shortly after midnight the two brigade commanders assembled their battalion commanding officers to further review the revised plans. At 4th Brigade headquarters, Brand arranged that the staff of the two battalions leading the attack — Lieutenant Colonel Peck's 14th and Drake-Brockman's 16th — would establish joint headquarters at the railway cutting. Battalion commanding officers were informed of minor changes to the plans of the previous morning which would affect their men. The companies were to again lead off in artillery formation — four companies in line and in single file by platoons. Artillery support was also similar with flanking barrages put down against enemy troops expected to be massing around Riencourt and Bullecourt. At around 1.00 am gas would be fired.

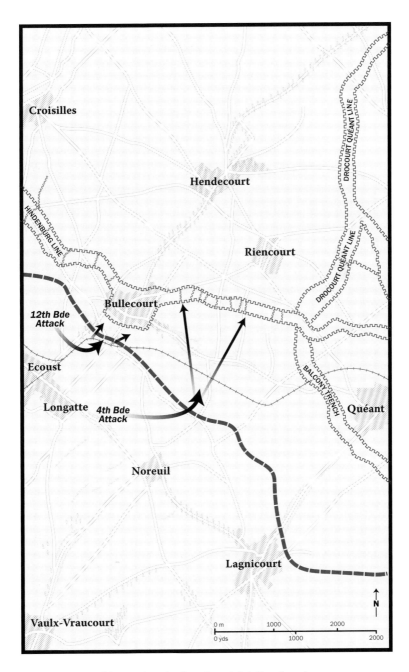

Map showing positions of the two Australian brigades and their line of attack.

A subsequent report noted that 'Gas was projected successfully into Bullecourt – enemy replied with rifle and machine gun fire.'[30]

Similar discussions were taking place at 12th Brigade headquarters. Brigadier General Robertson wrote that the 'tank commander was also present and explained the cooperation of the tanks.' Drawing special attention to support expected from the 12th Machine Gun Company, Robertson told his battalion commanding officers that six machine-guns positioned close to the railway line would provide cover for the infantry advancing alongside the tanks while another three guns would 'search and sweep with indirect fire the roads between Bullecourt and Riencourt.' The noise from those guns was also expected to help 'drown the noise of the Tanks when moving forward to their starting point.' A couple of 'mobile gun crews' were ready near the railway embankment to help consolidate the objective following its capture. And, somewhat inexplicably, five other machine-guns were to be 'held in reserve'.[31] With little more than an hour until the attack, orders were still being amended. It was not until 3.00 am that the 47th Battalion was told to have two companies ready to reinforce Lieutenant Colonel Howard Denham's 46th Battalion.[32]

Battalion commanding officers then reviewed the plans' finer details with their junior officers. Drake-Brockman discussed tactics with his company commanders until around 2.00 am, 'sorting out the final dispositions of the companies'.[33] Captain David Dunworth recalled that orders were again mixed up. 'We were ordered to wait until the Tanks had reached the enemy's position, pressed down the wire, and mopped up the machine guns, whereon they were to show us a coloured light as a signal to come on. Then this order was shortly after cancelled and we were told to give the Tanks 15 minutes start and follow them.'[34]

One of the 16th Battalion's better known and more courageous leaders, Major Percy Black, was told that he would be the senior officer among the attacking troops (effectively the 'de facto commander in action') in addition to his usual command of B Company. Prior to joining his men, Black told Drake-Brockman of a premonition: 'Well good-bye colonel – I mayn't come back, but we'll get the Hindenburg Line.'[35] Black's close friend, Captain Harry Murray, was again leading A Company. The usually optimistic and agreeable officer was, for once, less than sure how the attack would proceed. Before receiving his 'final orders, he had found himself hoping that the attack would be called off, but as always, now that the die was cast, he put aside his doubts to focus on the task before him.'[36] At 13th Battalion's headquarters, Durrant wrote that he had a 'final conference with OCs' before telling them 'to HELP 15th Battalion if necessary.'[37]

Portrait of Lieutenant Colonel Henry William Murray (1883–1966), VC, CMG, DSO and Bar. Murray was awarded his VC for outstanding courage when, as a captain, he led his company in an attack on Stormy Trench near Gueudecourt during the night of 4/5 February 1917. Over a period of 24 hours the company repelled numerous German counter-attacks (AWM ART00101-1).

***

Meanwhile, under cover of darkness, the troops had once more assembled in the sunken road. In addition to his standard equipment, each man carried an extra 200 rounds of small arms ammunition, two Mills hand grenades and two sandbags.[38] 'Before the men left, man after man shook hands with me and bid me good-bye', wrote Captain Chataway of the 15th Battalion,

> … they knew … their hour had struck … I felt … very bad. The element of surprise was lost – the tanks could never make up for it. Eight hundred yards of open country to be traversed and not a gun to be fired as cover for the advance, nor the destruction of the barbed wire entanglement before the enemy position. The tanks were to do all this.[39]

By 3.30 am the troops were in position, ready to attack.

They waited anxiously. At 3.00 am the first tank arrived at the railway crossing, some 600 yards from its starting-off point. Some five minutes later, two others arrived — they had just 15 minutes to be in position ready to attack. Brigadier General Brand clearly considered this beyond them and contacted divisional headquarters to ask that the tanks 'start … at 4.15 a.m.' Given their slow speed and the time it would take to get to the wire, it was a perfectly logical request. He subsequently revealed his understanding that 'the Tanks, unless they started earlier, would only be a hindrance instead of a help.'[40] But Brand's request was overruled by Holmes.

By 4.00 am three tanks, not the promised six, were lined up in front of the 4th Brigade's 'jumping off place … separated by gaps of approximately 100 yards.' Captain White recorded that, of the others,

> One had had an 'accident.' One complained of 'engine trouble,' and the other had lolloped into a sunken road whither it had gone contrary to the directions by a 14th [Battalion] officer. These tanks were out of action before the battle commenced, and, not only the three that had arrived, but the others had made squeals, screeches and sparks that must have warned the enemy. Our men cursed them and the 'silent artillery'.[41]

Another tank was preparing to move into the gap between the two Australian brigades. None had appeared in the 12th's sector. The doubts harboured by Birdwood and many other senior Australian officers had proven correct. As predicted earlier, a number of the tanks had yet again experienced some form of mechanical difficulty; some were even unable to move off from their assembly place. Others required assistance to extricate them from the gluey mud.

Victor Groutsch recalled his thoughts at the time: 'there is a lot of preparation for an event like that. Unfortunately they couldn't get [all of] the tanks up [on time]. The stupid bastards, they didn't give us any artillery at all! It was all going to be a surprise. God strewth! Terrible mistake.'[42] Captain Albert Jacka was guiding another tank forward when it became bogged in the muddy sunken road. Never one for formality, Jacka became so furious that Australian soldiers had to prevent him shooting the British tank officer. When told by the young British lieutenant that the tanks could not possibly reach the German wire before the infantry, Jacka again went into a rage. On this occasion, he ranted against those responsible for planning the attack. 'The organisation seemed to be bad,' Jacka subsequently wrote, 'and no-one appeared to be in direct command of the show. Personal safety and comfort seemed their sole ambition.'[43]

However it was unfair to solely blame the tank crews. Staff officers at I ANZAC headquarters and indeed divisional headquarters should not escape censure. As the tanks moved closer to the front, those same officers should have commanded the machine-gun crews to commence firing. But, in 'another lapse from best practice, the ANZAC staff failed to transmit orders for massed machine gun fire to be used to mask the sound of the tanks deploying for the attack, and an alert enemy was able to prepare its response more carefully.'[44]

Recognising the disaster that was likely to befall their men if the attack proceeded, a few Australian officers attempted to have the offensive cancelled or, at the very least, have the time of the attack amended so that the assault would begin once all the tanks were in position. Drake-Brockman was probably the most outspoken, reporting the disorganisation and chaos in his part of the line to divisional headquarters, noting particularly his waiting troops' frustration. But it was all to no avail. With another catastrophe in the offing, he was instructed to 'Stick to the program.'[45] Birdwood, too, made one last desperate attempt to have the attack called off. Aware of the futility of directly seeking out Gough, and in contravention of military protocol, he informed GHQ of the arrival of only some of the tanks and suggested a postponement. Should the attack proceed that morning, Birdwood at least wanted more artillery support for his infantry. Again, his appeal proved futile. On this occasion it was Kiggell who overruled the corps commander.[46]

***

Photograph c. 1947 of the Bullecourt diorama at the Australian War Memorial, Canberra, depicting the attack on the Hindenburg Line near the village of Bullecourt by the 4th Australian Division on 11 April 1917. The figures were sculptured by Leslie Bowles and the original backdrop painted by Louis McCubbin (AWM X50358).

At precisely 4.30 am Australian gunners began laying down the flank barrages.[47] Captain N.A. Nicolson was commanding the 114th

Battery from the 5th Division Artillery which had been called in to assist with the barrage. 'Out at 4a.m. and stood by the guns,' he wrote, 'we fired in the flank barrage – fired 1,200 shells including 430 smoke. Fired into the Hindenburg Line from Queant towards Bullecourt and kept putting in smoke to obscure the Germans' view of that flank attack.'[48] The 'light' fire was hardly sufficient to do much damage to the enemy positions. Inexplicably there was no fire from British and Australian heavy artillery on enemy gun emplacements sited to the rear of the villages.

A couple of minutes behind schedule, three tanks (one 'male' armed with 6-pounder guns and two 'females' with machine-guns only) leading the 4th Brigade advance commenced their trek towards the enemy wire. German officers, already on the lookout for an attack, had been alerted by the noise of the vehicles as they moved forward. Their guns were ready. German artillery opened up. With no counter-battery response from Australian guns, German artillery seemingly fired at will. Machine-guns from the direction of Riencourt and the Six Cross Roads then commenced their own barrage, firing a storm of bullets into the Australian infantry preparing to advance. Many were killed before they had even started. 'German heavies were enfilading us from Queant,' Captain David Dunworth wrote, 'I saw one section of the 15th wiped out by a heavy shell – I ordered the troops into lines of skirmishers.'[49]

Intelligence reports later confirmed what aerial reconnaissance had failed to notice — more of those expertly positioned German machine-gun nests. 'Machine-guns were firing from the front and rear of the [German] line,' one report noted. 'They appear to be placed in a semicircle from Bullecourt, over the high ground over the rear line, round to Riencourt. Most of the machine-gun fire came from the villages.'[50] Another shell decimated one of the 4th Brigade's mortar batteries. German trench mortars also caused havoc. Three bombs fell in a trench where an Australian machine-gun crew was firing on known enemy strongholds. A later report noted that 'the whole crew with the exception of one man had been blown to pieces.'[51] Similar carnage was not uncommon along other parts of the Australian front. Private Gallwey, about to go into battle for the first time, recalled that 'Mountains of dirt … timber, human bodies, all were thrown up.'[52]

Then it was the turn of the infantry to move forward. At 4.45 am the 16th Battalion (on the right) and the 14th (on the left) led off the advance. Moving in four successive waves they were soon followed by the 13th and 15th battalions.[53] Captain Dunworth wrote later that, 'Without a single protective shell we advanced. A hail of machine gun bullets met us.'[54] In almost no time at all, the infantry overtook the snail-paced tanks. Gallwey recollected that the men stretched 'illimitably to right and left … a glorious sight.'[55]

Another Australian soldier, Eric Simon, was less upbeat, recognising that 'the Germans were prepared.'[56] Donald Fraser (13th Battalion) remembered that,

> … the famous tanks were making so much noise that the enemy must have heard them coming for many miles … At 4.45a.m. the 16th Battalion rose and started to advance. The 13th [Battalion] followed behind them. There were 3 tanks in front, kicking up a terrible din, and drawing the enemy machine gun fire. Their progress was very slow. Shells and mortar bombs now covered the whole area back to the railway cutting. The 16th Battalion suffered very heavy casualties.[57]

Another account described how the infantry was required to 'advance about 1000 yards to reach the first objective; there was not any cover – the ground was as flat as a billiard table. Unprotected by a barrage, the attacking force was absolutely at the enemy's mercy until it reached the wire.'[58]

Advancing in four long lines — 'almost in parade order' — silhouetted against the snow, the Australians in their khaki uniforms were easily spotted by German observers. Flares lit up the pre-dawn sky. Horatio Ganson (16th Battalion) later recounted that, when the Germans 'heard us coming, the Very lights went up in hundreds, all different colours. They were like big fireworks. It was a beautiful sight, but it made it like day, and the Germans could see us.'[59]

Troops in that first wave had various recollections of what happened next. Sergeant A.L. Guppy noted that,

As soon as we start Fritz opens on to us with whizzbangs and 5.9s [shells] and   whole sections of men are wiped out. As we push on his machine guns open with a rattle and a perfect hail of bullets. As one looks around him in the breaking dawn with the ground white with snow, he sees everywhere hundreds of figures moving calmly forward … with here and there men falling as a bullet strikes home.[60]

Corporal Claude Benson remembered that 'our orders were not to get in front of the tanks … My Company was on the left flank, and my section on the extreme left. We advanced in waves and I was in the last wave. As we crossed No Man's Land "Fritz" opened up on us with machine gun and rifle fire, and our casualties must have been very heavy.'[61]

Crossing no man's land, the tanks found themselves in all sorts of trouble. The leading lines of the 14th and 16th battalions were about halfway across, moving through a slight crest, when the men noticed that they were outpacing the tanks. 'About half way to first objective 2 Tanks stopped,' Brigadier General Brand reported, 'and commenced to open fire thus giving away the position and proclaiming an attack. The infantry now under Machine Gun fire decided to push on alone … The third Tank had now also reached the first objective and [was] crossing over but failed to reach the second objective and was then immediately put out of action by a gun near Riencourt.'[62]

The British account differed somewhat. Two of the tanks that were hit by German machine-gun fire were positioned on the extreme right of the 4th Brigade's attack front. Before they could provide assistance to the infantry, and without getting anywhere near the wire, the crews reported mechanical problems and returned to the railway embankment. Another tank turned to the right, crossing the German trench at the *Balkon-Stellung*, some 500 yards outside the Australian advance area. *Die Ulmer Grenadiere an der Westfront* (*123rd German Regiment*) reported that the crew fought courageously to the end before it became 'stuck for some time in the wire, and after crossing the first trench was … put out of action by streams of armour-piercing bullets'.[63]

Three tanks, not the agreed four, advanced in the gap between the two brigades. For the Australians to have any chance of success it was essential that these vehicles cut through the wire and roll over the two lines of enemy trenches. Yet, as the same British account reveals, the first of the tanks 'was hit in the track and another in the cab. The third reached the wire, where it stopped for some reason, to be hit by a shell which exploded the petrol tanks.'

Durrant, however, noticed that two of the tanks had been hit by artillery and were burning, while another was stuck in the mud, unable to move. The British crew from one incinerated tank showed great courage, leaving their burning vehicle to fight with Lewis machine-guns alongside Australian infantry. Eric Simon recalled vividly what happened to another two. 'The others had been shot down or broke down at the starting,' he penned, 'but the crews of these two tanks were heroic. One tank got on to the wire and was crippled by a shell. The other went across it breaking the entanglement down in one place and firing with all its power at the German defenders. There was no doubt that this single tank frightened them.'[64]

Not all tank crews behaved bravely. For some Australian infantry, there was not only enemy artillery, machine-gun and small arms fire to avoid, but it was also necessary to steer clear of tanks. Ernest Etchell, a Lewis gunner with the 15th Battalion, was outraged by the actions of one crew. 'They were running over men wounded, killing them outright,' he recalled with indignation, 'by hell I'd have shot them if I could have got the door open … The tank killed more of our wounded than it killed Germans.'[65]

Pooley recalled that he 'saw one tank where we were … [with] a gang of machine-gunners in it. The others were working further down the sector. We were jogging along, wanting to get into the German trenches and out of the way … I don't know what happened to the tank, after that. We couldn't look behind. But the tank must have been blown up when it got to the wire. I know it didn't go any further.'[66]

Another tank (possibly that noticed by Pooley) was caught in the wire. Durrant noted that it was a 'good target on snow'.[67] Fraser remembered later the sight of

> … bullets flying off [the tanks]. We'd keep away from them because they were   drawing the "crabs" [artillery and machine-gun fire]. They nearly all blew up   before they got over there. And some of the tank crews were taken prisoner as well. They were – I seen two that went on fire … They were singed. Their hair was singed. They crawled out the back of the things. They were lucky to be   alive … [The tanks] were useless.[68]

Another Australian soldier also pointed out that the tanks, their 'shapes outlined by the sparkling of bullets', were attracting considerable German artillery, machine-gun and even rifle fire — fire which otherwise would have been directed at the infantry.[69]

'Very lights', in fact, had highlighted the only surviving slow-moving tanks, making them easy prey for enemy gunners. Shells from a German field gun, cleverly camouflaged among some trees, hit another. Attempting to escape the burning vehicle, the crew were mown down by a nearby enemy machine-gun.[70] Australian infantry, waiting behind the support line, also noticed that whenever a 'Very light' illuminated the sky, 'the battalions perfectly aligned as they moved steadily across the open ground' were cut down by enemy machine-gun and small arms fire.

A few Australians were not quite as critical. 'Some tanks moved off before the infantry,' Company Sergeant Major C. Emerson (15th Battalion) recounted, 'but we passed them halfway across No Man's Land. I saw one tank, away on the right, that had reached the enemy wire and had gone through the wire several times backwards and forwards, leaving substantial gaps where it passed.'[71] But, despite reports of some crack German troops fleeing at the sight of the tanks and the fact that, in the early part of the advance, enemy artillery concentrated their fire on the vehicles to the benefit of infantry, the majority of Australian troops still felt let down by the performance of the tanks.[72] Guppy was speaking for those Australians when he commented bitterly, 'the tanks have failed us'.[73]

***

Leaving the tanks well behind — and with the wire still largely uncut — the Australian infantry continued to advance across no man's land. Many of their more experienced officers paid little heed to the dangers, particularly the deadly machine-gun fire, and led their men from the front. Lance Corporal B. Knowles (a section leader from A Company) never forgot the courageous way Captain Harry Murray imposed his authority, 'strolling along as if death was something which came only with old age'.[74] Major Percy Black knew only one way to lead. Never one to be afraid of danger, he advanced in front of his men, offering encouragement — 'Come on boys, bugger the tanks!' he shouted.[75]

German artillery fired at a frenzied pace, shell after shell landing among the Australians. George Mitchell wrote of the

> ... tornado of thunder and flame ... The blast of one shell would send me reeling forward, while another would halt me with a wave of driven air. A headless man fell at my feet, as I rolled over him a sheet of flame fanned over the blinding light. A score of men just in front melted in bloody fragments as a big calibre shell landed. The air was dense with crackling bullets, and thick with the blood-chilling stink of explosives. The plain was carpeted with bodies, mostly lying still, but some crawling laggingly [sic] for cover. A man cannoned into me and fell, leaving a bloody patch on my shoulder. But there was no sound of human voice in all the storm.[76]

Jim Wheeler also clearly recalled the Germans 'shelling us with "heavies" … Out between the lines there must have been 800 or 1,000 of our brigade, and the Germans just tore them to pieces with bloody shell fire. One shell lobbed very close to me and got our Lewis gunners. They were practically no more after the explosion, blown to pieces.'[77]

Lieutenant Colonel Durrant's 13th Battalion, which was following behind the 16th and had 'orders to mop-up Riencourt', was soon in trouble. Durrant noted that, when his men started their advance, 'loss from shell fire commenced at once'.[78] The battalion was again caught in the open by heavy and accurate machine-gun fire coming from the direction of the Six Cross Roads. The right flank lost its direction, moving more towards the centre and following a sloping road which crossed its advance. Captain Murray quickly came to the rescue. Corporal Knowles recalled that he 'strode across and simply said "Right incline, 13th," and it was done without any fuss.'[79]

Pressing on a few yards further, the battalion met another torrent of deadly machine-gun fire. At least 30 men were killed — within a few seconds one section of 15 men was reduced to just three. With their mates falling around them, the men of the 13th Battalion pressed on, trying to find any gap in the wire made by the leading tank. According to one of the Australians, the wire was 'concertinaed together and held up on heavy wooden posts dug in about three feet high. The wire coiled right up and over the posts, and stretched out about twenty feet in width.'[80]

Not far ahead, the 16th Battalion had problems of its own. Attempting to find further gaps in the wire, more men were mown down. A few openings and passages were found, used by German patrols to enter no man's land. Simon recalled that his section 'ran through the [gap] and … jumped into the first line, the occupants of which surrendered without a fight after we had thrown our bombs in the trench.'[81] Observing the already numerous casualties from the 16th Battalion, officers from the 13th ordered their men to assist. Yet again, Murray was in the lead. 'Come on, 13th! The 16th are getting hell!' he was heard to scream. The battalion raced across the remaining 100 or so yards to the wire at a frantic pace. At the same time more machine-gun fire rained down on the men. According to one unsubstantiated account, further on, 'a single tank following behind the 16th had flattened a path through the first wire belt but had been stopped in the second belt.' With Murray leading the way the '13th charged up the narrow gap in the wire'. But the men could not get around one side of the tank. Murray instinctively dashed 'around to the other side' where he caught sight of 'only ten metres away in a short trench projecting into the wire belt, the machine gun that had caused many of the 13th's casualties in the approach. With suicidal courage, the German crew was still firing even though they were now surrounded. They were quickly shot, but they had done great damage to the Australian ranks.'[82]

What was left of Benson's section had now reached the 'enemy's first wire entanglements'. He recalled that they 'passed through a gap which had been made by a tank … My section … continued the advance and entered the first enemy trench … [which] was held by the remnants of our other battalions.'[83] Horace Rumble remembered later that he 'went through a gap in the wire …, but it was a death trap really. I don't know how I made it into the first line of trenches … Bodies were strewn either side of the wire. I suddenly felt a bang, and I looked down and there was my hand all shattered.'[84] Others were just plain unlucky. Lieutenant George McDowell wrote that he 'lost my old pal Charlie Kaler. He was wounded in an attack … and went into a small dugout … Half a minute after a shell burst at the entrance of the dugout and killed Charlie outright, mortally wounded our M[edical]O[fficer] and badly wounded our Major, also killed about six more who were … mostly wounded as was Charlie. I have felt rather rotten since.'[85]

Those Australians who remained unscathed continued to search for other ways through the wire as machine-gun fire swept the area relentlessly. Men were killed and lay where they fell, while the less fortunate were left hanging on the wire badly wounded (often in the abdomen) many suffering a terrible, painful death. Nothing could be done for them. The bitter fighting continued. One man apologised to his comrades for not being able to shake their hands; a bullet to the abdomen meant that his own hands were occupied holding his bowels inside his body. Another fought off seven of the enemy before being shot in both knees. He then declined the aid of a stretcher-bearer because his mates had more serious wounds. And a young soldier of around 17 'who had his knee slit clean open' refused to surrender, instead bombing enemy troops until the end.[86]

As the light gradually improved, some of the men encountered further complications. Ganson later recalled moving across no man's land where

> … there was no shell holes to get into. It was a case of lie down, or keep on going. When I got to the wire it wasn't broken at all. I don't remember how I got through it. I had wire cutters and bombs, and a flaming shovel on my back. I must have used the wire cutters … and smashed everything down and got through. I didn't go through where the tanks were. I was out on the right of that. I eventually … fell into the German trench.[87]

Lieutenant Albert Marshall (15th Battalion) recounted that a considerable number of men from his platoon were killed or wounded well before reaching the enemy trenches. Finally, when 'you got through the German wire, and then you got into their front line trench,' he recalled, 'it was all a mess of … wounded and dead … Barbed wire is awful stuff.' Marshall was unable to send a message back to battalion headquarters in the sunken road. 'We had no telephone,' he explained, 'they would have had to have … nearly a thousand yards of wire.' Instead 'runners' were used to relay messages across no man's land, often killed by the deadly machine-gun fire before they could get anywhere near their headquarters.[88]

Those troops who managed to fight their way into parts of the forward trench were surprised at how well built it was — 'from 8 to 10 feet deep' and 'about 10 feet wide with three fire steps and contained dug-outs'.[89] Others described how the trenches were deliberately constructed to trap Australian infantry, with 'entrances to the dugouts ... arranged that on the trench being taken they were fully exposed to German bomb and trench mortar fire.'[90]

***

Much later, Emerson wrote that 'crossing No Man's Land we lost heavily. Of 27 men in the platoon ... only 22 reached the enemy trench ... We started off in artillery formation ... [but] we deployed into skirmishing order and we were under heavy rifle and machine gun fire. Our artillery was doing nothing ... All dependence seemed to have been placed on the tanks. I reached the enemy front line.'[91]

Along other parts of the attack front, the Australian infantry faced a daunting scenario. The lucky men were killed outright; the less fortunate were forced to wait for inevitable death in no man's land, usually nursing horrendous stomach wounds, their innards hanging out, and with little hope of being reached by stretcher-bearers. Some troops managed to pass through gaps in the wire where many suffered the same fate as their mates in no man's land. As Bean writes, the survivors 'now ... [were] facing precisely the situation that the ANZAC leaders had feared – being without artillery support in [the] face of only half-cut wire. Hesitation would have been fatal, and their officers led magnificently.'[92]

Battles quickly descend into chaos and Bullecourt deteriorated faster than most. The randomness of being killed or left in no man's land with life-threatening wounds was possibly the most difficult prospect for the men to face. Lewis Sharp (13th Battalion) remembered very little apart from the indiscriminate way his mates met their fate. He visualised 'the poor buggers getting killed. When they are dying alongside of you – you don't think of it. One [bullet] will just miss you and get the bloke behind you, and over he'd go.'[93] Clarence James, also from the 13th Battalion, recalled that he 'got over into the first line of trenches when – the others had been there in hand-to-hand fighting – and they'd run out of ammunition.'[94]

Ernest Etchell, one of the 15th Battalion's Lewis gunners, was more prepared for the masses of wire. 'I had a plank and a bag under my arm to throw over the wire,' he asserted,

> … I was going to throw the plank over the wire and walk across it. I didn't go   through the sally-ports. They were covered by machine guns. I was prepared to   get over the wire in some way. No-one else that I saw had a plank like I did … But I was happy. I was over there on my own, and I had my gun going good. I was busy shooting at the Germans, and they were busy trying to get out of the way of the Lewis gun. They were really frightened by the Lewis gun … [I] kept firing … in a line … You can mow one hundred [enemy soldiers] down in a couple of minutes.[95]

Etchell's enjoyment was short-lived: he suffered a wound to his leg and was overpowered by a group of Germans.

Lance Corporal Bert Knowles' section had been reduced to just three men. He later recalled that, during the carnage, he had heard 'the same wonderful voice in front'. That voice belonged to Captain Murray whose words of encouragement had the desired effect. Those of Murray's troops who were within earshot rushed the enemy trench, oblivious to the bullet-riddled bodies of their comrades, most hanging dead on the wire creating a ghastly picture. Adding to this image of hell was the nearby remnants of a tank. The charred and blackened remains of the crew were arranged in macabre fashion around the burnt-out hulk.[96]

Guppy recalled his section reaching 'the barb wire entanglements [to] find that we have to file through narrow gaps. How many lived during that hail and how the men pushed on and finally rushed the machine guns in the front line was little short of marvellous … We find ourselves in the first line in a very wide deep trench with no cover except dugouts which are at frequent intervals.'[97] Along other parts of the advance, bitter hand-to-hand fighting and bomb-throwing erupted as more Australian infantry jumped into the German trenches.

Just before 5.15 am, and after only around 30 minutes of savage fighting and 'very heavy casualties', troops from the 16th Battalion captured sections of the OG1 trench, part of the brigade's first objective.[98] Most German troops in those parts of the trench had already taken flight. Those remaining were swiftly forced from their dugouts by bombs or at the end of a bayonet. The fate of their mates still uppermost in their minds, some Australian soldiers showed little mercy to those enemy soldiers who surrendered. A few were bayoneted or shot. Most, however, were sent back to the Australian lines under armed guard. The 13th Battalion, for example, sent back 60 German prisoners.[99] Meanwhile, the attack pushed on. Without so much as a pause or a rest, officers ordered the 16th Battalion to advance against the second line of German trenches (OG2) almost 200 yards further on.

***

However, worse luck had befallen the 12th Brigade. The first tank had only arrived shortly before 4.45 am. Chaos ensued — confusing Australian infantry for German front-line troops, the crew commenced firing. A soldier from the 46th Battalion later recalled that, following 'much abuse from the incredulous Australians, and finally realising his mistake, the commander of the tank showed himself and asked … in which direction was the enemy?' The second tank took another 15 minutes to arrive. Both tanks immediately began to fire 'continuously … for about 15 minutes' on the enemy positions. German 'artillery retaliated and "strafed" the area near the tanks very considerably causing heavy casualties.'[100] In the meantime, the pitifully inadequate British-Australian barrage had lifted.[101]

By now the waiting troops had become extremely anxious. Numerous bungled orders added to the already chaotic situation. On

9 April 12th Brigade headquarters had issued an order stipulating that the infantry were only to move forward when the tanks were in front of their starting line.[102] Throughout the following day those orders were amended frequently. One change had the tanks advancing before the infantry. Only when they reached the German wire were officers to show a green disc directing the waiting troops to 'come on'.[103] Adding to the confusion were later verbal orders from both the 4th Division and 12th Brigade headquarters demanding that the infantry 'Advance at 0445 hours irrespective of whether or not the tanks had reached the Hindenburg Line.' But there was no written order. Countering this was an order issued by the commanding officer of the 46th Battalion, Lieutenant Colonel Howard Denham, that 'infantry will not advance until fifteen minutes after the tanks pass the jumping-off trench and will move right forward into their objective following behind the tanks.'[104]

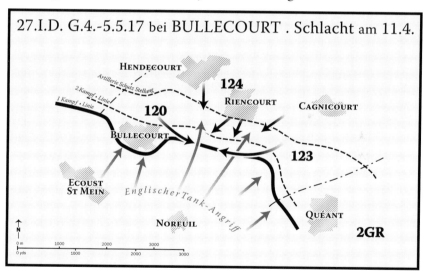

German map of the *27th Wurttemberg Infantry Division* showing the English tank attack at Bullecourt, 11 April 1917.

A little after 5.10 am, and shortly before first light — more than 40 minutes behind the scheduled start time — the two tanks commenced moving forward. Not long afterwards Denham recognised his mistake and the order went out for the infantry to commence their attack. It was now 5.15 am and the 4th Brigade had been advancing for around 30 minutes. Making matters worse, the British artillery had lifted its fire from the flanks of Bullecourt and Riencourt to allow infantry and tanks unrestricted entry into the villages, which it was assumed had already been taken.[105]

Lieutenant L. Challen (48th Battalion) recorded that 'the lads got up quickly and advanced at a quick pace, almost at a run.' The German artillery was prepared. Challen added that the 'enemy barrage was thick both with HE [high explosive] and shrapnel and was supported by MG [machine gun] fire which caused heavy casualties.'[106] One of the tanks was soon knocked out by artillery fire. The other encountered mechanical difficulties and could go no further. Infantry in that part of the advance were on their own, battling not only heavy enemy machine-gun and rifle fire but, more significantly, the largely uncut wire. At 5.19 am Lieutenant Colonel Raymond Leane (commanding officer of the 48th Battalion) sent off a wire to brigade headquarters. Pointing out the enormous number of casualties, he asked: 'On account of lateness of advance have arrangements been made to keep barrage longer on flanks of Bullecourt?' He was told 'nothing could be done'.[107] In fact, both the 46th and 48th battalions encountered heavier enemy machine-gun and artillery fire then their sister battalions from the 4th Brigade, in part due to the lack of any sustained artillery support and the late start of the attack.

Many officers and men were by now mystified as to what had taken place. And, more importantly, they were confused over what to do next. For almost 15 minutes very little happened. Fear was beginning to show on most faces. Something had to be done to arrest the situation before it deteriorated into complete chaos. Encouraged by some of the more battle-hardened officers, the men were told to push on with the advance. But, without support, the attack was doomed. Heavy rifle and machine-gun fire, most coming from the direction of Riencourt and Bullecourt, inflicted even more casualties among the advancing troops, many falling before they came close to the wire.

The right flank of the 46th Battalion followed the one tank which had managed to smash part of the wire, close to the ridge between the brigades. Countless more Australians were mown down by a hail of accurate machine-gun fire as they tried to find other openings in the wire and leap into the forward German trench. At around 5.50 am, Major Victor Waine sent a message to his commanding officer, Lieutenant Colonel Denham, asking for reinforcements. Denham ordered every soldier from Captain Frank North's A Company (47th Battalion) to load up with extra ammunition and bombs. As they neared the front, the men became tangled up in the confusion. However, many men from the 46th Battalion managed to find some way through the wire and capture parts of OG1. The left and centre sections were particularly fortunate, finding most of the wire cut. Bombing their way through the trench they forced the German defenders to pull back to their second line of trenches.[108] The 48th Battalion also somehow managed to force its way through into parts of the first line of trenches.

***

However, pushing on to OG2 became increasingly dangerous as the assaulting Australian infantry found waiting enemy soldiers who were better prepared. Many Germans who had survived the first onslaught withdrew to the second line of trenches through underground tunnels, while other reinforcements moved through the communication trenches from Riencourt. The right flank of the 48th Battalion was particularly luckless. Having found the wire in front of OG2 mostly uncut, the men faced strong opposition from reinforcements and newly sited machine-guns and suffered an enormous toll of casualties. Yet the Australians fought on, bombing their way through to a section of the trench near Central Road where they established a defensive position. Leane recorded that 'it was not until 6.18 that my men were able to reach 2nd objective.'[109]

Along other parts of the brigade front the troops met stronger resistance. In the 48th Battalion all company commanders except one had been killed or wounded. Only a few platoon leaders survived. Led by non-commissioned officers (NCOs) — or in some instances, where there were no NCOs, the more resourceful soldiers — the men pushed on.[110] Raymond Leane recalled that a

> … third tank arrived at about 6.30a.m. and asked me for orders. A machine gun nest near Bullecourt and a trench mortar on our left were giving us considerable   trouble. I therefore requested the officer in command of the tank to silence them. "Consider it done sir!" and immediately moved firing his guns. After going about 400 yards, the tank returned to my Battle position and the crew vacated the tank leaving the engine running. I caught one man who told me when asked why the crew had deserted the tank, "That it was too hot!" He also told me that tank was in good order. Captain Fairley went out to try and salve this tank, but was severely wounded by a sniper. The 12th Brigade received no assistance from tanks in this action.[111]

Against such overwhelming odds the two battalions fought on courageously with only one purpose — to take all of their objectives.

Lieutenant C. Sheldon was commanding Number 9 Platoon, C Company, 48th Battalion, on the extreme right flank of the attacking line. He later recalled that:

> When we arrived at our objective … we found that the enemy had already   evacuated and we established at the road which runs through the enemy line …   Lewis guns were placed to cover our flank and one gun was sent forward in front of our line about 30 yards to enfilade the enemy support line on our right. A bombing post was established … on the road to prevent enemy bombing parties entering the trench. The riflemen dug a firestep on the reverse side of the trench, and our consolidation was complete within half an hour of our occupation of the trench.[112]

There they waited for the anticipated counter-attack.

Despite the overwhelming odds, at 6.50 am Brigadier General Robertson reported that his 12th Australian Brigade had gained most of its objectives. However, the 48th Battalion had been unable to extend its left flank beyond the Bullecourt to Riencourt road, while the right flank of the 46th Battalion had been savagely mauled and had also failed to take part of the enemy trench. The two Australian battalions now found themselves in an unenviable position — rather than one behind the other as planned, they were now almost level and not overlapping sufficiently.[113] At around 7.00 am, Major V.J. Waine (46th Battalion) sent a message that his troops were desperately short of bombs and ammunition. Captain John Millar's B Company was ordered forward to assist.[114] By now any push against Riencourt was almost out of the question, as more German reinforcements scurried into the village where they soon set up additional machine-gun nests, while snipers were spotted on the roofs of some of the remaining buildings.

***

Along the 4th Brigade's advance front, the situation was becoming increasingly dire. The assaulting troops realised that many of the narrower belts of wire in front of the German support trench (OG2) were largely intact. Cut off from their own line by enemy shells falling in no man's land, as well as incessant rifle and machine-gun fire from the direction of Riencourt (a little under a mile away), the men were becoming indecisive, uncertain of what to do next. Junior Australian officers, with little experience of combat, were also unsure and began to panic. As they ordered their men to advance their luck held and they came across gaps and passages used by enemy patrols. Grim hand-to-hand fighting was not uncommon. Using anything that came to hand — bayonets, rifle butts and bombs, even their spades — the Australians fought grimly, killing a large number of Germans. Many others fled. However the Australians also suffered enormous casualties.

Captain David Dunworth's company was reduced to less than half its complement. Dunworth later recalled that the '14th and 15th [Battalions] were thoroughly mixed up owing to the heavy fighting.' He gathered

> ... a small body of men of both units in the first line and made for the second line overland. I was wounded and my men pushed on but recovering I pushed on to the front line. There gathered about 14 or 15 [troops] what I thought were 15th [Battalion] men (I afterwards found some were 14th) and ordered them to follow me. My objective was Riencourt and my idea was to push on whilst some NCOs to whom I had given hurried orders were to collect the rest of my company ... We pushed on towards the six roads ... At the same moment an enemy machine gun post opened up on the small party behind me. It kept a continuous fire on them and when later on I looked round – every man had been killed ... The enemy were on our flanks and in front.

German machine-gun fire 'swept the ground', slaughtering many Australians still desperately seeking a break in the second line of barbed wire.[115]

Other Australian troops closed in on OG2, in the process silencing a number of the deadly machine-guns. Clarence James described how one outnumbered German machine-gun crew fought on courageously until they were all killed. Others were less suicidal. When a section from the 13th Battalion took part of a trench, they found a number of Australian and German dead and wounded as well as almost 60 enemy soldiers who willingly surrendered.[116]

Major Percy Black was still out in front of his men. He instructed a runner to take a message back to battalion headquarters: 'Tell them the first objective is gained and I am pushing on to the second.'[117] Black soon discovered an opening in the wire and, as he was leading his men through, he was struck in the head by an enemy bullet and was killed almost instantly. Inspired by Black's courage, his men filed through the gap, the junior officers attempting to emulate his fearless leadership. Ganson was a member of the group. At the entrance to a German dugout, he 'could see about forty steps going down ... My officer, Jack Courtney ... said "Horrie, sling a bomb down there ... and when the Jerries come up you take charge of them. I'll go and bomb the other dugouts." About 30 Germans soon came up.' After finding someone prepared to take the prisoners back to the Australian line, Ganson 'went forward along the trenches and joined up with some other boys.' He happily 'drove Jerry back, fighting from one dugout to another, until ... [they] got to the end of the line where the trenches went out onto plain ground.'[118]

Other parts of the OG2 trenches were also taken, albeit at a huge cost. Myriad dead and wounded Australians, lying two or three deep in the trenches or hanging from the wire, testified to the bitterness of the fighting. Frank Massey (13th Battalion) recollected that the survivors were

> ... tired ... [and] the 16th and 14th [Battalions] were already cut to pieces getting through the wire ... it was horrible, because the men that had attempted to cut through the wire, a lot of them were still there ... It was ... marvellous that they got through. The wire in the Hindenburg Line was unbelievable ... With about   several strands of wire, with exits for the troops to get out for ... patrols. And all   exits were covered by machine guns.

Soon after, Massey 'copped a shell ... and put a field dressing on.' He later recalled that he 'could walk with difficulty ... so I carried on. And the first thing that I saw was the 14th Battalion man shot clean through the head – looking over the parapet.'[119]

Emerson later recounted that, in his sector, 'it was impossible to proceed further as the enemy second wire had not been cut.'[120] Guppy, too, recalled the 'wire entanglements between the first and second lines ... [being] almost intact and the slaughter there has been terrific.' He added that 'machine gun fire coming from the second line reserves and machine gun posts in the village [Riencourt] behind is terrific.'[121]

Confusion reigned. Men from different sections, platoons and companies came together and fought alongside one another. In a few places — most noticeably where there were gaps in the wire and in captured communication trenches — there was some semblance of order. Men from Captain F. Stanton's company scrambled into the second line of trenches through enemy 'communication trenches' while Lieutenant R. Hayes and a smaller number of troops 'consolidate[d the] first line trench'. What was left of Benson's section had also fought their way into one of the 'communication trenches'. 'It was my duty to clear this trench of the enemy,' he noted. 'We did so and any German left alive retired to the village [Riencourt].'[122]

Lieutenant M.J. O'Day's experience was not uncommon. He was commanding a platoon from D Company (15th Battalion) whose task was 'to establish outposts on the left of Riencourt'. O'Day recalled the vicious fighting along that part of the line. His men had fought their way through the first enemy trench before reaching

> ... the second trench with my sergeant and about eight men. It was impossible to go on. We defended ourselves for about 5 hours in the second trench. The enemy bombed up the trench from both flanks ... and put heavy machine gun fire over the top of us. It was impossible to advance or retire, and when our ammunition was exhausted, I, with a few men I had left surrendered. We were completely surrounded at this time.

O'Day added emotionally that 'Captain Leslie was in charge of the wave my platoon was in and was killed ... I was the only officer of my Company to reach the second trench.'[123]

Also among the dead was another popular company commander, Captain F.B. Stanton, whose depleted company had managed to fight its way into OG2. Emerson later recalled that:

> In the enemy front line I saw ... Captain Dunworth my OC was wounded going over just as we reached the trench. He

had been shot in the back and had to retire into a dug out. I collected what men I could, [about] 30, and attempted to connect with the 46th Battalion on the left, about 400 yards away. We bombed along the trench for over 200 yards when we were held up by a strong-post. I went to Lieutenant Sanders and got the trench mortar to bear, but we could not shift it … I formed a strong point in the trench and kept the enemy at bay until our supply of bombs ran out.[124]

Murray and his larger group of men were also encountering similar setbacks. Encouraged by the irrepressible Murray, they moved on into one of the many communication trenches, in the process killing and maiming many Germans. From the communication trench which led into OG2, they bombed their way into their second objective.

Captain D. Aarons was another officer whose philosophy of leading from the front was rewarded. With little thought for his own safety he led his men in attack after attack against the second line of trenches with whatever weapons they could find —rifles, bombs, bayonets or clubs — until they forced the few surviving Germans to flee or surrender. Reginald Colmer (13th Battalion) remembered that 'there were a lot of attacks … But we had bombs and everything else there to fight with … and rifles and things like that. It wasn't like Gallipoli where you only had the bullet and bayonet.'[125]

The Australian infantrymen learnt quickly and exploited the German communication trenches. Avoiding being caught in the open between the two lines of trenches, a number of sections bombed their way into OG2 through those same trenches, killing any Germans they came across. No prisoners were to be taken. Finally, not long after sunrise, all four battalions reported that they had taken their objectives. Although 'depleted by losses of probably sixty per cent in killed and wounded', the 4th Brigade had captured almost 500 yards of the enemy's first line and support trenches.[126]

***

But the gap between the two attacking brigades had increasingly become a liability and was proving difficult to close.[127] Australian officers blamed the 'failure of the tanks' which they believed should have closed this gap. According to Holmes' official report, it 'was never successfully closed and was a continual source of worry and danger to both brigades.'[128] Still the Australians continued to consolidate their gains, setting up defensive positions in anticipation of counter-attacks.

Murray was certain that, without artillery support, his men could go no further, or for that matter, defend the positions that they now held against those counter-attacks. With Black dead, Murray was regarded as his heir apparent. Troops along the 4th Brigade's front waited for the enemy, now looking to Murray for leadership. His first task was to secure the right flank and he instructed the men to build a barricade to hold the Germans at bay. He then devised other defence mechanisms — positioning Lewis machine-guns and placing groups of riflemen in crucial defensive positions, later assisting in building further barricades with whatever materials came to hand. Using grenades and weapons recovered from dead Germans and Australians, they waited for the coming assault.

Artillery support was still conspicuous in its absence. Having already sent a brief message requesting support, Murray wrote a detailed outline of the position. Around 7.15 am he sent a runner to battalion headquarters with a message that his men now

> … hold first objective and part of second. Have established block
> on the right of both objectives. In touch with 14th [Brigade] on
> the left. Expect heavy bomb fighting in evening. There are six
> tanks at a standstill, apparently damaged – just behind the first
> objective there are four, and two near second. Quite impossible
> to attack village. 'A' Company 13th [Battalion] badly cut about by
> machine gun fire in wire, some of all other 13th companies here
> all O.K. We will require as many rifle and hand grenades as you

can possibly send, also SAA [small arms ammunition]. Most of Lewis machine guns are O.K. Have four Vickers guns. Fear Major Black killed. Several officers killed and wounded … Have plenty [of] men. Have about 30 prisoners of 124 Reg[imen]t. Will send them over at dusk. Look out for S.O.S. signals. Send white flares (as many as possible). With artillery support we can keep the position till the cows come home.[129]

More requests for artillery support came from other experienced officers (like Captain Dunworth) in similar positions to Murray. No artillery responded.

Shortly after 7.00 am, other small groups of men from the 13th and 16th battalions had fought their way into a vital communication trench (nicknamed 'Emu Alley') which would take them almost into Riencourt. Moving further along the trench they crept to within 150 yards of the remaining buildings where they spotted well-positioned enemy snipers and machine-gunners, all with a clear field of fire on the Australians. They also saw more German soldiers assembling, preparing to counter-attack. When Lieutenant Colonel Durrant was informed, he asked for an immediate barrage. Yet again none was forthcoming.[130]

The counter-attack soon came. At around 7.30 am Durrant noted, 'Germans counter attack [by *124th Infantry Regiment*] bombing from Riencourt. Beaten back to 100 yards from Riencourt. [Another] counter attack on right [by *120th Infantry Regiment* from around Bullecourt].' Then, at around 8.00 am, he added, 'Flares lighted … our men reorganising and consolidating. Two small bombing attacks on left beaten off.'[131] Soon afterwards, the German artillery turned its attention to the Australian front line. Probably the worst damage was inflicted by a direct hit on Durrant's 13th Battalion headquarters, which killed six staff officers and wounded another five, although Durrant escaped unscathed.

At 8.10 am Brand had been given the latest news on the situation and told his artillery liaison officer to lay down a barrage on the

Australian right flank, some 200 yards behind the second line of German trenches. But the Fifth Army artillery commander in charge of the sector, Lieutenant Colonel R.L.R. Rabett, chose to believe other reports coming in from artillery observers and aviators which told him that the attack was proceeding as planned. One outrageous account went so far as to suggest that the tanks were well ahead of the infantry who had already taken Riencourt and were moving against Hendecourt. Another report described British troops entering Bullecourt. Concerned that shellfire might inflict greater casualties on those British and Australians already 'in the villages', Rabett refused to sanction the barrage.[132]

Robertson and Brand were both outraged that Rabett — a British officer — could override their order. Holmes, too, was devastated. He contacted Birdwood who also chose to believe intelligence reports from artillery observers and aviators from No. 4 Squadron, RFC. Birdwood — indeed all the divisional staff — must accept some criticism for their failure to take any action. How information coming in from the front — and from experienced and dedicated field officers such as Murray and Durrant — could be ignored or shelved defies belief. Additional requests from Murray, Dunworth and Durrant (among others) were never received or were simply ignored. Those same Australian officers were also curious and distressed over the British division's failure to attack, as they had anticipated that the British action would divert the Germans' attention from their men.

***

Not surprisingly, throughout the 62nd British Division, officers and men alike were apprehensive and cautious. Considering what had happened a little over 24 hours previously, who could blame them? Shortly before his men were due to leave their trenches, Lieutenant Colonel Hastings had advised his divisional commander that 'no tanks had arrived and that nothing was known of the results of the Australian attack, and they had certainly not entered Bullecourt.'

Major General Braithwaite ordered his troops to stay put. It was not until around 7.30 am that British divisional headquarters received an unconfirmed report that the Australians had taken the first line of German trenches.

However all the other reports reaching the British officers at the front were less than optimistic. Lieutenant General Fanshawe, the British V Corps commander, also received the same false message concerning troops and tanks entering Hendecourt and Riencourt. A little before 8.30 am, having heard of the rumoured capture of Bullecourt, he went so far as to suggest that the advance should push on regardless, 'without waiting for tanks'. But, as one observer commented, the task was 'quite impossible'.[133]

Braithwaite was keen to confirm that the Australians had taken enemy positions around Bullecourt. Following the calamity of the previous morning, senior British divisional officers, particularly Braithwaite, were unwilling to commit their troops to battle without proper reconnaissance. Patrols were despatched to report on the situation and ascertain whether the 2/6th West Yorks should push forward. One patrol described the catastrophe unfolding in the south-west part of the front where 'snipers and machine guns were active in Bullecourt where men could be seen moving about among the houses: that the wire was practically uncut and that any attempt to storm the village would need very great sacrifice.'

Another patrol reported almost the opposite. Little enemy resistance was being encountered 'in the south east and eastern roads of Bullecourt ... and that the Corps [Australian] on the right were advancing and that the enemy was shelling the northern edges of the village.'[134] The attack by the British division was never launched. Not long after, Fanshawe was given the latest information that the Australians had 'never reached the Western edge of Bullecourt on our right flank.'[135] Not surprisingly, Fanshawe rescinded his earlier order and the British troops were instead instructed to wait.

Gough was so convinced of the accuracy of intelligence reports that, just after 9.30 am, he ordered Major General A. Kennedy's British 4th Cavalry Division to attack the Hindenburg Line 'and move through Bullecourt'.[136] A section of cavalry which attempted to penetrate part of the line where the wire was uncut (and not far from where the 4th Brigade was being mauled) suffered similar catastrophic consequences. A British report noted that 'the cavalry assembling in "splendid formation" behind the embankment were heavily shelled. Colonel Melvill (commanding 17th Lancers) saw more than 30 large calibre 5.9" rounds fall right in the middle of a squadron pole-axing riders and horses alike ... After this debacle, the brigade was swiftly withdrawn ... and was proof that massed cavalry no longer had a role on the Western Front.'[137]

By 11.00 am British officers were well aware of the Australians' mixed fortunes in the advance. Another patrol had further established 'that the Hindenburg Line was [still] held' by the enemy. With three battalions from the 185th Brigade waiting 'in same position as previous night', Braithwaite again ordered his men to stay put. Fifteen minutes later he received confirmation from V Corps headquarters that any further advance by his men would be futile. He was told that 'the Division might have to place 1 brigade at the disposal of the 4th Australian Division who was holding the Hindenburg Line but not Riencourt and Hendecourt.'[138]

By now, however, the Australians' position was even more precarious. A short while later Braithwaite was asked to assist by delivering a flank attack. He justifiably refused. The terrain over which the British brigade was expected to operate was entirely flat. An attack in broad daylight without artillery support and against an expectant enemy would have meant another massacre, probably on a scale even greater than that of the previous morning.

***

Meanwhile, by 9.00 am, the 12th Brigade was still consolidating its hard-won positions in the enemy trenches. Lieutenant C. Sheldon remembered that,

> Our Lewis guns and rifles were very effectively employed in dispersing enemy   working parties, and bodies of men which could be seen behind his lines … Between 8 a.m. and 10 a.m. the situation was quiet. After 10 a.m. the enemy fired trench mortar bombs into the line held by the 46 Battalion and into the communication trench between the two lines. A battery of field guns which was   situated in or near the village of Bullecourt enfiladed our line with HE [high   explosive] and "whiz-bangs" doing considerable damage to the trench.[139]

Sheldon and his men waited for the expected German counter-attack.

Not long after nine o'clock Brand yet again attempted to secure an artillery barrage. Rabett once more dismissed the idea. Unsatisfied, Brand contacted Holmes at divisional headquarters. Holmes agreed that a barrage must be put down and conveyed his concern to Birdwood. But I ANZAC Corps and, indeed, Fifth Army headquarters, still believed the false reports that were continuing to arrive describing Australian troops supposedly in 'Hendecourt and Riencourt'. Brand was subsequently informed that his infantry must push on without artillery support. The Australians greeted this news with disbelief. At the front, Durrant wrote that his 'Battalion in close formation [was being] shot up.' Murray attempted to bring some order to an otherwise desperate situation. Durrant wrote that 'Murray went along whole line – 1,000 yards [and] reorganised the Brigade front.'[140]

At around 9.30 am Lieutenant Colonel Raymond Leane was informed that enemy troops, at almost battalion strength, were moving from the direction of Hendecourt towards his 48th Battalion positions. His brother, Captain Allan Leane, was also in a dire situation with more Germans preparing to counter-attack his position. Colonel Leane sent a desperate message — followed by a wire — to brigade headquarters requesting artillery support. As before, none came.

Soon after, the Germans commenced their expected counter-attacks (the *120th* and *124th infantry regiments* had now been joined by battle-hardened troops from the elite *123rd Grenadier Regiment*

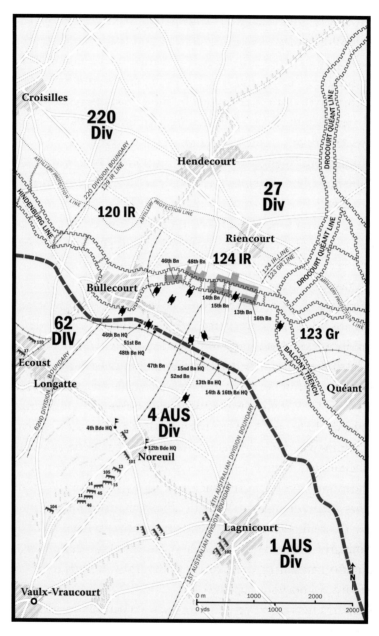

The situation at around 9.30 am on 11 April 1917 after troops from the 4th Australian Division had captured part of the Hindenburg Line. Note that the tanks are shown in the approximate positions where they were put out of action.

which had been holding major defensive positions around Queant) 'along both Hindenburg trenches on either flank, against the inner flanks, over the open on the right and down the two communication trenches east of the "central road".' On the 4th Brigade front alone, six different attacks came from large parties of enemy troops. Using their 'stick' grenades effectively, the Germans inflicted numerous casualties on the Australians. The Australians replied with their heavier and more lethal Mills bombs and deadly, accurate fire from the Lewis machine-guns positioned in shell holes in front of the trenches. The 4th Machine Gun Company, which had followed its infantry into the attack, had also placed its Vickers machine-guns in the best positions to sustain the highest number of German casualties. That they did to great effect. The first of the enemy attacks was beaten off. But the Australians knew that others were on the way.

More desperate than ever for artillery support, the beleaguered Australians fired multiple flares. Still no support came. With their ammunition and bombs dwindling, and their casualties mounting from hostile artillery and machine-gun fire, battalion commanders pleaded for reinforcements and a good quantity of grenades. Holmes, however, recognised the danger associated with sending reinforcements in broad daylight, particularly without artillery support — although why Holmes was not more vocal in demanding that support has never been adequately explained. Some groups volunteered to help their comrades and showed great pluck in moving through the maelstrom that was no man's land. The same dangers confronted those small groups of men who braved the hazards of German artillery and machine-gun fire to secure supplies of fresh bombs and small arms ammunition and bring these to their comrades, with many remaining in the forward positions to assist.[141]

At the same time, Australian troops continued to collect more grenades and weapons from the countless dead and wounded, both Australian and German, before preparing to fight off the expected counter-attack. In the 4th Brigade's sector, the troops improved their barricades, also placing their Lewis and Vickers machine-guns in positions that would allow them the maximum field of fire over the advancing Germans.[142] But, without artillery support, most knew that this was all in vain: with a limited supply of ammunition and bombs, it was only a matter of time before they would be dead or forced to withdraw.

And it was not long before other large groups of enemy troops were seen massing, preparing to launch another series of larger and deadlier counter-attacks along all parts of the line. The 'gap' between the 4th and 12th brigades — where the tanks were to have positioned themselves — now became the focus of their attention. From here the Germans would be in position to outflank both brigades. Other enemy troops launched a frontal attack, but were kept at bay by bombs or accurate machine-gun and rifle fire. The Germans, however, were quickly able to take control of the area in and around the 'gap' and thereby attack the flanks.

The Australians soon exhausted their supply of grenades, killing and wounding many Germans. However, through sheer weight of numbers, enemy soldiers either killed the Australians or forced them to withdraw. With their backs to the wall, Australian officers ordered their men to move out of the trench and into the nearest shell holes, where it was hoped that they could hold out until dark. Murray made another plea for artillery support. Finding another volunteer runner to relay his request to headquarters staff was relatively simple. Many volunteered to attempt what seemed the impossible. While the runner survived, by the time he arrived the Australian position had become even more precarious.

Many Australian troops were now without bombs and low on ammunition. The right flank of the 4th Brigade had become particularly vulnerable. Corporal Lancelot Davies (13th Battalion) noticed that, as the fighting intensified, 'bombs ran out' and

> German stick bombs and egg bombs were collected, and also every bomb that they could get from a dead Australian. Captain

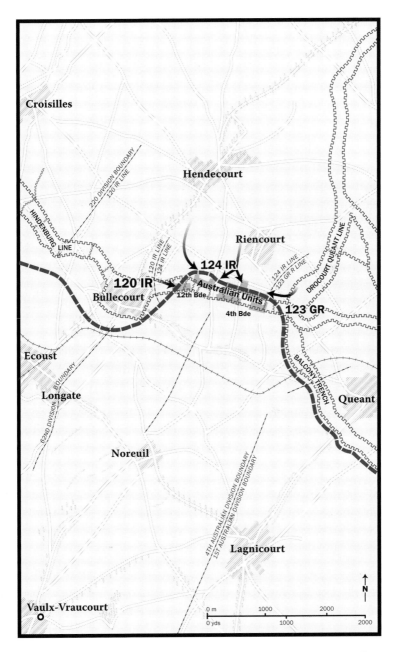

Map showing the position of German counter-attacks around Bullecourt during the morning of 11 April 1917.

Somerville (16th Battalion) was   there cheering his men when things were looking blue, as was Lieut. Watson (16th Battalion), the latter pulling the boys together as the situation began to look very bad, and continually cheering them.[143]

From the communication trenches, German infantry were bombing their way closer to the Australians sheltering in OG1. Using their stick grenades to deadly effect, they destroyed a number of machine-gun posts, killing all the crews. With little resistance — by now only a few riflemen had ammunition — German infantry launched a devastating frontal assault. Inevitably, the flanks of the Australian position were crushed. The remaining Australians in OG2 were now perilously close to being totally cut off. Sensing their danger, Australian officers, once again led by Murray, assisted those they could to find their way back to OG1.

As the morning wore on the number of requests for artillery support had grown to 18. All went unanswered. By now both brigades were in a similar position — desperately holding on against the odds. Still, Gough and Birdwood continued to receive a very different picture to the reality at the front. The Germans were virtually given free rein to move men, equipment, ammunition and supplies anywhere on the battlefield without fear of retaliation from Australian or British guns. Enemy machine-gunners and mobile field artillery were constantly on the move, locating better positions from which to inflict maximum casualties on the Australians, while cutting them off from supplies, including much-needed ammunition and bombs.

Some Australians were still holding out in the communication trench nicknamed 'Emu Alley', from where they observed the growing number of enemy snipers and machine-gun nests around Riencourt randomly killing their comrades. Private Simon noticed that the Germans

... did not cease firing with a shell fire barrage and with machine guns on the area we had crossed and made it practically impossible for anyone to approach or for anyone to go back to headquarters. Consequently [many] runners sent back with messages were killed … More machine guns opened fire at the top of our trench and it was very dangerous to leave them. Then trench mortars from the direction of Queant commenced to fire at our trenches … Many men were hit as the enemy methodically increased his range a few yards after each salvo and with almost every shot scored a direct hit on the trench … [as] the survivors were forced in the centre of the trench line from both flanks. The relentless enemy could command all the line with his mortars and the men were sentenced to death. The crowd of men who could not use their weapons … filled the trench that remained intact knowing they were doomed if they remained there.[144]

German artillery fire intensified. Private Frank McGinty (13th Battalion) recalled that 'they were using howitzers on us'.[145] Horace Rumble was convinced that 'we lost too many people by having no artillery support … there were shells flying everywhere and machine gun bullets. There was no chance of getting back to our line.'[146] Most Australian officers recognised the hopelessness of their situation. They knew they had to withdraw or face that last resort that few Australian soldiers could bear to contemplate — surrender.

General Holmes was informed of the latest situation and finally heeded the requests for more grenades. This time, however, the Germans were prepared, and watching for resupply teams. 'Efforts to send forward more bombs failed,' Holmes wrote, 'all the parties that attempted to go forward being mown down by machine gun from Riencourt and Bullecourt.' Holmes was all too aware that the situation was becoming more critical by the minute, adding that, 'unless more bombs etc. could be got up it would be impossible to hold on.'[147]

As the morning drew on, German troops delivered attack after attack on the dwindling number of survivors from both brigades.

Other enemy soldiers launched attacks from Riencourt, 'bombing down' the few remaining communication trenches held by Australians. Casualties mounted as another large group of crack enemy infantry gathered close to the sunken road, ready to launch a further series of attacks on the flanks, now held by a small and desperate band of Australians.

Pooley's group of 30 men waited for the enemy to counter-attack amid growing uncertainty. The constant danger from snipers unsettled the men. 'We couldn't see any Germans,' he recalled, 'but we thought there might be some about, and I had got up on the parapet with my rifle … [which] had become clogged-up with mud so I got back down to clean [it].' Another soldier took his place. 'But just as he got up, he got shot right through the head … All he said was "Mother." Then he died … A sniper had been lining up on my field.'[148]

Wheeler recalled the whole dreadful affair. He summarised the senselessness of it all, describing the horrific sight when 'the Germans started shelling us with heavies. Oh god. Out between the lines there must have been 800 or 1,000 of our brigade, and the Germans just tore them to pieces with bloody shell fire. One shell lobbed very close to me and got our Lewis gunners. They were practically no more after the explosion, blown to pieces.'[149]

By 10.45 am another series of counter-attacks had all but destroyed the Australians' morale. Durrant wrote of 'six attacks in all' against a string of positions where his men were desperately holding out. The largest, described as 'very severe', was again directed at the 'gap between [the] two Brigades'. The Australians 'gave ground' — including the important communication trenches 'Emu' and 'Ostrich' alleys. And, as Durrant added, there was still 'no response to SOS' for artillery assistance.[150] A report originating from the 2/5th Battalion (62nd British Division) — which was still anticipating an advance of its own — noted that the 'ANZACS have been counter attacked and are now on the original line. We are in our original positions as Bullecourt was never cleared by the Australians. Would you please send your exact dispositions?'[151]

A few groups of Australians still managed to fend off some of the less severe counter-attacks. But even they could not hold on much longer. Corporal Lancelot Davies (13th Battalion) 'never imagined the situation as critical as it was' until,

> Suddenly! We were subjected to a rain of light shells which scored good hits, owing no doubt to prearranged registration. Some fell right on the edge of the bay and wounded two of our party. More shells followed and another man went down. Their moans and appeals called for attention, so the remaining comrade and myself set to work endeavouring to relieve the wounded ones. I realised that an attack was imminent, but did not know from which quarter. The artillery fire had intensified, and was now joined by the rattle of machine guns and rifle fire. Within a few seconds … confusion seemed to reign, and I could see numbers of our men retiring from their various positions. Quite a lot fell as they were caught by the enemy's fire. From my position I could not see the advancing Jerries, who were then in the trench ahead … On looking up I beheld several Jerry bombers with bombs.[152]

At around 11.00 am Captain Aarons informed Brand of what he considered 'the terrible position at the front'. Anxious over the fate of his brigade, Brand 'was worn with anxiety. He was pale and haggard.'[153]

Along the 12th Brigade's front the situation was deteriorating by the minute. Major V.J. Waine (46th Battalion) pleaded for 'more ammunition, bombs, and rifle grenades. Vickers [machine-gun] requires 4 gallons water and at least 6,000 rounds SAA [small arms ammunition]. Enemy [*124th Infantry Regiment*] massing in Riencourt – Rifle grenades most important.' Waine was sent no rifle grenades nor, for that matter, small arms ammunition, just '4 petrol tins of water'. By a little after 11.00 am the 48th Battalion's position had become hopeless. Desperately outnumbered, the men's options were to withdraw or surrender. Continuing the fight could only result in certain annihilation.

German counter-attacks were becoming increasingly ferocious. Holmes wrote that 'a strong flank attack developed against the left of the 12th Australian Infantry Brigade.'[154] The sadly depleted 46th Battalion, still in the first line of enemy trenches, was the first Australian unit to attempt to withdraw and, not long after 11.15 am, a number of troops 'were seen evacuating the objective'.[155] However, they failed to alert the 48th Battalion further behind, leaving the 48th oblivious to the fact that it was totally cut off. Private Herbert Dunnett (A Company, 47th Battalion) risked his life to warn the 48th that the 'other battalions are being bombed out. You are surrounded', he told Lieutenant Colonel Raymond Leane, the 48th Battalion's commanding officer.[156]

Sensing the inevitable, Leane sent a message to divisional headquarters informing his superiors that his men were 'being bombed on both flanks' and were taking 'very heavy' casualties.[157] Once again he requested artillery support. Holmes passed on the request. Birdwood, on this occasion, agreed. Without contacting Rabett or indeed Gough, at Fifth Army headquarters, he ordered the Australian artillery to put down a 'flank barrage ... to cover the left of the left brigade' — but only in the area behind Riencourt.[158] No shells fell on German positions. Nor was there any counter-bombardment of enemy artillery.[159] In an action that aptly demonstrated the poor command and control at corps and divisional level, as well as the appallingly inadequate communication, the 46th Battalion war diary recorded, 'heavy barrage commenced on the enemy trenches'. However, the shells not only fell on enemy trenches but also on sections of the 48th Battalion 'who had fought their way back to the 46th's position when they realised that their comrades had retired without telling them.'[160]

Instead of surrendering *en masse*, Leane's only other slim option was to lead the remnants of the 48th — now critically short of ammunition and bombs — through one of the communication trenches and back to the railway embankment. However, as they attempted to bomb their way through, the men found themselves effectively cut off from reinforcements or supplies. Leane ordered them to turn and fight with their few remaining weapons. That they did. Bloody hand-to-hand fighting ensued.[161]

Confusion spread through divisional, brigade and battalion headquarters. D Company, 47th Battalion, commanded by Captain Frank Davy, was ordered to reinforce the 48th Battalion. Davy led his men courageously through constant artillery and machine-gun fire — somehow without taking casualties — until they reached Leane's men. Lieutenant Albert Paterson was ordered to take 136 men — the remaining reserves of the 47th Battalion — to support the 48th. Other Australians engaged behind the lines — even some of the cooks — all led by Lieutenant George O'Connor, were also directed to help. A number of these men had already contributed more than their fair share, having 'made the dangerous journey across the flat snow-covered fields more than once, carrying bombs, water and ammunition, or as stretcher bearers.'[162] But there was little that any of the reinforcements could offer by way of assistance; their only option was to join the withdrawal.

***

Based on the reports he had been receiving all morning, Holmes now understood all too well the plight of his two brigades. His men could allow themselves to be captured, or they could attempt to pull back to their own front line, running the risk of being killed or wounded by unrelenting enemy fire. Or they could remain and fight until they were killed or seriously wounded. The decision was in the hands of the men and their officers. Birdwood, when informed of the escalating scale of the catastrophe, immediately contacted Fifth Army headquarters 'and got permission to withdraw us'.[163]

Despite being appalled at the very idea, Murray had begun to organise an orderly withdrawal along his sector. Calling together his remaining officers and NCOs, he informed them of what needed to be done. Soon afterwards, Murray addressed troops from a 14th Battalion Lewis gun section: 'Well, men, we are just about out of ammunition, and it doesn't look as if anything more can be done. We either stay here and get skittled or be taken prisoners, or we can get out while our luck is in. What do you say?' Lance Corporal Bamford echoed the men's overwhelming support: 'We're with you, Harry, whatever you do.' Murray said simply: 'Well boys, out we go. Hand over all your ammunition, except ten rounds, to the Lewis gunners.' Turning to the machine-gun crews, he added: 'But listen you chaps, don't be too long after we go.' Officers moved along the trenches, informing their men of what to expect from the enemy in terms of crossfire from the machine-guns and rifles still peppering no man's land. Ever the realist, Murray told as many troops as possible that 'There's two things now – either capture or go into that!' Again bidding farewell to the courageous Lewis machine-gunners — who inevitably would be killed helping their retiring mates by allowing them a fighting chance of escape — he wished the men the best of luck in their dash across no man's land.[164]

Murray, as to be expected, yet again led from the front. One of the last to leave, he witnessed the massacre of many of his men. The German wire, which earlier had halted their advance, now obstructed their withdrawal. Murray accompanied a group of 10 other men. As enemy troops drew closer, he destroyed all copies of code signal lists before leading the group into the open. Chased by eager Germans, the small group huddled in a shell hole, expecting the worse. However luck again played a part. Confused enemy machine-gunners fired on their own men, killing many. The others fled. Murray and his party made their way safely back to the Australian lines.[165]

Lieutenant General Sir William Birdwood (centre) presenting Captain H.M. Murray, VC, DSO, DCM (16th Battalion), with a bar to his DSO for bravery during the first attack on Bullecourt. Towards the rear is Major General William Holmes, GOC 4th Australian Division (AWM E00450).

In another part of the line held by Massey's section, riflemen and bomb-throwers (with their few remaining grenades) kept the Germans at bay for a time. Inevitably, superior numbers forced the Australians back. Massey later recalled that they remained in

> ... the trench until the Hun ... came through the saps and communication trenches, and outnumbered us ten to one. And we had no hope of getting [out] – an order came through from Captain [G. Gardiner as] most of our [other] officers were killed or wounded [to] hop out and form up in front of the Germans about two ... hundred yards back ... It was like a hornet's nest buzzing round me. I don't know why I was not killed.[166]

***

Despite the dangers, Leane, too, had little option but to order the continued withdrawal of all his remaining men. According to Bean, at around 12.30, 'a full hour after the other troops – with proud deliberation, under heavy fire, picking its way calmly through the wire, helping the walking wounded, its officers bringing up the rear – the 48th Battalion came out.'[167] But the 48th returned without a number of fine young officers, including Captain Allan Leane (Lieutenant Colonel Raymond Leane's brother), who had been badly wounded while making his way back and had been captured. He died a little while later.

***

Shortly afterwards it was all over, Homes noting that the 'original line along the railway and in the Sunken Road to the north of it was reoccupied by German infantry.'[168] Despite being forced to withdraw, Australian soldiers had achieved what had previously been considered almost impossible — attacking and capturing parts of the heavily fortified Hindenburg Line without adequate artillery support. This was not all. For almost five hours they had held on, against relentless German counter-attacks, until finally ordered to pull back or surrender. Faced with the prospect of capture, many others chose to fight to the bitter end. Still others struggled back to the sunken road. Some 1200 surrendered.

CHAPTER 7

'Where all were gallant.'
THE WITHDRAWAL

While Australian soldiers had captured and held parts of the formerly unassailable Hindenburg Line, by mid-morning the attack on Bullecourt had turned to tragedy. Captain G.G. Gardiner was one of the many officers who believed it was time for a speedy withdrawal, the men taking their chances and avoiding surrender under any circumstances. The thought of spending the rest of the war behind wire in a German prisoner-of-war camp was unbearable. On the other hand, the prospect of death did not seem to bother him or his men.

Others also chose to fight — and die — without even attempting to pull back to the sunken road. Outnumbered more than 10 to one, the Australians remaining in the trenches had little hope of surviving. More counter-attacks and a surge in machine-gun fire continued to decimate their ranks. Groutsch recalled seeing 'these men struggling in the bloody trench. And trying to get back through the wire. That was the sad part.'[1]

***

Some officers and NCOs never heard the order to withdraw. Corporal Jim Wheeler was one. For almost the entire morning his small party of troops had held a crucial position on the left flank separated from the main part of the attack. When the time came to decide what his section would do, he 'told his men to hold on and "fight it out like Australians."'[2]

Along other parts of the front, Australians gathered in little knots, determined to fight to the end. All but out of ammunition, they had chosen almost certain death. Some used the butts of their rifles as clubs in a desperate effort to fight off the enemy. Others, however, had already had enough. Sensing the futility of continuing the fight, they capitulated. Wheeler was among those unable to 'get back', allowing himself to be captured.[3]

Corporal Lancelot Davies recalled that 'elite' German infantry 'had been counter-attacking for an hour or more'. As noon approached, his section was 'without ammunition' and 'our casualties had been severe'. German artillery again shelled that part of the front. 'Some [shells] fell right on the edge of the bay and wounded two of our party,' he remembered.

More shells followed, and another man went down. Their moans and appeals called for attention, so the remaining comrades and myself set to work endeavouring to relieve the wounded ones. I realised that an attack was imminent, but did not know from which quarter. The artillery fire had intensified, and was now joined by the rattle of machine gun and rifle fire. Within a few seconds … confusion seemed to reign, and I could see numbers of our men retiring from their various positions. Quite a lot fell as they were caught by the enemy's fire. From my position I could not see the advancing Jerries, who were then in the trench ahead … Again looking to the three wounded alongside, I stopped to aid one … Having bandaged number one, I was in the act of helping number two, when I was suddenly surprised to hear a gruff voice demand, "Come on Australia." On looking up I beheld several Jerry bombers with bombs – of the "potato-masher" type – each pointing a revolver.[4]

Davies was left with two options — death or surrender. He chose surrender.

Emerson's group had no grenades and was rapidly running out of ammunition. 'We managed to keep the enemy off … [until] about midday,' he penned,

… I was still there with about 20 men. Our right had been overpowered and the enemy were bearing round on our left. We emptied two panniers of Lewis gun ammunition into the enemy on our left. Then seeing that capture was inevitable I ordered the destruction of our Lewis gun and of a German machine gun that we had captured. The Germans were in overwhelming force and we eventually surrendered.[5]

When Wheeler 'ran out of bombs', he also laid down his arms to 'a lot of Germans … coming down a communication trench.'[6]

***

Not long after midday Brand received the latest report from an aviator, fresh from flying over the front. Although the aircraft was badly damaged, the pilot managed to land close to 4th Brigade headquarters. He told Brand the awful news. 'Everything has gone wrong,' he revealed,

'I was flying around and I saw a crowd of men walking along the road. Believing they were the enemy I came down lower with the intention of machine gunning them and I saw they were Australians.'

'How many would there be?' someone asked, and the airman replied: 'There would at least be five hundred men.' Continuing he said: 'I moved across the trenches. Here I saw Australians running across the open space back to their own lines and enemy fire rained on them from the trenches just left, so I knew they were retreating. I dropped some bombs on the enemy when my plane was hit and I managed to get here.'

Brand's worse fears were confirmed. But more was to follow.

Watching the few remaining survivors from his brigade returning to the sunken road, Brand became overwhelmed and sobbed. 'To hell with the tanks,' he cried, 'I've lost my brigade over them.'[7] Soon after, he left his headquarters to speak personally to his men. Chataway takes up the story:

Through the entrance came a bowed figure, his face twitching with emotion, as if the full knowledge of his tragic loss had penetrated his soul – the Brig. He passed among us, spoke to us, and gazed at us, a friend seeking friends. The outstanding gallantry of our men became fully known to us. The withering machine gun fire met with at the barbed wire, the desperate efforts made to cut through it, the human stairs. Of all the battles Australians were in, nothing to equal Bullecourt was ever experienced. Dying men flung themselves across the wire so that their comrades could climb over them. And when at last the lane of death was formed through the wire so as to enable the troops to get into the German line, they captured the position, only to sacrifice it again owing to their heavy losses. And as we learnt this pride took the place of sorrow, the deadly numbness of defeat and sense of loss was ousted.[8]

***

Murray was one of many who successfully fought his way back to his own line. Others were not so fortunate. They were slaughtered in what Murray described as 'like expecting to run for hundreds of yards through a violent thunderstorm without being struck by any of the raindrops.'[9] Clarence James was another who returned safely. 'We could only frog-hop from shell hole to shell hole' he recalled, 'because … [of] enfilading fire from both ends and both sides of the front, everywhere. We lost a hell of a lot of men … [getting] back to the Sunken Road.'[10] Fraser summarised with stark brevity what was happening around him: 'A lot of men killed. It was a hell of a morning.'[11]

Percy Bland was escorting a German prisoner and became one of the first Australians to reach his own line. Somewhat curiously, his first recollection was of a cook who had been killed by an enemy shell the previous day at the sunken road. 'I was in charge of the Pioneers then and we buried him,' Bland said, 'and after when we went over the next day, when we retreated back, after getting knocked to billy-oh … and where we had buried him was all blown to pieces – he'd been blown out, blown to pieces again.'[12]

When G.D. Mitchell's squad ran out of bombs, he was ordered to take the survivors back to the sunken road. 'I glanced round the trench as I swung my [Lewis] gun on [my] shoulder,' he wrote:

Bright mess-tins lay about, There was half a loaf of bread with an open tin of jam beside it, and, and bloodstained equipment lying everywhere. The dead sergeant still lay massive on the parapet. Other dead lay limp on the trench floor. Wounded sprawled or sat with backs to the parapet, watching us with anxious eyes.

"You are not going to leave us?" one asked of me. I could not answer him, or   meet his eyes as I joined the party moving down the sap. For some reason I felt that the guilt of deserting them was mine alone.

Here was a tangle of dismembered limbs and dead men. The air was heavy with the reek of explosives. One man with his foot blown off, leaned wearily back. He had a Mills [bomb] in his hand with the pin out. He would not be taken alive.[13]

Mitchell was another who returned safely.

***

Meanwhile, Sergeant Guppy had noticed that some of his group were surveying the 12th Brigade's front. Their curiosity was particularly drawn 'to the 48th Battalion, which on our left attacked Bullecourt [now] withdrawing in confusion and the men in retreat being mowed down by machine gun fire.'[14] The survivors were stunned at what had happened. An 'icy, contemptuous anger possessed' them.[15]

Possibly more maddening than anything else — particularly to those who had safely reached their own lines — was the knowledge that Bullecourt was finally being shelled. At around 2.00 pm, almost 10 hours after the first tank had rumbled forward, the front around Bullecourt fell silent. Brand, probably more than anyone else in the 4th Australian Division, was bowed by the sheer magnitude of the losses. Some 3000 troops from the 4th Brigade had taken part in the attack — of these 2239 were reported as casualties or prisoners of war.

Durrant recorded that his battalion suffered 'about 80%' losses.[16] The 12th Brigade's losses were less severe. Roll calls revealed 950 casualties from the almost 2250 soldiers who had attacked the Hindenburg Line. Close to 1200 Australians had become prisoners of the enemy. German losses were reported as six officers and 132 soldiers killed. A further 11 officers and 520 soldiers were wounded. The *124th Infantry Regiment*, which bore the brunt of the Australian attack, suffered losses of 434.[17]

Having received reports of the horrendous casualty figures, Birdwood's greatest torment was now the large number of Australians who had surrendered or were prisoners of war. The Germans boasted that, of the 3500 Australian casualties, 40 officers and 1141 men — as well as 53 machine-guns — had been captured.

***

Captain David Dunworth clearly remembered the aftermath. 'The wires looked awful with dead men strung on them like clothes pegs,' he wrote.

Those who were kept in the dugouts till later told me that they felt sick when they saw the blood pools in the snow. I was told of Major Black (16th) 'bravest of the brave' shot ... as he was coolly cutting his way through the wire, all the time encouraging his men. Of my own unit Lt. Eibel whilst fighting hard against the German bombing attacks turned to a man and gave him his papers saying 'give these to Capt. Dunworth and tell him I'm finished.' 'But,' said the man, 'you're not dead.' 'No,' quickly replied Eibel, 'but I will be by that time' and fighting to the end he proved right.[18]

By 3.00 pm German troops had reoccupied all their trenches. Now they began to clear the battlefield and search for wounded German and

Australian soldiers stranded in no man's land. Many were so terribly injured or maimed that they had had no hope of recovery. Some had crawled into shell holes. Others waited — lying and suffering in the open — for the inevitable. They all knew that they were incapable of moving back to safety across the bomb-cratered battlefield littered with the bodies of the dead. Death, for most, must have come as a blessed relief.

Even while the Germans were searching for wounded, Australian artillery was sporadically pounding no man's land. Machine-gunners also fired into the ranks of the German soldiers. Firing ceased only after an officer spotted enemy 'medical orderlies attending the wounded in the shell-holes of no man's land and on the wire ... After display of a white flag, for some two hours ... [Australian stretcher] bearers and fifty infantry were permitted to assist in collecting wounded. Most of those who were picked by the Germans off the wire were carried by them to their own trenches.'[19]

Other accounts differed noticeably. Bean, for instance, wrote that numerous Australians 'were wounded and lay about the wire until captured or put to death by a merciful enemy.' A number of German soldiers were not quite as benevolent. Several were seen firing at

> ... the stretcher-bearers, but after about 4 p.m. upon [Lieutenant J.] Julin's taking his party boldly towards the wire with Red Cross flags flying, the sniping ceased and for two hours the wounded were collected without impediment, the Germans carrying to their own trenches most of those from the wire, but in a few cases placing badly wounded men beyond its outer edge to be picked up by their opponents. Although they also took full advantage of the informal truce to repair gaps in their wire, the concession was welcomed by every Australian. It lasted until 6 o'clock, when snow began to fall and the Germans, probably fearing an attack under this screen, shouted 'finish hospital!' and both sides withdrew. Nevertheless, throughout the night, which was still and frosty,

not a shot was fired, and for several days afterwards, odd survivors crawled or were helped back to the railway.[20]

A few Australians who had hidden, either in shell holes or, in some instances, beneath their dead comrades, also attempted to scramble back to their own lines. Many were unsuccessful. German machine-gunners had little problem picking off the khaki-clad figures silhouetted against the snow-covered background. Very few managed to beat the German guns and return safely.

Australian stretcher-bearers also worked frantically to help recover the wounded. As the afternoon wore on, small groups of troops, many recently returned from the fighting, assisted the exhausted stretcher-bearers. Major Eric Lewis from the 47th Battalion clearly believed that they 'were the means of bringing and saving the lives of a number who, lying wounded in the snow, would most probably have perished from exposure.' Private Frank Coyle was one of the luckier ones. He was discovered stretched out, badly wounded, beside his Lewis gun. Coyle had managed to drag himself more than 100 yards before turning his gun on enemy troops who were chasing him.[21]

Ernest Etchell was another of the wounded who, quite by chance, came across stretcher-bearers who took him to the sunken road. But the move was not without incident. 'I was crawling outside the second line, when a machine gun opened up on me,' he recollected,

… I had another look and there was just a little hole where a bullet had come in   through the lace-holes of my boot and out my heel. The wound never bled. I   decided I'd better get rid of my gun … Not just leave it for the Germans to get and use … I hung onto my revolver. Then I had to get myself back on one leg.   Once I got back to this platoon in reserve, they looked after me. They got me on   a stretcher and sent three jokers to carry me back … We was going back down the road when a battery of 18 pounders come up the road at full gallop, and the Germans started shelling them. These jokers dropped me in the middle of the bloody road and cleared off … When the shelling had stopped, these three jokers came creeping back. I said to them "You're damn fortunate I left my revolver with Sergeant Lonergan, or I'd have shot the pair of you." And I would have done. I said, "At least you could have put me on the road. But you was in too big a hurry to get away."

The stretcher bearers carried me back to a motor ambulance … [where] one of the doctors put his head inside. "Any 15th [Battalion] in here?" he asked. I leaned up on my leg. "Yes, I'm one," I said. "How are the boys getting on up there?" he said. I said, "Getting shit chopped out of them."

After receiving medical treatment Etchell returned to the 15th Battalion.[22]

***

For other Australian soldiers who chose or had no option but to surrender, the prospect was bleak. They faced an uncertain future as prisoners of war. There was the gloomy prospect of being shot by enemy troops, even after surrendering, either because of confusion or (more likely) as some form of reprisal for the attack. They also had to endure interrogation by German soldiers, known to be well practised in the art. What would happen if they did not answer questions or, more likely, did not know the answers?

Among those who considered themselves unlucky to be captured was Richard Whittington. 'I threw away everything I had,' he remembered. 'But when I got half way across to our lines, still out in no man's land, there was a bit of a lull. Well I got into a deep shell hole … I was going to go home when it got dark, but when I popped up to have a look, the blighters [Germans] were all over no man's land!' Whittington gave himself up to a small section of enemy troops. 'I cursed myself after,' he murmured, 'that I didn't look around earlier. I could see them collecting stragglers. They just collected a lot of us up.'[23]

Lancelot Davies was captured during the fighting. Ordered to move out of the trench, Davies looked at 'a scene I shall never forget … before us our previously planned objectives. Bullecourt on the left, Riencourt in front, with Queant, a German stronghold, on the right. Confusion was rife as the Huns were still coming over in great numbers to the attack … No ill treatment had so far come my way.' Adding to the mayhem, a 'British plane hovered around, and appeared to be endeavouring to sum up the whole position as it swooped down and then ascended again. Suddenly its machine guns rattled … and I could see men scatter, many of our chaps among them.' Davies joined a group of other prisoners and was escorted to 'an area of much more calm, as the British strafe is not falling here.' Soon the men were 'joined by many other prisoners from the lines … The excitement of the battle, and its ultimate result, is now passed off, and we find ourselves in a sort of "family group".'[24]

Len Pooley was in the second line of enemy trenches when his section was suddenly 'surrounded by a lot of Germans'. Ordered to discard every piece of 'equipment' including 'rifles', the 17-year-old Pooley was convinced he and his companions were on the verge of being shot. He remembered that the Germans 'marched us out and they lined us up … I thought they were going to put the machine-gun on us … Anyway, it was only to count us, and ask us a lot of questions.' Pooley was being escorted to Riencourt when British-Australian artillery opened another round of barrages. Pooley knew that 'the strafe was too late to be of any use to the Australians.' He recalled shells falling 'among both friends and foe … a few of our chaps were hit, apparently by British shells.' Pooley added that 'somehow all fear had departed' as 'shells continued to crash'.[25]

Horatio Ganson's section of 'seven or eight' was cut off from what was left of the battalion. 'It was about midday when we were driven back,' he recalled, 'we had nothing at all to fight with … We had fired everything.' Trapped at 'the end of a trench' they 'couldn't go any further'. Enemy snipers were 'everywhere'. Rather than die, they 'took the bolts out of our rifles and flung them away … and with our last bomb we blew the rifles to smithereens. Then we waited for about half an hour. The first thing we saw was a stick bomb poked around the corner of the trench. We didn't know whether they were going to lob it or not … Then we heard his first word in German, "Loos!" That's what he said. "Come on! Get out of it!"[26]

During the 'late afternoon', Thomas Taylor and another wounded mate were still lying low, trying to 'reach our own lines'. But, within sight of that line, they were forced to evade the many snipers who were firing at them, taking refuge in a shell hole. Then the machine-guns opened up, 'killing our boys by the score. We decided then that the shell-hole would do us until darkness should give us an opportunity to again seek safety unobserved.' Before they could return to safety, Taylor noticed 'a German passing from shell-hole to shell-hole, evidently looking for prisoners.' Taylor was fearful that the soldier would 'stick that bayonet into us' as they 'had nothing whatever to defend ourselves with, as we had thrown everything away.' His anxiety was over quickly as the German 'made us his prisoners and we were taken back into their lines' where, for some time, enemy soldiers gave 'us a very fair "spin".'[27]

A.L. Guppy was also taken prisoner in the late afternoon while German soldiers were clearing the battlefield. He remembered feeling 'nearly frozen with the cold, when a strong party of Jerries with some of their stretcher bearers out looking for wounded came across me.' Guppy was taken to a trench behind enemy lines which was 'full of Germans'. Surprised at the treatment that he received, particularly at 'not being molested or searched in any way', Guppy was escorted just beyond Riencourt. Along the way he was 'horrified to see everywhere the bodies lying in trenches and in shell holes and in heaps in the open; how terrific had been the slaughter of our boys.'[28]

Captain D. Wells painted a rather different picture of his captors. 'No attempt was made to remove the wounded till dark,' he recollected, 'when German orderlies removed them, handling them very brutally without regard to the nature of their wounds.' Wells was particularly disappointed by the treatment he received from enemy officers. He remembered in particular that a 'German major put himself out to aggravate me and robbed me of all my belongings and badges of rank.' He also thought that the handling of medical cases was 'disgusting' and that many 'lives could have been saved had the patients received treatment in time, whilst others, instead of being permanently incapacitated, could have been completely cured. I can quote numerous cases of wilful brutality to helpless wounded men.'[29]

Whatever their treatment, the majority of those Australians regarded capture, and being a prisoner of war, as dishonourable. They believed that they had 'let their mates down' — the same 'mates' who had chosen death rather than the shame of becoming prisoners of war. Almost all those captured attempted to justify their surrender. Corporal Lancelot Davies was one. 'As the alternative meant death,' he wrote, 'and I was in a helpless position, one must naturally excuse my choice … I was compelled to submit to the most humiliating experience of a lifetime, surrender!'[30]

Horatio Ganson could not come to terms with his capture. He remembered that, immediately afterwards, 'it was a case of not knowing what to think. Your mind's given way. Everybody sat down more or less dumbfounded. We never thought of being a prisoner – never … You don't know what's going to come ahead of you, that's the trouble.'[31]

***

Those Australians who believed that they would be safe once in the hands of their captors soon discovered that they were sadly mistaken. Moving further behind the enemy front, some of the men were again mistakenly fired on by Australian artillery. Donald Fraser recalled that 'when the barrage came down, the Germans crouched up against the front wall of the trench as close as they could get. They didn't care where we were! Some of our fellows were killed.'[32]

The absurdity was not lost on most of the captured Australians. They continually condemned their own artillery commanders, believing that, had their guns fired when requested during the attack, they could probably have held the trenches, and thus would not be in their present predicament. Horatio Ganson had little doubt that 'if we'd had that barrage, we could have walked through the Jerry lines.'[33] Ernest Chalk recalled going 'through one of our own barrages and this gave us to realise very vividly what it really meant to be the object of a British bombardment. It was accountable for the lives of a great many of our boys, and ... our Hun guards suffered very heavy losses as well.'[34] Adding to the catastrophe — and their appalling luck — some other Australians were targeted by a British fighter aircraft flying low over the front. Fortunately, casualties were few. The aviator clearly believed that he was shooting at retreating enemy troops.[35]

German artillery now commenced a barrage which inflicted yet more casualties. An enemy report revealed that when 'the Australian prisoners trudged out watched by our escorts several shells exploded among them, fired from our artillery, which ignorant of the sudden turn of events in the fighting situation, took these for advancing enemy attack troops.'[36]

The ordeal was far from over. Davies recalled that his group of prisoners plodded 'along to an unknown destination'.[37] First came interrogation and Ganson was alarmed at the methods used. Guards 'searched you before you went out of the line', he remembered. 'Everything was spread out on the ground. You had to empty out. They take everything off you, although they didn't take personal things ... [only] anything that was dangerous.' Then they were questioned. The Germans were particularly interested in discovering all they could about the tanks. The soldiers, however, knew very little.[38]

German interrogators were even more eager to find out what the officers knew. Officers, it was assumed, would prove a more valuable source of information. Lieutenant Garner Veness confided to his diary that a 'small party of us [officers] ... were separated for cross examination purposes … [which] was unsatisfactory although they did try to draw us by speaking of what other [officer prisoners] had said.'[39] Removed from the men they commanded, another group of some 'two-dozen officers' was taken to a nearby French village where they were permitted to take a bath before being questioned.[40] German intelligence officers, expert in the art of interrogation, hoped to discover details of the operation of the tanks. But little information was forthcoming as Australian officers, like their men, knew very little. A machine-gun officer, Lieutenant Albert Marshall, had surrendered against his will. Selected for questioning, he was 'taken into a yard where [he was] interviewed and asked questions … The Germans talked to all the men to see what they could get … well, they were getting a little information from everybody.'[41]

The prisoners were later divided into separate parties. Over the next few days they were escorted by armed German guards (most of whom were too elderly for front-line service) to a number of villages behind the front where they were sorted into further categories. Most officers and some NCOs were transported to prison camps in Germany. The wounded were taken to hospitals. The majority, however, were escorted to the infamous Fort MacDonald near Lille — appropriately nicknamed 'the Black Hole of Lille'.

'For seven days we were confined in Fort MacDonald,' Lancelot Davies wrote. 'Each day we became more despondent in our misery.' Davies questioned why the prisoners were subjected to such humiliation 'and neglect. Had we been forgotten by some superior officer, under whose charge we came as prisoners?'[42] Claude Benson asserted that he and his comrades were 'wretchedly treated … the food … and sanitary arrangements were awful.'[43]

Worse was to follow. Believing that they would be sent to prison camps in Germany, the men were horrified to learn that they were to perform work 'behind the lines'. Ignoring the Hague Conventions of 1899 and 1907, which prohibited the use of captured soldiers to perform work to aid the enemy, Australian prisoners of war laboured in work that ranged from burying dead German troops to manufacturing 'anything from ploughshares to railway engines' in specially built foundries.

They were also expected to load machine-gun belts with ammunition. Keith Tamblyn remembered helping his 'mates' and continuing to fight the enemy by taking 'four or five … bullets out [at a time] and empty the powder out of the case [then] put the bullets back in.' The Australians were not averse to attempting other methods of sabotage, even taking the 'pall springs out' of machine-guns to prevent the weapon firing.[44]

At the end of each day the prisoners were returned to a cold and damp cell in a specially designed camp. A meagre diet combined with insufficient warm bedding, unhygienic sanitary conditions and poor medical attention led to illness. Dysentery became rife. Not unexpectedly, many Australian prisoners died as a consequence of this neglect. Horatio Ganson recounted that his group 'worked behind the lines from April to December' where there was also the possibility of being killed by shellfire from their own artillery.[45] By early 1918 most of the surviving Australians who had laboured behind enemy lines were in a somewhat safer environment, having been sent to prison camps in Germany. The wounded from Bullecourt (now physically if not psychologically recovered) had also been transported to those camps. The first battle of Bullecourt was but a distant memory for most.

***

Those Australian soldiers who had survived the fight and had returned to the safety of their own line remained overwhelmed with anxiety. Not only were they appalled at the performance of British officers and staff, they were beginning to question the wisdom of a few of their own commanders and staff officers, particularly those responsible for planning the attack.

Other Australian soldiers thanked their good fortune. Edmund Spencer (16th Battalion) was one. He had been on leave. 'We went down to the coast of France', he remembered, and 'had a whale of a time … at Tricourt … [while] all the boys were getting killed … We had a roll call, when I got back … just after they came out… There was a hell of a lot taken prisoner.'[46]

Even after their terrible ordeal the survivors were allowed little rest. Private C. Etherton recalled that he and his comrades were only in the line at Bullecourt for 'three days, got such a "doing" that we had to be relieved.'[47] Already exhausted, they marched through a blinding snowstorm to Bapaume, then boarded railway carriages which took them to a camp at Shelter Wood near Fricourt (where they had earlier trained for battle) before they were moved to more comfortable surroundings at Bresle, on the outskirts of Albert.[48] Despite their anguish, some of the troops attempted to mask their trauma with a happy face, singing as they 'marched into' the camp.[49]

***

Most, however, were still utterly disconsolate over what had happened. Toft's first thoughts were for a 'meal and a sleep, how one appreciates these common things when they are much needed. One saw the reaction of the men who had taken part in the battle. They were listless and difficult to interest.'[50] Many were simply attempting to come to terms with the tragedy. Recriminations against those responsible would soon begin.

CHAPTER 8

'This cursed futile British staff.'
AFTERMATH AND RECRIMINATIONS

On 11 April Haig reported the 'Mishap of 4th Australian Division at Bullecourt.'[1] For his part, Gough told the 4th Australian Division that he 'was satisfied that the effect upon the whole situation by the Anzac attack had been of great assistance.' How anyone — let alone those responsible for the incompetence and blundering — could suggest that the carnage at Bullecourt had 'greatly assisted' British army morale was bewildering, and the suggestion was considered both offensive and ludicrous. The two responses represented serious understatements and were indicative of the British reaction to the disaster and a precursor to subsequent ill feelings between Australian soldiers and the British High Command.

The 4th Australian Division never fully recovered from the carnage of Bullecourt. Corporal J. Armstrong remembered the battle 'as a bad dream'.[2] Most, if not all of the men questioned the ability of British officers and their staff. Some officers and men were looking for other scapegoats than the British, and began casting doubt on the quality of Australian leadership at both senior and junior levels. Recriminations continued for days, weeks and even months.

***

A few days after the battle, Captain Albert Jacka (14th Battalion) penned a letter to the sister of his good friend, Captain Fred Stanton, describing the circumstances of his death:

It was in the early morning of the 11th April, in our attack on the Hindenburg Line, in which Fred and his company took part. They had gained the first objective, and were pushing on to the second. A German machine gun was firing from the wire in front of the second line, and Fred went forward with five men to knock it out. He was successful in his mission, but paid dearly for his great gallantry. He was shot almost through the heart … Death was instantaneous. Fred's conduct throughout the fight was most gallant and all ranks are loud in their praise of his noble work. We can ill afford to lose such a brilliant officer as your brother.[3]

Jacka had written enough bereavement letters to make no mention of the inept planning and botched attack. He also neglected to add that Stanton, like too many other Australians, had needlessly lost his life.

***

Countless Australians unfairly blamed the officers and men of the 62nd British Division. Captain N.A. Nicolson (a veteran of the attack at Fromelles) was an artillery officer commanding a battery which put down a 'flank barrage' around Bullecourt. 'Our infantry made a fine attack', he wrote,

> … but the same old thing happened again that has so often happened before. The English Division on the left failed to co-operate. This cursed futile British staff. Too many social successes on it – useless in any capacity – absolute passengers … Today this snobbery has caused the 4th Australian Division to be cut to pieces. Its magnificent infantry went triumphantly forward and took the villages, its commanders relying on their left to do what they had promised. Too late the English staff let the Australians know that they had messed it up. The Australian flank was unprotected and where the Aussies had expected the British to be, were the Germans concentrating for a flank attack. This attack drove in and cut a lot of our infantry off and the others had to fight their way back.[4]

In his haste to blame the British, Nicolson was sadly astray in the finer points of the operation. That it was Australian staff who had failed to notify the same British division the previous day of the attack's cancellation and the fact that orders for 11 April clearly stated that British troops should advance only once the Australians had captured enemy positions around Bullecourt, appear to have escaped Nicolson. In addition, his description of 'our infantry' taking Riencourt-les-Cagnicourt and Hendecourt was a less than accurate portrayal of the events of the day.

Gough too (although not unfairly) continued to be handed a significant portion of the blame. Newton Wanliss was in no doubt that the

> ... whole plan seems to have been based on numerous misconceptions, and was the handiwork of someone dominated, not by reason, but by impulse. The decision to persist with the attack on 11 April, under the same original conditions after the fiasco of the previous day, was a lamentable and unfortunate error of judgement, entailing the most disastrous consequences. It seems inexplicable, and can only be explained as another example of their intense spirit of optimism which permeated British leadership throughout the entire war, and which seemed almost immune to the many and bitter fruits of experience. Though the battle was splendidly fought, it was crudely planned.[5]

Another Australian soldier, J.H. Case, asserted that 'Gough again proved his inefficiency as an organising General at the cost of many Australian lives.' And Case was another who believed that, had Gough made available an artillery barrage, 'the troops could have held the ground won, and a wedge would have been driven into the German lines which would have had far reaching results.'[6]

***

On 22 April 1917 Lieutenant Fred Appleton (14th Battalion) scribbled a letter to his sister Vera in Australia. He was recovering in the 3rd London General Hospital at Wandsworth from a wound to his left thigh. 'I got hit in an attack on the German Trenches', he wrote,

… unfortunately for us it was a costly experiment in the use of Tanks. We had no artillery to help us, 12 tanks were to do the job but the three allotted to our battalion were hit by German shells and did not do anything, so we had to go without them. I only got as far as the second row of German barbed wire and lay there in a shell hole from 5a.m. to 12noon, when our men having ran out of ammunition and bombs; none having been able to be brought up to us through the number of German machine guns firing from our flank … I had to crawl 1,200 yards on my hands and knees to get home, sooner than to stay to be made a prisoner. It was an awful experience. It had been snowing for two days previous, and I was almost frozen and, of course, the exertion opened up the wound and the blood began to flow again. I was pretty sick by the time I got to the dressing station, and had it bandaged up properly … I am waiting anxiously for news from the battalion to hear how many are left. I am afraid it was a most disastrous affair and would not be surprised if half the battalion is out of action. I know quite a number of the officers are killed or missing. Very few managed to get back. They were so seriously wounded.

However, unlike many, Appleton did not directly hold the tanks accountable.[7]

The muddled performance of Gough and his staff, notably his artillery officers, in the lead-up to the attack, is particularly worthy of criticism. Even taking into account the shortage of heavy artillery, howitzers and ammunition (all needed for the main Arras offensive), there was inadequate preparation. The performance at Bullecourt tends to suggest that the necessity for a strong preliminary barrage to cut the enemy wire was a lesson that had not been learnt from the Somme. The serious shortage of shells equipped with the new type of fuse (designed to explode and cut the wire) was all too evident. Officers at Australian artillery headquarters — particularly once the attack had commenced — should also be held accountable for not responding to the numerous requests from officers in the field for support. Likewise, Gough and other British staff officers, most notably Lieutenant Colonel R.L.R. Rabett, the officer responsible for artillery along the Bullecourt front, must also shoulder much of the blame. That they ignored countless requests for support from experienced and battle-hardened officers such as Captain Murray, instead choosing to believe the fanciful reports coming into headquarters, defies belief.

Charles Bean took a noticeably different stance. 'The artillery of the 4th Division acted as it was told to do', he wrote,

The attack was to be made without bombardment, and as far as I know, or could   see at the time, the divisional artillery carried out its task as ordered. Its   instructions were, as far as I know, to barrage the German trenches as soon as the troops were driven from them. At such a time it is inevitable that there should be wounded lying about the ground which its own artillery is shelling. The alternative would be to withhold shell-fire, but that would only allow the enemy to pour his fire upon any troops who might be later than the others in retiring, and on this occasion the 48th Battalion was in the line on the left an hour longer than the others.

Although Bean emphasised that he 'had not yet been able to study the orders given' throughout the action, he somehow had reservations that 'the artillery could be fairly blamed'. However, in allocating 'the blame', he was another who pointed the finger squarely at Gough.[8]

***

Long after the attack, accusations persisted over the performance of the tanks and, more significantly, the crews. Chataway, for one, was fierce in his condemnation. However he never forgot the valour of his mates. 'The element of surprise was lost', he wrote, 'the tanks could never make up for it. Eight hundred yards of open country to be traversed and not a gun to be fired as cover for the advance, nor for the destruction of the barbed wire entanglements before the enemy positions. The tanks were to do all this. And afternoon saw the pitiful few making their way home. The tanks had failed.'[9]

Brigadier General Brand was another who never stopped blaming the tanks and their crews.[10] The 4th Division's commander, Major General Walker, had little doubt what was responsible for the near annihilation of two of his brigades. 'Owing to the Tanks giving no assistance whatever to the Infantry', his report stated,

> … the latter had to advance under heavy machine gun fire across open ground and clamber over wire which was in many places undamaged. This caused heavy casualties and the troops, when they reached their objectives, were in considerable confusion and very reduced in numbers.
>
> Owing to the tanks failing to do their work a large gap was left between the two Brigades, which could never be closed and when the enemy delivered repeated counter-attacks, owing to Bullecourt not being attacked, and the idea of "squeezing it out" with the help being an impracticable one, it commanded the open ground and made it quite impossible for carrying parties to get forward with bombs etc., although large forward dumps had been formed N[orth] of the Railway Line.
>
> If Bullecourt had been attacked, as originally intended, and if our attack had been carried out under an Artillery Barrage – even with the wire only partially out as it was – I am confident that the ground gained could have been held.

Walker went on to sanitise the artillery's contribution, although he laboured over the way in which poor staff work, communications and 'forward observation' had figured in the reasons the gunners had failed to support his infantry. And, considering the failure of the guns to respond to numerous requests by officers leading the attack and the subsequent number of Australians killed by so-called 'friendly fire', Walker believed that 'the Artillery were considerably handicapped by doubt as to the position of our troops, but they answered all calls made on them, and the prompt barrage they put down when the troops were forced to retire saved many casualties.'[11]

General Walker's censure of the tanks was repeated elsewhere throughout the 4th Australian Division. Private Campbell Stewart, for instance, confided to his diary that 'The day of the great attack resulted in dismal failure, owing to lack of organisation, failure of tanks, shortage of bombs, want of artillery barrage and loss of officers. Our losses were heavy.'[12] Ernest Etchell was more direct. 'The whole history of it is scandalous', he said, 'it was the greatest bugger up of the war.'[13] 'We just went over like a lot of sheep', asserted William Fitzpatrick.[14] John Norris was a signaller attached to 16th Battalion headquarters. He, too, believed that 'Bullecourt was the stupidest tragedy of the whole war', and recalled the aftermath when the battalion 'came out with about 130 men out of just on 800. And there were 127 men – not men, 127 corpses – lying there ready to be buried … A bloke must have been so overcome with the whole business … that he got that full [intoxicated] that he was laid out with the dead.'[15]

Durrant argued that poor planning, coupled with the failure of the tanks, was 'unfair to brave men'. More optimistically, however, he put his faith in 'the lessons' gained. For instance, he considered that the attack was 'too small a scale', allowing the enemy 'to concentrate' their resources on a narrow front. Such an attack required a 'deep thrust [through a] narrow point [then] tanks were to give momentum.' The failure of the Third Army 'sealed our fate'. However he also believed that it would have been 'better if we attacked at 10p.m. [as] … we were equipped for open warfare [with] not enough bombs.'[16]

Sometime later Captain Jacka produced a useful, if rather unflattering report on how the tanks had failed. Distorted by Birdwood to suit his future ambition to command an army, it nonetheless noted that 'in future, tank crews and infantry should always be trained to cooperate in battle and that tanks should come under the direct orders of the infantry commander.'[17] Brigadier General Robertson, among others, agreed with Jacka's assessment. Robertson considered that the 'failure of the Tanks to carry out the programme completely upset the attack.' He was particularly critical of their lack of action in the 'space between the two Brigades which … was untouched and the result was that we were counter attacked from both Flanks and the enemy dominated the approach to the two objectives from Bullecourt and the untouched Trench East of Bullecourt.'

However, Robertson's major complaint was directed at 'the tactics of the Tanks in opening fire so early in the operation and the reason of the diversion from the programme laid down requires an enquiry.' He was just as adamant in his conclusion that the 'heavy casualties occasioned in my Brigade [the 12th] and finally our inability to hold the positions taken were to a great extent due to the failure of the Tanks. This failure has occasioned a loss of confidence in the Tanks by all ranks.'[18]

Ray Leane never excused the tank crews. At the time he made a case that his battalion would have suffered far fewer casualties without the tanks. He reasoned that his men's achievement 'was in no way due to the assistance given by the Tanks. In fact they were a hindrance, not a help. The men would have gone forward at once under cover of darkness, instead of having to wait in the open from 4a.m. until 5.16a.m. by which time it was daylight, for Tanks that never advanced. Had we been able to get forward half the casualties would have been saved.'[19]

Twenty years later, Leane was still making his case that 'Tanks were of no assistance in the attack – in fact [they] proved a menace.' He added that,

> … the tank personnel neither had confidence nor did they stay with the tank once subjected to fire. The decision to make the attack at this time on Bullecourt was ill conceived and badly arranged and personal experience proved to me that it was not understood by certain of the Higher Command. I agree that had we received artillery support prior to and during the action the result would in all probability have been different.[20]

Tom Chataway curtly summarised the feeling of almost all the men who took part in the attack — 'The tanks had failed.'[21]

But how justified was the criticism directed against the British tanks and tank crews? To some extent it appeared fair, if a little misguided and only partially accurate. Certainly the two officers from the Heavy Machine Gun Corps, Lieutenant Colonel Hardress Lloyd and Major Watson, who not only planned the tanks' role but encouraged Gough to proceed with the attack, are deserving of some blame. However they, too, were initially surprised at the haste with which Gough sought to launch the attack. And, while more of the blame should be levelled at a few of the crews, particularly those guilty of running over Australian soldiers and others for making dreadful decisions, much of that dissatisfaction appears unwarranted.

In April 1917 very little doctrine existed within the British army regarding the proper use of tanks in an attack, much less for tank-infantry cooperation. Most of the young British soldiers who made up the crews who manned the tanks were inexperienced. In fact, they had little concept of the battlefield that lay beyond the cramped, claustrophobic, closed cabin where their only picture of the outside world was provided by 'vision slits'.[22] Early tanks were not built for combat, but rather primarily designed for the limited training then in place. Protected by thin armour, the men inside not only had to endure the deafening noise of the over-strained engine, but also the hideous stench of exhaust fumes and leaking oil. That the tanks 'quickly suffered a 100 per cent casualty rate in machines and fifty per cent in crews' was hardly surprising.[23]

One tank was vulnerable — a company of tanks more so — to enemy artillery and machine-gun fire. The thin armour afforded little protection. Crews knew that a direct hit would most likely cause a tank to catch fire with the probability of a lingering, painful death, or send shrapnel bouncing around the cabin producing appalling, disfiguring wounds, usually so bad that the more fortunate among the crew were killed instantly. It is worth noting Watson's unsettling post-battle report. Of the tanks that went forward:

… [Captain 'Fanny'] Field's section of three tanks were stopped by the determined and accurate fire of forward field guns before they entered the German trenches. The tanks were silhouetted against the snow, and the enemy gunners did not miss. The first tank was hit in the track before it was well under way. The tank was evacuated, and in the dawning light it was hit again before the track could be repaired.

[2nd Lieutenant Eric] Money's tank reached the German wire. His men must have 'missed the gears.' For less than a minute the tank was motionless, then she burst into flames. A shell had exploded the petrol tanks, which in the old Mark I were placed forward on either side of the officer's and driver's seats. A sergeant and two men escaped. Money, best of good fellows, must have been killed instantaneously by the shell.

[2nd Lieutenant Arthur] Bernstein's tank was within reach of the German trenches when a shell hit the cab, decapitated the driver, and exploded in the body of the tank. The corporal was wounded in the arm, and Bernstein was stunned and temporary blinded. The tank was filled with fumes. As the crew were crawling out, a second shell hit the tank on the roof. The men under the wounded corporal began stolidly to salvage the tank's equipment, while Bernstein, scarcely knowing where he was, staggered back to the embankment. He was packed off to a dressing station, and an orderly was sent to recall the crew and found them still working stubbornly under direct fire.[24]

What should not be forgotten is that some tank crews put their own lives on the line by drawing fire away from advancing infantry, helping to save the lives of many Australians. Others who managed to escape their broken down or destroyed vehicles put themselves in further danger by taking up rifles and assisting the infantry. And, as a confidential intelligence report revealed: 'Prisoners report that our tanks produced a great moral effect on their infantry and caused a large number of casualties.'[25]

The 1st Tank Brigade compiled its own report. Considering the catastrophe that had befallen the tanks and the crews, it concluded that had there been 'four times the number of Tanks, of even the present type, the probabilities are that the line Bullecourt-Vis en Artois … could have been occupied … for generally where Tanks proceeded the infantry attack succeeded. Further from all accounts the Germans were in a very demoralized state.'[26]

A subsequent German report from the *27th (Wurttemberg) Division* somewhat agreed. Describing the achievements of the tanks, it further challenged the Australian critique that they were of no use:

On reaching or passing our trenches the majority of tanks turn to the right or left, to assist the infantry in the mopping up of trenches. Odd tanks go ahead to enable the infantry to breach our lines. Ordinary wire entanglements are easily overcome by the tanks. Where there are high, dense and broad entanglements, such as those in front of the Hindenburg Line, the wire is apt to get entangled with the tracks of the tanks. On 11 April one tank was hopelessly stuck in our wire entanglement. Deep trenches, even eight feet wide, seem to be a serious obstacle to tanks.[27]

Later Australian reports, unanimous in attributing the disaster to the poor performance of the tanks, also agreed with Leane's assessment that, had the enemy front been pounded by a stronger preliminary artillery bombardment (rather than the small barrage directed at the flanks) — and had the attack been made under the protection of a creeping barrage — the offensive would, most probably, have been more successful, and the positions could have been held. While nothing is certain in war, a scheme for employing the tanks in combination with some artillery support might also have met with success. But to stake all on the tanks' ability to cut the wire, while at the same time supporting the infantry, appears to have been a case of placing too much trust in a largely untried machine.

***

The reality is that the role of tanks was generally inconsequential when compared with Gough's tactical mistakes — particularly his plan to attack a re-entrant. Gough should have been aware that every attack against a restricted salient or re-entrant had provided an easy target for the Germans who would outflank the attacking unit and subsequently launch counter-attacks. Once the re-entrant was closed, well-positioned machine-gun fire from directly in front and from the flanks of the advancing infantry set up a model trap. Not only were the men cut off from any support, they were also unable to receive much-needed reinforcements and supplies of ammunition, weapons and equipment. With the only means of communication runners, flares or carrier pigeons, it would be close to impossible for the Australians to hold the positions they had so grandly taken.[28] Gough's poor planning did not go unnoticed by other senior British officers. His tactics were subsequently used by British army instructors in lessons on how *not* to plan an offensive.

Charles Bean was another who became increasingly scathing in his criticism of Gough. He never forgave the British general for his incompetent tactics and planning at Bullecourt. Many years after the Armistice, Bean wrote to the British Official Historian of World War I, Brigadier General Sir James Edmonds:

I have never heard his [Gough's] tactics on this occasion defended by anyone, British or Australian, and they are more criticised in the AIF than any other plans or decisions in the war. We here have always felt that Gough's action on this occasion was far more worthy of censure than his leadership of the Fifth Army in 1918, and the Australian divisions felt so strongly about it that the prospect of serving under him in the third battle of Ypres would have been depressing in the extreme. As it was, the battles of Bullecourt were the last muddled engagement [in] which the AIF took part … But Bullecourt was a nightmare.

Edmonds' assessment was similar:

I expect I shall be in full accord with you over Bullecourt. I was at Gough's HQ at the time, and remember that my opinion of him fell lower and lower. When the news of the Australians being cut off came he was furious and shouted over and over again, 'They ought to have been supported,' and began to look for scapegoats.

Another Australian, Colonel D. Bernard (a staff officer attached to the 4th Australian Division), had 'grave misgivings' over the entire operation, and had no doubt that Gough had ordered the Australian brigades 'to what was really certain destruction'.[29]

Gough never accepted condemnation for the failure. He maintained to the end his solemn belief that the Germans would not defend the village and its surrounds in force. The attacks on either side of the village were aimed to 'pinch it out'. For that reason, he had considered that a large preliminary barrage was not necessary, believing that the tanks would be more than sufficient to assist the infantry to break through. He deserves particular carping for having no alternative plans and for not anticipating that the enemy would refuse to give up Bullecourt, especially considering that, at the time of the attack, the village and its surrounds were a significant cog in the German defences given their proximity to the junction of the Hindenburg Line and the Drocourt-Queant Switch. As an army commander he should have grasped the significance and understood that German officers had every intention of defending it, come what may.

Many years later Gough was still justifying his rationale for attacking this part of the line. Pointing the finger squarely at the inadequate number of troops available to him 'to attack this formidable line of entrenchments on a very narrow front … [which] always leads to difficulties', he also laid much of the blame on Allenby and his Third Army for failing to advance as planned and linking 'hands with ours'. His logic was that a 'tactical defeat would be justified if it helped to secure the strategical success of the Higher Command.' Gough went on to record that the 'attack cost the Fifth Army a good deal, but if the Third Army had been able to advance its right and centre beyond Fontaine-les-Croisilles and Monchy-le-Preux, then the sacrifices would not have been made in vain. This essential condition, however, the Third Army was not able to fulfil.'[30] Clearly Gough was defending the indefensible. Blaming Allenby and his Third Army for his own tactical indiscretions was embarrassingly stupid, if it were not so serious. There was no mention of the already planned Flanders campaign and Haig's undertaking that Gough could be offered command. As much as anything, Gough wanted to demonstrate his 'offensive spirit' at Bullecourt to ensure his appointment.

***

Field Marshal Sir Douglas Haig also refused to accept any responsibility. Indeed, his diary entry for 11 April, relating to the battle, contained many inaccuracies highlighting yet again faulty British intelligence-gathering and inaccurate subsequent reports: 'The 4th Australian Division attacked at 4.30 this morning and preceded by 12 Tanks passed the Hindenburg Line between Bullecourt and Queant [which failed to occur]. They occupied Heudecourt [sic] and Riencourt [which they did not]. About noon the Enemy made a strong counter-attack from the direction of Cagnicourt [many counter-attacks, all much earlier, and from different directions] and drove the ANZACS back to their original line taking 400 [more than 1200] prisoners.'[31]

***

Nor can the roles of Birdwood and White be overlooked. Not only did they fail to effectively press a case against Gough's poor planning but, more importantly, they did not argue long or hard enough for a proper preliminary artillery barrage. 'Had Bullecourt been first unmercifully pounded by artillery', the famed British military theorist Cyril Falls reasoned, 'and had the whole attack been made under a barrage, it would have succeeded, and the position could have been held.'[32]

Birdwood, too, should have listened to Australian officers in the field. Their numerous requests for artillery support were ignored. Birdwood should also have demanded that Lieutenant Colonel Rabett order the Fifth Army guns to lay down a barrage. Australian artillery officers must also accept some blame for failing to act, continually refusing later requests for support due to confusion over where Australian troops were, and choosing 'to ignore numerous SOS rockets from the men fighting'.[33]

Sydney Cochrane from the 4th Australian Signals Company probably summarised Birdwood's acceptance of his own guilt as well as anyone. 'As to who was to blame for the disaster', Cochrane wrote, 'General Birdwood came over with General Brand and virtually apologised to the survivors. Apparently Birdwood was pretty choked up. The scuttlebutt was that he had tried unsuccessfully to get Gough to change his mind.'[34] Little wonder that many Australian soldiers were soon referring to Birdwood as 'a bastard of a man'.[35]

Birdwood, for his part, attempted to conceal his reluctance to seriously confront Gough, particularly prior to the attack. A few days after the battle he addressed officers and men from the 4th Brigade. Lieutenant Edgar Rule recorded what he told them:

'Boys, I can assure you that no one regrets this disaster that has befallen your brigade more than I do'; and again, 'I can assure you that none of your own officers had anything to do with the arrangements for the stunt'; and lastly, 'We did our utmost to have the stunt put off until more suitable arrangements could be made.'[36]

However, Birdwood was first and foremost a British officer, and owed any chance of promotion to Haig. He also came from an institution with a tradition of unquestioning loyalty to immediate superiors. Generally, Birdwood was far too deferential to GHQ and Haig and, of course, Gough. Only when it was too late did he attempt to confront GHQ and, subsequently, took it upon himself to order a barrage. But, by then, it was a case of much too little, much too late. White, on the other hand, was an Australian officer. He, however, had the bad luck to be attached to the Fifth Army — referred to as 'the graveyard of staff officers'.[37] When their criticism of Gough's planning was rejected — particularly the use of tanks — both Birdwood and White had the option of resigning. In reality, however, that course of action would have achieved no useful purpose except to rob the British-Australian war effort of two experienced senior officers, even if of limited backbone and questionable ability.

***

Without taking into account the appalling statistics, two Australian brigades had performed what Bean referred to as a 'previously unbelievable feat'. They had 'seized for a time part of the Hindenburg Line without a barrage. The tanks had indeed drawn much of the fire on themselves and scared many Germans; but, except for that, the infantry had been left to assault the famous fortification almost unassisted.'[38]

It was left to Tom Chataway to outline the stark reality of the outcome. 'And afternoon saw the pitiful few making their way home', he wrote. 'It is useless to talk about gallantry, where all were gallant. None of my [machine-gun] crews returned to me ... When I thought of big quiet Ernie Chalk and cheerful little Joe Reardon [later confirmed killed] in the hands of the enemy or on their last journey, I felt so depressed that life scarcely seemed living. Then news arrived ... Captains Dunsworth and Binnington wounded prisoners ... and Chalk a prisoner ... and Percy Black of the 16th Battalion dead upon the wire. The whole brigade had disappeared in that one wild dash.'[39]

Percy Bland was also disturbed by what had happened. 'The next morning they had a roll call', he recalled, 'it was the saddest thing I've ever stood in. They counted us, and named us ... there was Jacka – there were only two officers there ... All the brains was gone, the brains of the [14th] Battalion. There were only the stragglers ... And you were that cold and wet and miserable. It's the first time I've seen crying amongst your cobbers ... it was sad.'[40]

Over time Durrant made a complete reassessment, asserting that 'We lost much but we gained honours.' The attack was 'a most glorious achievement', and the outcome 'shook [the] enemy's confidence in [the] Hindenburg Line.'[41] After the war Brand, too, reconsidered what had happened. He was far less glum. Instead he was proud of what his men had accomplished:

> ... the most disastrous, the most bloody and yet the most glorious day in the history of the 4th Brigade. With its sister Brigade, the 12th, it advanced 1,000 yards over open country under terrific frontal and enfilade fire, hacked a way through a mass of wire entanglements, seized the famous Hindenburg Line, and, cut off from reinforcements or assistance of any kind, held on without artillery support for six hours, repelling several counter-attacks backed up by powerful artillery. As a feat of arms surely there was nothing finer in the whole war.[42]

***

Other Australian divisions soon heard news of the disaster and, more intrinsically, as it transpired, the foolhardiness of the British battle plan. Following the disasters at Fromelles and Pozieres the previous year, the reckless concept of attacking without artillery cover only reinforced the perception among many Australians of the callousness and bloody-mindedness of British officers and their staff. Senior Australian officers, particularly 'red-tabbed' staff, did not escape criticism. And, with little exception, all passed poor judgement on British tanks and crews.

More unfair flack was directed at the 62nd British Division. Considering the disaster that had befallen their comrades a little over 24 hours earlier, when Australian officers failed to notify the British of the attack's cancellation causing a large number of casualties, the disapproval was unwarranted and misdirected. Why blame the British division for not advancing on Bullecourt? Their orders were specific. They were to attack only *after* Australian infantry had entered the surrounds of the village — and not before. Despite faulty intelligence reports indicating otherwise, British officers at the front knew that no Australian troops had come close to Bullecourt. They had every reason for ordering their men to stay put, however much 'the Australians regarded it as another example of the unreliability of British troops'.[43]

***

For the Germans, Bullecourt was a vital 'victory in what had been a bad week elsewhere for the Sixth Army and its commander Freiherr von Falkenhausen.' The *27th (Wurttemberg) Division* understood that it 'had accomplished something extraordinary and had achieved a success that was rare for a division in defence.'[44]

On 12 April, the *27th Division* produced its account of the battle. Acknowledging that the tanks had an early psychological effect on German troops, it asserted: 'Yesterday the division inflicted a heavy defeat on the 4th Australian Division. The 4th and 12th Australian Brigades have been completely wiped out. Of the twelve attacking support tanks nine are destroyed, seven of which lie in or just in front of our lines.'[45] Of more concern to Haig and Gough was the capture of tank number 586, the first undamaged British tank captured by the Germans.

Two German officers with a captured British tank. The tank's serial number 586 is visible on the rear left-hand side. This tank is from Number 11 Company, D Battalion. Some reports claim that the tank penetrated as far as Riencourt and Hendecourt but, in fact, it was disabled close to the German trenches and left behind on the battlefield, becoming the first undamaged British tank captured by the Germans (AWM GO1534-1).

Considering the celebrated reputation of the 4th Australian Division and its leadership, senior German officers were well satisfied with their achievement, most noticeably the large number of prisoners taken. A later British report highlighted 'the German elation at the defeat of the 4th [Australian] Brigade. War Office records … show they specially feared our [4th] Brigade, and that their front line troops were always warned when the 4th Brigade was opposite them. Also that there was a reward of 1,000 marks for each Colonel of the Brigade and a larger one for the Brigadier General dead or alive. That they knew all these by name was proved to our prisoners captured at Bullecourt.'[46]

***

The First Battle of Bullecourt witnessed some of the most savage fighting in an already savage war. This battle deserves to rank alongside Gallipoli, Fromelles and Pozieres in the Australian national consciousness. Yet it has largely been forgotten. Like the three previous battles, Australian soldiers overcame enormous odds to secure what, at best, could be labelled a Pyrrhic victory. Fighting their way into the Hindenburg Line, the Australians achieved a short-lived triumph. Following their withdrawal, men from the 4th Australian Infantry Division never recovered from the shock of the fiasco at Bullecourt. They never stopped blaming senior British officers for the poor planning and tank crews for lack of support during the battle. Perhaps they also needed to look more closely at the performance of the Australian artillery and a number of their own senior and, indeed junior officers in the field, where at least some blame should be apportioned.

However, Gough's blunders stand out. The infantry plan, in which artillery was to play a part, was completely distorted by Gough's unexpected, badly timed and ill-considered eagerness to use tanks. Twelve tanks, providing all were available to lead off the attack, were hardly sufficient even along the narrow front. This overly ambitious arrangement was totally without precedent. Little wonder that Australian soldiers in France were disillusioned with tanks and that it took more than a year for these men to regain confidence in this new weapon.

While neither Birdwood nor White sufficiently championed the interests of their men, Gough's change of plan handicapped the Australian commanders. The cancellation of the artillery barrage in favour of the use of tanks undermined those plans already in place. Yet, somewhat ironically, it is far from certain that a preliminary barrage would have proven effective due to the shortage of heavy artillery and insufficient quantities of shells armed with the instantaneous fuse necessary to cut through wire.

***

Quite simply, too much was expected of Australian and British troops in a combined attack alongside largely untried tanks. Apart from the lack of artillery support, other issues also contributed to the tragedy. First, the attack was on too narrow a front and, more significantly, through a re-entrant, allowing the Germans to maximise their machine-gun fire from three sides. Second, intelligence reports failed to recognise that, when Australian troops managed to fight their way into the OG1 trenches, larger numbers of Germans could gather in the deep, tunnelled dugouts before moving through the maze of communication trenches to counter-attack. Third, following the Australian successes of the last couple of months (in the capture of the outpost villages) some of the men may have become more than a little complacent, believing rumours that the morale of German soldiers was low and that they were effectively on the run. Fourth, nowhere near enough attention was paid to those well-sited machine-gun nests around Queant and the Six Cross Roads which fired mercilessly on Australian troops while they were advancing and then attempting to pull back. Why no artillery fire had been directed against those positions prior to the attack remains something of a mystery. Fifth, why was there no heavy artillery fire from British/Australian guns on German artillery emplacements located behind the villages, from where they were able to pound Australian troops crossing no man's land and fire relentlessly on the tanks? And, finally, the failed attempt on 10 April served as a warning to the Germans. They were thoroughly prepared. Yet, war is at best unpredictable and, while 4th Australian Division may have been utterly dejected, a few days later, not far from Bullecourt, other Australian soldiers would exact some revenge.

CHAPTER 9

'We are well one up over this.'

THE LAGNICOURT COUNTER-ATTACK

Only a comparatively small number of Germans were listed as casualties in the attack on Bullecourt, particularly in comparison to Australian and British losses. Yet the commander of the German *XIV Reserve Corps*, General Otto von Moser, and other senior German officers, were concerned at the fact that an attack had taken place at all. Their concerns were compounded by the success of the Australians in breaking through what they had presumed were impregnable Hindenburg Line defences. Von Moser was looking for some form of retaliation which he hoped to launch before another expected Allied attack in the same area. In anticipation he ordered that some artillery be brought further forward and that his regiments be well prepared. For the moment, however, von Moser wanted nothing more than to demonstrate German strength by striking at the weaker parts of the Anglo-Australian line. The weakly defended Australian front around Queant was considered the best place to strike. What was left of the small village of Lagnicourt would be the centre of the attack.

***

Gough now found himself in an unenviable position. His Fifth Army had been considerably weakened due to Haig's decision to persist with the major British-Canadian offensive at Arras. More reserve units were taken from his already depleted divisions — so much so that only three divisions held the entire Fifth Army front. Two of these were already stretched Australian divisions. What was left of the decimated 4th was defending some 2750 yards of the front. The 1st Australian Division on its right held approximately 12,000 yards from slightly south of Riencourt to the Canal du Nord, not far from

Havrincourt. The British 62nd Division (on the Australian left) was defending another almost 4000 yards.

But Gough's temperament would not allow him to sit idly by, waiting for something to happen. With Haig's support, he had already commenced making plans to renew the attack on Bullecourt, which he wanted to launch as early as practicable. On 13 April Gough ordered that the guns of the 2nd Australian Field Artillery, required for the preliminary bombardment, be moved forward into the narrow valleys close to Ecoust, Noreuil and Lagnicourt. In his haste, Gough yet again had erred badly. The Australian guns were now more vulnerable to German heavy artillery and, moreover, almost invited some sort of infantry attack.

Gough also had other concerns, not least, Haig's requirement to follow the example set by the enemy and establish a reasonably strong 'in depth' defensive line. Considering the sizeable area that required defending and Gough's small number of troops, the idea was unwise and proved impractical to implement. Effectively three lines of defence were required: a reserve line (some five miles to the rear of the forward defences), a support line and then the front line, comprising small outpost trenches (commonly referred to as 'picquet lines') located directly in front of four outpost villages — Demicourt, Boursies, Hermies and Lagnicourt.[1]

***

On 13 April the last remaining units of the 4th Australian Division, holding the line near Noreuil, were withdrawn for rest and replaced by the 2nd Australian Division. In accordance with Gough's instructions two battalions, 'distributed in depth' from two of the brigades, were to hold the Noreuil front.[2] The 6th Australian Infantry Brigade was positioned on the left, with the road running north-east from Noreuil acting as the boundary with the 5th Australian Infantry Brigade.[3]

On the same evening the 1st Australian Division conducted a relief of its battalions, while moving the forward posts to within 1000 yards of the German OG1 line. Gough believed, erroneously as it transpired, that this would lead senior German officers to conclude that a renewed attack would not be launched at Bullecourt, but rather along that part of the front held by the 1st Australian Division. A worse consequence, and one not lost on enemy observers, was that the division's already thinly spaced forward observation posts were now dotted over small grassy inclines along the front which now covered around 13,000 yards. German intelligence officers were soon alerted.

In fact, that part of the front held by the 1st Division now resembled what could best be described as a 'fan' shape. The 1st Brigade was responsible for the line between the Cambrai road and Canal du Nord. The 3rd and 4th battalions were holding the front while the 1st was in support at Doignies and the 2nd in reserve at Beaumetz. The 2nd Brigade was in reserve at I ANZAC headquarters. The 3rd Brigade held the line from Louverval to the divisional boundary flanked by Noreuil and Lagnicourt. The two reserve battalions (the 9th and 10th) were at Morchies and Louverval while the 11th and 12th were in the front line.[4] The 12th Battalion's historian noted that all four companies were spread out in an apparently 'quiet sector of the line, and the Battalion held a frontage of 3,000 yards by small posts varying from fifty to one hundred yards apart.'[5] The Australians were confident that they could repel any German attack. Many, in fact, were experienced, battle-hardened troops having been in the thick of the Gallipoli campaign and, afterwards, the Somme offensive. Those inexperienced soldiers who had arrived in France towards the end of 1916 had been sensibly trained. Both divisions were led by respected and audacious senior officers and counted among their ranks a good number of first class junior officers and NCOs.

***

Troops from the 1st Australian Division had been the first to storm the beaches at Gallipoli on 25 April 1915 and the division had subsequently fought through the entire eight months of the peninsular campaign. Following further training and reorganisation in Egypt, the division had moved to France. On 23 July the troops took part in the Somme offensive, eventually capturing what was left of the village of Pozieres, albeit at a huge cost. Then, in August, came a successful German counter-attack — the division now needed to do it all again. Once fighting around the Somme finally concluded, the division was allowed to rest before joining the 'chase' to the Hindenburg Line in early 1917. During Bullecourt the 1st Division was in support on the left of the 4th Division near the village of Riencourt, where its men had witnessed much of the carnage.[6]

The division was fortunate in having a courageous leader — Major General Harold Bridgwood Walker, a comparatively elderly English officer at 53 years of age. A veteran of the Sudan and India, he also served in South Africa during the Boer War where he came under the command of Birdwood. When Birdwood was named commander of the ANZAC Corps, he took Walker as his Chief of Staff. At first, Walker was far from a natural leader, although he excelled in administration.

Major General Harold Bridgwood Walker, GOC 1st Australian Division (AWM ART03349).

Despite Walker's strong opposition to the Gallipoli landing (correctly, as it turned out, he argued that it stood little likelihood of success) he invested enormous effort in training the men and assisting the tactical planning. His courage was never in doubt. On 25 April 1915, Walker was the first headquarters staff officer to come ashore at Anzac Cove. Early the same afternoon he assumed command of the New Zealand Brigade when its commander fell ill. Within a few days he was commanding the 1st Australian Infantry Brigade. On 15 May, following the fatal wounding of its commander, Major General William Bridges, Walker took over temporary leadership of the 1st Australian Division. However this would last only until late May, when Major General James Walker Legge arrived from Australia to assume command.

In late July 1915 Legge was appointed commander of the 2nd Australian Division. Walker again took over as temporary GOC 1st Division, just in time for the failed Lone Pine offensive. He led the division through the remainder of the offensive, often exposing himself to danger by visiting his men at the front. In late September he was badly wounded and was evacuated from the peninsula. It seems that Walker gradually acquired his leadership skills; his men, frequently seeing him at the front, increasingly respected him for his courage and audacity.

In March 1916, with his appointment as GOC and promotion to major general confirmed, Walker returned to the division, then undergoing further training in Egypt, before moving to the Western Front. In France he commanded the division with distinction, first in the dreadful conditions at Pozieres and later in the 'chase' to the Hindenburg Line.

***

The 2nd Australian Division was formed in July 1915 from units training in Egypt. The next month, after further extensive training, the division was sent to Gallipoli where it played an active part in the fighting until the withdrawal. From Egypt, the division embarked for France, its troops becoming the first Australians to arrive on the Western Front. After more training in the 'nursery' sector around Armentieres, it also took part in the horrendous fighting at Pozieres, having relieved the 1st Australian Division on 27 July 1916. At enormous cost, it went on to capture the heights around Pozieres. Further actions followed in August and November before the division was granted some much-needed rest. In March 1917 a column of divisional troops helped 'chase' withdrawing Germans to the Hindenburg Line.

Major General Nevill Maskelyne Smyth, VC, GOC 2nd Australian Division (AWM ART00199).

On 28 December 1916 an English officer, Brigadier General Nevill Maskelyne Smyth, was named commander of the 2nd Australian Division, taking over from Legge. Smyth had served at Gallipoli, commanding the 1st Australian Infantry Brigade with distinction at the Battle of Lone Pine. He then took the brigade to France where he led it through the Somme offensive. A courageous officer, well respected by his men and by other AIF senior officers, his appointment and promotion to major general were well received throughout the 2nd Division.

***

Following the failed attack at Bullecourt, German General von Moser was given another highly regarded division — the *3rd Guards*. Otto von Moser shared at least one characteristic with Gough — he was not prepared to sit idly by. Moser was of the opinion that the best form of defence was attack.[7] He sought to launch an immediate strike of his own. Crown Prince Rupprecht of Bavaria (the commander of all German armies along this part of the British front) agreed. Not only would Australian artillery batteries be disabled, but Rupprecht also believed that a strong attack would prevent the British moving more men north and perhaps even draw some away from Arras.[8] Senior German officers supported Rupprecht's hypothesis. Keen to leave nothing to chance, Rupprecht decided to add another two divisions to von Moser's corps for the operation, given the codename *Sturmbok*.

Von Moser chose to attack with 23 battalions — almost four of his divisions — on 15 April. His plan was simple. German troops would launch a number of attacks along a six-mile front between Hermies and Noreuil. The village of Lagnicourt would be the focal point of the assault, from where his troops would fan out and advance against another seven villages, all located behind the weakest part of the Australian line. Capturing the villages was never part of von Moser's intention. Instead, he wanted nothing more than to occupy them for most of the day, while his storm troops searched for and destroyed whatever artillery batteries they could find in the valleys close to the villages, leaving British and Australian officers contemplating further German 'lightning' attacks.

The German general had already decided on a series of separate small-scale 'lightning' strikes. His infantry battalions were to attack in two waves, the first comprising three companies, all supported by a heavy machine-gun company. The second wave would include just one company of infantry and would also be supported by heavy machine-guns. Von Moser had chosen his main point of attack wisely. That particular part of France may have been pleasant, open, rolling countryside, dotted with many quaint villages (which before the war were postcard perfect) including Lagnicourt, Queant and Noreuil. But now all were in ruins. The terrain was almost completely flat, except for a few grassy slopes, which would also assist the Germans.[9]

A distant view of Lagnicourt from the west, showing the position from which German infantry rushed the Australian field batteries on 15 April 1917 during their unsuccessful attack through Lagnicourt (AWM E00633).

***

In the early morning of 15 April, all appeared as usual along the Australian front. Brigadier General R. Smith (GOC 5th Australian Infantry Brigade) reported that patrols were out in no man's land 'testing the enemy line to ascertain his strength ... and there was nothing in our front to indicate an attack of any sort.'[10] At around 4.30 am, however, almost 30 minutes before dawn, German artillery opened a barrage close to Longatte, cutting almost all the telephone communications.[11]

In fact, the preliminary bombardment had been well rehearsed, also targeting exposed Australian guns in the valleys. The gun crews were caught totally unprepared, the shelling causing 'their heaviest losses, so far, in the war'.[12] A number of Australian field batteries attempted to reply, including the 43rd Battery, not far from Ecoust, which was heavily shelled but managed to return fire until more than half its guns were put out of action and some 50% of the crews became casualties.[13] Gunner Mervyn Waller wrote that he had 'No sleep. Standing to guns – Fritz sending over [artillery barrage] very thickly falling on both flanks … Very lucky again, dud [shell] falling a few yards away, one a few feet from where we are lying.'[14]

A view of the area near Lagnicourt showing the gun pits at the front of the ridge where German infantry raided the 6th Australian Field Battery on 15 April 1917 during their failed attack through Lagnicourt (AWM E00638).

Australian infantry ensconced in their forward 'picquet lines' were aware that an attack was looming. Approximately 10 minutes later the enemy barrage lifted onto the villages. Sentries, positioned within earshot of the German front-line trenches, instinctively pulled back to the nearest 'piquet line'. A few were killed or wounded by enemy snipers, although most managed to reach their trenches. Soon after, battle-hardened German infantry launched the first of a series of strikes, the leading waves greeted by a salvo of small arms fire from the Australian piquet lines. Reinforcements from further back moved forward and joined the Australians now engaged in a bitter fight. Before long, however, they were seriously outnumbered and were forced to withdraw.

***

The main German attack (launched without a softening-up barrage) by the *2nd Guards Reserve Division*, slightly north of Lagnicourt and Noreuil — almost the exact spot where the two Australian divisions joined — came as a complete surprise. German troops swiftly overwhelmed the forward positions which were manned by sections from the 12th Battalion (3rd Brigade, 1st Australian Division) and the 17th Battalion (5th Brigade, 2nd Australian Division). Rapid gains were made. Soon after, the Germans made another strong thrust against the eastern edge of Lagnicourt, forcing the remnants of Captain James Newland's company (12th Battalion) to withdraw along a sunken road that ran between Doignies and Lagnicourt, where they became caught in crossfire coming from both sides of the road. Lance Corporal Leonard Bryant was not exaggerating when he confided to his diary that 'Fritz counterattacked … with seven picked regiments mostly from the Champagne area in mass formation and succeeded in breaking through thinly held defences being one man to 15 yards or two battalions to a Brigade front – on the left in the Lagnicourt village sector.'[15]

Captain A.S. Vowles' company (12th Battalion) was also caught in the fighting. With little time to prepare, he moved his men to what he believed was a better defensive position in another of the sunken roads that ran between Lagnicourt and Noreuil. When German troops came within range, Vowles instructed his Lewis gunners to commence firing, killing many Germans. But sheer weight of numbers finally told. With a growing casualty list, Vowles told his men to begin an orderly withdrawal, moving along the valley towards Vaulx-Vraucourt, where they joined other Australians in a similar predicament.[16]

From their vantage points Australian scouts reported more enemy troops advancing against both flanks. While the Australians fought bravely with little regard for their own safety, the outcome was inevitable and the Germans now threatened other parts of the line. The situation in the remaining Australian positions was deteriorating by the minute. With his own headquarters threatened, the 12th Battalion's commanding officer (Lieutenant Colonel C.H. Elliot) decided to act quickly, ordering what was left of D Company to pull back to another defensive line further to the rear. Some 50 men and two officers, with three Lewis machine-guns, managed to get back to the sunken road.

However, a German machine-gun nest, set up close to the village outskirts, accounted for more of the battalion as it attempted to reach the sunken road. Sergeant John Whittle was determined that he and his section would not withdraw without a fight. Lacking cover, and under continuous fire, he charged the enemy position, killing all of the crew and capturing their valuable machine-gun along with some ammunition. When German troops did attack, Whittle's men turned the machine-gun on them, holding the Germans at bay until they managed to reach temporary safety at the sunken road.[17]

Lieutenant Colonel Elliott now feared the worst. Attempting to hold out against other German troops rushing through the valley west of Lagnicourt, Elliott gathered not only all of the infantry he could muster, but also batmen and cooks, even officers and men on his staff at battalion headquarters, to establish a line along the edge of the sunken road. In addition, he ordered his few remaining officers to take the fight to the enemy. But overwhelming numbers soon told. Outnumbered 10 to one, and attacked from all sides, Australian officers had no option but to order their men yet again to pull further back to another prepared defensive spot south of Lagnicourt, where they were joined by remnants of the 9th Battalion.

Sometime after 5.00 am Brigadier General Smith at 5th Australian Brigade headquarters received the latest news on the situation — and on what was anticipated. When told that part of the 19th Battalion was still holding positions along the Noreuil-Lagnicourt road, Smith ordered a company-sized group to move to a nearby ridge to set up a defensive line which he hoped would offer better protection, while two Lewis guns were positioned nearby to provide covering fire.

***

Further north, on the other side of the Bapaume-Cambrai road, the German *38th Division* managed to break through several forward posts held by the 3rd Australian Infantry Brigade. At first, the Australians were shocked by a short, though no less intense, preliminary bombardment. On the left flank (in front of Louverval) some German troops were held up. Others moved through a gully, outflanking the Australians, who commenced an orderly withdrawal before reaching the same sunken road where other Australians were holed up. There, supported by that flanking machine-gun fire, they held off another German assault. Many Germans had been killed or wounded, while survivors reached an abandoned trench where reinforcements pushed through to them. Having reorganised, they attacked again, this time from all sides. The Australians found themselves surrounded.

A young officer — Lieutenant C. Pope (11th Battalion) — now took charge of what was a disastrous situation. Despatching a runner (Private A.G. Gledhill) to company headquarters, Pope requested reinforcements and a supply of ammunition and grenades. Captain R. Hemingway responded, sending one NCO and 15 men with guns and ammunition. But in the early morning light, enemy spotters noticed them moving down one of the valleys. Accurate machine-gun and rifle fire accounted for many and prevented the others from reaching Pope's position. In the meantime, however, Pope had been shot through the head and killed instantly.[18] While his position was eventually overrun, the courage and audacity of the men who held their ground provided valuable time, enabling some troops being held in reserve (assisted by several men from the 12th Battalion) to fortify their defensive line further to the rear.

**

At the same time infantry from the *4th Ersatz Division* were attacking positions held by the 3rd and 4th battalions (1st Australian Brigade) south of the Bapaume-Cambrai road. The Germans had put down a small preliminary barrage; despite this, Australian infantry were taken by surprise. Despite its mounting casualties, the 3rd Battalion held on grimly. Not so the 4th Battalion. The larger attack along its part of the front forced the remaining survivors to eventually withdraw to a line running through the outskirts of Boursies, finishing not far from Demicourt.

Other key positions were also under attack, requiring many Australians to pull back to what was known as the 'mail line', not far from the railway embankment. The 17th Battalion's commanding officer (Lieutenant Colonel C.R.A. Pye) ordered two of his more experienced officers, Captain W.H. Sheppard and Lieutenant C.H. Dakin, to move D Company to another of the sunken roads from which the exposed flank could be covered. Another platoon was ordered into a position 'astride the Lagnicourt-Noreuil road ... in order to prevent the enemy occupying a position from which the rest of the Company could be enfiladed.'[19] On the opposite flank more Germans were moving along l'Hirondelle River towards Noreuil. Captain Sheppard immediately ordered a platoon to follow him to a position close to the railway 'which commanded the approach to the village along the river', Sheppard later reporting that 'the platoon did some good shooting'.[20] Meanwhile, more enemy troops joined the attack. Sheppard acted swiftly, ordering his machine-gunners to lay down covering fire before leading the men in a fierce attack.

German officers responded by setting up a number of tactically well-positioned machine-guns on the other side of the valley. With Australian casualties mounting, the flank had become increasingly exposed, allowing enemy troops to toss grenades into Australian positions. Sheppard had little option but to pull back his dwindling number of men to a nearby trench. To reach the trench, however, they had to cross the deadly fire zone swept by German machine-guns. Many were killed or wounded. More enemy troops were discovered moving through the nearby valley, attempting to set up another machine-gun nest in front of Noreuil.

But the desperately outnumbered Australians held firm. Intense rifle and machine-gun fire, along with skilful bomb-throwing by the Australians, accounted for many Germans. One of the battalion's NCOs, Corporal Taylor, recalled that his section leader, Sergeant George Kirkpatrick's

… first bomb made a direct hit and accounted for three Germans. The sergeant was a tall man and, as he straightened himself for another throw, an enemy officer shot him in the forehead with a revolver. Jimmy and I threw our bombs together and the resultant explosion wrote finis to that German officer and his crew. But, to our left, on top of the trench, there appeared another crowd of Germans who threw a shower of "potato mashers" at us. But, luckily, they landed on the parados behind us. Fortunately, more of our fellows coming up from behind us accounted for this new menace with a copious discharge of well-directed Mills bombs.[21]

However, accurate enemy crossfire killed many Australians, including the brave Lieutenant C.H. Dakin (5th Machine Gun Company, 17th Battalion). The Germans were now in a position to place another two machine-guns at other critical locations. Not long afterwards, enemy infantry launched a successful attack. Finding themselves in a hopeless position, almost 30 Australians surrendered. Others courageously fought on until they inevitably succumbed. When the position was finally overrun, German soldiers found dead and wounded covering the ground, at least two deep. Yet that courageous rearguard action had provided their comrades valuable time to establish another more formidable defensive line.[22]

***

Birdwood was not told of the German attack until well after 5.00 am. His prime concern was the danger to a 'considerable number' of 18-pounder field guns. Nonetheless, he remained 'confident that, even though they [Germans] were making a strong attack, it was unlikely that they would attempt to establish themselves beyond their Hindenburg Line, so I felt pretty sure there would not be the real heart in it, as is the case with men who know they have definitely gone forward with no question of retirement.'[23]

Birdwood persisted in defending Gough's logic for ordering the guns moved 'to what undoubtedly is dangerous proximity to the German trenches'. Hinting at the incomplete planning for another attack on Bullecourt, Birdwood reasoned that 'this has been absolutely essential to enable the field guns to deal with those trenches at effective range.' Later he reconsidered the enemy's rationale for the attack, writing that their 'orders, apparently, were to occupy our advanced villages – capture our guns – remain there for twenty-four hours, and return the following night.'[24]

Brigadier General Charles Rosenthal (Commander Royal Artillery, 2nd Australian Division), commander of the three groups of Australian artillery in the valleys surrounding Lagnicourt, Noreuil and Ecoust, had other ideas. He believed that moving the field guns to within 'such a close proximity of the Infantry front line, not entrenched, was somewhat a risky proposition.'[25] And risky it proved. Shortly before 5.30 am, German troops broke through gaps in the outer and inner defence lines held by Lieutenant Colonel A.W. Ralston's 20th Battalion, which was responsible for defending the guns. Moving quickly, elite German infantry closed in on a number of Australian forward batteries belonging to the 1st and 2nd field brigades (2nd Australian Field Artillery) close to one of the sunken roads west of Lagnicourt. The guns had earlier been ordered not to fire due to the likelihood of hitting Ralston's troops. But, with the enemy now bearing down on them, the crews were instructed to fire — although only on obviously German targets.

The 5th Australian Division's artillery was also at the front, in anticipation of the next Australian attack on Bullecourt. The 114th Howitzer Battery had been positioned close to the 1st Division's left flank. When told that the enemy had broken through, Lieutenant Norman Nicolson (Forward Observation Officer) was ordered to the Battery Observation Post to report first hand. What he witnessed came as a shock:

> I could see enemy in possession of Lagnicourt, and the Battery positions of 2nd AFA Brigade. Our infantry were advancing to the cross-roads ... They reached the shelter of the sunken road here and were immediately attacked by enemy forces from Lagnicourt. At the same time I could see our infantry advancing across the ridge between the Lagnicourt-Vaux-Vraucourt Road ... At the same time Major Edmonds (OC 114th Howitzer Battery) turned the guns of the 114th Battery on to ... Lagnicourt at gunfire. The effect seemed splendid

and I am informed since by infantry … that there were about 40 dead Huns … many of who seemed to have been killed by shell fire.[26]

However, the situation for the Australian gunners had become far more desperate.

The prospect of being forced to abandon the guns was now a reality. Fearing much heavier casualties, Rosenthal bowed to the inevitable. He issued an order for the gunners to withdraw — but only after the removal of all breech-blocks and dial sights. 'The situation was such that no other course was possible,' he subsequently wrote. Rosenthal now decided that the enemy had already caused sufficient damage and ordered the heavy artillery, located in emplacements further behind the Australian line, 'to place a 60 pounder barrage East of Lagnicourt'.[27] He also recalled the confusion at 1st and 2nd Australian Divisional headquarters, as

> … by this time the guns of the 2nd AFA Brigade … had been over-run by the enemy … I then went to the Divisional Commander, 2nd Australian Division (then covering our front) and informed him and his GSO1 of what had happened. The GOC rang up 1st Australian Division who were responsible for the country in front of Lagnicourt. He … gave him [Major General Walker] the information … [Walker] replied that there must be some mistake, as he had been speaking to the Battalion Commander whose troops were East of Lagnicourt, and he had reported 'all quiet'… I then instructed my Brigade Major to communicate with the [Brigade Major] 5th Divisional Artillery, who were at this time supporting the 1st Australian Division … [He] had heard nothing of the attack, and protested against the Heavy Artillery placing the barrage East of Lagnicourt; he stated that posts of the First Australian Division Infantry were stationed there. He was then informed that the Infantry had fallen back through our guns.[28]

'The Lagnicourt Guns' by war artist, Will Dyson, depicts Australian troops inspecting field guns and ordinance at Lagnicourt. Although outnumbered almost six to one, the Australians successfully repelled a German attack directed against the artillery located around Lagnicourt and Noreuil (AWM ART02247).

***

By 5.45 am German troops had taken and occupied parts of Lagnicourt. Brigadier General Smith decided that his officers and soldiers needed to act more decisively and ordered his battalion commanders to move their men to the points where the Germans were making the greatest inroads. The 19th Battalion was directed to 'push a Company out to form a defensible flank … on the ridge running north east from Lagnicourt-Noreuil Road … and the 20th Battalion to establish a very strong post on the spur [near the Bois de Vaulx] … with 2 Lewis Guns to cover the watershed leading towards Lagnicourt.' He also instructed his machine-gun officers to move two of their Vickers crews 'to sweep no man's land towards Queant'.[29]

At around 5.50 am, fresh reinforcements arrived to assist the 17th Battalion which was still desperately holding the right flank. Two companies from the 20th Battalion moved to the crest of the ridge north-east of Vaulx-Vraucourt, while another company moved to the Vaulx-Lagnicourt road. At around 6.30 am Australian gunners began firing their 18-pounders and 4.5-inch howitzers on enemy positions in one of the valleys and on a ridge close to Hirondelle.

Meanwhile, close to Morchies, some of Elliot's group had linked up with a company from the 9th Battalion. Setting up a well-sited defensive position, their machine-gunners and riflemen killed a large number of Germans moving though one of the valleys. Sergeant H. Preston was in the thick of the battle. He noticed that German troops 'coming from Lagnicourt' were surprised as 'three [British] planes appeared here with machine guns on Huns, great slaughter, artillery and rifle fire from infantry, enemy retired … I saw men (Huns) round a machine [gun] looked to be putting it in position. I withdrew few yards and threw bombs in among them … I jumped into [one of the sunken] road [where there were] dead and dying everywhere.'[30]

German troops now found themselves fired on 'from all sides' as well as from the air and sought desperately to escape from the salient which they themselves had created. Shortly after 6.30 am that part of the attack was brought to a standstill. The few enemy survivors regrouped. But instead of again taking up the attack, they began withdrawing towards their own line. A few minutes later the 20th Battalion was ordered 'to push the enemy out of his position and move round Lagnicourt to outflank him'.[31] Assisted by well-positioned Vickers and Lewis machine-guns and by a blanket artillery barrage — and with little regard for their own safety — the exhausted Australian infantry moved against the enemy positions. Stunned by the Australians' dash and lack of fear, many Germans fled. Those who remained were killed. Australian guns continued to pound other enemy positions north-west of Lagnicourt — the exact place where those fleeing German troops were gathering. German casualties mounted until the few remaining survivors surrendered to advancing Australians.

At around the same time another party of enemy troops was spotted again moving towards Noreuil. The Germans were unwittingly caught in a trap of their own making. When they were no more than 50 yards away, over 200 Australian riflemen and others with machine-guns opened fire. The few Germans fortunate enough to survive beat a hasty retreat. Dead and wounded Germans littered the battlefield. Along all other parts of the front, the attack was in similar disarray. Lieutenant Nicolson (114th Howitzer Battery Forward Observation Officer), who witnessed what was happening, takes up the story:

The enemy attack on our infantry at the cross roads (same as in previous para) … did not succeed and about 20 minutes later our infantry made a very spirited attack and gained the left edge of Lagnicourt and the gun position … and the Lagnicourt-Vaus-Vracourt [sic] Road. I instantly communicated their progress to Major Edmonds, who placed his barrage between Lagnicourt and the enemy front line between Queant and Pronville, where enemy troops could be seen debouching from Lagnicourt in some disorder across the open ground. Here they got into a barrage which seemed most effective. They continued to retire in waves from Lagnicourt towards their front line. I estimate that I saw over 2,000 of them go across. They were harried by our artillery. I advised my OC of this and got the guns switched on to some of the thickest groups with good effect. I then asked for the guns to fire on the enemy wire and they did. Also the heavy guns and other batteries appeared to have concentrated here. They put up a splendid barrage and the enemy had to go through this. I should think the casualties would be very heavy here. In places I could see enemy troops running up and down the wire in this barrage evidently looking for a track through … This battery obtained good effect on a large body of hostile infantry retiring towards enemy lines … a section getting right into them with gunfire. The enemy appeared to frequently shell his own troops and had a barrage in front of his own lines before all his men had got across.

Nicolson also commented that a 'hostile battery ... concealed in a hollow ... must have had a bad time as our fire was very heavy there for a while.'[32]

By 7.00 am almost all of the surviving German troops were in an extremely precarious position. While a number had fought their way into the outskirts of Beaumetz, they had met stiff opposition. Others attempted to move into the village of Hermies, where they suffered massive casualties. And, while a few reached the outskirts of Boursies, they were quickly forced to withdraw. Only at Noreuil did they meet with limited success — in fact an advance party came to within 100 yards of brigade headquarters.

***

By now the position had become clearer to Birdwood. Implementing plans for a counter-attack of his own he ordered the artillery to lay another barrage between Noreuil and Lagnicourt and instructed the infantry in forward positions to hold their ground. Reinforcements were told to prepare to move forward. By 7.15 am all was in readiness for the counter-attack.

Not long afterwards, the 9th and 20th battalions began to advance towards enemy positions around Lagnicourt. Once the barrage had lifted, some men from the 19th Battalion attacked enemy troops ensconced around Noreuil. Along the entire front the Australians used clever tactics, advancing by alternate companies — one stopping and laying down covering fire while the other moved on — all under 'flanking fusillade fire'. One report noted that as 'a spectacle it was reminiscent of a field day on manoeuvres. As practical warfare in the open it was so brilliantly successful.'[33]

The Germans were overwhelmed by the sheer pluck of the Australians. 'It was the first time that I'd seen grown men brought to such a stage of terror and despair', wrote Sergeant Arthur Matthews (3rd Battalion) 'that they shrieked like terrified animals, and it was awful and awe-inspiring to watch.'[34] Seeing their opponents in such disarray, other Australians pushed ahead towards the enemy's flanks.

Faced with the certainty of death if they continued the fight, large numbers of Germans chose surrender. Many more were killed as they attempted to pull back.

Australian heavy artillery put down another blanket barrage, catching more enemy troops in the open before they could reach the safety of their own line. Another report noted that the withdrawing Germans were virtually stuck in the open, in no man's land, at the mercy of Australian guns. Heavy casualties resulted because 'there were few gaps in the [enemy] wire' through which they could retire.[35] British artillery soon joined in, bombarding Germans around the northern extremity of Lagnicourt. When the shelling stopped, more Australians moved forward, quickly reoccupying most of their former front line. However the Australians were still not quite finished. For over two hours their artillery — indeed some of the very guns that the Germans had earlier captured — pounded known enemy positions.

By 8.45 am the 20th Battalion, which had been primarily responsible for driving 'the enemy out of Lagnicourt', was mopping up and pushing forward 'to re-establish the original line of the 12th Battalion'.[36] There was a slight delay in reoccupying the northern part of the village — not because of enemy activity, but rather Australian gunners, who continued to exact revenge by shelling the withdrawing Germans. Just before 1.00 pm Australian officers reported that all had returned to the same positions that they had held less than nine hours earlier.

When informed of the surprise German attack, Field Marshal Sir Douglas Haig was pleased with the resolve and discipline of the Australians. He wrote in his diary that the 'whole of our line is re-established … The enemy pressed his attack with great energy. 4 Divisions were employed. He destroyed 4 of our 18 pounders and 4.5" howitzer and laid charges to destroy 8 or 10 more guns! Luckily our counter attack arrived soon enough to remove the bursting charges.'[37]

***

Wounded Australians were moved to dressing stations not far from the line and Sergeant Matthews visited a wounded mate. Taken aback by what he had witnessed earlier in the day, and the sight of his wounded comrades, he wrote:

One certainly gets very sick of the strong meat of war at times and I felt very much that spring morning, as I thought of all these men who sacrificed so much of their lives – and in many cases their lives – and live and sleep amongst the filth and wanton destruction of modern warfare, that others may live and sleep how and where they please.[38]

General Birdwood applied a more positive slant. Soon after, he visited the front, where he spoke to officers and men. 'Our counter attack fell upon them with complete success,' Birdwood reported,

... for the Germans found machine guns at them everywhere from front and flanks, with a real good artillery barrage behind them. They then realised that the game was up, and started retiring and surrendering all along the front. As they were driven further back towards their own wire, I got the whole of our heavies on to them ... [and] those of the corps on our left ... [where] they suffered the heaviest ... [W]e have actually counted over 2,000 dead [enemy] in front of us, while we took over 400 prisoners. Our own total casualties, including all very slightly wounded, are not 500, so I think we may say we are well one up over this ... It was only yesterday evening [16 April] that patrols, pushing further on, found German dead in a depression in the ground, lying in rows as thick as the Turks were in that big attack they made on us at Anzac on 20th May, when we calculated we had killed 3,000. This, as I am sure you will agree is very satisfactory, and is some slight compensation to us for previous losses [at Bullecourt], though I always feel that nothing makes up for them.[39]

Lieutenant R.G. Henderson (18th Battalion) was also upbeat over the outcome. 'We are all very cheery here', he wrote, 'as the Germans came over the other day and got well beaten, there are several thousands of men lying out in the open and our brigade got a large haul of prisoners.'[40]

**

The Germans had little to show for their casualties, which numbered 2313, rather than the 3000 reported by Birdwood. Hasty planning, an inadequate preliminary artillery barrage along most parts of the attack's frontage (perhaps von Moser should have followed the example set by the commander of the *2nd Guards Reserve Division* by calling off the barrage entirely, instead relying on stealth and surprise) and weak tactics certainly contributed to their failure. Captured German officers subsequently revealed that the

> … reason for the attack being carried out at short notice was that the enemy had come to the conclusion on April 14th that our line was lightly held and that a favourable opportunity presented itself to capture the artillery in the village nearest to the front if an attempt were made at once.[41]

Despite Birdwood's claim of only '500 or so' casualties, the Australians counted 1010, including four officers. The 11th Battalion suffered the most (245 casualties) while the 17th listed another 181 men as dead, wounded or missing. Australians captured by the enemy numbered around 300. The number of Germans captured was greater, and included 201 unwounded (four officers) and 44 wounded prisoners, seven machine-guns and two Australian Lewis guns.

If the offensive was expected to improve the morale of their troops, German officers were sadly mistaken. Four German divisions — two of them elite Guards divisions — had been stopped and forced back by what amounted to one Australian brigade. In addition, no British troops had been required from the Arras front. Yet British and Australian staff were aghast at how the enemy infantry had advanced more than one and a half miles while capturing Australian guns and holding them for close to two hours. A subsequent Australian court of enquiry found that:

> ... the infantry protection was inadequate, the right flank of the 2nd AFA Brigade was attacked and its rear threatened ... An escort of at least one Company of Infantry might have delayed the enemy's advance, but would not have prevented it.[42]

Birdwood, too, was of the opinion that his infantry had performed as well as they could under the circumstances. He was sure that they had demonstrated sufficient understanding of the techniques of 'defence in depth'. 'One of course hates the idea of ever losing a gun,' Birdwood added, 'but I feel I would far rather have five guns destroyed, than lose one good Australian soldier, for the former can be replaced, while the latter cannot.'[43]

Four 18-pounder guns from the 4th Battery, Australian Field Artillery, and one 4.5-inch howitzer from the 102nd Howitzer Battery were destroyed by the Germans using explosives. Two other guns 'were damaged by direct hits from hostile artillery fire'.[44] In fact, enemy troops wasted too much time going through the Australian trenches and dugouts looking for food and souvenirs. Had this period been used productively, all 22 guns could possibly have been destroyed, seriously hampering preparations for the next British-Australian attack on Bullecourt.

***

Following the failed German attack, little else changed along the I ANZAC Corps front, which still extended to the Canal du Nord. However, on 25 April, the two Australian divisions were reorganised. One brigade from the 1st Australian Division was sent behind the line south of Bapaume for some rest. The Australian brigade was replaced by the 11th British Division. Another Australian brigade was part of the corps reserve, ready to be rushed forward in case of another enemy attack. The 2nd Brigade, which had been temporarily assigned under command of the 2nd Division, was instructed to hold part of the line in the Lagnicourt-Queant sector, while the 5th and 6th brigades prepared for the next attack.[45] Sappers from the 2nd Brigade also contributed to the approaching attack by constructing a number of dummy trenches around Lagnicourt, somewhat optimistically hoping to deceive the Germans. In fact, throughout the next attack, enemy artillery would waste many shells bombarding those trenches.[46]

Another Australian division, the 5th, was camped nearby, east of Albert. The 4th Division was much further to the rear, still recovering after the mauling it had received at Bullecourt. The 62nd British Division was holding the V Corps sector of the line, along points to the south through to the south-east corner of Bullecourt. And while many may have had some inkling that they would soon be needed, they remained unaware of how advanced Gough, Birdwood and their staffs were in planning for the next combined British-Australian attack. This attack would be directed against those same enemy positions near Bullecourt.

CHAPTER 10

'To hold the enemy to his ground.'
PLANS AND PREPARATIONS FOR
THE SECOND ATTACK

Regardless of the mauling that the 4th Australian Division received at Bullecourt, General Sir Hubert Gough wanted nothing more than to swiftly launch a new attack in the same region, and proceeded with preparations to renew the offensive. He initially sought to launch the attack with Smyth's 2nd Australian Division on or about 15 April — this was the main reason the field artillery had been moved forward around Lagnicourt.[1] While Gough's recklessness may have been well known, to launch another offensive against such a well-defended re-entrant without the appropriate artillery barrage was nothing short of sheer recklessness. Had the attack gone ahead, the most likely scenario would have been a repeat of what had happened four days earlier, with the Australians cut to ribbons before they had even reached the German trenches.

But, due to three incidents (two of which were related) his plans were placed in abeyance. First, following the Lagnicourt attack, Gough had just the one Australian division (the 2nd) in the line, as the 1st Division was in reserve. Second, the Third Army's offensive had, for the moment, run out of steam. And third, at 6.00 am on 16 April, General Robert Nivelle launched his anticipated attack around Chemin des Dames, which the British assaults at Arras had been planned to support.

While Nivelle had intended a six-mile advance, after a few early gains the French plans unravelled. By the end of the day, the attack was little different to others that had preceded it — French *poilus* had managed to advance only around 600 yards. The head of the British Military Mission at the French army, Brigadier General Edward Spears, summarised the action: 'The attack gained ground at most points, then slowed down, unable to follow the barrage. As soon as the infantry and the barrage became dissociated, German machine-guns … filled the air with a whistling sound as scythes cutting the hay.'[2] Despite a solemn promise that he would cancel the attack within 48 hours if it became bogged down, Nivelle continued the assault for far too long, the action finally costing the lives of over 100,000 French troops.

Although Haig's thoughts were now, for the most part, directed at planning an offensive around Ypres in Belgium (with the purpose of relieving the Belgian coast and capturing the bases from which U-boats were menacing Allied convoys in the North Atlantic), he also needed to continue the attack at Arras to boost flagging French morale. The need became even more pronounced when a number of French soldiers instigated a mutiny which soon spread and saw General Philippe Petain appointed the French army's new commander-in-chief.

Yet, by late April, when the Arras offensive had all but run out of steam, Haig had a more opportunistic reason to continue his attack on Bullecourt and the Hindenburg Line. His actions also signalled clearly to the French commanders and politicians that his army was maintaining its pressure on the enemy, thereby securing their support for the Ypres offensive. And, for his part, Gough wanted nothing more than success around the tiny French village, if for no other reason than it would confirm his command of the 'big push' in Flanders.

Petain was an advocate of the 'bite and hold' strategy, adding to Haig's belief that the French army was incapable of any further large-scale attacks.[3] Haig wrote confidentially that British aims must include 'a good defensive line between Loos and Lagnicourt', and to prepare for 'several attacks to go in by surprise so as to hold the enemy, and *wear him out*.' The commander-in-chief decided on a succession of attacks by 14 divisions from the First, Third and Fifth armies, along a front extending almost 16 miles, to take place around mid-May.[4]

***

Haig had sanctioned another attack at Bullecourt by one Australian and one British division as part of the ongoing British offensive at Arras. He was also looking at other parts of the overall plan, writing in his diary that

> Fifth Army will continue to assist the Third Army by artillery fire and will also continue to prepare for, and seize, any timely opportunity to assault the Hindenburg Line from the south in cooperation with the advance of the Third Army. The first such assault, *already arranged for* will be in the neighbourhood   of Bullecourt, simultaneously with the forcing of the River Sensee at Fontaines- les-Croisilles and Cherisy by the Third Army. It is hoped to be able to effect this   in six or seven days from now …
>
> The Fifth and Fourth Armies in combination are also studying the question of an attack in combination, on the Hindenburg Line between the Canal du Nord and the Canal du Somme at Escaut: to be delivered simultaneously with, or immediately after, the assault on the Drocourt-Queant line by the First and Third Armies.[5]

Two days later Haig, the Chief of the General Staff (Lieutenant General Sir Launcelot Kiggell) and Chief of Operations (Brigadier General John Davidson) met with his army commanders and Major General Neil Malcolm (Chief of Staff, Fifth Army) seeking fresh ideas for a major attack, now intended for around mid-May. Following lengthy discussions, Haig instructed Gough to prepare for an attack close to Bullecourt in early May, hopefully to throw the Germans off guard. However, it seems little had been learnt from the previous battle as another 10 tanks were promised to Gough for 'the Bullecourt operation'.[6]

On 26 April Lieutenant General Kiggell met with senior French and British officers at Noyelle Vion to provide further details of how the 'Fifth Army would attack Bullecourt with Riencourt and Hendecourt as further objectives … In answer to the Third Army commander, he said that the present intention was for the Fifth Army

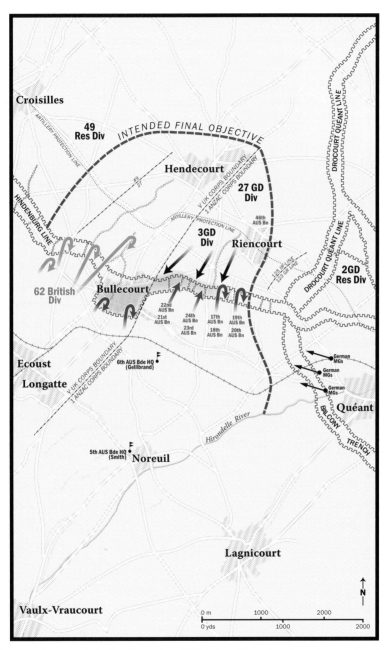

Bullecourt and surrounds showing disposition of British-Australian units prior to the second attack on 3 May 1917, and the projected final objectives.

to hand over Riencourt, after its capture, to the Third Army.' Those attacks, however, were just a prelude to Haig's larger attack, still scheduled for mid-May against 'the Hindenburg Line further south between the Canal de St Quentin and the Canal du Nord.'[7] Haig subsequently revealed to Gough his latest rationale for the Bullecourt offensive, which was to 'wear out' enemy troops and 'to work forward deliberately and methodically and without hurry to a good defensive line by the 15th May.'[8]

Another conference, presided over by Haig, was held on 30 April, and the date for the attack on Bullecourt was scheduled for 3 May, primarily to appease the French commander-in-chief, whose already calamitous offensive was to resume the following day. On 1 May Haig added that the 'enemy has already been weakened appreciably but time is required to wear down his great numbers of troops. The situation is not yet ripe for the decisive blow. We must therefore continue to wear down the enemy until his power of resistance has been further reduced.'[9] Haig, it seems, had lost interest in proceeding with the major attacks scheduled for mid-May. He was also unambiguous in his view that the Arras offensive must be brought to a close and was now beginning to concentrate all his resources for the Flanders offensive, which his armies must be prepared to commence within a couple of months. As the official British historian (Cyril Falls) asserts, the assault on Bullecourt, 'like the operations of the Third and First Armies on the 3rd May, was mainly designed to hold the enemy to his ground, to assist the French, and to encourage them not to break off their own attacks.'[10]

***

When Birdwood was summoned to Fifth Army headquarters he strongly protested at the use of tanks in the Australian attack. Gough eventually conceded. The clumsy monsters would instead be made available to the British division. Of more significance to Birdwood was the inclusion of something resembling a proper artillery plan.

Fearing heavier casualties from 'the great depth in which the hostile machine-guns are now disposed', Birdwood was told by Gough that 'a simple moving "barrage" (i.e. a curtain of fire) will not suffice. On the contrary, a methodical combination of Field and long range heavy artillery fire will often be found necessary to prepare the ground for attack by infantry.'[11] Birdwood (and for that matter all Australian officers and men) certainly had more faith in what Gough now proposed than in the tanks.

The 2nd Australian Division was to advance alongside the luckless 62nd British Division. Early plans had been issued to the Australian divisional commander on 18 April.[12] Three days later Smyth confirmed to his brigade commanders that the attack would proceed and that Gough had revealed that its objectives would depart little from those of 11 April. The advance was divided into three phases. The first would see Braithwaite's British division capture what was left of the village of Bullecourt and parts of the Hindenburg Line to the west. Australian troops were to take the OG1 and OG2 trenches in front of Riencourt. In the second phase, the Fontaine-Queant road, which ran anywhere from 200 to 1200 yards behind OG2 trench, was to be captured by both divisions, so as to provide a jumping-off line for the third phase: the capture of Riencourt by the Australians, and Hendecourt by the British.[13]

The events of a few weeks earlier had demonstrated to Birdwood just how challenging these objectives would prove. Cyril Falls was just as certain, 'the "fanning-out" of troops to secure the flanks of a salient having proved in the past a very difficult operation to control – and practically impossible to hold unless the VII Corps [advancing further north] were successful in joining hands with the attackers.'[14] Birdwood and Smyth decided that the 2nd Division would use two brigades — Brigadier General Robert Smith's 5th and Brigadier General John Gellibrand's 6th —both of which were to move forward along either side of Central Road, with the 5th on the right side and the 6th on the left.[15] This time there would be no gap between the brigades. Brigadier

General E.A. Wisdom's 7th Brigade was to be held in reserve, close to the Queant flank.[16]

Birdwood still harboured concerns over the 62nd British Division. He did not believe that its infantry could capture Bullecourt — after all, the British troops had never advanced with the support of tanks. Gellibrand proposed a plan (which would also assist his own troops) to smother Bullecourt with machine-gun and mortar fire. Birdwood agreed. Yet, Gellibrand's brigade was still provided only 48 of the 96 machine-guns which would support the advance.

***

Planning and preparation for both the artillery and infantry were somewhat improved following the earlier attack. Orders sent from army, corps and subsequently divisional headquarters involved much more precise detail. The artillery was also better prepared. From mid-April an additional six heavy and siege batteries from the First Army and one siege battery from the Third Army were sent from the Arras front, more than doubling the number of I ANZAC heavy batteries to 28. V British Corps had another 20 siege and heavy batteries to complement its one 15-inch and two 12-inch howitzer batteries. Effectively there was one heavy gun or howitzer to every 20 yards of the front line, almost the exact concentration required for an attack of this scale.[17]

The 2nd Australian Division's field artillery was likewise augmented by the batteries of the 1st, 4th and 5th Australian divisions.[18] All these field batteries were commanded by the Commander Royal Artillery (CRA) 2nd Division, Brigadier General G.J. Johnston. The 62nd British Division fared even better. Complementing its own field artillery batteries were those of the 7th, 11th and 58th British divisions and XVI Brigade Royal Horse Artillery from the 4th Cavalry Division (less one battery), all commanded by the CRA 62nd Division, Brigadier General A.T. Anderson.[19]

The administration and transport of ammunition for the hungry guns was also far better planned and organised. By the end of April sappers had completed a considerable amount of work repairing the roads and improving communications across the fields devastated by the Germans little more than a month earlier. An ammunition 'issuing station' was constructed at Fremicourt (slightly north-west of Riencourt) from where a light rail extended to Vaux, Beaumetz, Velu and Morchies. Another light railroad from Achiet le Grand to Mory enabled rapid transportation of ammunition to the gun batteries. Improving weather had allowed more work to be completed on the road network, making it easier to rapidly move troops and equipment to where they were most needed.

Since 12 April, when Gough's resumption of the attack was almost assured (only the date remained uncertain), batteries of British and Australian heavy and field artillery had been constantly pounding enemy positions near Bullecourt, Riencourt and Hendecourt. From 18 to 20 April, a much more extensive barrage had left what remained of the already ruined villages in rubble. However, the few remaining walls and the numerous underground cellars would pose a constant threat to the attacking troops. The enormous coils of wire in front of the Hindenburg Line were also cut in many places. Gunnery officers, however, appeared to have forgotten one significant target. Enemy trenches and machine-gun positions in and around Queant (and not quite 1000 yards from the Australian right flank) were, for the most part, left intact.

But Australian and British gunners did not have everything their own way. Indeed, they were usually forced to work under trying conditions. In what was the first occasion on this part of the front, enemy gunners were engaging in methodical counter-battery work. 'Noreuil Valley, which the Germans knew to be lined with guns,' Bean wrote,

> ... was constantly drenched with gas-shells. The gas officer of the Corps, Lieutenant H.W. Wilson, reported that on the night

of April 20 the Germans fired into it 3,000 lethal shells, the bombardment lasting for five hours with 1,000 lethal shells, and on the following night for an hour with 700 lethal and lachrymatory shells.[20]

By now, however, the Australians had gas shells of their own — and they were not afraid to use this deadly weapon.

Australian artillery barrages, in fact, were complemented by a not insignificant number of gas shells, causing death and terrible injury to enemy troops. On 27 April, a report noted that '350 gas projectors fired into Queant, 1.00a.m., by special Company Royal Engineers.' And, the following day, '1,000 4-inch Stokes gas bombs fired into Bullecourt [at] 10.00p.m. by special Company Royal Engineers.'[21] Enemy gunners always sought quick revenge. A V Corps operational report recorded that, during the early morning of 29 April, a successful gas release was followed by 'considerable retaliation'.[22] Australian soldiers had, however, been thoroughly trained in the use of their gas masks, attaching them immediately on hearing an alarm.

There were also Bangalore torpedoes — long metal tubes filled with ammonal — designed to blow away the thick belts of wire in front of the OG1 trenches, still held in place by stakes at least three feet high. An Australian report, dated 17 April, noted one occasion when,

Parties of sappers covered by infantry proceeded at 11.40p.m. to enemy wire ... 7 Bangalore torpedoes were inserted in wire at intervals of about 40 yards and at a given signal these were exploded. The enemy did not discover presence of our   men until explosion occurred, following which there was an increase in the number of flares ... As all torpedoes exploded together it is difficult to distinguish whether all had gone off but at least 5 or 6 were certainly successful.[23]

Two days later, Sapper Ernest Greenhill recorded another incident in which, shortly after midnight, he and 'a covering party ... carrying a tube of Ammonal 18 ft long ... had to go over no man's land eight hundred yards … [and] we had got within two hundred yards … when the other party blew their sector up, then Fritz started with his machine guns and flares.' After setting off his torpedo, Greenhill managed to crawl safely back to his lines, although two of the party were seriously wounded.[24] Other raids using Bangalore torpedoes were less successful. 'We seem to be trying to give the Germans the idea of where we are going to attack him,' one soldier wrote, 'on our right 2nd Division alone [used] 7 Bangalore torpedoes [which] were fired under his wire by the 2nd Brigade last night. Others were to be fired but Germans saw the parties and bombed them.'[25]

RFC aviators in their frail aircraft were also noticeable, constantly flying over German trenches. Not only were the pilots relaying information on the outcome of artillery barrages and advising corrections, they were also dropping bombs and firing their machine-guns at exposed targets, all with the purpose of assisting the infantry advance. However this came at a heavy cost in brave British pilots and their aeroplanes.[26]

***

Ongoing training and preparations for British and Australian infantry were no less intense and they relentlessly rehearsed all aspects of the operation. Very little was overlooked. Australian officers showed what could be achieved by first-rate leadership, organisation and staff work as well as constant rehearsal of all aspects of the advance. Needless to say, they also put to good use what had been learnt from the earlier attack. Smyth and his brigade commanders considered that they had prepared for most, if not all, possibilities.

For over three days the infantry were trained in the finer points of maintaining their direction in the dark while moving across ground complete with roads (close to the village of Favreuil) similar to the terrain they would encounter at Bullecourt. Tape, posts and wire marked the location of known German emplacements, including barbed wire, trenches and machine-gun nests. On 21 April specific objectives were designated to each battalion, right down to what each wave was expected to achieve in the time allocated. For instance, Gellibrand directed the first wave to 'carry and clean up enemy front trench at Zero plus 16, pushing two special parties to the left', describing further tasks through to the eighth wave, which was expected to 'establish posts, 3 per battalion, along spur from Le Brulle to Chateau, and maintain connection between 188th [British] Brigade and 5th A[ustralian] I[nfantry] Brigade.'[27]

Part of the 22nd Machine Gun Company resting along a sunken road near Noreuil, 23 April 1917, during preparations for the second attack on Bullecourt (AWM E00605).

April 25 was, however, a special day — the second anniversary of the landing at Gallipoli. Given the day off from training, most battalions celebrated with sporting events, usually one of the codes of football or cricket. Choice rations were prepared. The 4th Battalion's commanding officer and quartermaster decided to use most of the battalion's funds to allocate every soldier one bottle of beer, two packets of cigarettes and matches, one packet of biscuits, two chocolate bars and two sausages.[28] With the prospect of battle, and the chance of death or serious maiming not far from their minds, all the men appreciated the opportunity to momentarily forget what lay ahead.

At 3.30 am on 27 April the 5th and 6th brigades conducted their major rehearsal. Gough and Birdwood were both present. 'There were lines of white tapes,' Private Billy Williams recalled,

> … laid out on the ground to represent the German front lines. Each line was referred to as OG [Old German] from No. 1 to No. 8. We were divided into 8 waves and each wave had an objective. The first wave moving forward under a protecting barrage were expected to take OG1, and then the second wave had to frog hop over No. 1 wave and take OG2 and so on up to OG8. Most of us thought the rehearsal was farcical when the Light Horse were brought on the scene at night rehearsals, and bore lighted torches in front of the moving troops. The moving torches represented covering barrage.[29]

Officers once again revised all the details of the plan with their men, also using aerial reconnaissance photographs of enemy defensive positions.

Brigadier General Gellibrand was in the vanguard of training. He missed very little. During the final rehearsal he noticed the time that first light appeared. Afterwards he told the divisional commander that 'dawn broke before the first objective was taken rendering the attacking troops an easy mark for hostile fire.' Gellibrand believed that Zero Hour should be amended to 3.00 am from the scheduled 4.00 am, the time at which the men 'can be detected on the skyline [at about 500 yards'] distance.' He also recalled what 'danger enemy flares' could pose to troops advancing through the open spaces of no man's land.[30] He noticed the smallest of distractions, even remarking that the men's entrenching tools and bayonets made loud noises as they advanced. To overcome this, he instructed that these items be tied down. On 29 April there was a minor distraction when the troops had to refocus their thoughts and vote in the conscription referendum which had become a hot topic in Australia and at the front. Gellibrand understood the necessity, although he was still uneasy about his troops' preparation and ordered that another rehearsal be scheduled for 30 April.

Brigadier General John Gellibrand, GOC 6th Australian Infantry Brigade (AWM P01489.001).

Meanwhile, junior officers had been supplied with 300 highly detailed trench maps, allowing them and their men to commit to memory the gun emplacements and defensive positions they were most likely to encounter. Staff officers then devised the idea that the line of advance should be in the shape of 'half an ellipse'. Running to the west of Bullecourt the line turned north-east, so as to move behind Hendecourt, from where it curved further south, passing behind Riencourt then moving on towards Lagnicourt.[31]

Another obstacle encountered in the previous attack had been discussed at length. Maintaining supplies of ammunition and other essential equipment to troops when in the OG trenches was crucial. Planners decided that infantry and specialist units must move forward with more than enough ammunition and supplies to hold the OG trenches once captured. But that was not all. Each brigade established its own large supply dump not far from where trains discharged their loads, filling it with everything from spades and ammunition to sandbags. In addition, two other enormous supply depots were established at Igri Corner, not far from Noreuil, from where further supplies could be rushed to troops in the field as required.

Before the advance every infantryman was to be supplied with at least six Mills bombs and extra ammunition. Ordinary bombers and rifle grenadiers carried 10 while specialist bombers were issued 24. As the German 'stick-grenade' outranged the Mills bomb, specialists were supplied with a larger number of rifle grenades than usual. The men were also issued sufficient rations for two days and an additional water bottle as well as four sandbags — two secured around their legs, another two in their shoulder straps — to be used for reconstructing smashed parapets. Expanding wire netting and even mats to lay over uncut wire were supplied to a few of the men in the leading wave. Each wave was issued 16 picks and 32 shovels to be used for rebuilding damaged Germany trenches, although these were also handy and deadly weapons for hand-to-hand fighting in the trenches.[32] The typical load for each man was estimated to be a little over 100 pounds, no easy burden for the rapid crossing of no man's land. Gellibrand also suggested using one section (from four) in every platoon as 'general carriers', effectively 'pack mules' carrying extra supplies of ammunition, flares and Mills bombs. Only on reaching their objective were the troops to hand over the loads and take up their weapons.[33]

The men's comfort was not forgotten. Camps, comprising Nissen huts or specially built 'shacks', were assembled by the engineers close to the front, giving those rural areas 'the appearance of primeval prairie'. The same engineers also made temporary repairs to the few remaining habitable houses and barns in the nearby villages. Engineers located suitable positions and built headquarters dugouts, telephone exchanges and storage facilities for the large quantity of water required by the troops. And the recent surprise German attack at Lagnicourt, still fresh in the officers' minds, 'led to a hastening of work on the British [and Australian] defences'.[34]

The number of machine-gun companies assisting the infantry to advance across no man's land had also been dramatically increased. The 5th Australian Division was to provide two extra companies, making 96 machine-guns in all. Six of the guns were to move forward with each brigade while a few were held in reserve or used against enemy aircraft which might stray across the battlefield. Of the remaining guns, some 80 had been instructed to fire a barrage over the heads of the advancing infantry. Twelve Stokes mortars were also to provide support, six to each brigade.

A 6-inch long-range naval gun fires on German positions around Bullecourt from the outskirts of Beaumetz during 21 to 28 April, prior to the Second Battle of Bullecourt (AWM E02010).

From 25 April to 1 May the two brigade commanders suggested minor amendments to the plans already in place. Approved by Smyth, the new orders were passed on to battalion commanders who also 'continued to receive signals on a variety of subjects, such as advice to officers on maintaining direction in the dark and an order that ... [they] must personally supervise their units at the jumping-off line.'[35] Final orders issued to battalions were clear and comprehensive. Plans were detailed even down to the objective of every wave from each platoon, all complemented by detailed diagrams and maps.[36] And, only once the OG1 and OG2 trenches had been captured, were battalion officers instructed to fire different coloured flares to inform adjoining units and brigade headquarters.[37] The 2nd Pioneer Battalion also received extensive instructions directing that the men were to be ready and waiting for 'when 1st phase [of the] 3rd objective reached', and describing the size and shape of trenches that should be reconstructed. Pioneer companies were instructed to move forward alongside the infantry to help erect strands of barbed wire to the rear of the captured trenches, necessary protection for the flanks from counter-attack.

While the men were preparing for the advance, patrols continually braved the hazards of no man's land to report on enemy activity. During the early hours of 27 April, Australian patrols were sent out to locate a German forward post, examine 'enemy wire' and prevent 'if possible, hostile patrols approaching our posts'. A corps report noted that the 'work was carried out very successfully, a number of enemy posts located on our right divisional front and much useful information gained as to the state of the wire in front of our left division.'[38] One night later, British teams managed to secure 'useful information ... as to location of enemy posts and machine guns.' In their sector, Australian 'patrols reconnoitred enemy wire ... [reporting] that 6 Bangalore torpedoes were successfully blown in enemy wire ... [which] was well cut to a depth of 20 feet.'[39] Air reconnaissance also continued to contribute valuable intelligence information, adding to the enormous volume flooding into army and corps headquarters. One very interesting report, dated 29 April, indicating 'no signs of occupation of villages or occupation of village or trenches round Bullecourt', was passed to the Australian divisional headquarters.[40]

If the earlier advance was any guide, the first waves of attacking troops would, in all likelihood, be hammered by enfilade fire causing the flanks to 'brush past the wire at Bullecourt and Queant on either side of the re-entrant [so] the frontage was made narrower than the objective in the Hindenburg Line.' Parts of the objectives, including communication trenches, were to be 'bombed' by infantry moving along OG1.[41] Most, although regrettably, not all mistakes were corrected as they were identified. The trenches and machine-gun nests in front of Queant (the 'Queant Spur') still posed the greatest threat to the 5th Brigade, which would be attacking that part of the line. Intelligence reports also pointed to additional German machine-guns in 'Balcony Trench', located just 700 yards from the brigade's right flank. Yet Birdwood, White, Smyth and the I ANZAC Corps artillery commander, Brigadier General W.J. Napier, failed to take heed. White, in particular, continued to blame the tanks for the failure of the first attack, and seemed unaware of the dangers of attacking the re-entrant. Despite advice from officers who had led reconnaissance patrols — and even intelligence reports — he did not recognise 'the deadly danger from Queant' and refused to sanction a strong bombardment from the heavy artillery. And, while there may have been some disagreement over 'the control and command' of the heavy guns, Queant was fairly and squarely in the I ANZAC Corps sector and it was the responsibility of the corps staff (particularly Napier and White) and Smyth to work together and 'coordinate the plans of all arms'.[42]

The 17th Battalion's Intelligence Officer (Lieutenant John Wright) recognised the massive casualties that failure to deal with Queant could cause. He cautioned senior battalion and even brigade staff officers that German machine-gunners were presented with an almost perfect field of fire against advancing infantry. Yet Wright was uncercemoniously advised that the artillery could handle the situation. It also seems likely that Smith and Gellibrand were not being properly informed that artillery officers were targeting only certain sections of OG1 and OG2 trenches (those parts that were the main focus of the attack) and further flattening the villages of Bullecourt, Riencourt and Hendecourt.[43]

Yet, despite the well-deserved criticism, the artillery barrage preceding the advance was far better planned.[44] For a start, an excellent artillery observation post, with a direct telephone line to I ANZAC Corps headquarters, was established on the heights, some 1000 yards north of Noreuil, from which observers could pass information on the required adjustment of artillery fire to range on enemy targets. The heavy and field guns were to maintain a constant bombardment until shortly before the troops advanced. At that precise moment they were to lay a heavier barrage on German front-line positions. A lighter barrage would be fired on other targets. A creeping barrage — at first moving at a rate of 100 yards every three minutes, before easing down to 100 yards in five minutes — would also commence at Zero Hour.[45] Three other batteries, the 38th, 42nd and 43rd, formed the division's 'mobile artillery', and were to 'be held in readiness to advance to positions … as soon as the third objective had been gained.'[46]

A number of Australian trench mortar batteries had also been earmarked to help cover the British advance (Gellibrand's idea) while another medium trench mortar battery was sited to fire on German positions in OG1 and support lines as well as communication trenches used by German reinforcements. A further trench mortar battery was to be held in reserve, its officers maintaining direct contact with Australian brigade commanders to relay information on enemy activity.[47] If there was another prime flaw in the artillery plan, it was overlooking the opportunity to use smoke to provide some cover for the infantry, particularly considering that the first rays of light would appear much earlier.

***

On 1 May, the 5th and 6th Australian brigades were in position, making final preparations. Each brigade was to advance along a 650-yard front with two battalions ready to lead off and the other two 'in depth', waiting at the rear. The 7th Brigade was not far away, sited close to Noreuil, standing by to move forward if needed. The 1st Brigade (although part of the 1st Australian Division) was acting as divisional reserve and was also prepared to be used when and wherever needed.[48] Even at almost the last minute, orders were being changed; for instance, officers were directed that 'Dugouts will only be attacked with "P" Bombs under an Officer's instruction, as it is not desired to destroy any that may be suitable for our occupation.'[49]

Brigadier General Gellibrand was far more adventurous than Brigadier General Smith. He chose to establish his brigade headquarters some 550 yards forward of Noreuil, around 1400 yards from OG1 trench and just 500 yards behind the jumping-off tapes. Afforded only minimal protection by the railway embankment, Gellibrand had the advantage of being able to actually see how his troops were advancing. Coupled with information he was receiving from intelligence officers at the front, Gellibrand had a much clearer idea of what was happening than Smith who was more safety-conscious, placing his headquarters in Noreuil, over one mile to the rear of where his men would be starting. Thus Smith could not see for himself how the attack was progressing and messages from the front would take much longer to arrive at his headquarters.

On 2 May Gough and Allenby were called to GHQ where final plans were discussed. Haig reasoned that the major

> ... difficulty is on Gough's right [where] the Australians must cross some open   ground in the dark, while on First Army front opposite Oppy there is a wood   which can only be passed conveniently by day light ... If Gough went in early and the others attacked later, it is almost certain that enemy would become alarmed and barrage our front before the troops can get out of the trenches! So all must start to attack at the same hour.[50]

Zero Hour was subsequently scheduled for 3.45 am, not the earlier time that Birdwood had requested. This also suited General Braithwaite, who was concerned that his inexperienced British division had never before attacked in the dark.

The change was most likely the worst flaw in the plan and ultimately led to tragedy. If the attack was to have the maximum element of surprise and any chance of success, it needed to commence at least 30 to 60 minutes earlier so that the troops could set off and move through no man's land under cover of darkness. Birdwood, and to a lesser extent White, must accept blame for not pushing their case more purposefully, although it would have been difficult for them to have changed Gough's time for the attack, which had been fixed by Haig. Still, the majority of Australians were more certain of success than they had been a few weeks earlier. Captain L.C. Roth (2nd Pioneer Battalion) remained optimistic that all details had been considered as thoroughly as possible. His own men had been well prepared. 'There is a fair sized stunt on,' he wrote,

> ... and we are to go over the top. We are all rather excited but are looking forward to some fun ... we have rehearsed the stunt often enough ... We are right out in the open now well ahead of the old lines near Bapaume ... Our camps look for all the world like training camps at home and are really just the same except for the roar of the guns ... The Hindenburg Line is much knocked about as it is, our job is behind his second line so there should be some fun all round.

Roth, however, may have been a little over-zealous, predicting that 'Tomorrow morning Fritz will get absolute hell pitched onto him as our barrages are to be the most fearful yet played onto his line.'[51]

***

However the Germans were not completely caught off guard by the impending attack. Intelligence reports, gathered mostly from aviators and spotters in their balloons, assisted by reasonably good weather, and British/Australian prisoners, pointed out the build-up of troops and equipment behind the front around Bullecourt. The Germans, of course, were expecting another attack. Increased artillery fire only heightened their anticipation. However they were unsure of the day and time. Two downed German aircrew must have surprised their Australian captors when one asked nonchalantly 'What time is zero?' Captain John McDonald was hesitant in his reply. 'There's no zero! We're not thinking of attacking.' The German airman was not easily put off, telling McDonald 'Oh, we know you are.'[52] Private Williams, too, was 'sure that "Fritz" knew our every move, because when the real thing started at 3a.m. [sic] May 3rd 1917, both barrages on each side opened up simultaneously. It was so thick that I wondered how a flea could come through it unscathed.'[53]

General von Moser had earlier constructed a more comprehensive defensive line of his own, using a novel system based on recent *Flachen und Lucken* (defence in depth) doctrine,

> … designed to disintegrate the attacking force, it is like a filter that lets some parts of it go through – at a cost – and holds back other parts. And it is also like a net that encloses the most powerful part of the attacking force, and shuts it into a part of the defence position where the most favourable conditions exist for destroying it.

Quite simply, this meant that German troops, secure in their defensive positions, did not 'immediately … attempt to halt' infantry crossing no man's land head on, but rather 'concentrated on weakening and splintering the attacking force by constant threats from the flanks.'[54]

The *2nd Guards Reserve Division* was ordered to move into that part of the line which it was quite correctly anticipated would provide attacking troops their greatest obstacle, namely 'Balcony Trench' and Queant. This freed up the *27th Wurttemberg Division*, saving it from the necessity of engaging the exposed flanks. Making the task of the Australian and British infantry all the more difficult was the fact that the heavy bombardment did not have the desired effect on German troops sheltering in their deep dugouts.

On 2 May, a British intelligence report highlighted that German batteries from 'The Riencourt Group opposite Bullecourt' had been relocated to 'a number of new positions ... East of the Drocourt-Queant Line', from where it was anticipated they would inflict heavier casualties on advancing infantry.[55] Birdwood and White, in consultation with Smyth, needed to quickly amend plans and orders for the 5th Australian Infantry Brigade which would be attacking this part of the front. But, primarily for selfish reasons (Birdwood fearing recriminations in his almost certain promotion to command an army and White, because he lacked spine in his dealings with Birdwood), they did nothing.

***

Shortly after midnight on 2 May British and Australian artillery commenced a continuous barrage against known enemy positions around Havrincourt, Riencourt, Hendecourt and Bullecourt. Gaps along the German wire fronting OG1 were also 'kept under intermittent fire to prevent repairs being affected'. Australian machine-gunners figured prominently, firing tens of thousands of rounds at German communication trenches and the approaches, as well as at gaps in the wire to prevent enemy sappers making repairs. In the early hours of the morning, Australian patrols were sent out to check on and report which parts of the wire may have been repaired and what further damage had been done.[56]

Early in the morning of 3 May, not long before the attack was scheduled to commence, Fifth Army headquarters passed on a 'secret summary' of Gough's final directives to corps and divisional headquarters — effectively a definitive timetable. 'The 1st stage', it read, was

> ... to capture the trenches South of and running through the village [Bullecourt, by the 62nd Division] and to push strong

bombing parties further forward. This attack to take place before midnight tonight [3 May].

2nd Stage. To capture the trench North of Bullecourt to establish a junction with the left Brigade [of] 2nd Australian Division and to form a strong flank.

Artillery officers were further reminded of the necessity to lay a strong, accurate and synchronised 'creeping barrage' to prevent additional casualties.[57]

***

A few days earlier, Haig had outlined his real motivation for the attack. Sure that the 'decisive blow' of the war would be delivered by his British armies in a couple of months in Flanders, he needed to keep the ailing French on side. The only way was to persevere with the British attack along the Arras front. Haig was convinced that the French would then continue to maintain their support. On 1 May he confided to his diary: 'The enemy has already been weakened appreciably but time is required to wear down his great numbers of troops. The situation is not yet ripe for the decisive blow. We must therefore continue to wear down the enemy until his power of resistance has been further reduced.'[58]

***

Bean wrote that, from shortly before 10.00 pm on 2 May, Australian patrols were out in no man's land 'protecting the engineers who were laying the tapes. When the moon was sinking, at about 2.15 [am], the markers had gone out to their positions.'[59] Fifteen minutes later the leading battalions were moving out from locations around the railway cutting into their jumping-off positions. Both brigades had their two forward battalions — the 22nd and 24th battalions (6th Brigade) on the left of Central Road (the road that again separated the two brigades) while the 17th and 19th battalions (5th Brigade) were on the right. Directly behind were the 21st and

23rd from the 6th Brigade and the 18th and 20th from the 5th. All battalions were arranged in the attacking formation of eight waves. The men waited expectantly for the order to advance. They were confident that the artillery barrage had done its job, confident that the creeping barrage would outdo the pitiful protection offered by the tanks and confident that their officers had made the best possible preparations and plans.

CHAPTER 11

'On that day every man was a hero.'
THE SECOND ATTACK:
3–6 May

By 3.20 am on 3 May, the leading battalions from the 5th and 6th Australian brigades were preparing themselves for the attack, having taken up their positions in front of the embankment along the sunken road. German guns continued to maintain a heavy barrage, inflicting at least 30 casualties. Yet most Australian soldiers, steeling themselves for what lay ahead, did not flinch. At 3.45 am the creeping barrage opened. 'The big stunt started', Lewis Wilson wrote, with a 'terrible bombardment [and] no sleep.'[1] Within seconds, the signal was given to start the advance. With only a few feet separating each soldier, the first waves of Australian infantry began moving forward from almost exactly the same positions as the 4th Division in its ill-fated attack a few weeks earlier. Lieutenant C.E. McCardel was one of many junior officers who commented that the 'Hop out was successful.'[2]

Since the first attack the weather had improved appreciably — gone was the snow that had blighted the previous operation. The small number of remaining trees left dotting the countryside behind no man's land were beginning to blossom. And, in a few places, the grass was even showing signs of irregular growth. The Australian infantry noticed little of this as they moved forward. Their gaze was drawn to the dense clouds of dust, visible in the early dawn, which the barrage had produced and which were now being fanned across the enemy front-line trenches. They also noticed the green and orange flares sent up by the Germans which gave an odd, macabre colour to the battlefield. An enemy searchlight, coming from the direction of Hendecourt, added to the sense of surrealism.

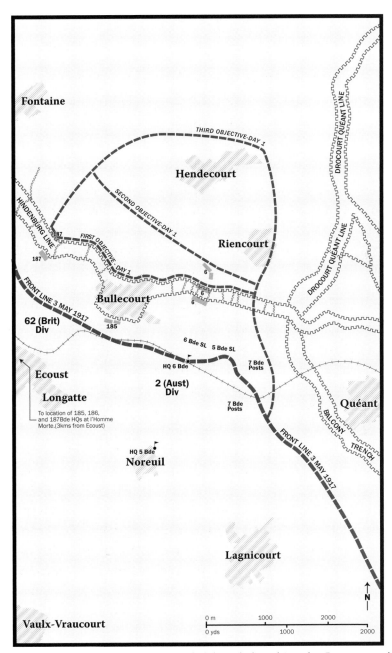

Map showing how the 62nd British Division attacked alongside the 2nd Australian Division, on either side of Bullecourt on 3 May 1917, and the general situation along the entire front line 3-4 May 1917.

By the time of the attack, German troops had become well versed in the latest changes to their flexible defence-in-depth tactics. German gunners had, likewise, learnt to match British counter-battery doctrine, and were said to be 'less vulnerable' to its effects. And there was another setback for the Australian infantry. Despite earlier predictions, insufficient British and Australian heavy artillery support had been scheduled, and there was a less than adequate supply of ammunition for the creeping barrage.[3]

Veteran German soldiers from the *27th Wurttemberger Division* and the *2nd* and *3rd Guards Reserve divisions*, along with those from several of the *Grenadier* and infantry regiments, secure in their dugouts, had been preparing for the attack. Ignoring the threat from the creeping barrage, machine-gunners raced to the parapet, cutting down many of the attacking Australians before they could approach the wire. Then it was the turn of the German heavy guns and *minenwerfers* to commence counter-battery fire against Australian and British artillery emplacements. Five minutes into the attack the barrage lifted and began tearing into no man's land, killing or maiming many more Australian infantry caught in the open.[4]

The 24th Battalion was leading the 6th Brigade's advance, with the 23rd Battalion close behind. Sapper Ernest Greenhill was still waiting to move forward. He later wrote that, when the last wave

… went over Fritz started to bombard us … then our Artillery started the greatest Bombardment ever Known we were against a railway embankment in our communication trench but we had to dig in from shrapnel fire but only got small cover when high explosive shell struck just where I was and smothered me with dirt and put me in a heap the first thing I done was to see if I had the use of my limbs thank God I had. I crawled along trench to get away from the fumes then came back after I pulled myself together only to find our Corporal killed. He was sitting at the side of me he had half his head blown open, [as] the chaps buried him another of our party got wounded.[5]

Defying machine-gun and artillery fire, the leading waves madly dashed across no man's land hoping to find gaps in the wire. In many places they discovered that it was still intact — a few dead and wounded Australian soldiers were already hanging on its rusty barbs, testament to the power of the German response which was far greater than anticipated. Casualties mounted as those who entered OG1 trench came face to face with more *Wurttembergers* racing towards them.

Deadly hand-to-hand combat and 'bombing' duels were common although, fortunately, short lived. At 4.01 am Australian officers set off a pair of red flares to confirm that the 23rd and 24th battalions had taken most of the objectives in OG1. Four minutes later another set of flares lit the sky — a sign that the men were moving against the next objective. Suffering few casualties they raced across the 50 or so yards separating the two lines of trenches on that part of the front. At around 4.20 am they entered the trench where violent hand-to-hand fighting and ferocious 'bombing' contests became more widespread. Enemy defenders fought boldly, at first surrendering very little ground. But the Australians kept coming. Forced to pull back, German soldiers managed to regroup before launching what became a disorganised counter-attack.[6]

The 21st and 22nd battalions, advancing on the left, fared worse. Enemy machine-gun nests wreaked havoc among the leading waves. And, as the men moved further forward, the German artillery barrage became heavier, taking 'the form of a cross on the centre of the 22nd Battalion'. More machine-guns opened up, the relentless firing sowing panic, splitting some companies in two and sending them further to the left, closer to Bullecourt and the Diagonal Road where the men came face-to-face with even more machine-gun nests, cutting what remained of their ranks to pieces, 'practically splitting these units in half'. The toll of casualties continued to climb.[7] With their numbers dwindling, the men who lived through the wall of machine-gun fire and deadly torrent of 'potato-masher' stick-grenades had little option but to pull back.

During the German withdrawal to the Hindenburg Line, Captain William Braithwaite (22nd Battalion) had witnessed how accurate and deadly those German stick-grenades could be, particularly in the hands of experienced soldiers. Well-trained *Wurttembergers* were masters of throwing the grenade, which Braithwaite called 'spudmaster bombs'. 'You couldn't imagine it,' he wrote, 'one minute would be quiet, the next you would see some "spudmaster bombs" coming through the air and you would know you were being shown the way out.'[8] Yet many Australians refused to withdraw, instead choosing certain death over the dishonour of retreating. Pushing on, they courageously fought their way through any gaps they found in the wire until cornered and killed.

The right flank of the 22nd Battalion found the going a little less arduous as the accuracy and severity of the creeping barrage forced enemy soldiers to shelter in their dugouts. Shortly after 4.00 am part of a company led by Captain E.M. Bland bombed its way into OG1. However, enemy soldiers soon appeared, and more deadly bombing duels and hand-to-hand fighting erupted. Unable to set up and use their machine-guns or trench mortars, the Australians were soon overrun and forced to withdraw. Regrouping and reorganising they attacked again, on this occasion, successfully.[9]

After mopping up and securing the first objective, other Australians further to the right were moving against OG2, where they met stronger resistance. More bloody hand-to-hand fighting ensued before the Australians gained the upper hand, forcing the few surviving Germans to withdraw. Soon after 4.10 am, another flare was set off signalling that this part of OG2 had been taken.

At around the same time a number of men from the 21st and 22nd battalions who had become disoriented and lost in the fog of battle joined the 24th Battalion now advancing towards the next part of their objective — an enemy tramway near the Six Cross Roads. A few of the men, however, appeared to be 'a little over eager getting at times too close to the barrage'.[10] Along the way they took another section of OG2 trench, moving then to take the enemy position at the start of Diagonal Road. The Australians could now see what was left of Bullecourt around half a mile in the distance.

German prisoners captured by the Australians in the opening phase of the Second Battle of Bullecourt, 3–4 May 1917, on their way to a prisoners' 'cage'. Close by is a dressing station to receive troops wounded in the battle. Note the passing motor ambulance, a prominent red cross painted on the roof (AWM E00491).

***

Shortly before 5.25 am Captain Gordon Maxfield, who was leading D Company, 24th Battalion, sent off a flare signalling that his men were making inroads. In fact, they had advanced almost another 500 yards past the OG2 line of trenches to the Six Cross Roads and were closing in on their final objective, Riencourt, some 550 yards to the south-west. Maxfield was unaware of a stronger than expected German presence in the village, which was to make its capture all the more difficult. However by now he had realised that the right flank had become exposed, and that Smith's 5th Brigade was nowhere to be seen. Worse was to follow for Maxfield's company, which now encountered a reinforcement of enemy troops.

However, relief arrived with the appearance of B and C companies, 23rd Battalion. Just before 6.00 am Maxfield set up his advanced headquarters in OG2. Any thought of moving against Riencourt was, for the moment, put on hold.

In fact, the two forward Australians battalions were on their own, and in the worst possible position, virtually trapped in a salient and holding a precarious part of the line, a little over 500 yards wide and some 1350 yards from where they had set off. When informed that the left and right flanks were both exposed, with a 'wall of fire' blocking 'the way across the re-entrant in the rear', Gellibrand ordered an immediate 'protective barrage' close to OG2 and 'around the pocket his brigade held'.[11]

***

Meanwhile, the 5th Brigade's attack was turning to a rout. Early in the advance, the 19th (on the right flank) and 17th battalions had unexpectedly moved closer to Queant and Balcony Trench, approaching the same strong German defensive positions that the Australian artillery had not bothered to silence. A few of the more inexperienced junior officers panicked and became disoriented, creating a deadly gap between the two battalions, into which the 17th's last few waves were apparently funnelled. A few observant battle-hardened junior officers from the 19th Battalion recognised the approaching disaster and ordered the men to move further left. But this only further congested the Australians, providing the German machine-gunners even better targets.

In the growing light of day, German marksmen had little difficulty distinguishing officers and NCOs. Essentially leaderless, the men were easy prey for enemy machine-gunners firing from Queant and Balcony Trench. Another artillery barrage had also begun to range in on the survivors who found themselves in a helpless position. Shrapnel shells killed and mutilated many more. Pieces of flesh, arms and legs, along with fragments of brain, spattered those close by. Decapitated bodies lay everywhere. It was not unlike a vision of hell. Private Ernest King was in the first wave. He remembered that 'there was considerable confusion … I went about thirty yards and have a dim recollection of falling into a huge shell hole and was immediately wounded in the face, right arm and chest.'[12]

But many of Smith's men, despite the hopelessness of their situation, pushed on with the advance — most in the face of certain death or mutilation — to try to gain their objective. Some reached the wire only to find enemy troops boldly standing on the parapet, paying no attention to British shells bursting nearby, and shooting point-blank at the attackers. The slaughter continued relentlessly. Against the odds, some Australians fought their way into a section of OG1 not far from Central Road. No sooner had they set off their flares to signify that they had successfully captured the objective, than they were surrounded by Germans. Anyone who refused to surrender was killed mercilessly.

At 4.57 am Smith was told that his brigade's advance had stalled and seemed certain to fail. Predictably, as the official British historian wrote, 'someone lost his head and gave the order to retire.'[13] Survivors began the trek back to the sunken road fronting the railway embankment. Many more were massacred attempting to pull back. Somewhat ironically, Lieutenant John Wright, the very same officer who had earlier issued the dire warning concerning the risks of not shelling Balcony Trench and Queant, was ordered to find out what had gone wrong. 'It was daylight', he recorded, 'and I had ample opportunity to see the machine-gun barrage, which was perfect. I had to screw myself up to plunge into it and after a few steps I was hit, the bullet entering about the centre of the abdomen and passing out the left side.'[14]

***

Gellibrand, meanwhile, had taken control. From his command headquarters close to the front, he watched the situation unfold, recommending to Smyth at divisional headquarters that Smith move closer to the action. The request fell on deaf ears. Instead, Smyth ordered Gellibrand to send a company of reinforcements from the 26th Battalion (7th Brigade) with orders to assist the leaderless troops from the 5th Brigade and join the fight.[15] Private Frank Fitzpatrick of the 6th Machine Gun Company was one of many encouraged by the arrival of the reserve company. 'The ground they had to traverse was a regular inferno of bursting shells', he wrote, 'and swept by Fritz's machine gun fire, but the magnificently steady and determined way in which those men moved through the welter to aid their comrades was something to remember. We were all Australians that day!'[16]

By early morning — indeed throughout most of the day — Gellibrand 'was to all intents and purposes in control of the effective attack on the whole front.'[17] With all apparently lost along that part of the 5th Brigade's advance, Gellibrand ordered a small number of junior officers helping out at 6th Brigade headquarters, and even members of his brigade staff, to move into the line and gather the stragglers. Lieutenant D.N. Rentoul (6th Brigade Signals Officer) and Lieutenant S.W. Gritten (5th Brigade Liaison Officer) were two who attempted to take charge — Gritten on the right and Rentoul in the centre.

Captain Walter Gilchrist was another who heeded the order. Shortly before 5.30 am he came across a group of around 100 disoriented men attempting to withdraw on the left of the stalled advance, not far from the railway embankment. Along with a company of reinforcements from the 7th Brigade, led by Major P.J. Thorn, Gilchrist led the men back into the cauldron of battle, attempting to capture parts of the enemy trenches and move on to lend support to the 6th's planned assault on Riencourt.[18]

Although Gilchrist had earlier been awarded the Military Cross, he was not an experienced infantry officer, rather a 27-year-old engineer officer on Gellibrand's staff. However, he was a natural leader who inspired his troops, and was heard to remark, 'These men are all right. All they want is a leader.' At around 5.45 am Gilchrist and his group reached a spot on the sunken road where almost 200 men, the remnants of Lieutenant Colonel George Murphy's 18th Battalion, had assembled. Encouraged by Murphy, the two groups joined forces and began moving towards their objective 'at a steady walk, rifles slung or at the trail, through the German artillery barrage and under fire of a few snipers until near the entanglement.'[19] All this without artillery support.[20]

However, German machine-gunners spotted the men advancing and waited until they moved closer to the wire before firing. Charles Bean described what happened next:

The stream of bullets from two guns could be seen ripping up the ground and raising two small dust-clouds which gradually converged until they met. The troops were now passing shell-holes crowded with their mates, who had been sheltering there since the first attack, and they began to take cover. Of the leaders, who were systematically picked off by German snipers, many of the finest were again hit. Rentoul had been wounded before reaching the wire, and was later killed ... The 18th Battalion ... lost, killed or wounded, 12 of its 22 officers engaged, and 61 of its 84 NCO's. Colonel Murphy moved across to steady first the right and then the left [both under enfilade machine-gun fire] but the advance ended slightly beyond the wire.

Gilchrist was one of the survivors. Leading his dwindling number of men, he moved forward to take almost another 200 yards of OG1. On Gilchrist's right, another two small groups, led by Lieutenants E.L. Davies and A.W. Irvine, used parts of the sunken road as cover to fight their way into OG1.[21]

Gilchrist repeatedly took the fight up to the Germans. He and his group bombed their way further along OG1 before stumbling across another small party from the 24th Battalion led by Lieutenant E. Smythe.[22] Provided with a 'situation report', Gilchrist continued along the trench, meeting other survivors who were endeavouring to bomb their way further eastward. Shortly before 6.00 am the Germans launched a strong counter-attack east of Central Road.

Again Gilchrist led from the front, gathering another mixed group of men from different companies and even battalions. Once more his natural leadership came to the fore. As Charles Bean wrote later:

> None of the other officers and men present knew who their leader was, but for half-an-hour or more he would be seen, bareheaded, tunicless, in grey woollen cardigan, his curly hair ruffled with exertion, continually climbing out of the trench to throw bombs or to call to the men in shell-holes, begging them to charge the position in front while the trench party bombed up it. The Germans were forced back past their strong point at the entrance of cross-trench [known as] "G." One of their machine guns was captured and turned upon Riencourt … But at some stage … the grey cardigan and curly head were missed, they were never seen or heard of again.[23]

Not long after Captain Gilchrist's death (at around 7.00 am) and with their numbers dwindling, survivors from the mixed group — now once again virtually leaderless — were forced to withdraw to Central Road.

Other Australians still in the thick of battle, and in German trenches, were in a more desperate position. The many communication trenches still controlled by the Germans, which connected OG1 with OG2, made defence all but impossible. In the closing salient, and now threatened with attack from all three sides, most surviving Australians — encouraged by their officers and NCOs — chose to take the fight to the enemy. But their efforts were to no avail. Sheer weight of numbers finally told, and enemy troops reoccupied almost the entire trench. Other Germans quickly moved through the nearest communication trench killing or capturing those few Australians grimly attempting to hang on.

Quick and decisive action was needed to save the 5th Brigade. Smyth ordered another two battalions from the 7th Brigade into the attack. The 26th Battalion was instructed to move under cover along Central Road. By now, the rapidly decreasing number of 5th Brigade survivors still sheltering in OG1 appeared in danger of being wiped out. But, inexplicably, instead of being ordered to take up the fight and assist the 5th Brigade, the 26th Battalion was instructed to act as carrying parties, delivering mortars, bombs, rifle-grenades and ammunition to those still holed up in the trenches.[24]

The other battalion, Lieutenant Colonel E. Norrie's 25th, also received puzzling orders, instructed to assist the British attack. In addition, Smyth unwisely ordered the battalion to push forward from a position close to the railway embankment and move against Bullecourt from the south-east, which required the troops to cross the exposed countryside in the light of day against a hail of machine-gun bullets. Gellibrand could not believe what he had been told. He reasoned with Smyth that it would be almost impossible for these men to move close to the Australians holed up in OG1, let alone try to attack Bullecourt. Gellibrand argued that, for the attack to have any chance of success, it must originate from the south-west. Smyth refused to listen. Gellibrand had no option but to obey Smyth's order, compromising by using just two platoons rather than the entire battalion.[25]

Lieutenant Colonel Norrie was a careful and deliberate officer, always attentive to the needs of his men. Understanding that they would need to advance across exposed, open ground he accepted Gellibrand's suggestion to employ just two platoons. Shortly after 7.00 am the men left the relative safety of the embankment. Capturing the Germans off guard, they moved rapidly until they reached a point less than 300 yards from the forward trench, where they were greeted by a deadly hail of machine-gun fire. Forced to flee, the survivors found shelter in neighbouring shell holes where they waited for the expected counter-attack.[26] Gellibrand's prediction that most of the men would be slaughtered well before they came close to the trench, let alone Bullecourt, had been realised and cast further doubt on a number of Smyth's decisions in the heat of battle.[27]

***

Shortly after 7.00 am, the Germans launched a series of local counter-attacks (all planned at divisional headquarters) directed against the 6th Australian Brigade in those parts of OG1 and OG2 considered the most exposed. At first the Australians held fast, in some places even pushing the enemy further back and seizing another 200 yards of trench. Fighting along OG1 ebbed and flowed with the Australians taking hold, only for the Germans to regroup and counter-attack to regain the trench. However, the fighting in OG2 took on a different complexion, with Australian troops hard pressed to even hold those parts of the trench they had captured.

In the space of some 60 minutes enemy troops had made numerous inroads. By 8.00 am many more Australians had been forced back to the point where Central Road joined OG2. There what remained of Captain J. Pascoe's company came to the rescue. Pascoe ordered his men to move from a position close to the Six Cross Roads and help cordon off OG2 at its junction with a communication trench. A trench mortar was also hastily moved up from OG1. The Germans were pushed back to 'Ostrich Alley'.[28]

At 8.45 am German infantry commenced the first of seven major (or 'general') counter-attacks (planned at corps headquarters), their primary objective the right flank of the 6th Brigade and the Australian-held positions close to Central Road. Supported by an artillery barrage, enemy troops moved into OG1 and OG2, engaging the Australians in more fierce hand-to-hand fighting. Many from both sides fell victim to the bayonet or bomb. If the Australians were to hold on, more artillery support was needed — particularly for the small number desperately clinging to positions along the Fontaine-Queant road. However, the Australian gunners had been firing their guns for almost six hours — a dangerous length of time for both crew and weapons. Without artillery protection, the already exhausted survivors from the 23rd and 24th battalions were unable to withstand such strong and relentless counter-attacks. Shortly after 11.30 am several began to drift back towards the railway embankment.

Gellibrand again attempted to curb the disarray, ordering every available man from his headquarters staff (even cooks, grooms and batmen) to assist in collecting the wounded and moving necessary equipment and ammunition to the Australians in the front line.[29] Taking ammunition and equipment to the front was relatively easy — particularly compared to the dangerous and distressing job of moving the wounded. Not only was there an enormous number of dead and dying Australians scattered throughout the trenches and in no man's land, it was also difficult for a young, inexperienced cook or batman to distinguish badly wounded soldiers from those already dead. And, once the wounded had been carefully placed on stretchers, the bearers had to traverse no man's land to Central Road which at least afforded some cover. However, they then needed to cross the most hazardous part — the next mile or so of open ground to Noreuil.

Yet, against the odds, the men performed their duties courageously. Bean described 'two stretcher bearers [who] were carrying a wounded man when one of the stretcher bearers was killed ... [Private] Carlson then dashed across, and, taking the end of the stretcher, helped to bring the wounded man in.'[30] Many, however, suffering horrendous wounds, died along the way. And, many more would have succumbed to their wounds, if not for the courage of those temporary bearers. Private Brown recalled one dead soldier — no more than a boy — 'with uncovered face smiling serenely at the sky ... If he was as happy now as he looked, how much better would it be to be with him than in this miserable mess! Did he catch that smile from Someone welcoming him Home?'[31]

A German artillery shell bursts on the Bapaume road, north-east of Noreuil, 4 May 1917. Stretcher-bearers bringing back wounded soldiers from the fighting around Bullecourt had a particularly nasty time on this road. In this photograph a bearer party is obscured by smoke from the shell burst (AWM E00442).

From the collecting points, the wounded were transported to advanced dressing stations — tents set up, usually well back from the front — 'awash with blood'. Joseph Cue was the 2nd Division's senior chaplain. He recalled the point at which

> ... the wounded had begun to arrive, for the battle had started almost at dawn. We were therefore at once thrown into the work. The main tent where the four doctors were, was quickly filled with stretchers. These were moved to await their turn; but the tent was not large enough; rows of men were lying outside, and the sun was getting strong. This was bad for men in pain, and having lost much blood. The ADMS then asked the chaplains to clear other tents to get the men under cover ... It did not seem very long and every tent was crowded and another had to be put up ... Hot drinks (lovely soup or cocoa) sandwiches or biscuits for cases where the abdomen was not wounded. Very simple jobs were very comforting, even the taking off of the men's putties and boots ... "Thank you very much sir, I have

not had my boots off for 6 days" said one man … It seems the very first thing that comes to a man when he has been hit, is the thought of the folk at home. "To whom shall I write?" "Write to mother, and say I am alright, only slightly wounded you know Padre." Mothers were in great numbers, wives came next, then sweethearts, uncles, aunts, and cobbers.

Cue also had to tend to the spiritual needs of those soldiers who knew that death was close. He vividly described the scene when a shockingly wounded soldier

… with his head badly knocked about, his face (what could be seen of it) covered with blood … his eyes were practically covered; his jaw smashed, and so unable to speak; this battered man, unrecognisable, was vomiting blood badly at the time. I went to him to see if I could help him. He pointed to his mouth and shook his head, meaning I cannot speak, and then made signs with his hand, as if he were writing. I therefore got his paybook from his pocket and found out his next of kin and wrote it down in my book and told him what I had done. No doubt he was glad of this, but it did not satisfy him, for he still propped himself on his elbow and made the sign of writing. I concluded he wanted to write a message somehow himself, and put the pencil and book in his hand … [On a] bloodstained page [he wrote] "Tell him I am so sorry I was sick." How a man, suffering as he must have been, could be so thoughtful and unable to rest until he had apologised to the wounded comrade by his side, because he had been sick on the ground between them, and had to write it because he could not speak it, is beyond my comprehension. Surely such a man is worth knowing whose action was something like our Blessed Lord's, who was so thoughtful for others, when he was dying on the cross.[32]

***

Meanwhile the 62nd (West Riding) Division's attack (on the 6th Brigade's left flank) had faltered and was in danger of failing. Despite some of the men having taken part in the attack on 11 April, the 62nd was inexperienced and not battle hardened, although all three brigades had participated in a couple of rehearsals alongside tanks from D Battalion. Gough, it seems, understood the dilemma the men faced and ordered the 22nd Brigade (7th British Division) to act as the 62nd Division 'reserve', ready to move at a moment's notice. In fact, two of the brigade's battalions had marched to Mory in the early hours of the morning to await an order from Braithwaite.[33]

All three of the West Riding brigades had attacked side by side, albeit with nowhere near the promised artillery support. As in the previous attack, tanks were to assume that role. In fact, 10 tanks (from No. 12 Company, D Battalion) provided what British troops regarded as ineffective assistance. However, as Bean wrote, 'tank officers afterwards expressed the opinion, which German evidence tends to confirm, that the infantry left too much to the tanks … the British infantry on the other hand, alleged that some of the tank crews seemed half-hearted.'[34] Whatever the reality, it would be unfair to simply blame the poor performance of those lumbering armoured monsters for the initial British failure. Incompetent, even lazy, staff work, particularly in the 185th Brigade, was also a contributing factor.[35]

Gellibrand had previously sent his liaison officer, Major A.R. Wiltshire, to the 185th Brigade headquarters at l'Homme Morte, some five miles from Bullecourt. Wiltshire's first report was less than encouraging. He considered the staff remote from the troops. Witnessing the extravagance at a brigade staff dinner shortly before the advance, Wiltshire was reminded of Gellibrand 'in his tiny ground-sheet "bivvy" about [four miles] further forward, and with his fingers on every thread of command and all the time inspiring everyone with his magical leadership.'[36]

By 6.45 am, Wiltshire was certain that poor leadership in the field, combined with inadequate staff work, was the chief reason for the chaos at the front. He told Gellibrand of the 'scanty reports at 185th Brigade. People here received *none* from forward units, but Brigadier believes his men [were] in Bullecourt from aircraft reports via Division.'[37] In fact, the situation of the British troops was almost precisely the reverse.

Brigadier General V.W. de Falbe's poorly prepared and badly led 185th Brigade (less the 2/8th West Yorkshire Battalion, which was 'on loan' to the 186th Brigade) had been given the major task of capturing what was left of Bullecourt. However, apparently due to a bright moon, last-minute alterations had to be made to the already inadequate plans. Instead of leading off from the Lagnicourt-St Martin road, jumping-off tapes were placed almost 100 yards further to the rear, from where the 185th Brigade and the two forward battalions of the 186th were to lead off. Not unsurprisingly, de Falbe and his staff failed to take into account that both front-line battalions were nowhere near full strength.

The 2/6th West Yorkshire Battalion attacked on the right with the 2/5th West Yorkshire on the left. The same well-concealed German machine-guns that had accounted for a large number of Australians were also responsible for untold casualties in the 2/6th. Survivors were also forced to deal with smoke, blown back towards the British line by a strong north-easterly breeze. Blinded, they mistakenly moved further left, some joining the 2/5th West Yorkshires. Against the odds, the British troops fought on only to find very few places in which the wire had been cut. Still they moved forward, until eventually gaining OG1 and even parts of OG2.

The 2/5th West Yorkshire Battalion even managed to reach Bullecourt before making further ground through the village to its northern extremity. But its progress soon stalled. If the British were to hold the village, strong artillery support and reinforcements were required. Neither was provided in sufficient quantities. At around 7.10 am, one company from the 2/7th West Yorkshire Battalion (which was held in reserve) was sent out. Strong enemy rifle and machine-gun fire halted the men well short of their objective, forcing them to fall back to the railway embankment.[38]

Brigadier General F.F. Hill's 186th Brigade (further to the left of the village) had been given the task of taking another three challenging objectives — first, the capture of parts of OG1 and OG2 trenches before moving on to a second, and much more substantial target, parts of the *Artillerie-Schutzstellung* (the German artillery 'protection line') which generally followed the same direction as the Queant-Fontaine road. The third objective remained the village of Hendecourt.

The 2/5th Duke of Wellington's Battalion, advancing on the brigade's right flank, found most of the wire cut. Reaching its objective with few casualties, signal officers established contact with the 2/5th West Yorkshires already in Bullecourt. A command post was set up a little over 1000 yards west of Captain Maxfield's group of Australians. But, with no radio contact or, for that matter, any other means of communication, both groups remained unaware of the other's position. And, without support, the British then attempted to push on towards their next objective. Not unexpectedly they encountered strong German resistance, with machine-gun fire virtually obliterating their ranks.

On the left of the advance, the 2/6th Duke of Wellington's Battalion encountered strand after strand of uncut wire. Disaster followed. A wall of machine-gun fire cut both the first and second waves to pieces. Dead and dying British soldiers, many with horrific wounds to the head and abdomen, littered no man's land forward of the German trench. Many more lay dead or lingering on the wire.

The 2/4th Duke of Wellington's Battalion, which was following close behind, did not attempt to withdraw. Instead it, too, was drawn into the carnage. Most survivors from both battalions saw the folly of advancing any further. Realising that they were advancing towards certain death, they attempted to fall back to the railway embankment. A few succeeded. Many did not. Those who did reach the safety of the embankment were quickly herded together by officers and ordered to resume the advance. This time they did not even reach the Lagnicourt-St Martin road before they were greeted by another deadly hail of machine-gun bullets.[39]

Brigadier General R. Taylor (GOC 187th Brigade) had orders to secure a defensive flank but to move no further than OG2. The brigade's advance soon bogged down and stalled. However, on the right, a company from the 2/4th York & Lancaster successfully breached parts of OG1. But on reaching the second line of German trenches, it met solid resistance. On its left, the 2/5th encountered numerous setbacks, not least more uncut wire. The few troops who somehow managed to push into OG1 were confused, unsure which part of the trench they had taken or even where they were. Worse was to follow. Continuing on, they moved into the sunken Lagnicourt-St Martin road — not far from where German machine-gunners and riflemen were waiting. Another massacre followed. The few survivors had no choice but to try to return to the safety of the railway embankment.[40]

When news of these setbacks finally reached Major General Braithwaite at divisional headquarters, he ordered a fresh artillery barrage to support another infantry attack. 'The tanks of No. 12 Company, D Battalion, would on this occasion have been of invaluable service,' Cyril Falls wrote, 'could the infantry have followed them, as the enemy's artillery appeared to be almost smothered by the British counter-battery fire.'[41] But no tanks were available, all either out of action or mechanically broken down. At 9.30 am British troops advanced for a second time, only to meet another tornado of machine-gun fire. The fortunate survivors pulled back to the railway embankment.

Meanwhile, Gellibrand had watched the tragedy unfold from his forward command headquarters. Yet, to his amazement, frequent messages from 185th Brigade, which were authenticated at 62nd Division's headquarters, that British troops were advancing and 'bombing towards the Anzacs', were being 'swallowed' at 2nd Australian Division headquarters.[42] In fact, at 6.26 am, Gellibrand told Smyth that the 185th Brigade's assault was a disaster and advised that the Australians' best course of action was to clear up the mess on the 6th Brigade's left.[43] Smyth, inexplicably, chose to believe what was being fed to him by Braithwaite and ordered the 25th Australian Battalion to lend some support to the British, if and when required.

During what was left of the morning, the British brigades never ceased their attempts to take their objectives. But their efforts were to no avail. The result was simply an increasing toll of dead and wounded lying in no man's land. For instance, the few remaining survivors from the 2/5th Duke of Wellington's and the 2/8th West Yorkshire battalions were attacked by aggressive German bombing squads.[44] Forced to pull back to no man's land, they could only find shelter in the numerous shell holes.

By midday other British troops had been pushed out of the few parts of Bullecourt that they had earlier occupied and forced to withdraw to the railway embankment. The 2/6th West Yorkshires fared the worst; no more than 100 men returned to whatever protection their own line offered. And, having survived all the day's horrors, other British survivors were also back at the railway embankment or taking cover in the sunken road close to the position where, not 12 hours earlier, they had started their advance.[45] By mid-afternoon Braithwaite finally acknowledged that his division had been unsuccessful in its attempt to capture Bullecourt. He also faced the fact that his men were in no condition to renew the attack. Brigadier General de Falbe, at 185th Brigade headquarters, was told to prepare to quickly hand over what was left of his brigade's front to the 22nd Brigade (7th British Division.)

Many reasons contributed to the 62nd Division's failure and the loss of 116 officers and 2860 other ranks. Not least of these was ineffective leadership by a few officers in the field; the attitude and poor discharge of orders by some British troops; faulty handling of the tanks and, of course, incompetent staff work — something Everard Wyrall attempts to gloss over in his *History of the 62nd Division*. Instead, Wyrall seeks to shift culpability to the Australian brigades. 'The failure of the 62nd Division to capture Bullecourt,' he asserts,

> ... was due largely to a fault which certainly cannot be charged to the gallant troops who stormed the village and the Hindenburg Line in the vicinity. Neither could the Divisional Staff, which had laboured to make all the arrangements as complete as possible, be blamed. It was due principally to an error in tactics which had so often failed in the earlier years of the war – notably at Festubert in 1915. The Australian Division on the right of the 62nd Division did not launch its attack side by side with the 2/6th West Yorks, the flanking battalion of the West Riding Division. There was a gap – a fatal gap – in the line of attack between the Colonials and the Yorkshiremen ... Thus some hundreds of yards of the enemy's positions (unfortunately that portion which very strongly defended by machine guns) was left free to enfilade the 2/6th West Yorks as that battalion advanced: which indeed happened. In all justice to the Australian troops it must be noted that they reached their objective, but before they got there the West Yorkshiremen had been cut up and of all those brave fellows who had penetrated the village the greater number had either been killed, wounded or taken prisoner, only a hundred survivors getting back to their own trenches. The inky blackness of the night, which

caused much confusion during the forming-up operations, also contributed to the failure of the assault, many of the troops losing themselves and being entirely ignorant of the direction of the   enemy's trenches.

Gough subsequently entered the debate. He believed that the 62nd Division's failure was due to the fact that 'It was one of the last divisions to come out from England, and although its men were as stout of heart as any, they lacked experience and training, and their attacking bodies lost direction.'[46]

Gellibrand had little doubt that the 62nd Division was largely responsible for its own demise. He too laid much of the blame on Gough for again sending ill-prepared men into the advance. 'It was of course a very bad error to put the 62nd Division in at this time,' Gellibrand wrote later. 'From a number of sources we knew that the Division was in no sense a proud one. An … officer told us to expect nothing from these and contact with officers and men confirmed this apprehension.'[47]

***

At around midday, British observers in their fragile aircraft reported that,

> … the enemy were strongly holding Hindenburg Line West of Bullecourt our men having been driven out by strong counter attack … The situation in Bullecourt was still uncertain but our troops had fallen back from West side of the Village. Six tanks were back at the starting point, but four of them appeared to be derelict between there and Bullecourt. One of the derelicts was burning.[48]

In fact, the attack on Bullecourt had become virtual siege warfare, with the Australians desperately holding onto those parts of the enemy trenches they had earlier captured. Germans troops were just as desperate to win them back. Shortly before noon, enemy troops from the *124th Infantry Regiment*, who had been hiding in underground tunnels around Riencourt, commenced a second 'general' counter-attack, against the Australian-held parts of OG1 and OG2. The insufficiently defended right flank was the primary objective, and the ferocity of the assault forced the few survivors to withdraw.

Some 45 minutes later the *123rd Grenadier Regiment* launched a series of smaller scale counter-attacks from around Queant. Firmly ensconced in their well-prepared positions in OG1 and OG2, the Australians held fast, their accurate, prolonged rifle and machine-gun fire — and the deadly bombing of trench mortar crews — beating back the enemy. Now it was the turn of the Australians to reorganise and attack. However, a heavy German artillery barrage put paid to their plans. Another enemy counter-attack followed, on this occasion, a much stronger 'general' assault that had been planned at corps, rather than divisional headquarters. The Australians, yet again with their backs to the wall, fought off the attack, although both sides incurred heavy losses.[49] Witnessing the valiant effort of his colonial partners, a British airman decided to boost their spirits by dropping a note with the simple words 'well done, Australia!'[50]

Shortly after 1.30 pm two battalions from the 7th Australian Infantry Brigade were ordered into the attack: 'one to assist the British to capture Bullecourt, and come up on Gellibrand's left'. The other (the 26th) was instructed to 'form a flank from the Six Cross Roads to the Hindenburg Line further east, which, it was assumed, the 5th Brigade would have recaptured.'[51] Lieutenant Colonel G.A. Read's 28th Battalion was first into the fight, advancing through Central Road then bombing along both trenches. Major A. Brown was commanding the two companies that took part in the attack against OG1 while Captain A.M. Montgomery was in charge of another two companies moving through OG2. Montgomery's fresher troops soon took parts of the trench before meeting accurate and almost non-stop machine-gun fire coming from the communication trench designated 'F', and more heavy fire from other cleverly concealed positions located behind the Riencourt-Noreuil road. His casualties mounting, Montgomery realised that his men could go no further and ordered them to pull back as far as a barricade previously constructed not far from communication trench 'G'.[52]

After initially encountering some resistance, the two companies commanded by Major Brown were more successful. Bean was loud in his praise of the way the men performed their task:

Covered by a Stokes mortar – which, however, eventually had to be stopped through its erratic shooting – and by four Lewis guns stationed on the bank of Central Road, the Western Australians advanced, seizing two bays of the trench at each rush. The corps observer telephoning to corps headquarters from the spur beyond Noreuil, reported that he could see bombers working in the open, rushing with great spirit along the parapet. After the attack had progressed 100 yards, an additional Lewis gun was placed out in shell-hole south of OG1, to cover the further advance. The Germans were quickly driven as far as cross-trench "F," and the mouth of this was next captured and barricaded; but beyond that point the enemy's resistance stiffened.[53]

However, by mid-afternoon Brown's men, desperately short of ammunition and grenades, were taking casualties at a rate they were unable to sustain. Around 4.00 pm the Germans attacked in even larger numbers, forcing Brown and his men to withdraw to Central Road. Brown called for one more supreme effort. Encouraged by a fresh supply of bombs and ammunition, the troops recommenced the attack. By 6.00 pm they had fought their way into the trenches closest to the Riencourt-Noreuil road.[54]

However, as on previous occasions, the Germans regrouped. Shortly before 7.00 pm they counter-attacked the parts of the trench held by Brown and his men. For almost 60 minutes the battle ebbed and flowed, with the German infantry breaking into the trench before fierce hand-to-hand fighting and bombing duels forced them to again withdraw. But the few remaining Australians were exhausted and, without reinforcements and nursing a rapidly diminishing supply of ammunition, they could not hold on for much longer. Brown had little option but to consider another withdrawal. Soon after 8.15 pm, they pulled out.[55]

With the onset of darkness, the ever-dwindling number of Australians (some 300 men, most of whom had been engaged in heavy fighting for much of the day) was precariously holding just 500 yards of German trenches. They were weary, disorganised and, in some instances, leaderless, their officers and NCOs having been the targets of enemy snipers and machine-gunners. Private Percival Luke later wrote that 'German machine gun fire is deadly. Our artillery goes all day … Our Brigade are reinforced but [has] made little progress … Engineers and pioneers stand to and assist … Our lines hold well … [but I] have little sleep.'[56] However, with dusk approaching, Smyth ordered that those captured parts of OG1 and OG2 be held at all costs. And Gellibrand made one further request, instructing his men to bomb their way down OG2, through to the communication trench 'L'.[57]

***

During the late afternoon Smyth had been informed that, due to heavy casualties, the 62nd British Division would be withdrawn immediately. The 7th British Division was already taking over. As early as 6.30 pm, before they had time to settle in, two of the fresh battalions from the 22nd Infantry Brigade were ordered to renew the attack on Bullecourt before pushing on to the next objective.

Smyth told Gellibrand to prepare those men just recently out of the line to assist the British. Yet again, Gellibrand could not believe what he was hearing. How could his exhausted troops be expected to comply with such an order? Gellibrand confronted

Smyth. After an often heated discussion, Smyth was persuaded of
the futility of sending tired men into battle. Despite this he was
keen for them to resume the attack after a rest and a good meal.
The British were subsequently informed that their attack had been
postponed until 10.30 pm. Smyth added that his rested Australians
would 'cooperate with the 7th British Division's attack, but would be
relieved in OG2 by two battalions of the 1st Brigade [1st Australian
Division] which, with the 5th Brigade, would advance to the second
objective when the 7th Division did so.'[58]

But, not for the first time, Smyth's plans were put on hold due
to enemy counter-attacks which forced much of the 28th Battalion
(which by now was primarily assisting the British) to withdraw. Soon
after, enemy artillery began firing on Australian positions close to the
railway embankment. Counter-battery fire from Australian guns was
ineffective — some shells falling well short of their designated target,
others falling far too close to other Australians clinging to parts of
OG2, not far from where the trench joined Diagonal Road. And,
as a 6th Brigade report added, 'The Australian position had become
critical with only a few sections from the 23rd and 24th battalions
holding on in parts of OG1 and OG2.'[59]

Gellibrand's immediate concern was a possible German 'pincer
movement' that could wipe out those troops. Mustering all the
available men and some of his own headquarters staff, Gellibrand
ordered them to take up positions along the railway embankment,
which was to be the main line of defence if the enemy decided to
push their attack further. Gellibrand's courage was on show for all to
see as he encouraged his men, moving along 'the embankment with
a rifle'.[60] The Germans, however, had no intention of attacking any
of the Australian positions. For the moment they invested all their
effort in counter-attacking OG1 and OG2 while strengthening their
defences in and around Bullecourt.

Sentries from the 8th Battalion in the western part of OG1 after capturing part of the Hindenburg Line in the fight for Bullecourt. Lieutenant W.D. Joynt is standing closest to the camera (AWM E00439).

Meanwhile Birdwood had decided that Gellibrand's 6th Brigade had done enough and had already ordered its relief by the 1st Brigade. Major General Walker was also told to prepare his 2nd and 3rd brigades to take over the other positions still being held by the 2nd Division. Gellibrand, however, remained behind until shortly before midnight on 4 May to advise Lieutenant Colonel Iven Mackay (the 1st Brigade's acting commander) on the most urgent task — to strengthen the Australians' hold on OG1 and OG2 close to Central Road.

By this time a large number of severely wounded Australian soldiers lay in OG1 and OG2 and also in no man's land. With another German counter-attack likely, all available troops were sent to man the front line and none could be spared to locate and rescue the wounded. Since late afternoon only those men who were slightly wounded — those who did not need help from stretcher-bearers — had been able to return safely to the Australian line. The cries of anguish coming from the battlefield were distressing for their comrades now preparing for a likely enemy attack.

Soldiers from the 6th Brigade bring one of their field kitchens into position in the Noreuil Valley near Bullecourt during the heavy fighting close to the village on 3–4 May 1917. The food may not have been nutritious, but it kept the troops sustained during combat (AWM E00437).

Captain Stanley Savige (24th Battalion) recalled a soldier, little more than a boy, with an abdomen wound so bad that he was clutching his entrails. Instead of troubling his mates, and despite being in terrible pain, the young man remained outwardly calm. Although unable to move, he was smoking a cigarette when Savige moved past him, telling him, 'Stick it out lad.' 'Don't worry about me, sir,' was the reply, 'but give the bastards hell!' Soon afterwards, the young soldier ended his suffering by shooting himself.[61] Savige subsequently wrote of the fierce fighting that his battalion endured throughout that awful day and night. 'Men fought until they dropped,' he recalled, and 'success rested on the knowledge that the small isolated groups many without leaders would fight on … Time seemed to be lost. We appeared to have reached an eternity of day without night. On that day every man was a hero.'[62]

***

At around 10.30 pm, two battalions from the 22nd British Brigade renewed the attack on Bullecourt — this time launching their assault in 'two stages'.[63] Their first objective was part of what was known as 'Tower Trench', which ran in a south-easterly direction around the southern extremities of the village; they would then push on and take 'Bullecourt by dawn tomorrow'.[64] Having taken the ruined village, they were then expected to move against their final objective — 'Bovis Trench', held by battle-hardened troops from the German *120th Infantry Regiment*, some 250 yards north of the village.[65]

Not only was the idea of two infantry battalions (around 1500 men) successfully assaulting and capturing 'Bovis' and 'Tower Trench', two of the best defensive positions on the Hindenburg Line, and advancing against what remained of Bullecourt, fanciful in the extreme, but the plans failed to take into account the troops' lack of preparedness and unfamiliarity with the terrain in that part of the front. In fact, during the day, the Germans had sent more troops into the village to reinforce the already strong defensive lines and ordered additional machine-gun nests and mortars placed in the most tactically significant positions around 'Bovis' and 'Tower Trench'.

The Germans were certainly prepared. Intelligence reports had highlighted the further build-up of British troops during the evening, indicating that another attack was inevitable. As the British moved forward, relentless machine-gun fire opened up from the forward trench and flanks, cutting the first waves to pieces. The survivors pressed on only to find the wire still only partially cut. Nonetheless, both battalions, against the odds, courageously fought their way into 'Tower Trench'. Following non-stop and often ruthless fighting, the British were successful, taking almost 50 prisoners before commencing the move towards what remained of Bullecourt.

Not unsurprisingly, that part of the attack soon encountered major obstacles. Parts of the 2nd Battalion Honorary Artillery Company fought its way into the village — several men were even reported to have made the second objective, 'Bovis Trench'. But the Germans soon responded. For a time, the British held out against a strong and fearsome counter-attack. However, with casualties mounting, the few surviving British soldiers were inevitably forced to withdraw. The 1st Battalion, Royal Welsh Fusiliers, was faring even worse, with a wide gap opening as the men attempted to form a defensive flank. Seizing their opportunity, enemy troops quickly mounted an attack. By 2.30 am the few surviving Welsh Fusiliers, unable to hold on, had withdrawn to their 'original line'.[66]

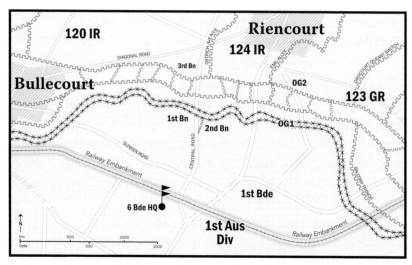

Situation map of area around Bullecourt on 4 May 1917 showing the numerous communication trenches that made the Australians' objective resemble a ladder, while highlighting the problems they experienced fending off German counter-attacks.

***

Despite the failure of the two British battalions, Major General Walker was told that, shortly before dawn on 4 May, other British units were to broaden the attack while fresh troops from his 1st Australian Brigade would assist by extending their flanks and pockets of resistance. The Germans, however, were not only preparing for another British/Australian attack, they were already planning a counter-attack of their own.

Not long after midnight, the 1st Australian Brigade had begun to take over those positions held by the 6th. But the men who moved into the trenches were in for a shock. The numbers of dead and badly wounded were so thick in places that the incoming troops had to scramble over their bodies. Bean wrote of the respect of the officers and men for what the dead had achieved:

> An officer of the 2nd Battalion records that his incoming troops, forced to trample on the dead crowded in those narrow trenches, were at great pains during that day to avoid stepping on any whose sleeve carried the red and white patch of the 24th Battalion. "We understood that it was they who took this position," he says simply.[67]

Before the last remaining troops of the 23rd Battalion could withdraw, the Germans launched their fourth 'general' counter-attack. Quickly gathering their weapons, they successfully helped fight off the enemy, killing around 30 and taking one prisoner. As Cyril Falls wrote, 'Then and then only did the remnants of the 6th Brigade file out, having added one of the most glorious pages to the annals of Australian arms.'[68]

Bean was also proud of what had been accomplished. He noted that 'tired, unkempt, reduced in numbers but bursting with pride the 6th Brigade came out. Its men looked for no recognition of their victory, and none awaited them.' In fact, with the exception of the 1st Canadian Brigade, the 6th Australian Brigade had accomplished the only triumph along the 'whole sixteen miles of battle-front'. Bean also had unequivocal praise for Gellibrand, although he tended to overstate the situation by suggesting that the brigade's 'achievement on this day had few parallels in the history of the AIF … The Landing [at Gallipoli,] the capture of Lone Pine, and the holding of the head of Monash Valley by the 4th Brigade are the achievements most nearly analogous to it.'[69]

Field Marshal Haig was also informed of what the 2nd Division — and the 6th Brigade in particular — had accomplished. 'The capture of the Hindenburg Line East of Bullecourt,' he told Birdwood,

… and the gallant manner in which it has been held by the 2nd Australian Division and the troops associated with it under General Smyth's command against such constant and desperate efforts to retake it, will rank high among the great deeds of war, and are helping very appreciably in wearing out the enemy. The fine initiative shown by all Commanders down to the lowest is admirable.[70]

Aerial view of Bullecourt after it was shelled by Australian artillery during the second attack. Note the destroyed buildings and trench lines. The photograph was taken on or about 5 May 1917 (AWM A01100).

Birdwood, however, knew that the 2nd Division was totally spent. The division was desperate to leave the fighting and rest while it received its complement of reinforcements and was refitted. Not long after, he advised Gough that those 'at present in the line will not be in physical condition to retain the ground won.' Gough agreed. But, with limited men and equipment under his command, he had little choice but to inform Major General Talbot Hobbs to prepare his 5th Australian Division for an imminent move to the Bullecourt front.[71]

***

Regardless of the plaudits, of the 2897 men from the 6th Brigade who went into battle, only 1348 returned. Several Australians again laid the blame squarely on the British. While elements of the criticism appear warranted, the performance of the 5th Australian Brigade and Brigadier General Smith in particular, was certainly less than satisfactory. Soon after the withdrawal, a number of explanations were advanced as to why the 5th's push had faltered, including that some parts of the brigade's 'jump-off tape had been wrongly inclined' and that there had been too few experienced officers leading the assault.[72] But it is Smith who must accept the bulk of the criticism, particularly for his decision prior to the attack that he needed a nucleus of veteran officers to remain behind so as to rebuild the brigade (once the battle had claimed its inevitable toll of casualties) and for sending too few battle-experienced officers to lead the men. Whatever the reason, the 5th Australian Brigade lost a significant number of officers and men. Among the 1523 reported casualties were 60 officers.[73] Incompetent leadership at brigade level through to uncertainty in the field on the part of several junior officers led to the dismal performance that Bean described when he wrote that 'the 5th Brigade had not taken its first objective; met by a deadly cross machine gun fire at the entanglement, it had hesitated, thus missing its chance of getting in. A second effort made soon after, without barrage, proved hopeless. A handful of men on the flank of the 6th Brigade had seized a few bays of the Hindenburg trenches there', although they were unable to hold on.[74]

The most compelling explanation as to why the 5th Australian Brigade failed appears to have been lost to history. Well before the assault, Lieutenant John Wright (the 17th Battalion's Lewis, Intelligence and Scout Officer) had told headquarters staff that the 'limit of the attack was badly chosen, the 5th [Brigade] being a skyline target for enfilade machine-gun fire from the right flank, i.e. from the

German trench [Balcony] which swung towards Queant ... I was told to shut up, that artillery would keep his nest of machine guns quiet.' Artillery officers cannot be wholly blamed for not putting down a sufficiently strong barrage against German machine-guns around Queant. It was the responsibility of corps and divisional headquarters staff, particularly Smyth, Birdwood and White. They should have heeded the advice of intelligence officers such as Wright that the 'the field of fire [coming from around Queant] was perfect, the kind of thing a Machine Gunner dreams about.' And, as Wright concluded, 'It was just another example of underestimating the enemy. The effect of his fire in the dark must have been demoralising.'[75] When added to the litany of other blunders (many even before the attack commenced), the 5th Brigade stood little chance of success.

***

At 3.45 am on 4 May, the 2nd Battalion, Royal Warwickshires, and 20th Manchester (Pals) Battalion commenced an advance to try to gain the so-far illusive — but, crucial — objective of Bullecourt. The British had to capture Bullecourt if the Australians were to have any chance of holding on to their gains. However, A.P. Burke, an English soldier with the Manchesters, was pessimistic, writing that 'our brigade would attack and try and take the village which a full division and 8 tanks failed to do.'[76]

Shortly before the scheduled time for the advance, Gellibrand was informed that the 1st and 3rd battalions — which had relieved his 6th Brigade — were also expected to provide support to the left of the British attack 'by bombing [westward] along OG1 and OG2.'[77] The 2nd and 4th battalions were to 'make their way up the Central Road and bomb their way eastward', to capture what the 5th Brigade had failed to do the previous day.[78]

The 2nd Australian Pioneer Battalion had provided considerable assistance to the infantry, making their task somewhat more achievable. Throughout the previous day and into the evening the sappers had laboured hard, taking numerous casualties, to build a communication trench of their own, which they appropriately named 'Pioneer Avenue'. 'Tonight we are going out again consolidating our advance position,' Sapper Ernest Greenhill wrote,

> … and making a strong point so that we can take Bullecourt, a very strong salient. We got a rough time of it going out, Fritz was putting all his big H.E. [high explosive] into our communications trench but no one got wounded. We got orders to get out and go over open country till we struck the railway embankment … We got on to our job [and] we had just started when Fritz opened up and shelled us off the job. We were ordered to look for cover, three of our chaps wounded. After Fritz eased off we went back on to the job again but he knew we were there and started again … After a very exciting time we got out of danger zone. My word I was lucky to escape … there was two Tommy Royal Engineers killed about twenty yards from where I was working.[79]

An Australian stretcher-bearer, Private E.C. Munro, recalled passing 'a line of pioneers who said they had dug a sap nearly up to Fritz's line.'[80]

In the early hours of 4 May, the 1st and 3rd battalions began moving through 'Pioneer Avenue' before bombing their way further westward along OG1 and OG2, capturing almost another 150 yards of German trenches, while assisting the two British battalions moving against Bullecourt. However, a report noted that, at 4.30 am, enemy troops again 'attacked on right and left of OG2 for half an hour'. After successfully fighting off the attack, the Australians counted 30 dead Germans and took one prisoner.[81] More deadly bombing duels and bayonet fighting followed as they fought their way past German defences around Central Road not far from where OG2 linked up with Diagonal Road, and almost 200 yards closer to Bullecourt, from where they attempted to establish contact with one of the British battalions 'in a communication trench which joined the fire trenches'.[82]

But much had already gone wrong as both British battalions were hit by another intense enemy bombardment as they left their jumping-off point, inflicting heavy casualties. An Australian officer, Lieutenant C.E. McCardel, recalled that enemy guns 'put up a barrage in front of us at 0310 … Fritz was [reportedly] going to attack us at 0800 but owing to the stunt on the left it did not eventuate.'[83] At precisely 3.45 am the British moved forward. Some 15 minutes later Private Burke was waiting, alongside the other Manchesters, for the order to advance when:

> … news came thro' that so and so and so were fighting a terrific hand-to-hand   battle and were slowly retiring. One battalion took their objective four times –   each time being bombed out, at last they had to retire having run short of bombs. Whilst we were waiting our time to go over, the wounded were coming down in dozens and we were under the severest bombardment I have ever known Fritz to send over. We knew it was certain death for all of us – orders are orders in the army and we have to obey them. Had we been lucky enough to take our objective we certainly could not have held it and having no one behind us – well you can guess the result. At 4.00a.m. we advanced but owing to other battalions retiring (coming towards us we were hopeless and could not get thro' his barrage) … then we had to line up, dig ourselves in and prepare for his counter attack … Daylight was rapidly approaching so it was a case of having to get away whilst it was dark so we had orders to go back to the original trench we started off from. Oh we had terrible casualties … Our company went in 104 strong came out 44.[84]

Somewhat surprisingly, considering the few men left in the badly mauled battalions, British troops initially performed well, albeit with some assistance from the Australians.[85]

The Royal Warwickshires managed to gain part of OG1 before boldly fighting their way into OG2 on the outskirts of the village. But, as a subsequent report noted, they were unable to 'occupy this trench … which is full of both Boche and our dead … because they are sniped from the houses.'[86] The Germans soon counter-attacked, forcing the few survivors to pull back. However, another 50 British soldiers and three officers held the enemy at bay in the part of 'Tower Trench' where it intersected with Longatte road. A company of 20th Manchesters had also fought its way into the south-eastern fringe of the village.[87]

At around midday a British reconnaissance team finally shed some light on the situation in Bullecourt. Despite not reaching OG1, almost 80 Welsh Fusiliers (from the first attack) were discovered still holding out close to the part of the German front known as 'The Crucifix' while an even smaller number of Royal Warwickshires were struggling to maintain their position near Longatte road. The nearby part of OG1 was found to be deserted apart from countless dead British and Germans. Meanwhile, survivors from the British battalions who had managed to scramble back to their line near Ecoust had assembled for roll call to ascertain how many of their comrades had been killed, wounded or were missing.

The 22nd British Brigade was clearly 'in no condition to repeat the attack'. Yet, in the late afternoon, the 2nd Battalion, Royal Warwickshires, and 1st Battalion, Royal Welsh Fusiliers, were ordered to do exactly that. Moving forward, the men were greeted by intense machine-gun and small arms fire from enemy strongpoints in and around Bullecourt, forcing the few fortunate survivors to mount a hasty retreat.[88] Throughout the day the 22nd British Brigade made other attempts, attacking German defences in front of Bullecourt. Without exception, all were forced back with no appreciable gains. By day's end the 22nd Brigade had lost 32 officers and 747 soldiers killed, wounded or missing.[89] Survivors were ordered out of the line. Senior British officers, from the safety of their headquarters well behind the front, now finally understood that the Germans had established even more formidable defensive positions around the village and would not relinquish their prize without a fight.

***

By early morning on 4 May the 1st Australian Brigade had finally occupied its positions. However, the 1st and 3rd battalions, to the left of Central Road, and the 2nd and 4th battalions on the right, remained temporarily under the command of Brigadier General Gellibrand. During the morning Gellibrand ordered more bombing raids by the 1st and 3rd battalions along both lines of enemy trenches. Assisted by mortars from the 6th Australian Brigade, the fresh troops fought ferociously before reaching another of the communication trenches, designated 'L', some 700 yards from Central Road. Aware that another counter-attack was inevitable, the officers ordered their men to construct strong fortifications in and around the trench. Lieutenant G.H. Leslie (3rd Battalion) wrote:

> To reach the captured German lines where the hardest fighting was going on we   had to travel along a communication trench about 1,000 yards long which was   being constantly shelled. From where we entered it I could see its whole length   and the continuous bursting of 5.9" shells close to and sometimes in the trench   caused many casualties and there was a continuous call for stretcher bearers. I've since wondered whether it was sheer courage or just a plain acceptance of fate that made us walk along that 1,000 yards.[90]

Throughout what remained of the morning, and into the afternoon, the Australians continued their bombing raids down OG1 and OG2. By early afternoon some of the men had reached as far as that part of OG2 which intersected with the Cross Roads. Others had progressed a few hundred yards further along OG1 before constructing blockades against German counter-attacks and establishing 'a flank along communication trench between these points'.[91] More German troops attacked and captured the same parts of OG1 and OG2. The severity of the fighting was evident in the numbers of Australian and German dead, by now three or four deep in the trenches. Indeed, the battle had developed a pattern all of its own — Australian troops would capture part of the enemy trench; German troops would regroup, calling in reinforcements and artillery, and counter-attack. The Australians would request artillery support and the battle would unfold all over again.[92]

But not everything went according to plan. For instance, a barrage was ordered to assist an attack, but the gunners had to wait for a resupply of shells, forcing the infantry advance to be delayed almost 75 minutes. When that attack commenced, it served little or no purpose, as it had been planned to assist a British attack further to the left. At around 2.50 pm, Australian infantry began moving east along OG1 and OG2 before becoming involved in ferocious hand-to-hand combat with some *Wurttembergers*. Not for the first time, confusion reigned among Australian troops. In the small confine of the trenches, littered with the dead and wounded of both sides, it was difficult to distinguish friend from foe. Fighting became more bloody and desperate. Despite massive casualties, the Australians went on to capture — or recapture — a further several hundred yards of enemy trenches, as far as communication trench 'G'.

Not surprisingly, German troops were quick to regroup and, with fresh reinforcements recently lorried into Bullecourt, counter-attacked. Forced to pull back again, Australian officers called in another artillery barrage before once more resuming the attack, bombing their way back down both lines of enemy trenches. The Germans responded with their own grenades. What followed was another fierce bombing duel. Although the British Mills grenade was more deadly and accurate in close-quarter fighting, the German stick grenade had the advantage of a longer range. Too few Australians had been equipped with rifle grenades, which would at least have allowed them to fight on more even terms.

By late afternoon a reserve company from the 4th Battalion had come to the rescue, moving quickly through the enemy trenches. Along with a few remaining groups of Australians, they demonstrated great tenacity, continuing a bombing duel while capturing further parts of the enemy's trench. By the end of the day the Australians were in a position slightly east of communication trench 'F'. Experience told them that the Germans would not surrender that part of the trench lightly. With little time to prepare for the expected counter-attack, the men repaired barricades and ensured that their reasonably good supply of ammunition and bombs was close at hand. Officers ordered their men to ready themselves and form a strong defensive flank.[93]

German artillery shells searching for Australian batteries in Noreuil Valley on 5 May 1917, two days after the Australians renewed their attack on Bullecourt (AWM E00515).

Meanwhile, enemy artillery continued pounding known Australian positions in OG1 and OG2. Lieutenant Albert Orchard wrote that his men were 'Heavily shelled by hun … Hottest time I ever had.'[94] Two smaller scale counter-attacks were designed to test the resolve of the Australians and determine their strength. Both were easily repulsed with the Germans suffering heavy losses. The fifth 'general' counter-attack soon followed at 6.00 pm. Fresh German infantry moving through 'Ostrich Alley' were halted by sections of the 1st Australian Battalion, still holding out in OG2 as far as communication trench 'L'. Other Germans, moving down Diagonal Road close to the same cross trench, had more success against sections from the 3rd Battalion, retaking OG2 to the point where it met communication trench 'K'.

At approximately 9.00 pm, another 'general' counter-attack, this time down 'Ostrich Alley', directed against the left flank of the 1st Battalion, was kept at bay by a deadly hail of machine-gun and small arms fire. The Australians were able to hold their position in OG1 as far as communication trench 'L'. However another enemy attack, through Diagonal Road (near the same communication trench) was directed against the right flank of the exhausted 3rd Battalion. Australian officers called in artillery support. But the fresher German troops were relentless and succeeded in retaking more of OG2 as far as communication trench 'K'. By now Australians and Germans alike were thoroughly exhausted. Rest proved elusive, however, as both sides served up prolonged artillery barrages throughout the night.[95]

***

Aerial view of Bullecourt showing further damage, 5 May 1917 (AWM J00277).

By early morning on 5 May, the situation along the entire front had become clearer. Fatigued and depleted Australian battalions were in desperate need of relief. The 1st Australian Brigade was still holding positions on the left of Central Road. Brigadier General Gellibrand was also thoroughly spent, having had little sleep for close to 48 hours, and was finally relieved by Lieutenant Colonel Iven Mackay, the temporary commander of the 1st Australian Infantry Brigade. Likewise, the 3rd Australian Brigade was also led by a temporary commander (Lieutenant Colonel L.M. Mullen). Mullen's troops were dispersed to the right of Central Road, the 11th Battalion holding positions in OG1, adjacent to the road while, alongside on the right flank in OG2, was the 12th Battalion.

An Australian soldier sleeping in his trench shelter in the second line of trenches (OG2) near Riencourt during the second attack on Bullecourt. Note his pack and various tools positioned close to the opening of the shelter (AWM E00455).

Attack and counter-attack continued along the entire front throughout the morning, until Australian troops had become so exhausted that they were incapable of further fighting. Compounding their situation, as Lieutenant Orchard noted, German 'snipers [were] active with machine guns and rifles'.[96] Instead of pushing on with the advance, Major P.S. Woodforde (commanding officer of the 1st Battalion) decided it was time to consolidate his men's gains. The advance would continue only when his depleted battalion could be reinforced. But the Germans had no intention of halting their counter-attacks. At 10.30 am they again bombed along OG1, checked only by determined Australians with rifle grenades, before withdrawing. Then came another German barrage followed, at 1.00 pm, by a bombing raid further down OG1. Fortunately, only minutes earlier, a reserve company from the 1st Battalion had moved up. After 10 minutes of ferocious fighting, the Germans were again forced to withdraw.[97]

The 2nd Battalion fared little better. Private B. Harris from C Company wrote:

At 12.30 the next morning 5th May, we moved up the trench we had dug to   support the 2nd Division. We remained in this trench until midday on 5th when we moved into the German line. We bombed along this trench using rifle grenades and when our supply of these were exhausted, had taken some eighty yards of trench. At this point it was decided to erect a bomb-stop across the trench and while this was being done, a Lewis gun was posted on the near bank of the trench ... Almost immediately the Germans commenced a counter attack, as we were out of rifle grenades, they succeeded in driving us back about fifty yards. However, rifle grenades again being supplied, we once more drove the enemy back. He made several attempts to dislodge us, once a number appeared in No Man's Land and by the signs they were making it was believed that they wished to surrender. We waved them in but when they arrived at a point about 20 yards from our trench they dropped into shell-holes and gave us a plastering with potato-mashers (stick bombs). Despite this, they did not succeed in entering the trench although our numbers had been greatly reduced by casualties. When this attack failed, our attention was directed to the environs of Queant. Here a considerable number collected and commenced moving towards us. They did not, however, get very far as they presented an excellent machine gun target. After sunset the battle quietened down which was just as well for us, as we had only about one fifth of our original number. About midnight the few of us who had survived were relieved by the 12th Battalion.[98]

However, more Australians were killed or wounded, including another fine young officer, Lieutenant Ernest Harris of the 3rd Machine Gun Company, who was fatally wounded by an Australian artillery barrage while trying to rescue one of his own men.[99] Corporal W.H. Anderson wrote later that a platoon, out on a bombing raid, encountered like-minded enemy troops moving towards them 'when a shell came over and killed eight and wounded two.'[100]

Meanwhile Birdwood and his staff were searching for some means to assist the 3rd Australian Brigade to expand its line further to the east. Inexplicably, they devised a hare-brained scheme that the 11th and 12th battalions should swap their positions in OG1 and OG2 to allow the 11th to lead another attack. But two powerful German artillery bombardments, which caused massive casualties, left the 3rd Brigade so short of men that the attack was inconceivable.

The same night, enemy artillery continued its unrelenting bombardment, which went on well into the next morning. Not only were Australian positions in OG1 and OG2 blown to pieces, but the barrage also targeted 'Pioneer Trench' and Australians waiting close to the railway embankment. Most had seen enough of the apparently ceaseless barrage. 'Shells landing everywhere,' wrote Private W.H. McKenzie,

One landed right in the sap we were walking through killing an officer and wounding several men. It was something awful to hear the cries of the wounded in the dark. The sap being so narrow that only one man at a time could pass along so we had to walk over dead and wounded ... We put in three days and nights of the most awful bombardment ever I wish to see or hear, in fact the old hands say it was the worst they have had since the war began.[101]

The British division was suffering through the same experience. 'For thirty hours we stayed in the bottom of the trenches awaiting our end,' Private Walter King wrote, 'Officers and men were continually going out with shell shock ... I shall never forget the ghastly sights of it all, and the stench of the dead was horrible ... We have had great praise [as] ... we held the line against it all. Fritz came over in massed formation and got a terrible thrashing, leaving the dead four deep.'[102] Charles Bean agreed that the enemy artillery fire, which commenced on 5 May and continued for 'some eighteen hours ... [was] intense methodical shelling – the only bombardment ever justifiably described by the Australians who suffered it as "perhaps worse than Pozieres"' the previous year.[103]

***

'Still fearful fighting raging around Bullecourt, and our men holding their ground', Captain N.A. Nicolson confided to his diary on 6 May.[104] In fact, by dawn German officers were so confident that their artillery had virtually obliterated the Australian positions that they ordered another 'general' counter-attack — their sixth and most vigorous — against what was left of the 1st Australian Brigade still gamely holding the trenches to the west of Central Road and the 3rd Australian Brigade, to the east of Central Road.[105]

That the 1st Brigade was able to hold the enemy at bay was due in no small part to an artillery barrage which had previously been planned to assist the cancelled infantry attack. But the 3rd Brigade was not so fortunate. Elite German infantry from the *3rd Guards Division* using that most ghastly of weapons, *flammenwerfers* (flamethrowers), made extensive gains, forcing the 11th and 12th battalions back as far as Central Road. 'When the Germans were about forty yards away,' Sergeant Pat Kinchington recalled,

I saw a fellow shoot a jet of flame into the bank. It was the first *flammenwerfer* I had seen. I fired and shot the carrier through the belly; my bullet went through the *flammenwerfer* can, and it caught fire at the back. You could hardly see for   smoke. There was a hole in the road; the man fell into it, and about a dozen men   on top of him – they all appeared to catch fire.[106]

For many Australian soldiers the merciless squeal of the *flammenwerfer*s, followed by a garish crimson light that lit up the darkness, as well as the persistent artillery barrage that tore men's bodies to pieces was something akin to Dante's Inferno and was much more than most could stomach.

Some 200 survivors from the 11th and 12th battalions hastily commenced a disorderly withdrawal. Other Australians on the opposite side of Central Road, however, encouraged them to stay put. Lieutenant Tom Richards (1st Battalion) was at the fore, yelling, '"What will Australia think when she knows you deserted your posts and let your brother soldiers down?" That shifted some back to their trench and I saw Lieutenant Burton in the end with his revolver drawn and preventing the men from going further back.'[107]

Another of Richards' men, Corporal George Howell, demonstrated what was required. Noticing that the 1st Battalion was likely to be outflanked by another party of enemy troops, he assembled all the men he could find, then jumped onto the parapet of OG1 where he bombed his way along the trench until severely wounded.[108] This was exactly the tonic that the others needed; taking their cue from Howell, they launched a vigorous attack while disabling another *flammenwerfer* and killing its crew. The Germans became disoriented, withdrawing to their starting positions.[109] For his valour, Howell was awarded the Victoria Cross, the citation reading:

Seeing a party of the enemy were likely to outflank his Battalion, Cpl Howell, on his own initiative, single-handed and exposed to heavy bomb and rifle fire, climbed on to the top of the parapet and proceeded to bomb the enemy, pressing   them back along the trench. Having exhausted his stock of bombs, he continued to attack the enemy with his bayonet. He was then severely wounded. The prompt action and gallant conduct of this NCO in the face of superior numbers was witnessed by the whole Battalion and greatly inspired them on the subsequent successful counter attack.[110]

Portrait of Corporal George 'Snowy' Howell, VC, MM, 1st Battalion. Howell was awarded the Victoria Cross for 'conspicuous bravery' on 6 May 1917. Just one month previously he had been awarded the Military Medal for 'courage and devotion to duty while leading a rifle bombing section' during the battalion's capture of Demicourt (AWM J03080A).

***

One week before the attack, Lieutenant Richards had been confident all would go well. 'Fritz will get a hot time', he wrote. But, following the *flammenwerfer* incident, and all that had preceded it, Richards had become a broken man. 'It was a lovely sport shooting Germans with both revolver and rifle, as well as bombing them down in their dugout,' he wrote later,

> ... I think it is the 6th May at this moment ... We have been right into the gaping   jaws of Hell and for three whole days simply engaged the Germans in bombing   attacks and defences, and waited until the Hun artillery, or rather until the devil   closed his jaws and crushed us. The devil in fact did close his jaws heavy and   often ... but when the 1st Battalion got into touch with Fritz he got hell from our   rifle and hand bombs also from our snipers. But alas! there were blunders made by the 3rd and 11th and 12th Battalions that were shocking; they got away from the enemy ... like cattle stampeding.[111]

Another officer from the 3rd Battalion may not have wholeheartedly agreed with Richards' sentiment. Yet he echoed the same thoughts on the horrific conditions. Lieutenant G.H. Leslie wrote that 'Bullecourt was for us 3 days of heavy shellfire, much bombing and many German counter attacks day and night.' Worse was the number of casualties. Leslie added that 'our Battalion had lost 64 killed and 245 wounded, a total of 309 out of our starting strength of 570.'[112]

Charles Bean provided possibly the best summary of what Bullecourt meant to friend and foe alike, when he wrote that,

> ... the conditions in Bullecourt were extraordinary difficult, approximating to those at Mouquet Farm in the First Battle of the Somme. The place had been so battered that the trenches were barely recognisable, and the German garrison relied entirely on the deep dugouts. The general positions of these, covered as they now were with heaps of debris, were difficult to find even for the German guides who nightly led up the reliefs or the carrying parties with food and ammunition. The food

supply was irregular and the inmates of the dugouts lived partly on rations found in the haversacks of the British dead.

But, as Bean added, the Germans held one decisive advantage over Australian and British troops in that they

... no longer manned their trenches by day or night, but posted sentries above the dugouts while practically the whole garrison remained below. Even in the crucial hours of dawn they stood to arms not in the trench, but at the stairs of the dugouts, ready to rush from them upon the appearance of an attack. They thus escaped much of the loss and strain of the bombardments, and being troops of high morale, issued promptly to meet the attacking British [and Australians] ... Very soon the intruders would find the fire of machine-guns and trench-mortars coming from several enemy nests in the crater-field.[113]

***

A motor car and a wagon stand on the dirt Vaulx-Noreuil road where an Australian advanced dressing station has been set up to receive casualties from the fighting around Bullecourt on 6 May 1917. A soldier wearing a helmet (right) sits besides some rolled-up blankets and ground sheets. In the distance (centre left) smoke rises from German artillery shells exploding along the road from Noreuil as horse-drawn ambulance wagons travel along the road bringing casualties from the front (AWM P02321.064).

Senior Australian officers (at brigade and divisional headquarters) understood that their troops had done far more than what had been asked of them. Now, exhausted and incapable of advancing, the Australian line needed to be relieved. But, before this could occur, the men were required to assist a group of engineers under the command of Lieutenant F.F. Scarr, who had been ordered to block off parts of both trenches and lay charges slightly forward of communication trench 'F'. After blocking off parts of OG1, the sappers moved onto OG2. Spotted by enemy snipers, Scarr and a number of his men were killed.[114] Despite their losses, and the fact that the British had still not taken Bullecourt, by 6 May the Australians had advanced their hold on the Hindenburg Line to a front of almost 600 yards.[115]

During the afternoon, the Australian battalions were finally relieved (the 2nd and 4th taking over the positions held by the 3rd and 1st battalions) while the 9th Battalion (3rd Brigade) was placed at Lieutenant Colonel Mackay's disposal. Soon after dusk, Mackay ordered that it move up 'to the left of his line in order that a completely fresh unit should carry out, in concert with the 7th Division the fresh attack now in preparation.'[116]

***

After four days of solid fighting, the attack on Bullecourt, which was originally planned to assist the right flank of the Third Army, now resembled a desperate siege. Ground was being contested yard by dreadful yard. Yet, by 6 May, Haig was convinced not only that Nivelle's offensive had failed, but also that the British attack at Arras had come to nought.

Why continue to attack Bullecourt? And who was to blame for this latest fiasco? The first question was purely political. With his Flanders offensive fast approaching, Haig needed the French to continue their attacks in the south, if for no other reason than to keep German divisions away from Belgium. Haig was convinced that 'if the French do not act vigorously, the enemy will be free to transfer his reserves to oppose our attack in the north.'[117] But the French would only agree to Haig's plan if they were assured that the British were keeping their end of the bargain. British troops had to continue their attacks if only to divert German divisions from the south. Bullecourt was Haig's compromise — no more than a token show. But Bullecourt was also Gough's show. The egotistical Gough needed a victory, simply to show Haig and his two competitors for the Ypres offensive (Plumer and Rawlinson) that he was the right man for the job.

As for who should be held accountable, while Haig and, to a similar extent Gough, was certainly responsible for strategy, inadequate Australian staff work — at corps, division and particularly at 5th Brigade level — was the main reason the 2nd Australian Division failed so dismally. This is nowhere better demonstrated than in the indecision over the shelling of known German machine-gun nests. Had the Australian artillery been instructed to deal with those dangerous positions around Queant, the 5th Brigade's advance on 3 May would, most likely, have seen similar gains to those of Gellibrand's 6th Brigade. But staff officers (particularly White and the ANZAC artillery commander Brigadier General W.J. Napier) acted indecisively, while Birdwood, Smyth and Smith also cannot escape criticism.

British staff work was even poorer, leading to the hasty replacement of the 62nd British Division by the 7th. By the end of 6 May, these two divisions had suffered heavy casualties for little gain, and were spent. Gough had just two options, both of which he must have considered extremely unsavoury. He could request permission from Haig to withdraw his forces or he could send in more battalions to be battered like those that had gone before. Gough was not one to countenance withdrawal (after all his ambition to command the upcoming attack at Ypres was uppermost in his mind). Instead, unsurprisingly, he was already making preparations for another British-Australian attack on 7 May.

CHAPTER 12

'It was like passing through hell.'
THE SECOND ATTACK:
7–17 May

Given that the attack had not proceeded as planned and had now become bogged down, it was hardly surprising that Gough was keen to launch another assault on Bullecourt, which was also designed to protect the Australians' left flank.[1] On this occasion the 7th British Division was to lead off from the south against a limited objective, effectively a triangle in Bullecourt's south-east corner, while the 9th Battalion (3rd Australian Brigade) was to bomb its way down the German forward trench and link up with the British in Bullecourt. Plans had earlier been drawn up including detailed artillery support, which would be provided by heavy guns belonging to V Corps, complemented by field artillery from the 2nd Australian and 7th British divisions. An order, originating from the Fifth Army, directed: 'A creeping barrage will be put down 200 yards in front of OG1 and will remain on this line for two minutes when it will creep forward at the rate of 100 yards in 3 minutes until OG1 is reached, on which trench it will remain [for] 4 minutes. It will pick up the stationery barrage on this line, and both barrages will then creep forward 100 yards in 4 minutes.'[2] Another barrage, 'a feint', would be directed against the north-west corner of Bullecourt.[3]

Once the south-east corner had been captured, patrols were expected to fan out and dominate the road running through to the north of the village. And finally, one element that had been neglected in previous attacks was included. Artillery would deal with the deadly machine-gun nests in and around Queant as well as other machine-guns located west of the Longatte to Bullecourt road. The Australians were to shield the British right flank, through to their objective in the south-east corner of Bullecourt, by bombing westward along OG1.[4] The commander of V Corps, Lieutenant General Sir Edward Fanshawe, was confident of success. Not so Major General Herbert Shoubridge, GOC 7th British Division.

Shoubridge challenged Fanshawe principally over the limited time he was given to plan and organise the attack. Fanshawe responded 'that a delay of three days was a luxury they could not afford.'[5] Shoubridge passed on the order to Brigadier General H.R. Green whose 20th British Infantry Brigade (the same brigade that had been cut to pieces in front of the village of Mametz in July 1916) was to deliver the attack, adding that 'it was hurrying things forward very much. That all arrangements had been made for the 8th [May] and that the … Australian Division did not wish to do it before the 8th; the Corps Commander however said it must be on the 7th.'[6]

Green decided that the 2nd Gordon Highlanders should lead the advance, closely followed by the 9th Devons. After consolidating the first objective, the 'Blue Line' (basically parts of OG1 and 'Tower Trench' in front of Bullecourt), the Highlanders and Devons were to move against the second objective, the 'Green Line' in Bullecourt's south-east, where they were to link up with the Australians. The 'Brown Line', located in the northern extremity of Bullecourt, was the third and final objective of the combined British-Australian troops.[7]

On the same day, units from the spent and exhausted German *27th Division* had been relieved by others from the *3rd Guards Division*, which comprised tough and experienced troops from the *9th Grenadier*, the *Guard Fusilier* and *Landwehr regiments*. These were the same units that had attacked the 2nd Australian Division at Lagnicourt the previous month. But, now rested, refitted and better equipped, they occupied positions in what little remained of the buildings, or in underground cellars, on the western side of the village, eagerly awaiting the expected British-Australian attack.[8]

***

In the early hours of 7 May, Gordon Highlander and Devon units had formed up and were making last-minute preparations some 200 yards from the forward German trench, almost under the muzzles of enemy machine-guns. The German artillery was already giving those waiting British troops a particularly harrowing time with a 'triple protective barrage of 5.9's, Pip-squeaks and Machine-guns'.[9] At 3.45 am, the British infantry started moving forward.[10] A report noted that Lewis machine-gunners from the 3rd Australian Infantry Brigade, positioned in OG2, provided 'excellent assistance by firing on the enemy reinforcements coming from Riencourt-Les Cagnicourt. A strong enemy post ... received special attention and 30 to 40 enemy casualties are claimed.'[11]

German artillery shells burst over the Australian support lines near Bullecourt, 7 May 1917, shortly after the attack on Bullecourt had been renewed by Australian and Scottish troops (AWM E00517).

Advancing British troops nonetheless encountered stiff opposition. But they stubbornly fought on. At around 4.55 am the first objective was captured along with 38 prisoners. Fifteen minutes later the Highlanders had breached the second objective.[12] At about 6.00 am a report reached V Corps headquarters stating that both objectives were 'being consolidated'.[13] Gough was also being kept informed of the attack's progress, quickly relaying what he learnt to Haig. And, apparently content with developments, Haig confided to his diary that '5th Army reports 7th Division attacked Bullecourt from S[outh] at 3.45a.m. in conjunction with bombing attacks by I ANZAC Corps on right along Hindenburg trench. By 7.00a.m. touch with Australian Division was reported as established and 70 prisoners taken. Attack seems to have been most successful.'[14]

***

Meanwhile, the 9th Australian Battalion was bombing its way down OG1 hopeful of 'connecting' with the British. At 3.58 am, a number of platoons set off separately, 'leap-frogging' through the enemy trench. If the past provided any indication, the 'leap-frog' method had proven particularly effective: once a platoon had captured a length of German trench it swiftly commenced consolidation. Almost immediately, the following platoon would pass through and take a similar length of trench. The process was repeated until the objective was finally taken.

However, German troops were well prepared for the attack. The first of the Australian platoons encountered stiff opposition just some 70 yards into the advance. Hand-to-hand fighting was commonplace as enemy infantry desperately attempted to hold their position using whatever weapons came to hand, including 'egg-bombs', 'stick-bombs', 'Pineapple' mortars and machine-guns, even the bayonet. With Australian casualties mounting, the leading platoon was forced to withdraw. The following platoon used its rifle grenades to great effect, firing behind the German defenders, preventing any further supply of bombs or ammunition being brought forward. As they moved closer to Bullecourt, the Australians encountered even fiercer opposition — this time, the dreaded flame-thrower. But these Australians had been better trained and kept their distance thereby taking fewer casualties. And when the flame-thrower crew finally ran out of fuel, an Australian Lewis machine-gunner killed them without hesitation.

Well-positioned German machine-gun nests and snipers caused more casualties until Lewis machine-gunners and specialist troops with rifle grenades could silence them. However, another three flame-throwers and a 'Pineapple' mortar began firing on the Australians until Mills bombers disabled the crews, capturing some of the weapons when the surviving Germans took flight.[15] Despite their fatigue, the Australians pushed on to their next objective, before waging another fierce bombing duel, which lasted just a few minutes until the 40 remaining Germans, including a machine-gun crew, pulled back.

Sergeant H. Preston (9th Battalion) wrote that his section 'bombed our way through when one officer of Gordon Highlanders jumped into parapet and shouted Anzacs! Anzacs! still bombing throughout.'[16] Official British historian, Cyril Falls, was one who considered the Australian 'bombers' did remarkably well. 'Tactical skill of a high order was shown repeatedly,' he noted,

> ... especially in the Australian bombing operations, which in their kind were   probably never surpassed. Several of them were conducted with almost clockwork precision, the bombers fighting in relays, covered by lateral artillery barrages, by trench mortars, and by Lewis guns established on the flanks in shell-craters outside the trenches. Outranged by the German egg-bombs and even by the stick-bombs, the attackers outfought the enemy by firing barrages of rifle grenades beyond the hand-thrown Mills bombs.[17]

The Australians finally achieved their objective, linking up with the Highlanders.

'The attack was carried out by relays of bombers', a later Australian report stated, 'advancing under support of rifle grenades and Lewis guns in addition to artillery, mortars and Vickers guns. As each short length of trench was occupied by a party of bombers steps were taken against counter attacks whilst the next relay of bombers went through them.' The Australians counted more than 30 Germans 'killed in OG1'. However, their own casualties were heavier, totalling 71 in all. But those remaining Australians were able to establish a 'strong point ... [which] gave an exceptionally good field of fire and a Vickers machine gun as well as a telephone was established there.' The report concluded that the position was secured: 'Our left flank post and the right one of the Gordons were exchanged so that our flanks would actually overlap.'[18] Indeed, the left flank was considered secure due to the efforts of four Australian platoons fighting their way down OG2 to communication trench 'L', where they established another two strong defensive posts.[19]

The 7th Division's commander considered this success 'the result of a most dashing advance by your Australians as they had a long and difficult trench to bomb down.'[20] Cyril Falls was even more lavish in his praise: 'The Australian attack was conducted with great skill,' he wrote,

> ... it might, indeed, stand as an example of the art of the bombing attack in trench warfare at its highest. It was covered by an artillery barrage fired in enfilade along the Hindenburg Line, by the fire of a medium trench mortar and of three Stokes, by that of Vickers and Lewis guns, and by showers of rifle grenades, fired beyond the hand-thrown Mills. Bombers and rifle grenadiers worked in relays.[21]

However not all went smoothly. At around 5.15 am a party of Highlanders, courageously led by Captain Maitland Gordon, joined some Queenslanders (from the 9th Battalion) to consolidate their position. An enemy machine-gun opened fire close by, killing them all.[22]

Australian and British troops finally cleared and secured a part of Bullecourt — no matter that it was the small south-eastern sector, in which almost every building had been utterly destroyed. Yet, the British-Australian position remained precarious at best. As soon as

German officers discovered that their troops had withdrawn, they ordered their artillery to lay a blanket barrage. While the Gordons were securing another position, enemy infantry commenced a further 'local' counter-attack. The British held fast, eventually launching an attack of their own, forcing the Germans to again pull back beyond their starting position. Despite the small but significant victory, the Germans continued to hold most of the northern part and the south-west corner of Bullecourt — known as the 'Red Patch' — effectively the remainder of the village.[23]

At around 6.00 am, another German barrage, lasting close to an hour, was directed at the captured positions, while several groups of enemy storm troops, each estimated at company strength, were spotted gathering between Riencourt and Bullecourt, apparently organising a counter-attack. British officers relayed the information to divisional headquarters. An immediate barrage was put down which killed or wounded many of the enemy caught in the open. The survivors quickly fled to the safety of their own trenches.[24]

Shortly after 9.00 am German soldiers were reported massing for another larger counter-attack. Australian and British troops were ordered to prepare. But, fortunately for the battle-weary men, the attack did not eventuate.[25] Instead, German artillery continued its mission of constantly hammering the south-eastern part of the village, the barrage increasing in intensity throughout the morning. British-Australian counter-battery fire commenced at around 10.00 am. A few hours later, the 20th British Brigade's commander (Brigadier General Green) reported that 'Counter battery work is very good and hostile fire has slackened considerably.'[26] Soon afterwards, some 200 German storm troops were spotted moving from the north-west of Bullecourt, but were 'successfully dealt with by … [British] infantry'.[27]

Reports coming into 7th British Divisional headquarters reassured Shoubridge that 'progress is being made in the "Red Patch"'. He nonetheless increased pressure on the British brigade commander to move the 9th Devons further into the village.[28] Certainly enemy shelling had not discouraged the British infantry as they pushed on with their advance, reporting further 'satisfactory progress' through Bullecourt's south-west corner. But the Germans never abandoned their attempts to move more of their own troops into the village. An RFC airman observed that, by early evening, the enemy were rushing some 300 reinforcements into Bullecourt which, for the moment, halted any further British-Australian advance.[29]

In the interim, a British pioneer battalion (24th Manchester) assisted by the 528th Field Company (Royal Engineers) had finished constructing a communication trench stretching from the railway embankment to the British-Australian position in Bullecourt's south-eastern corner, making it possible to maintain a steady supply of weapons, ammunition and Mills bombs. Despite the fact that the village was now of no tactical significance, Gough was eager to quickly capture what remained, no matter the cost. Senior German officers were just as stubborn and were not prepared to yield another inch. They ordered as many counter-attacks as were needed to push Australian and British troops out of the village and away from the Hindenburg Line.[30] Information from enemy prisoners told of 'a large force now in the rear of this front – 8,000 troops reported at Oisy le Verger, [and] a large concentration of guns' which were in position to reinforce the besieged German defenders.[31]

***

Meanwhile, during the evening of 7 May, the 1st Australian Brigade was finally relieved by the 2nd, which had been out of the action for some three weeks holding positions around Lagnicourt.[32] The 1st Brigade was thankful to finally leave the front. Private W.H. McKenzie (3rd Battalion) wrote that, 'In the three days and nights we repulsed six counter attacks by the Germans, we were practically fighting the whole time and if we had not got relieved when we did I am afraid the Germans would have come over and found us all asleep at our posts for we were just beaten for the want of sleep.' However, if the men thought they were to be rested, they were sadly mistaken. 'After being relieved we had about two miles to go under heavy fire,' McKenzie added,

> ... and then were straight back to the line with a load of sand bags. One shell landed right amongst us, half burying myself and several others. Two of our party have not been heard of since, they must have either been blown to pieces or completely buried. All next day we stayed two miles behind the line ... The fighting is still fierce all around Bullecourt which we can see from our position.[33]

Captain L.C. Roth of the 2nd Pioneer Battalion was another Australian pleased to be out of the fighting. 'After Bullecourt I was very much run down and my nerves rather shaken,' he told his mother.

> First day I was knocked unconscious with a shell burst and [the] following day was knocked down several times by bursts and half buried at another time. I did not mind this so much as the continual banging of the shells themselves. After a while each crump seemed like a hammer hitting me on the head and the old wounds gave a jog as a gentle reminder that they were in familiar surroundings. The last time I came out is an absolute mystery to me. We finished our job alright and the men got home fairly well, but the whole place was one barrage of shells and those who didn't get home stopped. I must have walked straight through the barrage unconsciously.[34]

Those Australian soldiers from the 2nd Brigade now moving to the front line had already heard the dreadful accounts and knew what to expect. Chaplain J.J. Booth (8th Battalion) wrote that, 'With the main attack came a series of counter attacks and the whole area is still very disturbed which means a good deal of artillery and machine gun activity. We are now informed that we are to go in again to the right of Bullecourt ... which is the next sector to our old spot in the sunken road.'[35]

Australian gunners from the 1st Division had also seen enough. Most were thoroughly spent and could take little more. 'A terrible day. Month in action today', wrote Gunner Lewis Wilson on 7 May. 'Our camp getting shelled … No one hit. In shelter of a pit full of dead horses. Absolutely buggered.' However, for the moment they had to carry on, at least until they could be suitably relieved. Their guns, too, were becoming increasingly worn, which meant that the barrels were more likely to explode when fired, causing more casualties. Little wonder those same gunners became more despondent when they heard that the infantry were being rotated and rested.[36]

***

The following day (8 May), General Gough decided to make good his promise of forcing the enemy from the 'Red Patch'. He wrote to Haig, telling him that 'It hardly seems probable that the enemy will allow us to remain unmolested in the Hindenburg Line and in Bullecourt.' Somewhat illogically (considering what was happening around Arras) Gough scribbled in the margin that he 'spoke with General Malcolm who will get later in touch with Third Army regarding cooperation against the Hindenburg Line West of Bullecourt.'[37]

The fine weather that had seen the previous attacks launched over solid ground had now broken. Heavy rain made the battlefield muddy and more difficult for the infantry to traverse. At 11.00 am the inexperienced 8th Devonshire Battalion (20th British Brigade) attacked from the south. The troops began bombing their way through OG1, making good progress along the trench, now filled with gluey mud, until a strong counter-attack forced their withdrawal.[38]

The 8th Australian Battalion, with the 7th in support, was sent to create a diversion by bombing along another 150 yards of OG2 towards Bullecourt. At first the battalion encountered little opposition but, as the men moved closer to the village, German resistance strengthened. The Australians came to a grinding halt.

Then the Germans counter-attacked. Captain W.D. Joynt, VC (8th Battalion) recalled:

The Germans kept counterattacking from front and flanks without success; altogether twelve Hun counterattacks were defeated. None of them reached our front line, each attack disintegrating fully two hundred yards short of our trenches. German officers could be seen bravely attempting to lead their men on to come to grips with us, but the Huns wouldn't follow.[39]

The 7th Battalion was not required to take part in the attack. Instead some men were used to carry ammunition and supplies to troops from the 8th, holed up in OG2. 'We were supposed to attack,' Lieutenant S.E. McCardel (7th Battalion) wrote, 'but things were pretty quiet. Got busy and built our dugout up and made it *tres bon*. Had to get a fatigue party of 100 men out to carry ammunition up to the line as there was a stunt on. One of the Hun shells hit a GS wagon full of bombs and Mortars and killed 46 men and 4 horses.'[40]

Meanwhile, the Gordons had been relieved by the 2nd Border Regiment. In their first action during the night of 8/9 May, troops from the Cumbrian region successfully attacked the north-east part of the 'Red Patch', with 'many enemy dead left on battlefield'.[41] But, predictably, the Germans soon hit back. Throughout the early morning of 9 May, German artillery maintained a constant heavy bombardment.[42] At 9.10 am elite troops from the *123rd Grenadier Regiment* from around Riencourt launched another counter-attack. Caught in the open, they suffered massive casualties from the cross-fire of well-positioned Australian Lewis machine-gunners and Cumbrian riflemen, and were forced to withdraw.[43]

Major General Shoubridge was now confident that his men could take the remainder of Bullecourt. He ordered the 8th Battalion, Devonshire Regiment, to resume the attack. Late in the morning British and Australian artillery and a number of Stokes mortars put down a heavy barrage. At around midday the infantry set off. Well-equipped bombers led the way, followed by specialist troops with their rifle grenades and then the Lewis machine-gunners and Stokes trench mortar crews. Shoubridge had learnt from past indiscretions. He ordered that his heavy machine-guns be positioned along the railway embankment from where they could envelop the area north of Bullecourt and deal with expected German counter-attacks from around Queant.

However German observers in forward positions had caught sight of the British infantry as they prepared for the attack and a lethal enemy barrage caught the Devons in the open. Many casualties were inflicted, yet still the survivors pressed forward. The German artillery never relented. Fierce hand-to-hand fighting followed, particularly in trenches fronting the Bullecourt-Ecoust road. With casualties mounting, the British decided to pull back. Young Devon officers, however, stepped forward, encouraging their men to rally, also spurring reinforcements who had only just arrived, urging them to attack. The German troops were overrun. Forced out of their trenches, they were trapped by a volley of machine-gun fire coming from the railway embankment.[44]

A portion of the heavily wired area between Bullecourt and Riencourt, 9 May 1917. In the background thick entanglements are visible along the ridge as is the tank which reached this point in the attack on 11 April 1917 (AWM E00637).

By early evening a British report noted that the Devons had moved their 'original position' forward almost 100 yards and were setting up a safe line, slightly east of the Longatte road, while 'a large number of dead enemy have been personally seen by a Staff Officer'. However, the entire 20th British Brigade had been badly cut up and the survivors were exhausted. Eleven officers and 157 men had been listed as killed or missing and another 25 officers and 568 men wounded. And, while most of the brigade could be satisfied with having extended the hold on the south-east corner of the village, others considered that 'there was something unsatisfactory and depressing in these piecemeal attacks, repeated over the same ground and without substantial alterations of plan to hold out to each succeeding attack prospects of better fortune than had attended its predecessors.' Shoubridge ordered that the fatigued troops be relieved by Brigadier General H.R. Cumming's 91st Brigade. On 10 May, during a lull in the fighting, the 2nd Battalion, Queen's Regiment, took over the right flank while the 1st Battalion, South Staffordshire Regiment, established a position on the left. The 22nd Battalion, Manchester Regiment, was in support around Ecoust while the 21st Battalion (Manchesters) was in reserve, further to the rear.[45]

***

Meanwhile, headlines in a British newspaper, *The Daily Telegraph*, told its readers of the 'Continued Fighting at Bullecourt, Anzacs in Hindenburg Line', adding that,

> ... Anzac troops maintain and steadily extend their hold upon the Hindenburg Line ... The fighting here appears to have become a great bombing match, in which the individuality of the Australian soldiers has proved much superior to the machine-like methods of the Hun. Within the Bullecourt enclave the struggle continues to ebb and flow, and for the moment the German machine-gun fire seems to dominate the ruined village. But our artillery is continuously combing the place ... Our line

follows the outskirts of the village around three sides, and as our gunners have observation across the fourth side, the position is not a particularly good one for the Germans.[46]

The bravery of Australian stretcher-bearers under fire, particularly as they came to the assistance of wounded 'Gordons and Devons', was not lost on the British divisional commander, who passed on his commendation to his Australian counterpart.[47]

***

The 1st Australian Division was utterly exhausted. A few days earlier, Major General Talbot Hobbs had been told to prepare his 5th Australian Division for a move to the front. Immediately he intensified the division's training. On 7 May, Hobbs was taking part in a division sports day and horse show at Albert when he heard that British and Australian troops were poised to take the village. He knew that his division would soon be 'drawn into Battle of Bullecourt'.[48] But, as Hobbs told Birdwood (which was passed on to Gough), 'he regretted this, as they [his troops] were just getting to a stage in training when he felt that a further ten days would do them any amount of good.'[49]

The 5th Australian Division had only come together in February 1916. On 22 March 1916 the former commander of the 2nd Australian Infantry Brigade, James McCay, was appointed GOC and promoted major general. A capable, if not brilliant brigade commander, McCay was essentially an administrative officer, and was not popular with other officers and soldiers. He lacked the ability and temperament to lead them in the heat of battle. By 12 July 1916 the division had assembled in the relatively quiet Armentieres sector in France, essentially a training or 'nursery' section of the line. Barely a week later, the still largely inexperienced troops were hastily sent into a large-scale attack, the first Australians to participate in an offensive (rather than the much despised patrols and raids) on the Western Front.

The Battle of Fromelles has come to represent all that was wrong with British leadership in World War I. Instigated by the commander of the British XI Corps, Lieutenant General Sir Richard Haking — known to his men as 'butcher' — it was planned as a 'feint' to keep enemy soldiers away from the main Somme attack further south. Haking's reasoning for the attack was to straighten the line by reducing the small salient, nicknamed 'Sugar Loaf', located slightly north-west of the enemy-occupied village of Fromelles. As luck would have it, the 5th Australian Division faced the enemy on the northern flank of the salient.

At 7.00 am on 19 July 1916, British and Australian artillery commenced the preliminary bombardment. Eleven hours later troops from the 5th Australian Division went 'over the top'. The men were decimated as they tried to cross no man's land. In less than 24 hours, the Australians suffered 5533 casualties. The 5th Division was effectively out of action for some months afterwards, only re-entering the front line in late October 1916, by which time the extreme winter conditions were beginning to set in, and the Battle of the Somme was finally drawing to a close.

In February and March 1917 the 5th was one of the Australian divisions responsible for pursuing withdrawing German units to the Hindenburg Line, in the process capturing German 'outpost villages' including, on 2 April, Louverval and Doignies. By early May all the division's infantry brigades (less artillery) were being rested and refitted around Albert. Once Hobbs was told to prepare his division for a move to the front, however, he had increased his training, particularly infantry coordination with artillery and other arms.

***

When the Somme campaign ended, the AIF began to refit and restructure its depleted divisions. Senior commands were also reshuffled. Even after the disaster that was Fromelles, Major General McCay's performance as GOC was less than satisfactory. He had failed as a divisional commander. Deteriorating health provided the excuse and McCay was given a less strenuous post — command of AIF depots in the United Kingdom. On 18 December 1916, the 52-year-old Major General Talbot Hobbs had assumed command of the 5th Australian Division.

Portrait of Major General John Talbot Hobbs, GOC 5th Australian Division (AMWA 32).

Joseph John Talbot Hobbs was the ideal replacement — an educated, no-nonsense officer. In civilian life, Hobbs was a successful Western Australian architect with a practice in Perth. He also had a passion for part-time soldiering. Following his arrival in Australia from England, Hobbs had trained as a gunnery officer. He continued to learn the latest artillery techniques, often travelling to England (at his own expense) and even completed a 'gunnery' correspondence course conducted by the University of Sydney. When war broke out he put his experience and expertise to good use at Gallipoli and on the Somme, where he commanded the Australian artillery with initiative and pluck.[50] Bean, who personally witnessed Hobbs' impact on officers and men, wrote that 'success with the staff of the 5th Division was instantaneous, he secured the affection which had been denied to McCay and capably led the division.'[51]

***

The 14th Australian Infantry Brigade was first into the front line, taking over the sector east of Central Road from the 3rd Brigade during the night of 8/9 May.[52] Almost immediately the men began to understand that reports of the enemy pulling out of Bullecourt were little more than fiction. Sergeant Walter Downing believed that he was going into 'hell', in which

> … trenches were filled with corpses, over which men trampled and stumbled … Scraps of battered bodies obtruded from the obscene earth. The country became   more and more abominable, more and more desolate. Steel helmets, rusted rifles, parts of equipment, broken iron stakes, lengths of barbed wire were mingled in the tormented soil. The land was bare, except for stumps of trees, except for the railway lines, whose rails were broken and twisted … Doubling through a ravine, full of shattered limbers and guns, torn equipment, disembowelled mules and dead men, full of the noise and the stink of bursting shells, full of flying lumps of red-hot steel, burring and whizzing and whining – sweating as we wound through a battered trench, cringing and recoiling as the shells burst almost in our faces, we came to a place where a white-faced officer with a streak of blood on his brow sat under a bank of earth, directing the incoming men.[53]

German gunners had not paused their seemingly endless pounding of those parts of the village occupied by Australian and British troops. Casualties were high, particularly among 'units going to and from the trenches'. The recollections of Lieutenant Ronald McInnis were similar to those of Downing. He wrote that his platoon

… marched out in fighting order without our packs, through Vaulx to Noreuil. We had a very fine view of an intense barrage being put down by our guns. It was about finished when we got to Noreuil. Then we went on through an endless sap in the dark to the front line just opposite Riencourt. The support line of the captured Hindenburg Line is our firing-line. It was like passing through Hell from the railway-line to the front line. There were dead everywhere, and the ground was chewed up by shell-fire just as it was on the Somme. My platoon and another from B Company had to go up to reinforce C Company in the front line … We got in without a casualty and relieved the 12th Battalion. The relief was complete just before the dawn stand-to, and one can imagine what a devilish approach it was to the line when it took us all night.[54]

Australian soldiers in the second line of trenches in front of Riencourt in May 1917 clean their rifles in preparation for an attack (AWM E00454).

The 5th's historian, A.D. Ellis, added that 'not only were our front lines pummelled day and night, but every approach to them, especially from Vaulx-Vraucourt, through the well-named "Death

Valley" to Noreuil and thence to the Railway Cutting, was swept with a fine impartiality by an almost constant stream of high-explosives, shrapnel, and gas shells.'[55]

All day, and throughout the evening of 9 May, German artillery maintained the barrage, targeting front-line trenches and the railway embankment.[56] This was far worse than anything the Australians had experienced — the earlier Bullecourt and Pozieres battles paled in comparison. 'This is a very hot position in the line', Lieutenant McGinnis wrote. 'The Huns still hold the Hindenburg Line from about 70 yards to our right, and the trenches have sandbag "bomb-stops" across them which have to be carefully watched the whole time. Bullecourt is just to our left.'[57] Another Australian report noted that it was difficult to respond with counter-battery fire as enemy 'artillery fire came from both the front and from the right flank evidently from the vicinity of Queant. This latter fire enfiladed both the front line trenches and the Railway Embankment and was particularly damaging in its effect.'[58] The 5th's artillery, however, recorded that its guns were 'very active ... Bullecourt and Riencourt received special attention'.[59]

Major General J.J. Talbot Hobbs (second from left) talking to Australian stretcher-bearers carrying a wounded soldier near Noreuil during the fighting around Bullecourt, May 1917 (AWM E00441).

The inexperienced Australian troops, fresh to the front, were not only unaccustomed to such heavy shellfire, they were also never sure when the Germans would attack. The strain was unbearable. But no attack came. That same night, the 15th Brigade moved into positions west of Central Road formerly occupied by the 2nd Brigade. During the morning of 10 May, Hobbs moved into his divisional headquarters close to the front at Vaulx-Vraucourt, within range of enemy guns, having taken over command of all Australian troops around Bullecourt from Major General Smyth. However, his move came only after he had 'talked with Gellibrand about the experience of his brigade at Bullecourt and later Smyth'.[60] Hobbs' first order saw immediate improvements made to those defensive positions already in place.[61]

Lieutenant General Sir William Birdwood visits a cookhouse in the Australian support lines in one of the many sunken roads during the second attack on Bullecourt (AWM E02000).

At around noon on 10 May the Germans launched the expected counter-attack against the 'left bomb block', although only on a small scale. 'We had some good sniping', Lieutenant McGinnis recalled, Germans 'were coming to and from Hendecourt to a communication sap leading towards Bullecourt ... We kept the enemy running.'[62] Although the Germans initially gained some ground, an almost immediate response by Lieutenant Colonel C.A. Denehy's 58th Battalion (15th Australian Brigade) restored 'the situation'.[63] The remainder of the day and the next were relatively quiet along all parts of the front except for a minor incursion on the left of the 5th Australian Division.[64] And, while troops from the 5th Division were learning to deal with 'the Boche' and applying finishing touches to their defensive positions, plans were being drawn up for another combined British-Australian attack scheduled for 12 May, to be led by Brigadier General H.R. Cumming's 91st British Brigade which had previously relieved the exhausted 20th.[65]

***

By 12 May the fighting and loss of life around Bullecourt had become part of Field Marshal Haig's 'wearing out' strategy. On the same day he wrote that 'the capture of the Hindenburg Line east of Bullecourt, and the manner in which it has been held ... against such constant and desperate efforts to retake it, will rank high among the great deeds of the war and is helping appreciably in wearing out the enemy.'[66]

***

Yet again, the objective for the attack, on 12 May, was the capture of the 'Red Patch' followed by the expulsion of German troops from what remained of Bullecourt. On this occasion, however, planning was more methodical, with artillery officers adding their advice on the best way to lay barrages on enemy positions around Bullecourt. Agreement was reached that, after a short preliminary bombardment, advancing troops would follow a carefully calibrated creeping barrage and, to achieve the maximum advantage, 4.5-inch howitzers would fire 50 yards ahead of the 18-pounders. The 2/7th West Yorkshires (58th Brigade, located to the left of the 91st) was given the task of launching a feint attack at a point north-west of the 'Red Patch', known as 'The Crucifix', designed to draw enemy troops away from the main assault. As the RFC effectively had control of the sky around this part of the front, aviators would be available soon after dawn to assist the infantry by bombing and machine-gunning enemy positions and also pass information to headquarters concerning the situation on the ground below.[67]

Australian soldiers from the 5th Division bathe in one of the many shell holes around Bullecourt, 12 May 1917 (AWM E03925).

While the 5th Australian Division was not directly involved in the planning, Hobbs agreed with Shoubridge's request 'to assist as much as possible by ... 15th Infantry Brigade capturing cross roads NE of Bullecourt and ... by [divisional] Artillery participating in barrage fire under which the 7th Division would attack.'[68] Hobbs met the commander of the 15th Brigade, Brigadier General Harold 'Pompey' Elliott, and both men agreed that Lieutenant Colonel

C.A. Denehy's 58th Battalion, which was holding the part of the line directly opposite the crossroads, would advance, pushing forward some 14 minutes after Cumming's brigade had moved off, to allow them to steer clear of the British-Australian barrage.[69] Some machine-gun sections from the 14th Australian Infantry Brigade were also involved, albeit in a minor role, having been ordered to lay down 'machine gun fire' to help cover the attack.[70]

The main part of the Australian attack could not have been in better hands. Denehy, according to Elliott, 'worships his Battalion, and it really is very fine, but I believe he thinks of it all day and dreams of it at night.'[71] Denehy was well liked and well respected by all his officers and men. Prior to any engagement, he made careful preparations and Bullecourt was no exception. He decided that the first target must be the well-placed and strengthened machine-gun positions. Lieutenant Rupert Moon's platoon, part of A Company, was given the most perilous of assignments — to take out those enemy machine-gun nests, including one constructed entirely of concrete. Part of the nearby trench, known as the 'Bomb Block', which extended to the crossroads, was to be destroyed by Lieutenant N. Pelton's platoon from B Company. Another platoon from C Company, led by Lieutenant S.J. Topp, was to advance in two waves against the crossroads and parts of the nearby enemy trench.[72]

Hobbs, however, was only too well aware of the near impossible task confronting the battalion. Shortly before the attack he issued a memorandum, informing his officers of the need for more attention to detail as,

> It has been found, in the fighting round Bullecourt, that the troops are still inclined to depend too much on hand grenades, and are not using their rifles as much as they should. Commanders must impress on their men that the rifle and machine gun are the chief weapons of the infantry soldier. Much more execution can be done with these than with bombs which are only better than rifles in certain circumstances.

Troops are also inclined to rely entirely on artillery barrage to deal with counter attacks. Here again infantry must use their rifles and machine guns more, so that they can look after themselves better if at any time thick artillery barrages are not available for defence.[73]

It was also unfortunate that the Australians would be meeting fresh German troops from the *9th Grenadiers*, who had taken over that part of the line during the night of 10/11 May.[74]

*****

At 3.40 am on 12 May, the 2nd Battalion, Queen's Royal West Surrey Regiment, and the 1st Battalion, South Staffordshire Regiment, led off the British assault, 'covered by an artillery barrage, with a feint barrage by machine guns on the left flank of the attack'.[75] Despite support from Australian machine-guns, the left flank of the South Staffs soon struck trouble, encountering enemy troops well ensconced in the 'Red Patch', who inflicted heavy casualties, bogging down their advance. Progress slowed further.[76] The right flank, however, fared much better. Forcing a gap in the German defences, British infantry fought their way through to the north-west and northern extremities of Bullecourt. The attack along the Queens' front proceeded almost exactly as planned, albeit well behind schedule. By early morning the battalion had captured the entire right of its objective as far as the village church. A British report noted that this particular part of 'Bullecourt appears to be very quiet. Very little shelling and only occasional machine gun fire.'[77] The 'feint' attack by the 2nd Battalion (7th West Yorkshire Regiment) also initially fared well, reaching the point known as 'The Crucifix'. But the German *120th Infantry Regiment* soon regrouped, launching another strong counter-attack in which their bombers took the initiative and forced the British into a hasty withdrawal.[78]

*****

Studio portrait of Lieutenant Rupert Vance Moon, VC, 58th Battalion (AWM A02592).

Meanwhile, at exactly 3.54 am on 12 May, the Australians had begun moving forward. Lieutenant Moon and his platoon were the first into action. Showing little concern for his own safety, Moon positioned himself in the vanguard of fighting for the heavily fortified concrete machine-gun post. Enemy machine-gunners mounted a robust resistance but, after almost 10 minutes of bombing and hand-to-hand combat, the nest was secured, with surviving Germans pulling back to a support trench where they were subsequently spotted by a British aviator.[79] Despite being wounded, Moon remained with his men and encouraged them as they consolidated the position.

The simultaneous attack by B Company was not progressing as well. German soldiers fought with great gusto and determination. Elliott's subsequent report noted that their positions 'contained many dugouts from which the enemy constantly organised attacking parties of about 12-15 men with bombs and our advance was delayed for one hour although the successive enemy parties were killed or wounded by our rifle grenade fire.'[80] German artillery also pounded Australian positions in the trenches and the area in front, making it difficult for reinforcements to get through. Two platoons from A Company were, nevertheless, ordered to assist.

Finally, satisfied that the captured position at the crossroad was secure, Moon led what remained of his platoon in a 'spirited attack' across open ground against the German right flank.[81] But the Germans held firm, even launching regular counter-attacks against any ground the Australians seized. Wounded again, Moon never gave up. Instead, he and his men launched a copy-book 'flanking advance' which forced the ever-dwindling number of enemy survivors to flee. Over 100 surrendered to Moon.[82]

With the first two positions safely in Australian hands, C Company, supported by the 15th Australian Light Trench Mortar Battery and the 15th Australian Machine Gun Company, commenced its advance against the section of the enemy trench that lay beyond the crossroad. But problems were soon apparent. With the Queen's Battalion held up nearby, the Australians encountered the same hostile machine-gun and rifle fire from the left flank. A report from a British aviator confirmed that the 'men were in shell holes in front of [enemy] trench ... The trench itself was full of men whom I took to be Germans.'[83] Moon's platoon happened to be close at hand. Again showing little regard for his own safety, Moon led his men once more into the cauldron. Wounded yet again, this time by a machine-gun bullet, his leadership and courage inspired his men, contributing significantly to the eventual capture of the position.

Moon suffered a further wound when, during a discussion with other officers on where to place the best defensive line to secure the position, a sniper's bullet shattered his jaw. Never one to whimper, Moon returned to the Australian line to have all his wounds treated. The official report on Moon's achievements stated that, 'sitting down with blood and sweat pouring from him, he remarked "It was a hard fight boys; I've got three cracks, and not one of them good enough for Blighty."' For his leadership and exceptional courage, Moon was awarded the Victoria Cross.[84]

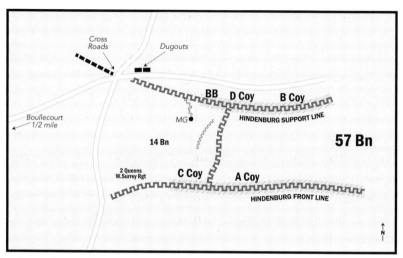

Map showing the area where Lieutenant Moon and his men fought so gallantly and where he won his Victoria Cross.

Despite its mounting toll of casualties, including many fine young officers, the 58th Australian Battalion had secured all of its objectives. Among those listed as killed was the battalion 'bombing officer', Lieutenant W. Barlow. 'His own portion of the work had been done,' Lieutenant Colonel Denehy wrote,

> ... but we were being very severely shelled and casualties were numerous. I lost   many good men that 12ᵗʰ of May and as report after report was brought to me   from different parts of the line that this officer and that had been put out of action Lt. Barlow came to me and said "I am not wounded at Headquarters, now sir let me go and take one of the leaderless platoons." I gave him permission to go and it was not 10 minutes before he was killed. His was the supreme sacrifice putting aside all thoughts of personal danger ... It was the spirit of men like him that won the day and gained for the 58ᵗʰ a splendid victory that will live in the history of the AIF.[85]

Another four promising junior officers were killed as were 30 of their men. A further 78 were wounded along with six young officers. More than 150 Germans were counted dead on the battlefield, while another two officers and 184 men were captured. Also seized were four machine-guns, three *minenwerfer* and two 'Pineapple' mortars.[86]

Almost immediately following the attack, the Germans responded with a heavier than usual artillery barrage. 'The sky was lit in the east with the flare and flicker of the German artillery,' Sergeant Downing recalled,

> ... It was a place where every sight, every sound, meant death – the screams of   someone dying in agony, the monstrous clash and rumble of the guns, flinging   hundreds of tons of shells each minute on our line ... There was nothing that was not ugly, distorted and horrible – nothing but the heroism of flesh contending with steel, and the flares in their diabolical beauty, filling with light that place of terror.[87]

The 15th Brigade reported 348 casualties, including 18 officers. Worst hit was the railway embankment, where support troops happened to be concentrating. The 59th Battalion headquarters also collected a direct hit from a gas shell, killing or seriously wounding all those nearby including the commanding officer, Lieutenant Colonel H.T. Layh.[88]

Hobbs informed Birdwood that he was pleased with the way the attack 'was ably planned at very short notice ... [and] immediately after some 12 hours [of] heavy shelling' had been skilfully executed by his officers and men. Although distressed by the number of casualties in the battalions, Hobbs believed that the outcome 'reflects great credit on all concerned'.[89] Reflecting Hobbs' thoughts were the numerous congratulatory messages which flowed into 5th Division headquarters over the next few days. Haig's was the most laudatory. 'I congratulate all your troops on the complete success of the various attacks made yesterday morning,' he wrote. 'These successes are very satisfactory, not only in themselves but as showing that the enemy is beginning to weaken under the repeated heavy blows inflicted on him during all the hard fighting of the past five weeks.'[90]

The reality was somewhat less certain. By the end of 12 May the British assault had been brought to a standstill, while the position in Bullecourt was unparalleled in the entire war thus far.[91] 'The British now held the entire village except for the "Red Patch",' Cyril Falls wrote, 'though there was a gap in the line at the north-west – but to that the Germans clung with grim pertinacity, apparently using the sunk road west of the village to communicate with it.'[92]

***

Meanwhile, during the night of 12/13 May, British V Corps headquarters had assumed responsibility for the Bullecourt front while, at the same time, the 173rd Brigade (58th London Division) had replaced the 15th Australian Brigade.[93] The 54th was the only Australian battalion in 'occupied' Bullecourt and maintained its hold on the right sector, with another battalion in support further to the rear. A further four Australian battalions were holding positions in the left sector, well behind the Bullecourt front — two battalions around Morchies-Vaulx and another two near Beugny-Ytres.[94]

***

On 13 May Major General Shoubridge decided to consolidate gains made by his British division the previous day. Brigadier General Cumming had his doubts. A not insignificant crisis of command now became apparent when Cumming approached Shoubridge to argue against any further attacks by his brigade that day. Instead, he suggested that the men make preparations for a 'surprise' attack, to be launched from the south-east preceded by a preparatory artillery barrage, designed to surprise the Germans and isolate their remaining soldiers still holed up in the village. Cumming stipulated that the attack should not be launched until the following morning — 14 May — to allow his men some badly needed rest. The delay would enable him and his fellow officers ample time to make suitable amendments to the plans.

But Shoubridge would not hear of it. He wanted the attack not only to commence without delay, but to be launched from the south-west. Cumming considered the idea outrageous as his exhausted men would be moving against the better defended enemy positions — straight into the storm of machine-gun and artillery fire — and their jumping-off line would provide enemy observers the most advantageous view of his troops as they commenced their advance. Another heated debate followed. Shoubridge refused to be told by a subordinate officer how best to plan his division's operations. According to another of the staff officers present, Shoubridge appeared 'somewhat annoyed'. Not long afterwards the divisional commander informed Cumming that he considered him 'too tired to cope with the situation ... [and that his] judgement was therefore warped.' Cumming was advised 'that he must relinquish his command'.[95] Shoubridge replaced him with Colonel W.W. Norman of the 21st Manchester Regiment. Norman agreed to Shoubridge's concept of an attack from the south-west, although a compromise was reached whereby Shoubridge permitted his new commander to pursue a simultaneous subsidiary attack, originating from the north-east.[96] Without sufficient time for proper planning — or, for that matter, for Norman to become accustomed to the area — the attack was always going to be challenging.

The 2nd Battalion, Royal Warwickshire Regiment (on loan from the 22nd Brigade), set off from the south-west, while two companies from the 22nd Manchester Regiment advanced from the north-east. Without adequate artillery support the attack stood little chance. In fact, the British barrage fell well short and into the waves of its own infantry, causing enormous casualties. With little option the remaining British troops withdrew. However, they were ordered to repeat the attack later in the day. Yet again, no ground was gained.[97] However Shoubridge was not one to give up easily. On 14 May he ordered further attacks against the 'Red Patch' from the east, this time by another battalion also on loan from the 22nd Brigade — the 1st Royal Welsh Fusiliers. Their first attack was another disaster — as was the second. Dead and dying British soldiers were scattered three to four deep in trenches and in no man's land. Shoubridge demanded another attack. At 2.30 pm the infantry again moved forward. However more bad luck intervened. A bomb dump, vital to the success of the attack, was blown to pieces. In some places the British took parts of the 'Red Patch', but without a ready supply of bombs and other crucial ammunition, the few remaining survivors had little option but to pull back.[98]

***

Meanwhile the 54th Australian Battalion was consolidating its position in the German trenches and shoring up its defences. The Australians were only separated from enemy troops ensconced in the 'Red Patch' by recently constructed barriers known as 'Bomb Blocks' which, in fact, formed a small salient. A communication trench, no more than a few dozen yards from where enemy troops could mass, formed the battalion's front line. Well-sited German machine-guns in the 'Red Patch' and in Queant (on their right) could also present problems by enfilading the Australians' position. Moreover, a sizeable number of *minenwerfer* were positioned within range, making the Australians particularly vulnerable to a surprise attack.

The 54th's commanding officer, Lieutenant Colonel S. Midgeley, expected the enemy to attempt to exploit those weaknesses, and did his best to prepare the men for an eventual attack. Throughout 14 May the Germans prepositioned even more *minenwerfer* and smaller field artillery as well as large supplies of ammunition. Storm troops from the *Lehr Regiment (3rd Prussian Guards Division)* were moved nearby, ready to attack at a moment's notice. An intelligence report noted that the German regiment had been trained specifically for this type of operation:

After two days of complete rest the [enemy] companies were taken out independently to practice the attack ... [at] the high ground East of Cemetery Wood ... A prisoner of the 2nd Battalion *Lehr Regiment* states that during the training and rehearsal ... chief importance was attached to practising the sections and platoons ... to drill the men to take up their positions automatically, and thus render them independent of their platoon or section leaders [should they] become casualties ... it was thus hoped to avoid hesitation or waiting for orders, with consequent risk of endangering the success of the enterprise.[99]

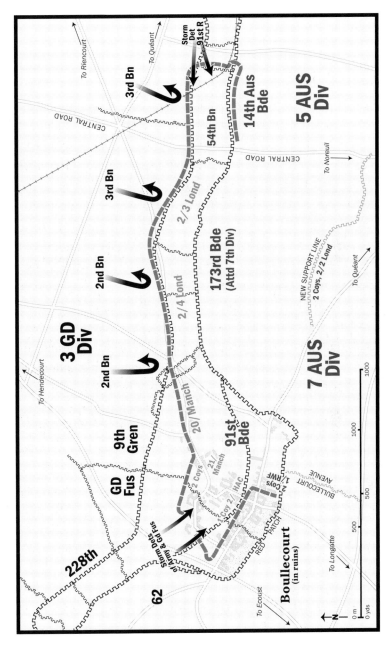

The last major German counter-attack of 15 May 1917 showing the positions of British-Australian units under assault and the location from which the German regiments launched their attacks.

A protracted artillery barrage during the night of 14 May frayed the nerves of Australian soldiers sheltering in their trenches. 'The bombardment mostly of the deadly fluttering gas shells, lasted continuously,' Lieutenant McGinnis wrote.

We had no sleep, and were forced to put our gas helmets on several times. We had shelters that were not shell proof, and were only safe in that they presented a wall of solid earth towards the enemy … Five of our shelters were blown in last night, but marvellous to relate, no one was wounded. It was the longest gas bombardment we ever had experienced, lasting five hours.[100]

A subsequent report noted that, as a result of the barrage, 'the trenches were very badly knocked about and our casualties were unfortunately heavy.'[101]

At 1.00 am on 15 May, the barrage intensified. At around 3.40 the *2nd* and *3rd battalions*, *Luhr Regiment*, supported by other well-trained German storm troops from the *Stesstrupp*, commenced their advance. 'Fritz attacked all along the line,' McGinnis noted, before 'our guns opened up splendidly – he had knocked out only one of our batteries, the 11th, with all his firing. Until about 4.30 the noise was deafening.' Yet, by 9.45 am, the Germans had achieved a partial breakthrough, according to McGinnis, along 'about 60 yards of trench held by the 54th'.[102] Hobbs attempted to take personal control. Telephoning the commander of the 14th Brigade (Brigadier General C.J. Hobkirk), he 'suggested that trench mortars be used from either side of the portion occupied by the Germans'.[103] A much heavier barrage was also put down by the division's 18-pounder field guns. I ANZAC reported that its own heavy artillery fired 'some 4.5's into the sunken road … and searched valleys either side of Riencourt and our heavies neutralised hostile batteries.'[104] McGinnis recollected that this resulted in 'every Hun being killed. He had very heavy casualties.'[105]

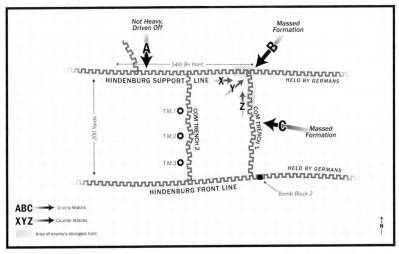

A more detailed map showing the direction of the strongest German attack and the 54th Battalion's counter-attack.

Reinforcements from the 56th Battalion were hastily sent forward to assist the 54th. Supported by Lewis machine-guns, the Australians launched an attack of their own, not once, but three times.[106] 'As soon as the enemy were seen in the open and all jammed up,' a battalion report noted, 'a third counter attacking party left our trench … throwing heavy showers of bombs into the now rather disorganised enemy.' Although cut off, and 'willing to surrender', the Germans were killed mercilessly, 'the whole party was wiped out.' Witnessing the way that other German soldiers had been massacred, the remaining survivors 'attempted to escape over the open, but all of these were mown down by our rifle and machine gun fire and if any escaped this fire … they were either killed or wounded by our barrage, which completely cut off their retreat.'[107]

Despite the distasteful killing of German soldiers who wanted nothing more than to surrender, quick thinking by Australian officers had reversed what was otherwise a dire 'situation'. At 10.50 am Hobkirk reported to Hobbs that the battalion was 'now established in the Hindenburg Line as we had been before the attack. The cause of the trouble … was German *minenwerfer* fire. A large number of Germans were killed.' The Australians 'had about 100 casualties'.[108]

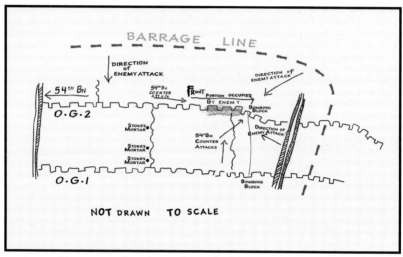

A trench map of the same area, drawn by an officer in the field, highlighting the numerous 'Direction of Enemy Attack'. Note the Barrage Line and where the Stokes mortars were placed for maximum effect and the position of the Bombing Block.

A couple of days later Hobbs described in more detail what had happened when, during

> ... the night 14th/15th all our Field Artillery Groups, and the Noreuil area were persistently shelled with gas shells and High Explosive. Information from a prisoner had been obtained that the LEHR Regiment had been warned for an attack to take place on the evening of the 13th ... and the attack was not a surprise. Artillery action had been considered and the prompt application ... contributed largely to the successful repulse and the infliction of heavy casualties on the enemy.

> The attack was made in strength, and ... it appears that the enemy was confident of ejecting us completely from the Hindenburg Line and from Bullecourt. Apart from the very heavy casualties inflicted on him ... it appears his morale is distinctly shaken by the defeat he has suffered.

After discussing other difficult decisions concerning the counterattack with his brigade commander, Hobbs wrote that, in his opinion, four reasons had contributed to the German demise:

a. The demoralization produced by our barrage and searching fire before the

b. [counter] attack.

c. The effectiveness of the S.O.S. barrage in cutting off the [enemy] retreat ...

d. The deadliness of the Lewis Gun Fire ...

e. The promptness and determination of the leader and troops who made the counter attack and killed all the Germans who entered our line

Since the repulse, the enemy has been noticeably inactive ... [and] it is evident that the blow has been a severe one for him.[109]

The majority of Australian soldiers were pleased with the outcome, albeit reflective over the fate of their mates. After walking over the area where the attack took place, Lieutenant McGinnis recalled that it was 'awful ... the place is literally covered with dead, and they are mixed up with the earth forming the communication sap.'[110]

**

Meanwhile, at 3.45 am on 15 May, the same counter-attack that had surprised the Australians was launched against the British front. Portrayed as 'the last and biggest', in the English sector alone it was preceded by 'some 60,000 rounds of high-explosive and gas shells', inflicting a high number of casualties and destroying a number of defensive positions. The Germans had planned well, their gas shells subsequently targeting British artillery which was about to commence counter-battery fire. Despite this, British gunners managed to don their gas masks and put down a barrage, described as a 'fantastic firework display as rockets of all colours were flung up, calling, it might be, for aid, for fire to lengthen, or for fire to shorten – no observer could in the confusion recognize signals or even tell whose were the rockets – made a truly awful and infernal battle picture, to which the din was fitting accompaniment.'[111]

Around 4.00 am, the same experienced German storm troops from the *Lehr Regiment* attacked to the left of the British front, while on the extreme right, units from the elite *Guard-Fusilier Regiment* began their assault. The English units were soon overwhelmed by sheer numbers. The *Guard-Fusiliers* captured almost 150 yards of OG1 and OG2 as well as some communication trenches. British field and heavy artillery responded swiftly and stunned German troops began to pull back. British infantry joined in the chase. The surviving Germans were massacred by artillery shells, machine-gun and rifle fire as they attempted to reach their own line. Further to the west, another brigade commanded by Brigadier General Bernard Freyberg forced a further party of Germans to retreat, taking six prisoners. With the enemy in retreat, two reserve companies from the 2nd Battalion (3rd London Regiment), reportedly 'a newly-arrived formation of Londoners who were for the first time entering the front line under battle conditions' and led by Lieutenant Colonel (the Rev) Percy Beresford, successfully attacked the few other parts of OG1 and OG2 still held by the enemy.[112]

German prisoners of war and Australian Red Cross wagons moving along the Vraucourt-Noreuil road during the Second Battle of Bullecourt. This road was the major route for ammunition supplies during the two battles (AWM E00446).

While they may have fresh to the front line, the Londoners retained memories of what they endured that day. 'I think the worst experiences were in the line at Bullecourt,' Private T.E. Crook (2nd Battalion) wrote,

> There wasn't much left to see of Bullecourt itself … [and] we were glad to leave   that part of the line … It must be remembered that from the front line trenches you had to go down communication trenches, to get back to the road, as you dare not walk overland as Jerry kept his machine guns and artillery going all the time … he always knew when troops in the line were being relieved.[113]

These young, inexperienced British soldiers had held the Germans at bay east of the Longatte road.

But the Germans struck with more venom and purpose in other areas of the British front. One well-organised attack retook parts of the south-eastern section of the village. The British, however, regrouped with another attack of their own — on this occasion by a company from the 20th Battalion, Manchester Regiment, to the left of the Londoners. After a vigorous bombing fight, followed by the all-too-familiar hand-to-hand combat, the plucky British regained that part of the front.[114]

***

Major General Shoubridge finally understood that his depleted and exhausted units could do little more. The 7th British Division had taken and held a large part of Bullecourt for 12 days. Now, all it needed was rest and refitting and a supply of new men to replace those killed or seriously wounded. Gough concurred. During the night of 15/16 May, 'the 7th Division handed over the Bullecourt position to another London Brigade – the 175th.' Major General H.D. Fanshawe's 58th London Division took over the entire Bullecourt front, 'held by its own troops comprising Bullecourt and the original left sector of the Australian front', while the 54th

Australian Battalion maintained a presence in the captured trenches east of Central Road.[115]

With fresh troops in the line, Gough was not keen to allow this opportunity to slip by, and ordered the immediate capture of the few remaining parts of Bullecourt. Staff officers at V Corps had been anticipating such a request. At 10.50 am, the corps commander, Sir Edward Fanshawe, informed his divisional commanders that troops from the 58th and 62nd divisions would move against those remaining enemy positions 'The advance will be carried out methodically,' the order confirmed, 'and attacks against the enemy holding a position in any strength will not be made without adequate artillery support.'[116]

At around 6.30 pm on 16 May, a company of the 2nd Battalion, 1st London Regiment (173rd Brigade) bombed its way along OG2 as far west as the road to Hendecourt.[117] However, senior German officers no longer saw the sense in holding on to what remained of an insignificant village and were preparing for an orderly withdrawal, albeit only after demolishing those remaining cellars and dugouts and preparing booby traps for unsuspecting British and Australian soldiers.

At 2.00 am on 17 May (before demolition and booby-trap work could start) and following a 'hurricane' barrage lasting barely two minutes, the 2nd Battalion (London Rifle Brigade) began a frontal attack from the south, targeting the few remaining enemy positions in the western part of the village. The plan was simple. And, not surprisingly, considering the Germans were preparing to withdraw, it worked. The Londoners swiftly took the area, with barely a whimper from enemy troops. Many Germans surrendered complete with their weapons, including machine-guns and 'Pineapple' mortars. Another single company from the 8th London Regiment (Post Office Rifles) soon passed across the 2nd Battalion's front, struggling through what was left of the western end of Bullecourt, before clearing the remainder of the village. German troops again offered little resistance

— like their comrades, several simply laid down their arms.[118] A few more 'small parties were seen digging, but they were dispersed by artillery fire'.[119]

***

'The quietest day the 5th Division have had here' came on 16 May although, towards midnight, the division sustained around 100 casualties due to an unexpected German artillery barrage. Australian patrols were not intimidated by the artillery fire, venturing into no man's land during the late night and into the early morning of 17 May. 'Everything was very quiet,' one report noted, 'no signs of any hostile patrols could be seen.'[120] Bean, too, considered that 'the Hun' gave the impression that he 'might really be going back – but I can't yet hear our guns on him.'[121] Hobbs, however, remained unconvinced. Believing that the Germans would most likely order another counter-attack, at 10.00 am on 17 May he ordered a section from the 285th Tunnelling Company (5th Pioneer Battalion) to lay down 'a defensive system of mining' in front of the sector held by the 14th Infantry Brigade.[122] The enemy attack never eventuated.

***

Although the Australians had taken little part in the final capture of Bullecourt, 'patrols' sent out from the 14th Brigade kept the British informed of German troop movements, particularly 'a large number of infantry moving along Lagnicourt-Pronville Road'. And, on 16 May, specialists from the 15th Brigade moved back to the Bullecourt sector to 'furnish the working parties … re the proposed mining operations in OG1 and OG2 – Hindenburg Line.'[123] Field artillery from the 5th Australian Division also assisted in laying barrages on 'enemy tracks and approaches' used by the Germans to move reinforcements to assist in rebuffing the British attack. Heavy and field artillery attached to I ANZAC was also ordered to assist, while taking 'advantage of the opportunity thus created of inflicting casualties on the enemy.'[124] Australian trench mortars and machine-guns were not forgotten, keeping 'enemy roads and communications under intermittent bursts of fire.'[125]

On 18 May the 5th Australian Division confirmed that 'things were very quiet on our front practically the whole of the day.'[126] Apart from occasional 'sniping and machine gun fire' the enemy's 'artillery was again very quiet'.[127] Official British reports now claimed that their troops 'have recaptured Bullecourt and a portion of the Hindenburg Line east of the village.'[128] After 15 days of at times horrendous fighting, what little remained of the village of Bullecourt and its surrounds was finally in British hands. And while the tiny hamlet was of no strategic or tactical value, Haig, in one of his many dispatches, acknowledged that the 'Australians during the past ten days having gallantly maintained their positions in this sector, repelling at least twelve determined counter attacks. We hold the greater part of Bullecourt.'[129]

Even in the horror of the Second Battle of Bullecourt, Australian troops never lost their cynical sense of humour. Here, at a cookhouse of the 5th Australian Division, some wag has scrawled 'The Vaulx Arms Hotel'. This photograph was taken on 20 May 1917, not long after Bullecourt was captured (AWM E02008).

Gough was less complimentary. The British general may have finally achieved his goal of taking Bullecourt, yet his mind (in common with Haig's) was already elsewhere, preoccupied with Flanders and planning for the Ypres offensive. Many years later, and regardless of his insistence that the attack on Bullecourt must continue, Gough devoted just two sentences to the events surrounding its capture: 'Finally the capture of the village was completed on 17th May by the 58th and 62nd Divisions, which had now relieved the 7th. The assault, except for an unsuccessful attack by the Third Army on 20th May, was the last incident in the Battle of Arras.'[130] Little mention was made of the human cost and the contribution of the four Australian divisions which took part in the two battles. Likewise, there was no mention at all of the enormous number of Australian and British casualties.

CHAPTER 13

'Would God I had died for thee.'
AFTERMATH

Not long after Bullecourt was captured and secured, Captain W. Maile, a British officer attached to the 2/3rd Home Counties Field Ambulance, wrote that the

> ... battle of Bullecourt was one of the fiercest and bloodiest of the war. Bullecourt was a village of a few hundred inhabitants very strongly held and fortified by the Hun. The only trouble was it caused a nasty bulge in our fairly straight front line. The Higher Authorities strongly objected to this and so decided it must be taken! After weeks of fighting and the efforts of four Divisions [sic] with all the necessary guns, it still held out. Of course hundreds of men were killed, but things like that seemed to be of very little importance to the high command. It probably inflated their ego. It required five divisions, roughly 60,000 men to take the village. We were the last division to have a go after four divisions had failed. Eventually we took it, but at a terrible cost in lives.[1]

And, under a headline declaring 'How Bullecourt was Won', a British periodical of the time attempted to apply a more positive slant to the battles, telling its readers that,

> ... fighting had been going on in Bullecourt since 3 May. It was then that the   Australians broke with magnificent dash into the Hindenburg Line upon the right of the village, and despite the fact that they had formed a most dangerous salient for themselves, held on tenaciously for ten days.[2]

Even with such favourable comments in the British press and Haig's insistence that the taking of the village was 'among the great achievements of the war', the sentiment among Australian troops could not have been more different.[3] The two battles of Bullecourt represent the AIF's lowest point on the Western Front. Prior to Bullecourt, Australian officers and their men had held out some hope that senior British officers and their High Command would do all they could to bring this horrendous conflict to a victorious end. Following Bullecourt the same Australians — providing they had the good fortune to survive the battles — had little trust in the competency of those senior British officers and their staff. One Australian, Major Garnet Adcock, summarised the sentiment succinctly. 'Everyone here is "fed up" of the war,' he wrote, 'but not with the Hun. The British staff, British methods and British bungling have sickened us.'[4]

Australian troops billeted in one of the sunken roads near Bullecourt on 19 May 1917, just two days after the fighting had ceased. Note the graves marked by crosses in the field beyond the road (AWM E02021).

***

However, a number of Australian officers, both senior and junior, and some of their troops, cannot escape criticism for their performance. While, in numerous instances, Australian officers and the men they led performed better than admirably, there were more than a few occasions on which their leadership was poor. Australian staff officers, including Birdwood and White, perhaps more than most, should be held accountable for the faulty planning at I ANZAC Corps headquarters, including their failure to order artillery to eliminate the deadly machine-gun nests at Balcony Trench, and around Queant, which caused massive casualties in the first battle. That they knew of the existence of the machine-guns and were aware of their deadly potential, but virtually chose to ignore it, is indefensible. Those machine-guns should have been targeted in the preliminary artillery bombardment. Inexplicably, the already inadequate artillery fire was, instead, directed against enemy supply lines.

Even more bizarre is the fact that they never learned from past lessons, and in the second attack they again chose not to target the very same machine-gun posts. Brigadier General Robert Smith was also at fault for establishing his 5th Brigade headquarters near Noreuil, too far behind the line to allow him to adequately direct his brigade's attack. Thus, when the attack went awry, Smith could contribute little. Had he sited his headquarters closer to the front, perhaps near the railway embankment — where Brigadier General John Gellibrand had established the 6th Brigade headquarters — the 5th Brigade's attack may have been more successful. As it was, it disintegrated into a rout, and for that Smith must accept much of the blame.

However, it is Haig who must bear prime responsibility for the overall strategy and for permitting Gough to continue the fruitless and unnecessary attacks on a village which, after early May — when the main Arras attack was to be halted — held no strategic (let alone tactical) value whatsoever. In January 1918 Haig (in another of his dispatches) provided some clues as to why he had permitted the slaughter to continue. 'A necessary part of the preparations for the Messines attack was the maintenance of activity on the Arras front,' he wrote, 'sufficient to keep the enemy in doubt as to whether our offensive there would be proceeded with. I therefore directed the

Armies concerned to continue active operations with such forces as were left to them.' Yet, later in the same dispatch, Haig was apparently at odds with himself when he wrote that,

> To secure the footing gained by the Australians in the Hindenburg Line on 3rd May it was advisable that Bullecourt should be captured without loss of time. During the fortnight following our attack, fighting for the possession of this village went on unceasingly; while the Australian troops in the sector of the Hindenburg Line to the east beat off counter attack after counter attack. The defence of this 1,000 yards of double trench line, exposed to counter attack on every side, through two weeks of almost constant fighting deserves to be remembered as a most gallant feat of arms.[5]

And Gough, it seems, had learnt little from the ill-judged attack on 11 April. Not only did he again consent to the use of tanks for the assault on 3 May (although on this occasion they provided somewhat limited support alongside the hapless 62nd British Division), his tactics remained inept. He erred badly by allowing a similar attack to proceed along the same narrow front against the same re-entrant without taking into account the well-sited German defences near Queant. Overall, Gough's planning and execution of the two battles was anything but impressive. When added to his failures on the Somme the previous year, it appears that he retained his command of the Fifth Army for no other reason than his close friendship with Haig.[6]

Despite the failure of the tanks, changes to artillery doctrine in early 1917 were still in some sort of limbo. It is not clear whether — even if enough artillery had been available to lay down a lengthy blanket barrage or, for that matter, a short intense bombardment on enemy trenches and gun emplacements — this would have been sufficient to influence the outcome of the battle. Certainly British planners were improving their doctrine and tactics, particularly following failures such as those that blighted the Somme offensives.

However they still had much to learn and much to develop before they could formulate anything resembling the successful combined arms doctrine that they would put into effect in mid to late 1918. German defences around Bullecourt and that sector of the Hindenburg Line were strong and well constructed, and the many strands of thick wire in front of OG1 and OG2 must have been daunting obstacles for attacking troops. More significantly, there were far too few high explosive shells readily available to the Fifth Army — the type of shells which could effectively cut the wire in sufficient places to allow passage into enemy trenches. Similar problems plagued the second battle. Still, the attack went ahead. And, for two weeks it became a virtual war of attrition — in the words of Haig a 'wearing out' fight. Ultimately, it was the Germans who chose not to sacrifice more badly needed troops for a village that meant virtually nothing to their changing strategic plans.

**

The human tragedy from both battles was overwhelming. During the lengthy second battle, many of the dead were simply left to lie in no man's land. A number from the first battle, their bodies already badly decomposed, also lay on the battlefield while others had been left hanging on the barbed wire and must have presented a ghastly sight to the assaulting troops. There were also numerous men whose scattered remains could not be identified having been macerated by the ceaseless artillery fire. A British soldier from The Post Office Rifles attempted to describe the scene not long after the village had been taken:

> By this time Bullecourt and its surroundings had become a veritable charnel- house, dead bodies and dead mules were lying in hundreds, and the place was so   offensive that it was a question whether it could be retained. Parties were   organised to clear up, and in a short space of time, in spite of every adverse condition, it was made tolerably healthy.[7]

Once the fighting had concluded, Australian troops were finally given some time away from the front line. For many, however, this proved to be but a brief respite. Sent further north to Flanders, within a few short weeks they were engaged, first in the attack at Messines then, not long afterwards, in the unimaginable horror that became the Third Battle of Ypres.

***

At the end of the Second Battle of Bullecourt the 2nd Australian Division listed 173 officers and 3725 men as casualties. The 1st Division had fared little better, losing 80 officers and 2261 men while the 5th sustained losses of 39 officers and 1204 men. British casualties were not quite as heavy. The 7th Division counted 128 officers and 2554 men as casualties while the 58th Division suffered losses of 39 officers and 680 men with the 62nd Division taking casualties of 143 officers and 3284 men.[8]

German losses, while significant in the fighting for Bullecourt, were not as heavy as the Australian or British. The *27th Wurttemberg Division* sustained casualties totalling 2176 while the *Lehr Division's* losses amounted to around 2000 and the *3rd Guard Division's* to 1146.[9] German officers were able to minimise their casualties, particularly during the earlier stages of the battle, by employing recent changes to *Flachen und Lucken* (defence-in-depth doctrine) which had worked remarkably well during the latter part of the British attack at Arras.[10] Experienced enemy soldiers quickly learnt what those changes involved.

Bullecourt also saw the deaths of a number of Australian and British aviators who fought and died in the confines of their frail flying machines in the skies above. Infantry struggling through the mud and horror in the trenches below must have wondered how pilots coped with being enclosed in those tiny biplanes. The airmen were also remarkable for the chivalry they displayed towards their enemy which was akin to that of the medieval knights. 'The environment in which they fought was still harsh,' writes Peter Pedersen, 'pilots sat in open cockpits, close to engines that were louder than a pneumatic drill and vibrated so much their bodies shook. At the routine altitude of 10,000 feet, sub-zero temperatures, oxygen deprivation and increased blood pressure kicked in, reducing efficiency by 75 per cent. Then came the physically draining forces of violent combat manoeuvres.'[11] Many of the German aircraft were superior in design, particularly the Albatross scout, piloted by experienced aviators the like of the feared Captain Manfred von Richthofen. Australians fighting at Bullecourt often spotted von Richthofen in his bright red triplane, occasionally witnessing his victory over a British aircraft which would plummet to the earth in flames. Without a parachute to allow them to escape the burning aircraft, those pilots often suffered a terrible death. The more fortunate were killed instantly. However, German aviators were not always on the winning side. For instance, on 12 May, Lieutenant Ronald McGinnis wrote of witnessing 'some fine aerial fights this morning in which our machines drove him off every time.'[12]

***

Following the first assault on Bullecourt on 11 April, German intelligence sources — usually photographs from aerial reconnaissance which showed the ongoing build-up of British and Australian men and equipment, or information divulged by captured British or Australian soldiers — revealed that another attack was imminent. The wily German general Otto von Moser moved some of his best troops from the *123rd Grenadier Regiment* into the most vulnerable part of the line. Prior to the attack, which German headquarters knew from reports and alterations to British artillery preparation would be launched on or about 3 May, more well-armed elite storm troops not only manned the trenches, but occupied well-concealed positions ready to counter-attack. When the attack came, those men were well prepared.

Von Moser, too, knew that tanks were again preparing to assist the advance. 'Once again the English had in vain put their hopes in the tanks,' he wrote, 'but, stripped of the protection which they expected, their infantry came upon fresh troops on the outskirts of Bullecourt who were prepared to hold on to this important strong point and fight to the last man.'[13] And, when the strong German defences were breached, von Moser ordered that reinforcements be prepared to move forward without delay to launch a large-scale (or 'general') counter-attack. Seven large scale ('general') counter-attacks were launched during the almost two weeks of the battle. While most were initially successful, Australian and British troops were usually able to respond with a counter-attack of their own.

The later German counter-attacks were far less successful. Certainly, the seventh and final attack during the night of 14/15 May was defeated so comprehensively that it led enemy officers to reassess their position. In the end the German High Command saw no point in continuing to drain its dwindling manpower by holding onto von Moser's so-called 'important strong point' and surrounding parts of the Hindenburg Line, which held little tactical value and certainly no strategic value. Senior German officers chose logic over stubbornness, and withdrew their men to another well-prepared position behind the original line.

***

Regardless of the Pyrrhic victory that Bullecourt has come to represent, many lessons were learnt by senior Australian and British officers — lessons which would prove invaluable, particularly when plans were being developed for forthcoming battles involving tanks. While a secret British report written by Major General Neill Malcolm on 17 May noted that Gough and the more senior tank officers had understood little from the first Bullecourt battle, particularly that 'the cooperation between Infantry and Tanks is not good', more significantly, it asserted that infantry officers would need to be permitted more involvement in future planning.[14] The following year, the Australian general John Monash, having already deliberated at length over the report by Jacka and other critiques of both battles, made certain that the newer and better protected Mark V tanks went into action completely shielded, and only after Allied artillery had blanketed the German artillery emplacements. He also made full use of air cover, a strategy that, up to this point, was virtually unknown.[15]

Innovations in close artillery support (covering an attack by Australian infantry) were largely a response to events in the early stages of the second battle. Australian artillery officers were quick learners. By mid-May, 'field artillery was handled with remarkable boldness as regards targets, and though, inevitably, the infantry on occasion suffered in consequence, these experiments in close support were in general successful.'[16]

More 'lessons' were realised at brigade and even battalion level. For instance, Major Maurice Wilder Neligan (temporary commanding officer of the 9th Battalion) reported that his officers noticed that protective steel helmets glistened 'when wet ... and are easily seen when flares go up', thereby attracting 'heavy shelling during reliefs'. Australian troops also needed further 'training in the use of German bombs'. Wilder Neligan argued that enemy 'bombs can often be used – thus saving carrying parties for our own.' However, his most significant observations concerned morale. Regimental aid posts, set up in 'the front line trench proved very valuable – both from point of view of morale and in dealing with wounded.' More crucial was the need to clear communication trenches 'of dead and wounded'. Wilder Neligan witnessed firsthand the often slow and painful death of numerous soldiers, noting also that many others sustained dreadful wounds. He described scenes in which the bodies almost covered the bottom of the trenches. 'Troops going into attack are naturally affected by this,' he wrote, 'besides ... that it blocks up the sap.'[17]

***

In 1933 Charles Bean's account of the two battles of Bullecourt was published in Volume IV of *The Official History of Australia in the War of 1914-1918*. Since then Bean has been criticised by Eric Andrews, among others, for being less than accurate in his account, particularly concerning the unsatisfactory staff work and for not revealing the deficiencies in some Australian divisions and brigades — primarily the 2nd Division and 5th Brigade — and the 'serious failures at Corps level'. Andrews asserts that, 'although the basic error, to attack a re-entrant, was made by Gough with Haig behind him, and although Gough's impetuosity led to the precipitate attack by tanks in First Bullecourt', poor planning by Australian officers, particularly Birdwood and White, constituted the major reason the attack was doomed even before it started. It is possible that Bean, because of his proximity to certain senior staff officers — particularly White — 'or perhaps even [his inability] to face the fact himself', attempted to cover up the simple truth that 'the Australians themselves contributed to the disasters'.[18] And, while there is almost no possibility that Birdwood and White could have persuaded Gough to call off the attacks, evidence suggests that they could have tried harder, at least to make suitable amendments to the plans.

Not unexpectedly, Andrews' main criticism centres on Bean's neglect to mention weak staff work, above all the failure of the Australian artillery to eliminate the German machine-gun nests around Balcony Trench and Queant. Yet, in attempting to find fault with Bean's description of the subsequent infantry attack, Andrews falls into a similar trap himself. Establishing that the artillery did not destroy the machine-guns, he goes on to question Bean's assurance 'that both [the 5th and 6th] brigades assembled on a two-battalion front of 680 yards.' Using one of Bean's own small maps as evidence, Andrews then disputes where the troops actually lined up to attack. And, while it is not possible to establish this by studying any of the documents or war diaries — something Andrews appears to accept — he somewhat inexplicably writes that 'if the right flank of the 5th Brigade did extend on a 680 yard frontage, the men on its far right would be only 700 yards from the German wire around Queant, not 850 as the Brigade calculated.' Andrews now implies precisely what Bean claims in his official history. 'The *exact position is impossible to determine*,' Andrews writes, 'but it *seems quite clear* that the soldiers were well on the "crest", insofar as there was one, and in clear view of the German lines. No wonder the 5th Brigade was slaughtered.'[19] The 5th Brigade was certainly slaughtered, for the most part due to poor staff work and some weak leadership by junior officers when confronted with the overwhelming firepower of enemy machine-guns from positions around Queant (a fact most certainly minimally acknowledged by Bean). Add to this Brigadier General Smith's mediocre command skills and his decision to establish his brigade headquarters too far from the action.

A little over a month after the second battle, Gellibrand resigned his leadership of the 6th Australian Brigade to take up a temporary training command in England. At the time he cited numerous reasons, not least the inability of the 2nd Division's 'G Branch' 'to assess critical information from other sources and formulate appropriate orders', using as an example the flawed orders to the 25th Battalion in its attack on Bullecourt.[20] Yet, on the face of it, this explanation was part of a smokescreen. Gellibrand, in fact, was deeply troubled by the 'old boy network', the incompetence and bad leadership at 2nd Division headquarters and Smith's inability to properly command the 5th Brigade — nowhere better demonstrated than in his bungling of the brigade's advance on 3 May.[21]

And, while Andrews may have been critical of Bean's account in the *Official History*, Gellibrand certainly disagreed following his reading of an early draft of the book. 'It is a book written from the heart and not a book written to order,' Gellibrand penned in response to Bean's account:

> I couldn't read some of it aloud to save my life and yet, as one reads, the gradual change to tragedy is imperceptible until one

is overwhelmed on realising what the words mean. If any reader happens to be an old hand, he will realise the agony of soul that made David lament, "Oh my son Absalom, my son, would God I had died for thee."[22]

Brigadier General Harold 'Pompey' Elliott was another senior Australian officer who, even after the war, condemned White and Birdwood for what he regarded as their ineffective leadership in both battles and for the indifference they showed over the unnecessary deaths of Australian soldiers at Bullecourt. Elliott also believed that their battle plans and tactics were ultimately flawed. Likewise, he had no doubt that the weak artillery preparation for the second battle was squarely a result of their poor planning, that they were also negligent for not considering the use of smoke to cover the infantry advance and for allowing the British to amend the time of the attack. As late as 1921 Elliott was still a bitter man. Recalling the careless use of tanks in the first battle, he told the Australian Senate that Birdwood and White should be held accountable because, rather than provide some concealment in the first battle, they 'sent the tanks forward when the ground was white with snow, so that every tank stood out like a nigger on a whitewashed fence.'

After the war, White was adamant that he and Birdwood did as much as possible to prevent the first battle from proceeding. Both, in fact, told Gough, on more than one occasion, that they were particularly uneasy about tanks advancing alongside Australian troops, most of whom had not even laid eyes on the unsightly monsters, let alone trained with them. Birdwood blamed Gough — not Haig — for insisting that the attack proceed. Once Gough had informed Birdwood and White that it was Haig's order to proceed, White

> … told Birdie that I didn't believe it. Gough is an Irishman and he wanted to do the attack. Unquestionably he was speaking to the Chief-of-Staff but I think he [Gough] made it an excuse for this story – I think he lied. There is no question that Gough wanted us to make this attack. He was anxious to do something.

He was up against Allenby [for command of the soon-to-be-launched Flanders campaign].[23]

Yet, without discounting White's account, Elliott's and Gellibrand's criticisms certainly appear justified and offer a plausible explanation as to why both battles turned to disaster for the AIF.

**

Apart from valuable lessons learnt for planning future battles, if anything positive could have come from the two battles of Bullecourt, then it could only have been shaken German morale. Australian soldiers demonstrated that the Hindenburg Line was not as unassailable as the German High Command believed. The first battle, in which Australian infantry succeeded without either artillery or, for that matter, suitable tank support, made enemy officers reassess not only the two lines of defensive trenches, but also rethink their changes to the defence-in-depth doctrine. The second battle, in which Australian and British troops successively recaptured and consolidated the OG1 and OG2 trenches, added to the enemy's woes and forced the German staff to again reconsider their doctrine. German units holding the village had sustained more casualties than their high command considered viable. The Germans were also forced to maintain reserve units — which were needed elsewhere — to the rear of the Bullecourt sector. Little wonder that senior German officers ultimately decided to withdraw their troops and surrender parts of the Hindenburg Line around the village. German commander General Otto von Moser assessed the nature of the battles succinctly when, following two weeks of horrendous and bloody fighting, he wrote that, by 'common consent … [it was] much bitterer than on the Somme.'[24] Australian soldiers who survived the bloodletting at Bullecourt would certainly have agreed.

POSTSCRIPT

Bullecourt Today

The tiny village of Bullecourt was rebuilt after the war and bears few scars to remind visitors of the horrors it witnessed all those years ago. Yet French villagers have never forgotten the debt that they owe the young men who travelled across two oceans to fight and die and, ultimately, to help liberate what remained of their great grand-parents' village. Every Anzac Day, those same local villagers organise and attend a special service to commemorate the sacrifice of the many Australian soldiers and their British brothers-in-arms.

Outside the small town hall the citizens have built a memorial, engraved with the moving words '*A la memoire glorieuse des enfants de Bullecourt morts pour la France 1914-1918*' ('To the glorious memory of the children of Bullecourt who died for France 1914-1918'). Opposite the town hall is the church of St Vlaast, which replaced the original church that was completely destroyed in the fighting. In front of St Vlaast is the 'Slouch Hat' memorial, listing all the Australian and British units that fought in the two battles and next to it part of a rusty tank track from one of the vehicles which took part in the first battle — a memorial to the tank crews from D Battalion, Heavy Branch Machine Gun Corps. All along the main road there are other, smaller memorials, dedicated to the sacrifice of Australian and British soldiers.

Not far from the church is the beginning of the sunken road. These days, walking along this same road, where all those years ago young Australian soldiers lined up to commence their advance, the only noise (and surprise) comes from French hunters often out looking for easy prey. Indeed the crack of rifle fire provides its own reminder of what those Australians experienced. Looking across the fields it is possible to see the spire of St Vlaast in the distance, while on the other side the village of Riencourt is clearly visible. The obstacles the British and Australian soldiers faced as they advanced up a slight incline become more evident, as does their clear and uninterrupted exposure to machine-gun fire from the direction of Queant, further to the left of the sunken road. And, in the fields, not far off the road, it is still possible to find a rusty shell case or even a button or badge from one of the soldier's uniforms.

It is also possible, as in the case of Sergeant John Wright of the 22nd Battalion, to find the remains of an Australian soldier, previously listed as missing. In November 1994, a farmer, ploughing his field close to where the sunken road meets the side road to Riencourt-les-Cagnicourt, came across Wright's bones, his identity disc still in place. One year later, in November 1995, six Australian soldiers carried his remains in a flag-draped coffin to the Queant Road Military Cemetery, not far from where he was killed. At the small church Wright was finally given a fitting military farewell. No doubt there are others, like Wright, still lying in those fields waiting to be found.

Back in Bullecourt, the Australian flag flies proudly outside the small museum close to the town hall while, close at hand, in the inn, numerous items of Australian memorabilia line the walls. By venturing down a nearby road, it is possible to imagine the difficulties confronting the 62nd British Division as the men lined up to attack the village from the area behind and slightly to the left towards Ecoust.

On the opposite side of Bullecourt is the *Rue des Australiens* — or, as it was called in 1917, the Diagonal Road, where the German support trench OG2 followed alongside the road. The *Rue des Australiens* now leads to the imposing Australian Memorial Park, located between the German front (OG1) and support trenches (OG2). In pride of place stands the bronze statue of the 'Bullecourt Digger', now watching over the broad, open, fertile farmlands. This is the same ground where, in April and May 1917, many thousands of Australian and British soldiers were killed or wounded as they struggled to capture and hold this part of the Hindenburg Line.

The Memorial Park was opened by the Australian Minister for Veterans' Affairs, Ben Humphreys, on Anzac Day 1992. Humphreys was disappointed by the emptiness of the park and suggested to the government that Melbourne sculptor Peter Corlett be commissioned to design some form of commemoration of the sacrifice of the soldiers which could be erected on the cairn already in place. Corlett's design not only portrays the individuality of the Australian troops who fought at Bullecourt in 1917, but captures the essence of the Australian soldier, ensuring its relevance for future generations.

Not long after being awarded the commission, Corlett discovered a personal connection. His father, Kenneth Corlett (4th Field Ambulance), had been involved in the first battle. Now Peter Corlett had a face to put to his 'Bullecourt Digger'. Corlett also took great care to replicate the Australian soldier's uniform and the equipment of the day. Shortly before the statue was unveiled, on Anzac Day 1993, Corlett revealed that he 'stood in the field and touched the cairn upon which my sculpture will eventually rest and felt a felt a wave of emotion run through me. I felt my dad's presence and everything went quiet.'

A little further along the *Rue des Australiens* there is a small memorial cross signifying the point where OG2 intersected the roadway from the fields to the left — the same spot that caused so much grief to Australian troops attempting to advance further along the trench towards Bullecourt. Over the years, many personal and heartfelt messages (in English and French) have been added to the cross and many remain to this day. From this site, not far from where Lieutenant Rupert Moon's gallant conduct saw him awarded the Victoria Cross, it is possible to view a panorama of almost the entire old battlefield.

Not much further on is the junction where Central Road joins the old Diagonal Road — the Six Cross Roads — with Riencourt a short distance away. From this exact spot, at the junction, it is possible to glimpse the point where Central Road joins the sunken road, while a distant row of trees signifies the railway embankment — the position from which the Australians commenced their advance, and the point to which they were forced to withdraw after the first futile battle. A short distance away is Riencourt and, further to its right, the village of Queant — best remembered as the village from which deadly machine-gun fire inflicted such heavy casualties on the 5th Australian Infantry Brigade.

Bullecourt and its surrounds witnessed some of the most dreadful fighting of the Great War. Yet, today, apart from its memorials, it is difficult to find any remnant damage or, indeed, imagine that the village was virtually razed to the ground. Australian flags are prominent, and serve as a reminder to those Australians who visit this place to commemorate the sacrifice of their grandfathers or great grandfathers alongside the local villagers who will never forget. Every Anzac Day this tiny village in a far-off country effectively becomes a little piece of Australia.

Endnotes

Introduction

1 See Eric Andrews, 'Bean and Bullecourt: Weaknesses and Strengths of the Official History of Australia in the First World War', in *Revue Internationale d'Histoire Militaire*, No. 72, 1990, pp. 25–47.

2 C.E.W. Bean, *Official History of Australia in the War of 1914–1918*, Vol. IV, *The AIF in France 1917*, University of Queensland Press, St Lucia, 1982 (1933), pp. 544–45.

Chapter 1

1 On 19 July 1916 the 5th Australian Division was ordered to attack enemy positions around the French village of Fromelles. In a badly planned and poorly executed operation, the division incurred casualties of 5533 officers and men. Most Australians blamed the commander of XI Corps (Lieutenant General Sir Richard Haking) for the disaster. On the broader canvas, following Fromelles some Australian officers began to doubt the wisdom of placing Australian forces under British command. The notion was reinforced a month or so later when the 1st, 2nd and 4th Australian divisions each suffered huge casualties attempting to take Pozieres, a French village located on the main Somme battlefield. But, for the moment, the majority of Australians still believed that General Headquarters (GHQ), senior British officers and politicians were doing their best to reduce casualties and bring the war to an end.

2 Jeffrey Grey, *A Military History of Australia*, Cambridge University Press, Oakleigh, Vic, 1990, p. 102

3 Peter Pedersen, *The Anzacs: Gallipoli to the Western Front*, Viking, Camberwell, Victoria, 2007, p. 185.

4 W.H. Downing, *To the Last Ridge: the First World War memoirs of W.H. Downing*, Duffy and Snellgrove, Sydney, 1998, p. 33.

5 F. Cutlack (ed), *War Letters of General Monash*, Angus & Robertson, Sydney, 1935, p. 155.

6 Sergeant Rupert Baldwin, Pedersen, *The ANZACS*, p. 186.

7 B. Gammage, *The Broken Years: Australian Soldiers in the Great War*, Penguin, Ringwood, Victoria, 1987 (1974), p. 179.

8 Cutlack (ed), *War Letters of General Monash*, p. 155.

9 F. Green, *The Fortieth: a record of the 40th Battalion AIF*, Government Printer, Hobart, 1922, p. 15.

10 For a recent analysis of the Somme campaign see Robin Prior and Trevor Wilson, *The Somme*, Yale University Press, New Haven, CT, 2005. The battle from the troops' perspective is best outlined in P. Hart, *The Somme*, Weidenfeld & Nicolson, London, 2005.

11 M. Neiberg, *Fighting the Great War: a Global History*, Harvard University Press, Cambridge, Massachusetts, 2005, p. 233.

12 I. Passingham, *All the Kaiser's Men: the life and death of the German Army on the Western Front 1914-1918*, Sutton Publishing, Stroud, Gloucestershire, 2003, pp. 139–40; M. Samuels, *Doctrine and Dogma: German and British Infantry Tactics in the First World War*, Greenwood Press, Westport, CT, 1992, particularly Chapter 3.

Endnotes

13   H. Herwig, *The First World War: Germany and Austria 1914-1918*, Arnold, London, 1997, p. 312.

14   Ibid., p. 315.

15   The strategy worked for a while. During the first six months when Germany expected to starve Britain into submission, monthly losses averaged slightly over 600,000 tons. On 19 June the new First Sea Lord (Admiral Sir John Jellicoe) informed the War Council that 'there is no good discussing plans for next Spring [as] we cannot go on.' Gerard De Groot, *Douglas Haig 1861-1928*, Unwin Hyman, London, 1988, p. 327.

16   Passingham, *All the Kaiser's Men*, p. 138.

17   A.D. Ellis, *The History of the Fifth Australian Division*, Hodder and Stoughton, London, 1920, pp. 175–76.

18   B. Doneley, *Black Over Blue: the 25*th *Battalion, AIF at war 1915-1918*, University of Southern Queensland Press, Toowoomba, 1997, p. 79.

19   General Hubert Gough, *The Fifth Army*, Hodder and Stoughton, London, 1931, p. 177.

20   Bean, *Official History*, Vol. IV, *The AIF in France 1917*, p. 113.

21   Gough, *The Fifth Army*, p. 177.

22   A. Farrah-Hockley, *Goughie: the Life of General Sir Hubert Gough CGB GCMG KCVO*, HarperCollins, London, 1975, p. 205.

23   McDowell to his father, 20 March 1917, George Stanley McDowell papers, AWM PR00276.

24   Summary of Operations, 8th Australian Infantry Brigade, 16–21 March, involving the occupation of Bapaume, AWM 26, item 177/2.

25   Signal, 5th Australian Division to I ANZAC Corps, 17 March 1917, AWM 26, item 173/9.

26   H.E. Elliott, 'Story of 15th Brigade's Advance,' German Withdrawal, No 260, Bean papers, AWM 38 3DRL606/260(1).

27   Gough, *The Fifth Army*, p. 178.

28   Passingham, *All the Kaiser's Men*, p. 140.

29   P. Sadler, *The Paladin: a Life of Major General Sir John Gellibrand*, Oxford University Press, South Melbourne, 2000, p. 115.

30   McDowell to his father, 20 March 1917, George Stanley McDowell papers, AWM PR00276.

31   5th Australian Division, Weekly Summary of Operations, 23 March 1917, AWM 26, item 173/9.

32   David Coombes, *The Lionheart: A Life of Lieutenant General Sir Talbot Hobbs*, Australian Military History Publications, Loftus, New South Wales, 2007, pp. 158–59.

33   Pederson, *The ANZACS*, p. 195.

34   26th Battalion, Operation Order, 26 March 1917, Lagnicourt, quoted from papers of Lieutenant W.F.J. Hamilton, 26th Battalion, AWM PR88/174.

35   J. King, *The Western Front Diaries: the ANZACs' Own Stories*, Simon & Schuster, Pymble, NSW, 2008, p. 244.

36   13th Infantry Brigade Report, Attack on Village of Noreuil, April 1917, AWM 4, item no 23/13/15.

37   1st Australian Infantry Brigade Order No. 24, 8 April 1917, AWM 4, item 1/42/27 part 1.

38   50th Infantry Battalion, War Diary 2 April 1917, AWM 4, item no 23/67/10.

39   L. Newton, *The Story of the Twelfth: a Record of the 12*th *Battalion AIF During the Great War 1914-18*, John Burridge Military Antiques, Swanbourne, Western Australia, 2010, p. 131.

40   Major General Walker's Report on capture of Hermies, Demicourt and Boursies by 1st Australian Division, 9 April 1917, AWM 4, item 1/42/27, part 1.

41   Bean, *Official History*, Vol. IV, *The AIF in France 1917*, p. 251.

42   Situation Wires, 9 April 1917, AIF Diaries, General Staff Headquarters 2nd Australian Division, April 1917, AWM 4, item 1/44/21, part 1.

43   Boursies had cost the 10th and 12th battalions 341 men; Hermies the 2nd and 3rd battalions 253; and Demicourt the 1st Battalion just 55 casualties. See Bean, *Official History*, Vol. IV, *The AIF in France 1917*, p. 249.

Chapter 2

1   Diary of Field Marshal Sir Douglas Haig, Monday 26 February 1917, G. Sheffield and J. Bourne (eds), *Douglas Haig War Diaries and Letters 1914-1918*, Weidenfeld & Nicolson, London, 2005, pp. 271–72.

2   Passingham, *All the Kaiser's Men*, p. 145.

3   Spears to Napper re attack against Arras, French sector, 9 March 1917, Major Spears papers, Liddell Hart Centre for Military Archives, Kings College, London.

4   Hew Strachan, *The First World War: an Illustrated History*, Simon & Schuster, London, 2003, p. 243; Gary Sheffield, *Forgotten Victory, The First World War: Myths and Realities*, Headline, London, 2001, p. 162.

5   Passingham, *All the Kaiser's Men*, p. 145.

6   Charteris to Haig, 28 January 1917, German Withdrawal, Arras, AWM 45, item 33/8.

7   Neiberg, *Fighting the Great War*, p. 235.

8   Kiggell to Malcolm, 5 February 1917, correspondence between GHQ and armies relating to German withdrawal, Arras, Bullecourt, 1917 (subsequently correspondence, German withdrawal) AWM 51, item 52.

9   Lieutenant General L. Kiggell, report of meeting at GHQ between Haig and his Army commanders, 26 March 1917, correspondence German withdrawal, AWM 51, item 52, author's emphasis.

10   P. Simkins, 'Haig and the Army Commanders' in B. Bond and N. Cave (eds), *Haig a Reappraisal 70 Years On*, Pen & Sword, Barnsley, 1999, p. 91.

11   Lieutenant General L Kiggell report of meeting at GHQ between Haig and his Army commanders, 26 March 1917, correspondence, German withdrawal, AWM 51, item 52.

12   Diary of Field Marshal Sir Douglas Haig, Monday 26 February 1917, Sheffield and Bourne (eds), *Douglas Haig War Diaries and Letters 1914-1918*, p. 271, Haig's emphasis.

13   J. Williams, *Byng of Vimy: General and Governor General*, Leo Cooper, London, 1992 (1983), p. xiii.

14   Simkins, 'Haig and the Army Commanders,' p. 91.

15   Williams, *Byng of Vimy*, p. 147.

16   M. Barrett, *Casualty Figures: How Five Men Survived the First World War*, Verso, London, 2008, p. 57.

17   L. James, *Imperial Warrior: the Life and Times of Field-Marshal Viscount Allenby 1861-1936*, Weidenfeld & Nicolson, London, 1993, p. 94.

18   P. Griffith, *Battle Tactics of the Western Front: the British Army's Art of Attack 1916-18*, Yale University Press, New Haven, CT, 1994, p. 85.

19   Neiberg, *Fighting the Great War*, pp. 237–38.

20   M. Farndale, *History of the Royal Regiment of Artillery: Western Front 1914-18*, Royal Artillery Institute, London, 1987, p. 165.

21   Sheffield, *Forgotten Victory*, p. 163.

22   Diary of Lieutenant General Sir (George) Sidney Clive, 8 April 1917, 2/4, Liddell Hart Centre for Military Archives, Kings College, London.

23   Passingham, *All the Kaiser's Men*, p. 149.

24   James, *Imperial Warrior*, p. 100.

25   G.W.L. Nicholson, *Canadian Expeditionary Force 1914-1919: the Official History of the Canadian Expeditionary Force in the First World War*, Queen's Printer, Ottawa, 1962, p. 253.

26   Ibid.

27   Neiberg, *Fighting the Great War*, p. 239.

28   Cutlack (ed), *War Letters of General Monash*, p. 171, Monash's emphasis.

29   Williams, *Byng of Vimy*, pp. 165–66.

30   Diary of Field Marshal Sir Douglas Haig, 10 April 1917, No 112, Vol. 15, April 1917, National Library of Scotland.

31   James, *Imperial Warrior*, p. 100.

32   Passingham, *All the Kaiser's Men*, p. 152.

33   Diary of Field Marshal Sir Douglas Haig, Thursday 12 April 1917, Sheffield and Bourne (eds), *Douglas Haig War Diaries and Letters 1914-1918*, p. 281.

34   Haig to his wife and diary entry, 13 April, Sheffield and Bourne (eds), *Douglas Haig War Diaries and Letters 1914-1918*, pp. 282–83.

35   W. Reid, *Architect of Victory: Douglas Haig*, Birlinn, Edinburgh, 2006, p. 347.

36   Gary Sheffield, 'Haig and the British Expeditionary Force in 1917' in P. Dennis and J. Grey (eds), *1917 – Tactics, Training and Technology*, Australian Military History Publications, Loftus, New South Wales, 2007, p. 7.

37   For an account focusing on one French division which explains the reasons behind the mutinies and the eventual outcome, see L. Smith, *Between Mutiny and Obedience: the Case of the French Fifth Infantry Division During World War One*, Princeton University Press, Princeton, NJ, 1994.

Chapter 3

1   R. Neillands, The Great War Generals on the Western Front 1914-18, Robinson Publishing, London, 1999, p. 369.

2   A. Clark, The Donkeys, Pimlico, London, 1991, p. 123.

3   G. Sheffield and D. Todman (eds), Command and Control on the Western Front: the British Army's Experience 1914-1918, Spellmount, Staplehurst, Kent, 2004, p. 71.

4   I. Beckett and S. Corvi (eds), Haig's Generals, Pen & Sword, Barnsley, 2009, p. 78.

5   Sheffield and Todman (eds), Command and Control on the Western Front, pp. 85–86.

6   Liddell Hart discussion with L[loyd] G[eorge] and Hubert Gough at Reform Club dinner, 29 January 1936, Liddell Hart papers, Liddell Hart Centre for Military Archives, Kings College London, LH11/1936/31.

7   N. Dixon, On the Psychology of Military Incompetence, Jonathon Cape, London, 1976, p. 373.

8   D. Winter, Haig's Command: a Reassessment, Viking, London, 1991, p. 278.

9   Gerard De Groot, The First World War, Palgrave, Houndmills, Hampshire, 2001, p. 44.

10   Rawlinson diary, 26 January 1917; Haldane war diary, 31 March 1917; Brigadier A.E. Hodgkin diary 14 March 1917: S. Robbins, British Generalship on the Western Front 1914-18: Defeat Into Victory, Routledge, London, 2006, p. 33.

11   J.M. Bourne, 'British Generals in the First World War' in G. Sheffield (ed), Leadership and Command: Anglo-American Military Experience Since 1861, Brasseys, London, 2002, pp. 93–116.

12   Bean to N. Wanliss, 8 May 1924, 14th Australian Battalion, 1st Battle of Bullecourt April 1917, AWM 224, MSS 143(A) part 10.

13   Gough to Paul Maze, 3 August 1918, Liddell Hart Papers, Vol. 6, Liddell Hart Centre for Military Archives, Kings College, London, LH 9/28/59.

14   For an account of the battle see Bean, Official History, Vol. IV, The AIF in France 1917, pp. 31–41.

15   Liddell Hart discussion with Duff Cooper, 18 January 1936, Liddell Hart Papers, Liddell Hart Centre for Military Archives, Kings College London, LH11/1936/27.

16   Discussion with L[loyd] G[eorge] and Hubert Gough at Reform Club dinner, 29 January 1936; Liddell Hart to Arthur Barker Publishers, 19 September 1954, Liddell Hart papers, Liddell Hart Centre for Military Archives, Kings College London, LH11/1936/31 and LH1/323/16.

17   Shirtley to his mother, 6 January 1917, Lieutenant William Shirtley papers, AWM 2DRL792.

18   T. White, Diggers Abroad: Jottings by a Digger Officer, Angus & Robertson, Sydney, 1920, p. 46.

19   P. Toft, 'Playing a Man's Game', The Queensland Digger, 1 February 1938, p. 10; 1 March 1938, pp. 8–9.

20   Pedersen, The ANZACS, p. 199.

21   Bean, Official History of Australia in the War of 1914–1918, Vol. III, The AIF in France 1916, University of Queensland Press, St Lucia, 1982 (1929), p. 45.

22   Ibid., p. 47.

Chapter 4

1   Kiggell to Gough, 5 February 1917, AWM 51, item 52, author's emphasis.

2   C. Falls, History of the Great War. Military Operations. France and Belgium, 1917, Vol. I, The German Retreat to the Hindenburg Line and the Battle of Arras, MacMillan, London, 1940, p. 357.

3   Kiggell to Gough, 5 February 1917, AWM 51, item 52.

4   Kiggell to Gough, 20 February 1917, AWM 51, item 52.

5   Bean, Official History, Vol. IV, The AIF in France 1917, p. 253.

6   Lieutenant General L. Kiggell report of meeting at GHQ between Haig and his army commanders, 26 March 1917, correspondence, German withdrawal, AWM 51, item 52.

7   Bean, Official History, Vol. IV, The AIF in France 1917, p. 254.

8   Falls, History of the Great War. Military Operations France and Belgium 1917, Vol. I, p. 358.

Endnotes

9   Bean, *Official History*, Vol. IV, *The AIF in France 1917*, p. 257.

10   Sheffield and Bourne (eds), *Douglas Haig: War Diaries and Letters 1914-1918*, pp. 280–81.

11   Griffith, *Battle Tactics of the Western Front*, p. 142.

12   General H. Gough, *Soldiering On: Being the Memoirs of General Sir Hubert Gough GCB, GCMG, KCVO*, Arthur Barker Ltd, London, 1954, p. 138.

13   Bean, *Official History*, Vol. IV, *The AIF in France 1917*, p. 258.

14   Ibid., p. 259.

15   G. Keech, *Battleground Europe. Bullecourt: Arras*, Leo Cooper, South Barnsley, 1999, p. 26.

16   The line was not expected to be open before 30 March, but due to industrious work by British soldiers it was reopened at Achiet-le-Grand on 28 March and at Bapaume one week later.

17   Notes on Proceedings of Army Commanders at Conference held at Rollencourt Chateau, 24 March 1917, AWM 45, item 33/9.

18   Falls, *History of the Great War. Military Operations France and Belgium 1917*, Vol. I, p. 358.

19   Bean, *Official History*, Vol. IV, *The AIF in France 1917*, p. 259.

20   Gough, *The Fifth Army*, p. 182.

21   Bean, *Official History*, Vol. IV, *The AIF in France 1917*, p. 264.

22   Diary of the General Staff Fifth Army, Bean, ibid., p. 260.

23   Kiggell to Gough, 2 April 1917, AWM 51, item 52; 'Report on Attack against Hindenburg Line', Appendix 39, 11 April 1917, 4th Australian Division, General Staff, National Archives, London, WO 95/3443.

24   Falls, *History of the Great War. Military Operations France and Belgium 1917*, Vol. I, p. 358.

25   Pedersen, *The ANZACS*, p. 198.

26   For an analysis of German tactics and strategy see Samuels, *Doctrine and Dogma*, particularly Chapter 4.

27   Passingham, *All The Kaiser's Men*, p. 151.

28   'Distribution of Artillery', 6 April 1917, Haig papers, National Library of Scotland, 3155/192(a) cf No 213C.

29   Sheffield, *Forgotten Victory*, pp. 137–38.

30   Griffith, *Battle Tactics of the Western Front*, p. 66.

31   Ibid., p. 143.

32   Narrative of the conference proceedings, Bean, *Official History*, Vol. IV, *The AIF in France 1917*, p. 260.

33   Bean, ibid., p. 261.

34   Falls, *History of the Great War. Military Operations France and Belgium 1917*, Vol. I, p. 359.

35   4th Australian Divisional Artillery, Order No. 68, 2 April 1917, AWM 4, item 13/13/11.

36   Bean, *Official History*, Vol. IV, *The AIF in France 1917*, p. 262.

37   Fifth Army Order No 49, quoted in Falls, *History of the Great War. Military Operations France and Belgium 1917*, Vol. I, p. 358.

38   62nd Division Weekly Summary of Operations, week ending 12 April 1917, National Archives, London, WO95/3068.

39   I ANZAC Heavy Artillery Operation Order No 42, 9 April 1917, National Archives, London, WO 95/993.

40   M. Evans, *Somme 1914-18: Lessons in War*, The History Press, Stroud, Gloucestershire, 2010, p. 135.

41   R.N.L. Hopkins, *Australian Armour: a history of the Royal Australian Armoured Corps 1927-1972*, Australian War Memorial, Canberra, 1978, p. 1.

42   At the time there were only 50 tanks in France. Of these just 36 were able to take part in the battle as mechanical and track failure further reduced the number. W. Churchill, 'Motor Digest', London, August 1941, p. 7, Hopkins, *Australian Armour*, p. 4.

43   Colonel Stern, 24 April 1917, Liddell Hart Centre for Military Archives, Kings College, London, Minutes 1/4/2, MWSD,

44   Falls, *History of the Great War. Military Operations France and Belgium 1917*, Vol. I, p. 360.

45   Ibid.

46   Liddell Hart discussion with Sir Giffard Martel, 29 March 1948, Liddell Hart papers, Development of Tank, Liddell Hart Centre for Military Archives, Kings College, London, LH 9/28/59.

47   Order No 1 by Lieutenant Colonel J. Hardress Lloyd, 9 April 1917, Diary of Tank Corps Headquarters, WO 95/91; 62nd Division, 185th Infantry Brigade, Order 9 April 1917, National Archives, London, WO 95/3082.

Chapter 5

1   Andrews, 'Bean and Bullecourt', p. 29.

2   Telegraphic Order by Fifth Army, 2 April 1917, C. Falls, *History of the Great War. Military Operations. France and Belgium, 1917*, Vol. I, *The German Retreat to the Hindenburg Line and the Battle of Arras. Appendices*, Macmillan, London, 1940, p.111.

3   4th Australian Division Report on Attack against Hindenburg Line, 11 April 1917, National Archives, London, WO95/3443.

4   Holmes, 'Report on Attack against Hindenburg Line by 4th Australian Division', 11 April 1917, AWM 4, item 1/48/13, part 2.

5   J.E. Hatwell, *No Ordinary Determination: Percy Black and Harry Murray of the First AIF*, Fremantle Arts Centre Press, Fremantle, 2005, p. 155.

6   Falls, *History of the Great War. Military Operations. France and Belgium, 1917*, Vol. I, p. 456.

7   'Preliminary Instructions for Operations,' 5 April 1917, 12th Australian Brigade, AWM 4, item 23/12/14.

8   Falls, *History of the Great War. Military Operations. France and Belgium, 1917*, Vol. I, p. 358.

9   Bullecourt, narrative by David Dunworth, April 1917, AWM224, MSS143(A)Part 10.

10   McDowell to his father, 20 March 1917, papers of Lieutenant George Stanley McDowell, AWM PR00276.

11   Private Walter King to his brother, Alf, 5 April 1917, Imperial War Museum, London, Catalogue No 275, 89/7/1.

12   Elliott to his wife Kate, 7 April 1917, Ross McMullin, *Pompey Elliott*, Scribe Publications, Carlton, Vic, 2002, p. 282.

13   Report on Attack against Hindenburg Line, WO 95/3443.

14   War Diary, 12th Infantry Brigade, 6–7 April 1917, AWM 4, item 23/12/14.

15   Durrant, 'What Took Place', and 'Particulars', papers of Major General J.M. Durrant, AWM PR 88/009.

16   Durrant, 'Notes on the Hindenburg Line,' papers of Major General J.M. Durrant, AWM PR 88/009

17   Tom Chataway, Death Rides Abroad, unpublished manuscript, Chalk collection.

18   D. Hunter, *My Corps Cavalry: a History of the 13*th *Light Horse Regiment AIF*, Slouch Hat Publications, McRae, Victoria, 1999, p. 51.

19   4th Australian Division, Special Machine Gun Instructions, 8 April 1917, National Archives, London, WO 95/3443.

20   Headquarters 4th Australian Division, 8 April 1917, AWM 26, item 169/37.

21   4th Australian Division, Report on Attack against Hindenburg Line, 11 April 1917, National Archives, London, WO95/3443.

22   Falls, *History of the Great War. Military Operations. France and Belgium, 1917*, Vol. I, p. 359.

23   C.E.W. Bean, *ANZAC to Amiens*, Penguin, Ringwood, Victoria, 1993 (1946), p. 329.

24   Griffith, *Battle Tactics of the Western Front*, p. 168.

25   Chataway, Death Rides Abroad, unpublished manuscript, Chalk collection.

26   Falls, *History of the Great War. Military Operations. France and Belgium, 1917*, Vol. I, pp. 360–61.

27   62nd Division, Order No 31, 8 April 1917, National Archives, London, WO 95/3068.

28   E. Wyrall, *The History of the 62*nd *(West Riding) Division*, Vol. I, John Lane The Bodley Head, London, 1924, p. 42.

29   1st ANZAC Heavy Artillery, Operation Order No 42, 9 April 1917, National Archives, London, WO 95/993.

30   I ANZAC Corps, War Diary, 10 April 1917, AWM 4, item 1/29/15, Part 1.

31   Falls, *History of the Great War. Military Operations. France and Belgium, 1917*, Vol. I, p. 361.

32   18th Australian Infantry Brigade Order No 134, 9 April 1917, AWM 4, item 23/12/14.

33   185th Infantry Brigade, Operation Order No 19, 9 April 1917, National Archives, London, WO 95/3082.

34   Durrant, 'The Tactical Plan', papers of Major General J.M. Durrant, AWM PR 88/009.

35   Holmes to HQ 4th Australian Infantry Brigade, 10 April 1917, AWM 4, item 23/33/17.

36   Bullecourt, narrative by David Dunworth.

37   Neillands, *The Great War Generals*, p. 356.

38   Bullecourt, narrative by David Dunworth.

39   Durrant, 'Strategy of Bullecourt', papers of Major General J.M. Durrant, AWM PR 88/009.

40   185th Infantry Brigade Operation Order No 18, 10 April 1917, National Archives, London, WO 95/3082.

41   185th Infantry Brigade Operation Order No 19, 10 April 1917, National Archives, London, WO 95/3082.

42   Durrant, 'Strategy of Bullecourt'.

43   43 R. Travers, *Diggers in France: Australian Soldiers on the Western Front*, ABC Books, Sydney, 2008, p. 139.

44   Falls, *History of the Great War. Military Operations. France and Belgium, 1917*, Vol. I, p. 362.

45   Ibid., p. 363.

46   Lewis Sharp interview, Chalk collection.

47   Hatwell, *No Ordinary Determination*, p. 158.

48   T. White, *The Fighting Thirteenth: The History of the Thirteenth Battalion AIF*, Tyrells Ltd, Sydney, 1924, p. 93.

49   Donald Fraser, Memoirs, unpublished manuscript, Chalk collection.

50   CSM C. Emerson, 'Statement by Repatriated Prisoner of War', 31 December 1918, AWM 30, item B13.18.

51   'Comments by Brigadier General R.L. Leane on 1st Bullecourt', 27 July 1937, Bean papers, AWM 38, 3DRL 7953/30, part 2.

52   Groutsch interview, Chalk collection.

53   Report on Attack against Hindenburg Line, 11 April 1917, 4th Australian Division, National Archives, London, WO95/3443.

54   White, *The Fighting Thirteenth*, p. 93.

55   Bullecourt, narrative by David Dunworth. It was while Dunworth was a prisoner of war in Germany that an enemy Intelligence Officer talked to him about the postponed attack. Dunworth was also informed that, as the Germans 'knew we would return to the attack they had rushed up strong reinforcements and they had seen our troops falling back and the cavalry riding away, hence they knew a serious attack had for some reason failed.'

56   Bean, *Official History*, Vol. IV, *The AIF in France 1917*, p. 284.

Chapter 6

1   N. Wanliss, *The History of the Fourteenth Battalion AIF: Being the Vicissitudes of an Australian Unit During the Great War*, Arrow Printery, Melbourne, 1929, p. 193.

2   White, *The Fighting Thirteenth*, p. 93.

3   Bullecourt, narrative by David Dunworth, 14th Australian Infantry Battalion, April 1917, AWM224, MSS143(A) part 10.

4   Hatwell, No *Ordinary Determination,* p. 160

5   J. Sheldon, 'Bullecourt Day of Disaster: the Assault Seen From the German Side of the Wire', *Wartime*, Issue 63, pp. 14–18.

6   Diary, CQMS A.L. Guppy, 10 April 1917.

7   Hatwell, *No Ordinary Determination*, p. 160.

8   Groutsch interview.

9   Toft, 'Playing a Man's Game', *The Queensland Digger*, 10 May 1938, p. 20.

10   Nicholls, *Cheerful Sacrifice,* p. 157.

11   Wyrall, *The History of the 62nd (West Riding) Division*, Vol. I, pp. 42–43.

12   I ANZAC Corps, War Diary, 10 April 1917, AWM 4, item 1/29/15 Part 1.

13   I ANZAC Corps War Diary, Order No 124, 10 April 1917, AWM 4, item 1/29/15Part 2.

14   Falls, *History of the Great War. Military Operations. France and Belgium, 1917*, Vol. I, pp. 363–64.

15   Sheffield, *Forgotten Victory*, p. 164.

16   White, *Diggers Abroad*, p. 40.

17   Falls, *History of the Great War. Military Operations. France and Belgium, 1917*, Vol. I, p. 364.

18   I ANZAC Heavy Artillery, Operation Order No 43, 10 April 1917, National Archives, London, WO 95/993.

19   Falls, *History of the Great War. Military Operations. France and Belgium, 1917*, Vol. I, p. 363.

Endnotes

20   I ANZAC Corps, Intelligence Summary No 254, 10 April 1917, AWM 4, item 1/30/15Part 1.

21   Neillands, *The Great War Generals*, pp. 356–57; Bean, *ANZAC to Amiens*, p. 330.

22   J. Walker, *The Blood Tub: General Gough and the Battle of Bullecourt 1917*, Spellmount, Staplehurst, 1998, p. 93.

23   Durrant, 'The Tactical Plan,' papers of Major General J.M. Durrant, AWM PR88/009.

24   Ganson interview.

25   I.L. Polanski, *We Were The 46th: the History of the 46th Battalion in the Great War of 1914-18*, Puttees and Puggarees, Townsville, Qld, 1999, p. 43; Ganson, interview.

26   Toft, 'Playing a Man's Game', *The Queensland Digger*, 10 May 1938, p. 20.

27   Brand, 'Tribute to the Digger', papers of Brigadier General C.H. Brand, AWM PRO00884.

28   12th Australian Infantry Brigade Order, 10 April, 1917, National Archives, London, WO 95/3082.

29   4th Infantry Brigade, Report 11th April near Riencourt, AWM4, item 23/4/19.

30   62nd British Division, War Diary, 11 April 1917, National Archives, London, WO95/3068.

31   12th Infantry Brigade, 'Report on Operations, Bullecourt' 15 April 1917, AWM4, item 23/12/14.

32   Craig Deayton, *Battle Scarred: the 47th Battalion in the First World War*, Big Sky, Newport, NSW, 2011, p. 94.

33   Hatwell, *No Ordinary Determination*, p. 160.

34   Bullecourt, narrative by David Dunworth, AWM224, MSS143(A)Part 10.

35   Bean, *Official History*, Vol. IV, *The AIF in France 1917*, p. 295.

36   Hatwell, *No Ordinary Determination*, p. 160.

37   Durrant, '11 April 1917', Durrant's emphasis, papers of Major General J.M. Durrant, AWM PR88/009.

38   Lieutenant L. Challen, Report on Operation 11th April 1917, Bean papers, AWM 38, 3DRL606/247(2).

39   Chataway, Death Rides Abroad, unpublished manuscript, Chalk collection. Chataway commanded the 15th Battalion's Lewis machine-gun section. At the time of the attack he was attached to battalion headquarters.

40   4th Infantry Brigade, Report 11th April 1917, AWM4, item 23/4/19.

41   Travers, *Diggers in France*, p. 142.

42   Groutsch interview.

43   Walker, *The Blood Tub*, p. 105.

44   Lee, 'William Birdwood' in Beckett and Corvi (eds), *Haig's Generals*, p. 43.

45   Hatwell, *No Ordinary Determination*, pp. 161–62.

46   Lee, 'William Birdwood' in *Haig's Generals*, p. 43.

47   I ANZAC Corps, War Diary, 11 April 1917, AWM 4, item 1/29/15, part 1.

48   Captain N.A. Nicolson, diary 11 April 1917, AWM 3DRL 2715.

49   Bullecourt, narrative by Captain David Dunworth, AWM224, MSS143(A)Part 10.

50   I ANZAC Corps, Intelligence Summary No 256, 12 April 1917, AWM4, item 1/30/15Part 1.

51 Australian Red Cross Wounded and Missing files, 1914-18 War, 330 Private Edward Knights, 4th Machine Gun Company, AWM 1DRL/0428.

52 Pedersen, *The ANZACS*, p. 201.

53 4th Infantry Brigade Report 11th April 1917 near Riencourt, AWM4, item 23/4/19; C. Longmore, *The Old Sixteenth: Being a Record of the 16th Battalion AIF During the Great War 1914-1918*, History Committee of the 16th Battalion Association, Perth, 1929, p. 135.

54 Bullecourt, narrative by Captain David Dunworth, AWM224, MSS143(A)Part 10.

55 Pedersen, *The ANZACS*, p. 201.

56 Toft, 'Playing a Man's Game', *The Queensland Digger*, 10 May 1938, p. 21.

57 Fraser, Memoirs, unpublished manuscript, p. 21, Chalk collection.

58 Travers, *Diggers in France*, p. 143.

59 Ganson interview.

60 Diary, CQMS A.L. Guppy, 11 April 1917.

61 Corporal C.C. Benson, Statement by Escaped Prisoner of War, 10 October 1918, Mitchell Library, ML MSS 885.

62 4th Infantry Brigade Report 11th April 1917 'Near Riencourt', AWM 4, item 23/4/19.

63 Falls, *History of the Great War. Military Operations. France and Belgium, 1917*, Vol. I, pp. 364–65.

64 Toft, 'Playing a Man's Game', *The Queensland Digger*, 10 May 1938, p. 21.

65 Etchell interview.

66 Pooley interview.

67 Durrant, '11 April 1917', papers of Major General J.M. Durrant, AWM PR88/009.

68 Fraser interview.

69 Travers, *Diggers in France*, p. 143.

70 Nicholls, *Cheerful Sacrifice*, p. 158.

71 CSM C. Emerson, Statement by Repatriated Prisoner of War, 31 December 1918, AWM 30, item B13.18.

72 Falls, *History of the Great War. Military Operations. France and Belgium, 1917*, Vol. I, p. 366.

73 Diary, CQMS Guppy, 11 April 1917, Chalk collection.

74 Knowles, 'Bullecourt Tragedy', *Reveille*, April 1931, p. 15.

75 Darryl Kelly, *Just Soldiers: Ordinary Australians Doing Extraordinary Things in Time of War*, ANZAC Day Commemoration Committee, Aspley, Queensland, 2004, p. 13.

76 G.D. Mitchell, *Backs To The Wall*, Angus & Robertson, Sydney, 1937, p. 92.

77 Wheeler interview.

78 Durrant, '11 April 1917', papers of Major General J.M. Durrant, AWM PR88/009.

79 Hatwell, *No Ordinary Determination*, p. 163.

80 Etchell interview.

81 Toft, 'Playing a Man's Game', *The Queensland Digger*, 10 May 1938, p. 21.

82 Hatwell, *No Ordinary Determination*, p. 163.

83 Corporal C.C. Benson, Statement by Escaped Prisoner of War, 10 October 1918, Mitchell Library, ML MSS 885.

84 Rumble interview.

Endnotes

85   Lieutenant George McDowell to his father, 15 April 1917, papers of Lieutenant George Stanley McDowell, 13th Battalion, AWM PR00276.

86   W. Davies, *In the Footsteps of Private Lynch*, Vintage Books, North Sydney, 2008, pp. 96–97.

87   Ganson interview.

88   Marshall interview.

89   'Narrative of Action, 11th April 1917', 15th Infantry Battalion, AWM 4, item 23/32/25.

90   I ANZAC Intelligence Summary, No 255 11 April 1917, National Archives, London, WO 157/565.

91   CSM C. Emerson, Statement by Repatriated Prisoner of War, 31 December 1918, AWM 30, item B13.18.

92   Bean, *ANZAC to Amiens*, p. 331.

93   Sharp interview.

94   James interview.

95   Etchell interview.

96   Hatwell, *No Ordinary Determination*, p. 163.

97   Diary, CQMS Guppy, 11 April 1917, Chalk collection.

98   Fraser, Memoirs, unpublished manuscript, p. 21.

99   Hatwell, *No Ordinary Determination*, p. 164.

100   Lieutenant L. Challen, Report on Operations 11th April 1917, Bean papers, AWM38, 3DRL606/247.

101   Falls, *History of the Great War. Military Operations. France and Belgium, 1917*, Vol. I, p. 367.

102   12th Infantry Brigade Order, No 134, 9 April 1917, AWM26, item 171/18.

103   12th Infantry Brigade Order, No 134, Continuation, 10 April 1917, AWM26, item 171/18.

104   Bean, *Official History*, Vol. IV, *The AIF in France 1917*, p. 304.

105   Falls, *History of the Great War. Military Operations. France and Belgium, 1917*, Vol. I, p. 367.

106   Lieutenant L. Challen, Report on Operations 11th April 1917, Bean papers, AWM 38, 3DRL606/247.

107   Lieutenant Colonel Raymond Leane, Report on Operation 11th April 1917, Bean papers, AWM38, 3DRL606/247.

108   Polanski, *We Were The 46th*, p. 40.

109   Lieutenant Colonel Raymond Leane, Report on Operations 11th April 1917, Bean papers, AWM38, 3DRL606/247.

110   Diary of C.E.W Bean, 11 April 1917, AWM 38 3DRL 606/75/2.

111   Comments by Brigadier General R.L. Leane on First Bullecourt, 27 July, 1937, Bean papers, AWM38, 3DRL7953/30Part 2.

112   2nd Lieutenant C. Sheldon, Report on Operations 11th April 1917, Bean papers, AWM 38, 3DRL606/247.

113   Falls, *History of the Great War. Military Operations. France and Belgium, 1917*, Vol. I, p. 367.

114   Deayton, *Battle Scarred*, p. 96.

115   Bullecourt, narrative by David Dunworth, 14th Australian Infantry Battalion, AWM 224, MSS143(A) part 10.

116   James interview.

117 Hatwell, *No Ordinary Determination*, pp. 162, 164.

118 Ganson interview.

119 Massey interview.

120 CSM C. Emerson, Statement by Repatriated Prisoner of War, 31 December 1918, AWM 30, item B13.18.

121 Diary CQMS A. Guppy, 11 April 1917, Chalk collection.

122 Corporal C.C. Benson, Statement by Escaped Prisoner of War, 10 October 1918, Mitchell Library, ML MSS 885.

123 Lieutenant M.J. O'Day, Statement by Repatriated Prisoner of War, 3 January 1919, AWM 30, item B13.18.

124 CSM C. Emerson, Statement by Repatriated Prisoner of War, 31 December 1918, AWM 30, item B13.18.

125 Colmer interview.

126 Hatwell, *No Ordinary Determination*, p. 164.

127 Falls, *History of the Great War. Military Operations. France and Belgium, 1917*, Vol. I, p. 367.

128 Report on Attack against Hindenburg Line, 4th Australian Division, National Archives, London, WO95/3443.

129 Bean, *Official History*, Vol. IV, *The AIF in France 1917*, p. 317.

130 Falls, *History of the Great War. Military Operations. France and Belgium, 1917*, Vol. I, p. 367.

131 Durant, '11 April 1917', papers of Major General J.M. Durrant, AWM PR 88/009.

132 Diary No 183, 11 April 1917, Bean papers, AWM 38 3DRL 606, item 183[3].

133 Falls, *History of the Great War. Military Operations. France and Belgium, 1917*, Vol. I, p. 368.

134 Wyrall, *The History of the 62nd (West Riding) Division*, Vol. I, p. 43.

135 War Diary, 62nd British Division, 11 April 1917, National Archives, London, WO 95/3068.

136 Ibid.

137 Walker, *The Blood Tub*, p. 102.

138 War Diary, 62nd British Division, 11 April 1917, National Archives, London, WO 95/3068.

139 2nd Lieutenant C. Sheldon, Report on Operations 11th April 1917, Bean papers, AWM38, 3DRL606/247.

140 Durrant, '11 April 1917', papers of Major General J.M. Durrant, AWM PR 88/009.

141 Falls, *History of the Great War. Military Operations. France and Belgium, 1917*, Vol. I, p. 367.

142 Durrant, '11 April 1917', papers of Major General J.M. Durrant, AWM PR 88/009.

143 L. Davies, A Narrative of POW Experiences, unpublished manuscript, Chalk collection.

144 Toft, 'Playing a Man's Game', *The Queensland Digger*, 10 May 1938, p. 21.

145 McGinty interview.

146 Rumble interview.

147 Report on Attack against Hindenburg Line, 4th Australian Division, National Archives, London, WO 95/3443.

148 Pooley interview.

149 Wheeler interview.

150 Durrant, '11 April 1917', papers of Major General J.M. Durrant, AWM PR 88/009.

Endnotes

151 Message 2/5th Battalion to 185th Infantry Brigade, 11 April 1917, National Archives, London, WO95/3081.

152 Diary of Corporal Lancelot Davies, 11 April 1917, quoted in Davies, A Narrative of POW Experiences, unpublished manuscript, Chalk collection.

153 Toft, 'Playing a Man's Game', *The Queensland Digger*, 10 May 1938, p. 20.

154 Report on Attack against Hindenburg Line, 4th Australian Division, National Archives, London, WO 95/3443.

155 46th Infantry Battalion War Diary, 11 April 1917, AWM 4, item 23/63/15.

156 Deayton, *Battle Scarred*, p. 97.

157 46th Infantry Battalion War Diary, 11 April 1917, AWM 4, item 23/63/15.

158 Holmes report on attack against Hindenburg Line, 11 April 1917, AWM 26, item 169/37.

159 Pedersen, *The ANZACS*, p. 204.

160 Polanski, *We Were the 46th*, p. 42.

161 2nd Lieutenant S. McKenzie, Report on Operation 11th April 1917, Bean papers, AWM38, 3DRL606/247.

162 Deayton, *Battle Scarred*, pp. 96, 98.

163 Bullecourt, narrative by David Dunworth, AWM 224, MSS143(A)Part10.

164 Sergeant Blackburn, quoted in Hatwell, *No Ordinary Determination*, p. 170.

165 Hatwell, *No Ordinary Determination*, pp. 170–71.

166 Massey interview.

167 Bean, *ANZAC to Amiens*, p. 334.

168 Holmes report on attack against Hindenburg Line, 11 April 1917, AWM 26 item 169/37.

Chapter 7

1   Groutsch interview.

2   Bean, *Official History*, Vol. IV, *The AIF in France 1917*, p. 333.

3   Wheeler interview.

4   Davies, 'A Narrative of POW Experiences: 11 April 1917-December 1917', AWM PRO0140.

5   CSM C. Emerson, Statement by Repatriated Prisoner of War, 31 December 1918, AWM 30, item B13.18.

6   Wheeler interview.

7   Toft, 'Playing a Man's Game', *The Queensland Digger*, 10 May 1938, p. 20.

8   Chataway, Death Rides Abroad, unpublished manuscript, Chalk collection.

9   Hatwell, *No Ordinary Determination*, p. 170.

10 James interview.

11 Fraser interview.

12 Bland interview.

13 Mitchell, *Backs to the Wall*, pp. 97–98.

14 Diary CQMS A.L. Guppy, 11 April 1917, Chalk collection.

15 Farrar-Hockley, *Goughie*, p. 206.

16   Durrant, '11 April 1917', papers of Major General J.M. Durrant, AWM PR 88/009.

17   Walker, *The Blood Tub*, p. 107.

18   Bullecourt, narrative by David Dunworth, AWM224, MSS143(A) part 10.

19   A.G. Butler, *The Official History of the Australian Army Medical Services in the War of 1914-1918*, Vol. II, *The Western Front*, Australian War Memorial, Canberra, 1930, p. 135.

20   Bean, *Official History*, Vol. IV, *The AIF in France 1917*, p. 341.

21   Deayton, *Battle Scarred*, p. 98.

22   Etchell interview.

23   Whittington interview.

24   Davies, A Narrative of POW Experience, unpublished manuscript.

25   Pooley interview.

26   Ganson interview.

27   Taylor, Peregrinations of an Australian Prisoner-of-War, unpublished manuscript, Chalk collection.

28   Guppy diary, 11 April 1917, Chalk collection.

29   White, *The Fighting Thirteenth*, p. 100.

30   Lancelot Davies, A Narrative of POW Experiences, AWM PR00140.

31   Ganson interview.

32   Fraser interview.

33   Ganson interview.

34   Chalk, Experiences as a Prisoner-of-War in Germany, unpublished manuscript, Chalk collection.

35   Walker, *The Blood Tub*, p. 104.

36   J. Williams, *Anzacs, the Media and the Great War*, University of New South Wales Press, Sydney, 1999, pp. 165–66.

37   Davies, A Narrative of POW Experience, unpublished manuscript.

38   Ganson interview.

39   Diary, Lieutenant Garnet Veness, 12 April 1917, AWM PRO1059.

40   Sanders, narrative, unpublished manuscript, papers of Captain Reginald Edwin Sanders, AWM 2DRL417.

41   Marshall interview.

42   Davies, A Narrative of POW Experience, unpublished manuscript, Chalk collection.

43   Benson, Statement by Repatriated Prisoner of War, AWM 30.

44   Tamblyn interview.

45   Ganson interview.

46   Spencer interview.

47   Etherton to 'Frank', 28 December 1917, papers of Private C.G. Etherton, AWM PRO1020.

48   4th Australian Division Order No 57, 18 April 1917, AWM 26, item 169/38.

49   Bean, *Official History*, Vol. IV, *The AIF in France 1917*, p. 344.

50   Toft, 'Playing a Man's Game', *The Queensland Digger*, 1 June 1938, p. 20.

Chapter 8

1   Diary of Field Marshal Sir Douglas Haig, 11 April 1917, Haig Diary, No 112, Vol. 15, April 1917, National Library of Scotland, Edinburgh.

2   Corporal J.S. Armstrong to Mr N. Wanliss, 6 November 1924, AWM 224, MSS 143Part 10.

3   Jacka to Stanton's sister, 15 April 1917, papers of Captain F.B. Stanton, AWM2DRL155.

4   Diary of Captain N.A. Nicolson, 11 April 1917, AWM 3DR2715.

5   Travers, *Diggers in France*, pp. 144–45.

6   Case, Lest We Forget, unpublished manuscript, AWM MSS 1365.

7   Appleton to his sister Vera, 22 April 1917, papers of Lieutenant Fred Appleton, Chalk collection.

8   Bean to N. Wanliss, 8 May 1924, AWM224, MSS143Part 10.

9   Chataway, Death Rides Abroad, unpublished manuscript, Chalk collection.

10   C.H. Brand, 'Who Broke the Hindenburg Line?' *Reveille*, April 1933, p. 7.

11   Walker, 'Report on Attack against Hindenburg Line by 4th Australian Division', 11 April 1917, AWM 4, item 1/48/13Part 2.

12   Diary of Campbell Nelson Stewart, 11 April 1917, Chalk collection.

13   Etchell interview.

14   Fitzpatrick interview.

15   Norris interview.

16   Durrant, 'The Lessons', papers of Major General J.M. Durrant, AWM PR88/009.

17   Walker, *The Blood Tub*, p. 105.

18   Brigadier General D. Robertson, Report 19 April 1917, AWM4, item 23/12/14.

19   Lieutenant Colonel R. Leane, Report on Operations of Tanks April 11th 1917, 19 April 1917, Bean papers, AWM38 3DRL606/247.

20   Comments by Brigadier General R.L. Leane on First Bullecourt, 27 July 1937, Bean papers, AWM38, 3DRL606/247.

21   Chataway, Death Rides Abroad, unpublished manuscript, Chalk collection.

22   R. Kershaw, *Tank Men: the Human Story of Tanks at War*, Hodder & Stoughton, London, 2008, p. 20.

23   Griffith, *Battle Tactics On The Western Front*, p. 163.

24   C. Campbell, *Band of Brigands: the First Men in Tanks*, Harper Press, London, 2007, p. 273.

25   I ANZAC Corps, Intelligence Summary No. 256, 12 April 1917, AWM 4, item 1/30/15Part 1.

26   1st Tank Brigade, Summary of Operations, April 1917, National Archives, London, WO 95/97.

27   Evans, *Somme 1914-18 Lessons in War*, p. 162.

28   Walker, *The Blood Tub*, p. 107.

29   Bean to Edmonds, 8 May 1930, Edmonds to Bean, 25 June 1930 and Bernard to Edmonds, 23 October 1930. T. Travers, 'From Surafend to Gough', *Journal of the Australian War Memorial*, Issue 27, October 1995, pp. 19–20.

30   Gough, *The Fifth Army*, pp. 182–84.

31   Sheffield and Bourne (eds), *Douglas Haig: war diaries and letters 1914-1918*, p. 280.

32   Falls, *History of the Great War. Military Operations. France and Belgium, 1917*, Vol. I, p. 369.

33   Pedersen, *The ANZACS*, p. 206.

34   R. Ramsay (ed), *Hell, Hope and Heroes: a Life in the Field Ambulance in World War I*, Rosenberg Publishing, Dural, New South Wales, 2005, pp. 115–17.

35   E.M. Andrews, *The ANZAC Illusion: Anglo-Australian Relations during World War I*, Cambridge University Press, Cambridge, 1993, p. 101.

36   Travers, *Diggers in France*, p. 145.

37   Travers, 'From Surafend to Gough', p. 20.

38   Bean, *ANZAC to Amiens*, p. 334.

39   Chataway, Death Rides Abroad, unpublished manuscript, Chalk collection.

40   Bland interview.

41   Durrant, '4th Division at Bullecourt', papers of Major General J.M. Durrant, AWM PR 88/009.

42   Brand, 'Who Broke the Hindenburg Line?', *Reveille*, April 1933, p. 7.

43   Pedersen, *The ANZACS*, p. 205.

44   Walker, *The Blood Tub*, p. 107.

45   Williams, *ANZACS, the Media and The Great War*, pp. 165–66.

46   White, *The Fighting Thirteenth*, p. 99.

Chapter 9

1   Keech, *Battleground Europe, Bullecourt*, p. 69.

2   2nd Australian Division, Report on operations of 15 April 1917, German Withdrawal, 14–25 April 1917, AWM 26 item 163/12.

3   M.C. Wrench, *Campaigning with the Fighting Ninth: In and Out of the Line with the 9th Bn AIF*, Boolarong Publications, Brisbane, 1985, p. 178.

4   Keech, *Battleground Europe, Bullecourt*, p. 70

5   Newton, *The Story of the Twelfth*, p. 133

6   For a worthwhile, well-researched account of the 1st Australian Division in both battles, see R. Stevenson, *To Win The Battle: the 1st Australian Division in the Great War*, 1914-1918, Cambridge University Press, Port Melbourne, 2013, particularly chapters 5 and 6.

7   Pedersen, *The ANZACs*, p. 206.

8   Bean, *ANZAC to Amiens*, p. 335.

9   Fifth Army Intelligence Summary, April 1917, National Archives, London, WO 157/209.

10   Fifth Australian Infantry Brigade, Report on Operations, 15 April 1917, Bean papers, Estray material, AWM38, E1.

11   2nd Australian Division, Report on operations, 15 April 1917, AWM 26 item 163/12.

12   Bean, *ANZAC to Amiens*, p. 335.

13   Ibid., p. 336.

14   Diary of Mervyn Napier Waller, 15 April 1917, AWM PR 87/007.

15   Diary of Lance Corporal Leonard Clyde Bryant, 15 April 1917, AWM PR 00142.

16   Bean, *Official History*, Vol. IV, *The AIF in France 1917*, p. 376.

17   Both Captain Newland and Sergeant Whittle were awarded the Victoria Cross.

18   For his courage Pope was posthumously awarded the Victoria Cross.

19 German Attack on Noreuil, 15 April 1917, Bean papers, Estray material, AWM38, E1.

20 Ibid.

21 Pedersen, *The ANZACS*, p. 207.

22 Bean, *Official History*, Vol. IV, *The AIF in France 1917*, pp. 380–81.

23 German attack on 1st ANZAC Corps front, 15/4/1917, General Birdwood's report, Bean papers, Estray material, AWM38, E1.

24 Ibid.

25 Brigadier General Charles Rosenthal, statement to Court of Enquiry re Abandonment of Guns of 1st Australian Division Artillery on 15th April 1917, AWM 26, item 63/12.

26 Ellis, *The Story of the Fifth Australian Division*, p. 197.

27 Brigadier General Charles Rosenthal statement to Court of Enquiry re Abandonment of Guns of 1st Australian Division on 15th April 1917, AWM 26, item 163/12.

28 Ibid.

29 Fifth Australian Infantry Brigade, 15 April 1917 Report on Operations, 16 April 1917, Bean papers, Estray material, AWM38, E1.

30 'Lagnicourt', papers of Sergeant H. Preston, AWM 2DRL811.

31 2nd Australian Division, Report on operations of 15 April 1917, German Withdrawal, 14–25 April 1917, AWM 26 item 163/12.

32 Ellis, *The Story of the Fifth Australian Division*, p. 198.

33 'Fight For Lagnicourt', Reuter's Special Service. Keech, *Battleground Europe, Bullecourt*, p. 69.

34 Matthews, 'The Campaign on the Somme,' W. Philpott, *Bloody Victory: the Sacrifice of the Somme*, Little Brown, London, 2009, p. 468.

35 I ANZAC Corps, General Staff, Report, 15 April 1917, National Archives, London, WO 95/982.

36 2nd Australian Division Report on operations, 15 April 1917, AWM 26 item 163/12.

37 Haig's Diary, No. 112, Vol. 15, 15 April 1917, National Library of Scotland, Edinburgh.

38 Matthews, 'The Campaign on the Somme', Philpott, *Bloody Victory*, p. 468.

39 German attack on 1st ANZAC Corps front 15/4/17, General Birdwood's report, Bean papers, Estray material, AWM 38, E1.

40 Henderson to his mother, 20 April 1917, papers of Lieutenant R.G. Henderson, AWM 1DRL 343.

41 'State of 11th Battalion Line, Lagnicourt', April 1917, AWM 27, item 312/1.

42 Proceedings of Court of Enquiry re Abandonment of Guns of 1st Aust Division Artillery on 15 April 1917, AWM 26 item 163/12.

43 German attack on 1st ANZAC Corps front 15/4/17, General Birdwood's report, Bean papers, Estray material, AWM38, E1.

44 2nd Australian Division, Weekly Summary of Operations 14 April to 20th April 1917, AWM 26, item 163/12.

45 I ANZAC Corps, War Diary, 25 April 1917, National Archives, London, WO 95/982.

46 R. Austin, *As Tough As Bags: the History of the 60th Battalion 1st AIF 1914-1919*, RJ. & S.P. Austin, McCrae, Victoria, 1992, p. 199.

Chapter 10

1   An order, dated 12 April, went on to affirm that the attack would commence on 15 April. Further dates were proposed 'not before' the 16th, then 'not before' the 17th, the 18th, the 20th, the 22nd, the 26th or 27th. Other dates, prefixed with 'probably' were suggested before Gough, and Haig settled on 3 May. See Falls, *History of the Great War. Military Operations. France and Belgium, 1917*, Vol. I, p. 455fn.

2   Pedersen, *The ANZACS*, p. 208.

3   Diary of Field Marshal Sir Douglas Haig, 24 and 26 April 1917, Sheffield and Bourne (eds), *Douglas Haig: War Diaries and Letters 1914-1918*, pp. 286–87.

4   Haig's diary, No. 112, Vol. 15, 29 April 1917, National Library of Scotland, Edinburgh, author's emphasis.

5   Haig's diary, No. 112, Vol. 15, 23 April 1917, National Library of Scotland, Edinburgh, author's emphasis.

6   Record of a conference held at Doullens, 25 April 1917, AWM 51, item 52.

7   Haig's diary, No. 112, Vol. 15, 26 April 1917, National Library of Scotland, Edinburgh.

8   Ibid.

9   Haig's diary, No. 113, Vol. 16, 1 May 1917, National Library of Scotland, Edinburgh.

10   Falls, *History of the Great War. Military Operations. France and Belgium, 1917*, Vol. I, p. 456.

11   Record of a conference held at Noyelle Vion, 30 April 1917, AWM 51, item 52.

12   2nd Australian Division Order No. 121, 18 April 1917, AWM 26, item 163/12.

13   2nd Australian Division Report of Operations against The Hindenburg Line, 3-10 May 1917, Bean papers, Estray material AWM38 E1; 2nd Australian Division Order No 121, 18 April 1917, AWM 26, item 163/12.

14   Falls, *History of the Great War. Military Operations. France and Belgium, 1917*, Vol. I, p. 457.

15   2nd Australian Divisional Order No. 124, 29 April 1917, AWM 26 item 164/1.

16   2nd Australian Division Report of Operations against The Hindenburg Line, 3-10 May 1917, Bean papers, Estray material, AWM38 E1.

17   Falls, *History of the Great War. Military Operations. France and Belgium, 1917*, Vol. I, p. 457.

18   Bean, *Official History*, Vol. IV, *The AIF in France 1917*, p. 414.

19   Falls, *History of the Great War. Military Operations. France and Belgium, 1917*, Vol. I, p. 458.

20   Bean, *Official History*, Vol. IV, *The AIF in France 1917*, p. 419fn.

21   War Diary, 7th Infantry Brigade, 27 and 28 April 1917, AWM 4, item 23/7/20.

22   V Corps, Summary of Operations 28 April-4 May 1917, National Archives, London, WO 95/748.

23   War Diary, I ANZAC Corps, General Staff January-April 1917, 18 April 1917, National Archives, London, WO 95/982.

24   Diary of Sapper Ernest Greenhill, 19 April 1917, AWM PRO3232.

25   Preparations for the Second Battle of Bullecourt, Bean papers, AWM 38, 3DRL606/77/2.

26   Bean, *Official History*, Vol. IV, *The AIF in France 1917*, pp. 426–27.

27   6th Australian Infantry Brigade Order No. 86, 21 April 1917, AWM 4, item 23/41/20.

28   4th Infantry Battalion War Diary, 25 April 1917, AWM 4, item 23/21/26.

29   L. Carlyon, *The Great War*, Pan McMillan, Sydney, 2006, p. 368.

30   HQ 6th Brigade to HQ 2nd Division, 27 April 1917, Sadler, *The Paladin*, pp. 129–30.

31   Keech, *Battleground Europe, Bullecourt*, p. 80.

32   Operation Orders, 5th Australian Infantry Brigade, AWM4, item 23/5/22.

33   6th Australian Infantry Brigade Order No. 88, 1 May 1917, AWM 26, item 167/6.

34   Falls, *History of the Great War. Military Operations. France and Belgium, 1917*, Vol. I, pp. 457–58.

35   Sadler, *The Paladin*, p. 130.

36   17th Battalion AIF Operation Details for 3 May 1917, National Archives, London, WO 95/3314.

37   Extract from 5th Aust Infantry Brigade Operation Order No. 99, AWM 26, item 155/8.

38   I ANZAC Corps Summary of Operations for week ended 27 April 1917, AWM 26, item 153/1.

39   I ANZAC Corps, War Diary, 28 April 1917, National Archives, London, WO 95/982.

40   V Corps, Summary of Operations 28 April-4 May 1917, National Archives, London, WO 95/748.

41   Falls, *History of the Great War. Military Operations. France and Belgium, 1917*, Vol. I, p. 459.

42   Andrews, 'Bean and Bullecourt: weaknesses and strengths of the Official History in the First World War', p. 41

43   Pedersen, *The ANZACS*, p. 209.

44   For a critique which argues that the 'artillery preparations for the second battle were badly, if not negligently, handled', see Andrews, *The ANZAC Illusion*, p. 101.

45   Falls, *History of the Great War. Military Operations. France and Belgium, 1917*, Vol. I, p. 459.

46   I ANZAC Artillery, 'Advance of Artillery in Close Support', 30 April 1917, AWM4, item 13/11/15.

47   2nd Australian Division Artillery HQ, 'Action of Trench Mortars', 30 April 1917, AWM4, item 13/11/15.

48   2nd Australian Division Report of Operations against The Hindenburg Line, 3-10 May 1917, Bean papers, Estray material, AWM38, E1.

49   'Amendments to Operation Memo No. 27/17 dated 23/4/17', 1 May 1917, AWM4, item 23/39/21.

50   Haig's diary, No. 113, Vol. 16, 2 May 1917, National Library of Scotland, Edinburgh.

51   Captain L.C. Roth to his mother, 2 May 1917, Roth papers, AWM 1 DRL554.

52   Pedersen, *The ANZACS*, p. 209.

53   Carlyon, *The Great War*, p. 386.

54   Samuels, *Doctrine and Dogma*, p. 66.

55   Fifth Army Intelligence Report, April-May 1917, National Archives, London, WO157/209.

56   I ANZAC Corps, War Diary, 2 May 1917, AWM 4, item 1/29/16 Part 1.

57   V Corps Secret Memorandum, 3 May 1915, National Archives, London, WO 95/748.

58   Haig's diary, No. 113, Vol. 16, 1 May 1917, National Library of Scotland, Edinburgh.

59   Bean, *Official History*, Vol. IV, *The AIF in France 1917*, p. 431.

Chapter 11

1   Diary of Gunner Lewis Wilson, 102nd Battery, 2nd Brigade, 3 May 1917, AWM PR00717.

2   Lieutenant C.E. McCardel, diary 3 May 1917, AWM1DRL0423.

3   Passingham, *All the Kaiser's Men*, p. 157.

4   Report of attack 3–4 May 1917, 6th Australian Infantry Brigade, 17 May 1917, AWM4, item 23/6/21.

5   Diary of Sapper Ernest Greenhill, 3 May 1917, AWM PRO3232.

6   War Diary; 'Part Taken in Attack on Hindenburg Line 3rd May 1917', 23rd Infantry Battalion, AWM4, item 23/40/20.

7   Report of attack 3–4 May 1917, 6th Australian Infantry Brigade, 17 May 1917, AWM4, item 23/6/21.

8   Papers of Captain W.M. Braithwaite, 22nd Battalion, AWM PR00349.

9   22nd Battalion War Diary, 3 May 1917, AWM4, item 23/39/21.

10   24th Battalion Summary of Operations on the Hindenburg Line 3–4 May 1917, AWM 4, item 23/41/20.

11   Falls, *History of the Great War. Military Operations. France and Belgium, 1917*, Vol. I, p. 461; Pedersen, *The ANZACS*, p. 212.

12   Papers of Private E.G. King, AWM PR 83/018.

13   Falls, *History of the Great War. Military Operations. France and Belgium, 1917*, Vol. I, p. 460.

14   Pedersen, *The ANZACS*, p. 211.

15   2nd Australian Division War Diary, Attack on the Hindenburg Line 3–9 May 1917, AWM 4, item 1/44.

16   P. Burness, *Bapaume and Bullecourt 1917: Australians on the Western Front, DVA*, Canberra, 2007, p. 12.

17   Falls, *History of the Great War. Military Operations. France and Belgium, 1917*, Vol. I, p. 461.

18   Report of attack 3–4 May 1917, 6th Australian Infantry Brigade, 17 May 1917, AWM4, item 23/6/21.

19   Bean, *Official History*, Vol. IV, *The AIF in France 1917*, p. 448.

20   Bean diary, 3 May 1917, AWM38, item 3DRL606/78/1.

21   Bean, *Official History*, Vol. IV, *The AIF in France 1917*, p. 448.

22   Summary of Operations on Hindenburg Line, 24th Battalion, 3–4 May 1917, AWM4, item 23/41/20.

23   Bean, *Official History*, Vol. IV, *The AIF in France 1917*, pp. 455–56.

24   Report on Operations, 2–3 May 1917, 26th Infantry Battalion, AWM4, item 23/43/22.

25   Sadler, *The Paladin*, p. 132.

26   War Diary, 25th Infantry Battalion, 3 May 1917, AWM4, item 23/42/21.

27   Gellibrand 'Chronology of Events, 3 May 1917', Gellibrand papers, AWM 3DRL 1473/102.

28   War Diary, Headquarters I ANZAC Corps, 3 May 1917, AWM4, item 1/29/16 Part 1.

29   Report on the Assault of the Hindenburg Line East of Bullecourt, 3 May 1917, AWM 4, item 23/6/21.

30   Bean diary, 4 May 1917, AWM 38 3DRL606/80.

31   Pedersen, *The ANZACS*, p. 213.

32   'With a Chaplain During a Battle (The Battle was Bullecourt)', Joseph Cue papers, AWM 1DRL/0625.

33   Falls, *History of the Great War. Military Operations. France and Belgium, 1917*, Vol. I, p. 463.

34   Bean, *Official History*, Vol. IV, *The AIF in France 1917*, p. 451.

35   Bean diary, 4 May 1917, AWM 38 item 606/77.

36   A.R. Wiltshire, 'Liaison with the British at Bullecourt', *Reveille*, May 1933, p. 3.

37   Wiltshire to Headquarters 6th Brigade, signal 3 May 1917, AWM 26, box 167, item 6.

38   Fifth Army, Summary of Operations, 3–4 May 1917, National Archives, London, WO95/519.

39   Fifth Army, Intelligence Summary, 3–4 May 1917, National Archives, London, WO95/748.

40   Fifth Army, Summary of Operations, 3–4 May 1917, National Archives, London, WO95/519.

41   Falls, *History of the Great War. Military Operations. France and Belgium, 1917*, Vol. I, p. 465.

42   Bean diary, 4 May 1917, AWM 38 item 606/77.

43   2nd Australian Division Diary of Attack on the Hindenburg Line 3–9 May 1917, AWM 26,167/1.

44   Fifth Army, Intelligence Summary, 3–4 May 1917, National Archives, London, WO95/748.

45   Fifth Army, Summary of Operations, 3–4 May 1917, National Archives, London, WO95/519.

46   Gough, *The Fifth Army*, p. 188.

47   Gellibrand to Bean, 23 January 1931, Bean papers, Estray material, AWM38 E1.

48   Fifth Corps, Summary of Operations 28 April–4 May 1917, National Archives, London, WO95/748.

49   2nd Australian Division Report on the Operations against the Hindenburg Line, 3–10 May 1917, Bean papers, Estray material, AWM38 E1.

50   Gellibrand to Bean, 16 January 1931, Bean papers, Estray material, AWM38 E1.

51   Bean, *Official History*, Vol. IV, *The AIF in France 1917*, pp. 453, 453fn.

52   Report on Operations 3–4 May 1917, 28th Infantry Battalion, AWM4, item 23/45/26.

53   Bean, *Official History*, Vol. IV, *The AIF in France 1917*, p. 472.

54   Report on Operations, 3–4 May 1917, 28th Infantry Battalion, AWM4, item 23/45/26.

55   Ibid.

56   Private Percival Luke, diary, 3 May 1917, AWM PR83/44.

57   Report on Assault of the Hindenburg Line, 3 May 1917, 6th Australian Brigade, AWM4, item 23/6/21.

58   Bean, *Official History*, Vol. IV, *The AIF in France 1917*, p. 480.

59   Report on Assault on the Hindenburg Line, 3 May 1917, 6th Australian Brigade, AWM4, item 23/6/21.

60   Bean diary, 4 May 1917, AWM 38 item 606/77.

61   Pedersen, *The ANZACS*, p. 216.

62   Carlyon, *The Great War*, p. 381.

63   Fifth Corps War Diary, 3 May 1917, National Archives, London, WO95/748.

64   Ibid.

65   7th Division War Diary, 3–4 May 1917, National Archives, London, WO95/1632.

66   Fifth Corps, Intelligence Summary, 3–4 May 1917, National Archives, London, WO 95/748.

67   Bean, *Official History*, Vol. IV, *The AIF in France 1917*, p. 488.

68   Falls, *History of the Great War. Military Operations. France and Belgium, 1917*, Vol. I, p. 467.

69   On this occasion Bean seems to have overlooked at least a few other notable 'achievements' of the AIF, including the 4th Australian Division capturing and holding the Hindenburg Line at Bullecourt, and the 5th Australian Division's heroic — though futile — attempt to capture Fromelles in July the previous year. See Bean, *Official History*, Vol. IV, *The AIF in France 1917*, p. 488fn.

70   Telegram, Haig to Birdwood, 10 May 1917, Papers of Brigadier General Robert Smith, AWM PRO1974.

71   HQ I ANZAC Corps to HQ Fifth Army, 5 May 1917, AWM26, item153/1; Falls, *History of the Great War. Military Operations. France and Belgium, 1917*, Vol. I, p. 473.

72   Pedersen, *The ANZACS*, pp. 210–11.

73   Bean, *Official History*, Vol. IV, *The AIF in France 1917*, p. 543.

74   Bean, *ANZAC to Amiens*, p. 339.

75   Wright to Bean, 14 September 1937, Bean papers, Estray material, AWM38 E2.

76   Burke to his brother, Reg, 6 May 1917, private papers of A.P. Burke, Imperial War Museum, London, Catalogue No 1665.

77   2nd Australian Division Report on Operations against the Hindenburg Line 3–10 May 1917, Bean papers, Estray material, AWM 38, E1.

78   1st Australian Division, Headquarters War Diary, 5 May 1917, AWM4, item 1/42/28; Falls, *History of the Great War. Military Operations. France and Belgium, 1917*, Vol. I, p. 467.

79   Sapper Ernest Greenhill, diary 4 May 1917, AWMPR03232.

80   Private E.C. Munro, diary 4 May 1917, AWM 1DRL526.

81   Report of attack on Hindenburg Line, 4 May 1917, 1st Australian Brigade, AWM4, item 23/1/22.

82   Falls, *History of the Great War. Military Operations. France and Belgium, 1917*, Vol. I, p. 467.

83   Lieutenant C.E. McCardel, diary, AWM 1DRL 423.

84   Burke to his brother Reg, 6 May 1917, private papers of A.P. Burke, Imperial War Museum, London, Catalogue No 1665.

85   Report on Operations against the Hindenburg Line 3–10 1917, 2nd Australian Division, Bean papers, Estray material, AWM38 E1.

86   7th Division War Diary, 4 May 1917, National Archives, London, WO95/1632.

87   Ibid.

88   Fifth Army, Summary of Operations 3–4 May 1917, National Archives, London, WO95/519.

89   Walker, *The Blood Tub*, p. 157.

90   Papers of Lieutenant G.H.. Leslie, Second Bullecourt, May 1917, 3rd Battalion, AWM PR8867.

91   Report of attack on Hindenburg Line, 4 May 1917, 1st Australian Brigade, AWM4, item 23/1/22.

92   War Diary, Headquarters, General Staff, I ANZAC Corps, 4 May 1917, AWM4, 1/29/16 Part 1.

93   Report on Operations against the Hindenburg Line 3–10 May 1917, 2nd Australian Division, Bean papers, Estray material, AWM 38 E1.

94   A. Orchard (ed), *Diary of an ANZAC: the front line diaries and stories of Albert Arthur 'Bert' Orchard M.C.*, Arthur Orchard, Otago, New Zealand, 2009, p. 124.

95   Report of attack on Hindenburg Line, 4 May 1917, 1st Australian Brigade, AWM4, item 23/1/22.

96   Orchard (ed), *Diary of an ANZAC*, p. 124.

97   Report of attack on Hindenburg Line, 5 May 1917, 1st Australian Brigade, AWM4, item 23/1/22.

98   Private B. Harris, memoir, in Keech, *Battleground Europe, Bullecourt*, pp. 102–03.

99   Statement by Lieutenant Baker-Finch regarding Lieutenant E.W. Harris on 5 May 1917, AWM2 DRL589.

100   Corporal W.H. Anderson, diary 5 May 1917, AWM PR82015.

101   Papers of Private W.H. McKenzie, 3rd Battalion, AWM PR0316.

102   Private Walter Tom King to 'Alf', 22 May 1917, Imperial War Museum, London, Catalogue No 275, item 89/7/1.

103   Bean, *ANZAC to Amiens*, p. 342.

104   Captain N.A. Nicolson, diary, 6 May 1917, AWM 3DRL2715.

105   Bean, *Official History*, Vol. IV, *The AIF in France 1917*, pp. 511–13.

106   Pedersen, *The ANZACS*, p. 217.

107   Lieutenant T.J. Richards, diary, 6 May 1917, AWM 2DRL0786.

108   For his courage and audaciousness Howell was awarded the Victoria Cross.

109   Falls, *History of the Great War. Military Operations. France and Belgium, 1917*, Vol. I, p. 469.

110   P. Kendall, *Bullecourt 1917: the Breaching of the Hindenburg Line*, Spellmount, The Mill, Gloucestershire, 2010, p. 265.

111   Papers of Lieutenant J.J. Richards, May 1917, 1st Battalion AIF, AWM2DRL786.

112   Papers of Lieutenant H.H. Leslie, Second Bullecourt, May 1917, 3rd Battalion, AWM PR8867.

113   Bean, *Official History*, Vol. IV, *The AIF in France 1917*, p. 490.

114   Ibid., pp. 519–20.

115   Report of attack on Hindenburg Line, 7 May 1917, 1st Australian Brigade, AWM4, item 23/1/22.

116   Falls, *History of the Great War. Military Operations. France and Belgium, 1917*, Vol. I, p. 470.

117   Haig diary, No. 113, Vol. 16, 3 May 1917, National Library of Scotland, Edinburgh.

Chapter 12

1   Bean, *Official History*, Vol. IV, *The AIF in France 1917*, p. 520.

2   Fifth Army Orders (1/4/1917–12/5/1917), 6 May 1917, WO95/248, National Archives, London.

3   Bullecourt narrative, 7 May 1917, Fifth Corps Intelligence Summary, WO95/748, National Archives, London.

4   Falls, *History of the Great War. Military Operations. France and Belgium, 1917*, Vol. I, p. 471.

5   Walker, *The Blood Tub*, p. 157.

6   7th Division War Diary, 6 May 1917, National Archives, London, WO95/1632.

7   Ibid.

8   Walker, *The Blood Tub*, p. 159.

9   Acland to Falls, National Archives, London, CAB45/116.

10   7th Division War Diary, 7 May 1917, National Archives, London, WO95/1632.

11   Report on Operations 3–10 May 1917, 3rd Australian Infantry Brigade, AWM4, item 23/3/19.

12   7th Division War Diary, 7 May 1917, National Archives, London, WO95/1632.

13   Bullecourt Narrative, 7 May 1917, V Corps Intelligence Summary, National Archives, London, WO95/748.

14   Haig diary, 7 May 1917, No. 113, Vol. 16, 7 May 1917, National Library of Scotland, Edinburgh.

15   'Story of Fight in OG1', 7 May 1917, Major M. Wilder Neligan, Temp CO 9th Battalion AIF, AWM4 item 23/1/22.

16   Papers of Sergeant H Preston, '2nd Bullecourt', AWM 2DRL811.

17   Falls, *History of the Great War. Military Operations. France and Belgium, 1917*, Vol. I, pp. 480–81.

18   Report on operations around Bullecourt, 7 May 1917, 1st Australian Infantry Brigade, AWM 4 item 23/1/22.

19   Ibid.

20   Shoubridge to Smyth, May 1917, AWM27, item 354/124.

21   Falls, *History of the Great War. Military Operations. France and Belgium, 1917*, Vol. I, p. 472.

22   7th Division War Diary, 7 May 1917, National Archives, London, WO 95/1632.

23   Ibid.; Sadler, *The Paladin*, p. 135.

24   Bullecourt Narrative, 7 May 1917, V Corps Intelligence Summary, National Archives, London, WO95/748.

25   Report of operations around Bullecourt, 7 May 1917, 1st Australian Infantry Brigade, AWM 4, item 23/1/22.

26   7th Division War Diary, 7 May 1917, WO95/1632, National Archives, London.

27   V Corps Intelligence Summary, 7 May 1917, National Archives, London, WO95/748.

28   7th Division War Diary, 7 May 1917, National Archives, London, WO95/1632.

29   Bullecourt Narrative, 7 May 1917, V Corps Intelligence Summary, National Archives, London, WO95/748.

30   'Fifth Army Appreciation' concerning Bullecourt, Fifth Army SG 78/212, 8 May 1917, AWM45, item 35/24.

31   7th Division War Diary, 7 May 1917, National Archives, London, WO95/1632.

32   Falls, *History of the Great War. Military Operations. France and Belgium, 1917*, Vol. I, p. 473.

33   Papers of Private W.H. McKenzie, 3rd Battalion, AWMPR00316.

34   Roth to his mother, 23 September 1917, papers of Captain L.C. Roth, 2nd Pioneer Battalion, AWM1DRL554.

35   'Bullecourt', papers of Chaplain J.J. Booth, 8th Battalion, AWMPR84/336.

36   Diary of Gunner Lewis Wilson, 1st Division, 7 May 1917, AWM PR0717.

37   Gough to GHQ, 8 May 1917, Fifth Army Orders, National Archives, London, WO95/248.

38   Falls, *History of the Great War. Military Operations. France and Belgium, 1917*, Vol. I, p. 473.

39   W. Joynt, *Breaking the Road for the Rest*, Hyland House, Melbourne, 1979, p. 118.

40   Diary of Lieutenant C.E. McCardel, 7th Battalion, 8 May 1917, AWM DRL423.

41   V Corps, Intelligence summary, 8–9 May 1917, National Archives, London, WO95/748.

42   7th Division War Diary, 9 May 1917, National Archives London, WO95/1632.

43   Falls, *History of the Great War. Military Operations. France and Belgium, 1917*, Vol. I, p. 473.

44   7th Division War Diary, 9 May 1917, National Archives, London, WO95/1632.

45   7th Division War Diary, 10 May 1917, National Archives, London, WO95/1632.

46   *The Daily Telegraph*, 7 May 1917, Keech, *Battleground Europe, Bullecourt*, p. 105.

47   Message GOC 7th British Division to GOC 1st Australian Division, 17 May 1917, AWM27, item 354/83.

48   Hobbs diary, 7 May 1917, Hobbs papers, Battye Library, MN1460, item5523A/3.

49   Birdwood to Gough, 9 May 1917, correspondence relating to Bullecourt, AWM51, item 52.

50   For an account of the 5th Australian Division and Hobbs' leadership see Coombes, *The Lionheart*.

51   Bean, *Official History*, Vol. IV, *The AIF in France 1917,* p. 25.

52   14th Australian Infantry Brigade Order No. 87, 8 May 1917, AWM4, item 23/14/14.

53   Downing, *To The Last Ridge*, pp. 65–66.

54   Diary of Lieutenant Ronald Alison McInnis, 8 May 1917, AWM PR00917.

55   Ellis, *The Story of the Fifth Australian Division*, p. 201.

56   5th Australian Division Intelligence Summary, 9–10 May 1917, AWM26, item173/13.

57   Diary of Lieutenant Ronald Alison McInnis, 8 May 1917, AWM PR00917.

58   Report of operations around Bullecourt, 9 May 1917, 1st Australian Infantry Brigade, AWM 4, item 23/1/22.

59   5th Australian Division Intelligence Summary, 10–11 May 1917, AWM4, item1/50/15Part 5.

60   Hobbs diary, 9 May 1917, Hobbs papers, Battye Library, MN1460, item 5523A/3.

61   Falls, *History of the Great War. Military Operations. France and Belgium, 1917,* Vol. I, p. 474.

62   Diary of Lieutenant Ronald Alison McInnis, 10 May 1917, AWM PR00917.

63   Ellis, *The Story of the Fifth Australian Division*, p. 202.

64   7th Division War Diary, 11 May 1917, National Archives, London, WO95/1632.

65   V Corps, Intelligence Summaries, 10 and 11 May 1917, National Archives, London, WO95/748; 7th Division War Diary, 11 May 1917, National Archives, London, WO95/1632.

66   Kendall, *Bullecourt 1917*, p. 317.

67   V Corps Operation Order No. 139, 11 May 1917, National Archives, London, WO95/748.

68   Hobbs diary, 10 May 1917, Hobbs papers, AWM PR82/153.

69   Operation Orders, 15th Infantry Brigade, 11 May 1917, Papers of Brigadier General Harold 'Pompey' Elliott, AWM2DRL0513, item 2/1.

70   5th Australian Division, Order No.146, 11 May 1917, AWM4, item 1/50/15Part 2.

71   Elliott to his wife, Kate, 21 July 1917, McMullin, *Pompey Elliott*, p. 286.

72   Ellis, *The Story of the Fifth Australian Division*, p. 202; 15th Australian Infantry Brigade, Report on action at Bullecourt, AWM4, item1/50/15Part 2.

73   5th Australian Division, General Staff Memorandum No. 137, 12 May 1917, AWM4, item 1/50/15Part 4.

74   5th Australian Division, Intelligence Summary, 11–12 May 1917, AWM4, item 1/50/15Part 5.

75   Narrative 12 May 1917, V Corps Intelligence Summary, National Archives, London, WO95/748.

76   War Diary 7th Division, 12 May 1917, National Archives, London, WO95/1632.

77   Ibid.

78   Falls, *History of the Great War. Military Operations. France and Belgium, 1917*, Vol. I, p. 474.

79   Narrative 12 May 1917, Appendix No. 19, National Archives, London, WO95/748; Report on action at Bullecourt, 15th Australian Infantry Brigade, AWM4, item 1/50/15Part 2.

80   Report on action at Bullecourt, 15th Australian Infantry Brigade, AWM4, item 1/50/15Part 2.

81   Ellis, *The Story of the Fifth Australian Division*, p. 203.

82   Report on action at Bullecourt, 15th Australian Infantry Brigade, AWM4, item 1/50/15Part 2.

83   'Phone Message from Corps', 12 May 1917, General Staff, Headquarters 5th Australian Division, AWM4, item 1/50/15Part 7.

84   Bean, *Official History*, Vol. IV, *The AIF in France 1917*, p. 531fn.

85   Denehy to Mrs Barlow, 7 October 1917, Barlow papers, AWM PR0030.

86   5th Australian Division Intelligence Summary, 11–12 May 1917, AWM4, item 1/50/15Part 5.

87   Downing, *To The Last Ridge*, p. 66.

88   Bean, *Official History*, Vol. IV, *The AIF in France 1917*, p. 533fn.

89   Hobbs, Report on Action at Bullecourt, AWM26, item 173/14.

90   Message from Field Marshal Sir Douglas Haig, 13 May 1917, Ellis, *The Story of the Fifth Australian Division*, p. 204.

91   V Corps, Weekly Summary of Operations, 12–18 May 1917, National Archives, London, WO95/748.

92   Falls, *History of the Great War. Military Operations. France and Belgium, 1917*, Vol. I, p. 475.

93   Bean, *Official History*, Vol. IV, *The AIF in France 1917*, p. 533.

94   5th Australian Division Order No. 147, 11 May 1917, AWM26, item173/14.

95   P. Simkins, 'Building Blocks: Aspects of Command and Control at Brigade Level in the BEF's Offensive Operations, 1916-1918' in G. Sheffield and D. Todman (eds), *Command and Control on the Western Front: the British Army's Experience 1914-1918*, Spellmount, Staplehurst, Kent, 2004, p. 160.

96   Falls, *History of the Great War. Military Operations. France and Belgium, 1917*, Vol. I, p. 476.

97   V Corps, Weekly Summary of Operations, 12–18 May 1917, National Archives, London, WO95/748.

98   War Diary 7th Division, 14 May 1917, National Archives, London, WO95/1632.

99   Intelligence Summary 5th Australian Division, 17–18 May 1917, AWM4, item 1/50/15Part 5.

100   Diary of Lieutenant Ronald Alison McGinnis, 14 & 15 May 1917, AWM PR00917.

101 'Report on Attack by Enemy on 54th Battalion', 15 May 1917, AWM4, item 23/71/16.

102 Diary of Lieutenant Ronald Alison McGinnis, 15 May 1917, AWM PR00917.

103 War Diary, 14th Australian Infantry Brigade, 15 May 1917, AWM26, item173/14.

104 Message, I ANZAC to Fifth Army, 16 May 1917, AWM4, item 1/50/15Part 9.

105 Diary of Lieutenant Ronald Alison McGinnis, 15 May 1917, AWM PR00917.

106 Bean diary, 15 May 1917, Bean papers, AWM38, item 3DRL606/78/1.

107 'Report on Attack by Enemy on 54th Battalion', 15 May 1917, AWM4, item 23/71/16.

108 War Diary, 14th Australian Infantry Brigade, 15 May 1917, AWM26, item 173/14.

109 Hobbs report to I ANZAC Headquarters, 17 May 1917, AWM26, item174/1.

110 Diary of Lieutenant Ronald Alison McGinnis, 16 May 1917, AWM PR00917.

111 Falls, *History of the Great War. Military Operations. France and Belgium, 1917*, Vol. I, p. 476.

112 Bean, *Official History*, Vol. IV, *The AIF in France 1917*, p. 533.

113 Papers of T.E. Crook, 2/8th Battalion, Miscellaneous 2165, Account of the 8th (City of London) Battalion – London Regiment, The Post Office Rifles 1914-1918, Imperial War Museum, London.

114 V Corps, Intelligence Summary, 'Narrative 15 May 1917,' National Archives, London, WO95/748.

115 War Diary, 54th Infantry Battalion, 15 May 1917, AWM4, item 23/71/16; Bean, *Official History*, Vol. IV, *The AIF in France 1917*, p. 533.

116 V Corps, Intelligence Summary, Appendix No. 29, 16 May 1917, National Archives, London, WO95/748.

117 V Corps, Weekly Summary of Operations, 12–18 May 1917, National Archives, London, WO95/748.

118 Falls, *Military Operations France and Belgium 1917*, Vol 1, p. 478.

119 War Diary, General Staff, Headquarters 5th Australian Division, 18 May 1917, AWM4, item 1/50/15Part 1.

120 War Diary, 56th Infantry Battalion, 16 May 1917, AWM4, item 23/73/16.

121 Bean diary, 16 May 1917, Bean papers, AWM38, item 3DRL606/78/1.

122 General Staff, 5th Australian Division, Order G8/68, 16 May 1917, AWM26, item174/1.

123 War Diary General Staff, Headquarters 5th Australian Division, 16 May 1917, AWM4, item 1/50/15Part 1.

124 V Corps Operation Order No. 142, 16 May 1917, National Archives, London, WO95/748.

125 5th Australian Division, Intelligence Summary, 17–18 May 1917, AWM4, item 1/50/15Part 5.

126 War Diary General Staff, Headquarters 5th Australian Division, 18 May 1917, AWM4, item 1/50/15Part 1.

127 War Diary, 56th Infantry Battalion, 18 May 1917, AWM4, item 23/73/16.

128 'Wireless News', 17 May 1917, General Staff, Headquarters 5th Australian Division, AWM4, item 1/50/15Part 5.

129 Murdoch, 'The Australians at Bullecourt', miscellaneous items, Chalk collection.

130 Gough, *The Fifth Army*, p. 188.

Chapter 13

1   Captain W. Maile account of Bullecourt, Imperial War Museum, London, IWM7266/76/65/1.

2   M. Pemberton, 'How Bullecourt was Won', *The War Illustrated*, 9 June 1917.

3   Kendall, *Bullecourt 1917*, p. 316.

4   Andrews, *The ANZAC Illusion*, p. 100.

5   Field Marshal Sir Douglas Haig, dispatch, 4 January 1918, London *Gazette*, Issue No. 30462.

6   Neillands, *The Great War Generals on the Western Front*, p. 361.

7   Kendall, *Bullecourt 1917*, p. 316.

8   Falls, *History of the Great War. Military Operations. France and Belgium, 1917*, Vol. I, p. 479.

9   Bean, *Official History*, Vol. IV, *The AIF in France 1917*, p. 541.

10 Samuels, *Doctrine and Dogma*, pp. 64–68.

11 Pedersen, *The ANZACS*, pp. 218–19.

12 Diary of Lieutenant Ronald McGinnis, 12 May 1917, AWM PR00917.

13 Otto von Moser, *Die Wurttemberger im Weltkrieg*, Keech, *Battleground Europe, Bullecourt*, p. 116.

14 Secret Report, Lieutenant General N. Malcolm, SG 67/43, 17 May 1917, AWM45, item 35/24.

15 P. Pedersen, *Monash as Military Commander*, Melbourne University Press, Carlton, Victoria, 1985, particularly Chapter 10.

16 Falls, *History of the Great War. Military Operations. France and Belgium, 1917*, Vol. I, p. 481.

17 Maurice Wilder Neligan, 9th Battalion, Lessons from Bullecourt, 10 May 1917, AWM4, item 23/1/22.

18 Andrews, 'Bean and Bullecourt', pp. 46–47.

19 Ibid., p. 40, author's italics.

20 Sadler, *The Paladin*, p. 137.

21 Andrews, *The ANZAC Illusion*, pp. 163–64.

22 Gellibrand to Bean, 14 October 1933, D. Winter, *Making the Legend: the War Writings of C.E.W. Bean*, University of Queensland Press, St Lucia, 1992, p. 183.

23 Bean, notebooks, May 1918, Winter, *Making the Legend*, p. 166.

24 Bean, *Official History*, Vol. IV, *The AIF in France 1917*, p. 541fn.

BIBLIOGRAPHY

Australian War Memorial, Canberra

AWM 4 AIF Unit War Diaries, 1914-18 War

    13/13, 4th Australian Divisional Artillery, AIF

    23/1, 1st Infantry Brigade, AIF

    23/3, 3rd Infantry Brigade, AIF

    23/4, 4th Infantry Brigade, AIF

    23/6, 6th Infantry Brigade, AIF

    23/7, 7th Infantry Brigade, AIF

    23/12, 12th Infantry Brigade, AIF

    23/13, 13th Infantry Brigade, AIF

    23/14, 14th Infantry Brigade, AIF

    23/21, 4th Infantry Battalion, AIF

    23/32, 15th Infantry Battalion, AIF

    23/33, 16th Infantry Battalion, AIF

    23/39, 22nd Infantry Battalion, AIF

    23/40, 23rd Infantry Battalion, AIF

    23/41, 24th Infantry Battalion, AIF

    23/42, 25th Infantry Battalion, AIF

    23/43, 26th Infantry Battalion, AIF

    23/45, 28th Infantry Battalion, AIF

    23/63, 46th Infantry Battalion, AIF

    23/67, 50th Infantry Battalion, AIF

    23/71, 54th Infantry Battalion, AIF

    23/73, 56th Infantry Battalion, AIF

    1/29, 1st ANZAC Corps, General Staff Headquarters, AIF

    1/30 1st ANZAC Corps, Intelligence Headquarters, AIF

    1/42, 1st Australian Division, AIF

    1/44, 2nd Australian Division, AIF

    1/48, 4th Australian Division, AIF

    1/50. 5th Australian Division, AIF

AWM 26 Operation Files, 1914-18 War

    153 1st ANZAC Corps, AIF

    155 5th Australian Infantry Brigade, AIF

    163 2nd Australian Division, AIF

164 2nd Australian Division, AIF

167/1 2nd Australian Division, AIF

167/6 6th Australian Infantry Brigade, AIF

169 4th Australian Division, AIF

171 12th Australian Infantry Brigade, AIF

173 5th Australian Division, AIF

174 5th Australian Division, AIF

177 8th Australian Infantry Brigade, AIF

AWM 27 Records arranged according to AWM Library classification

312/1, 11th Battalion, AIF, Lagnicourt, April 1917

354/83, 1st Division, AIF, Bullecourt, May 1917

354/124, 2nd Division, AIF, Bullecourt, May 1917

AWM 30 Statements by Repatriated Prisoners of War

AWM 38 Papers of Charles Bean

3DRL 606

75 Diary March-April 1917

77 Diary April-May 1917

78 Diary May 1917

80 Diary May-June 1917

183 Notebook, 1917

247 Folder, 1917-31

260 Folder, 1916-30

3DRL 7953

30 Correspondence, 1929-39

E1

Estray Material

AWM 45 Copies of British War Diaries and Other Records, 1914-18 War

33/8 Documents relating to German Withdrawal, February-May 1917

33/9 Army Commanders Conferences, German Withdrawal, February-May 1917

35/24 Australian Divisions at Bullecourt

AWM 51 AWM Security Classified Records (series of operational documents and high level
Correspondence between GHQ and Army commanders)

52 Correspondence, German Withdrawal, Arras, Bullecourt, 1917

AWM 224 Unit Manuscript Histories

MSS 143, 14th Battalion, AIF

Private Records

PRO0030, Lieutenant W. Barlow, 58th Battalion, AIF.

Bibliography

PRO0140, Corporal Lancelot Davies, 45th Australian Field Artillery Battery, AIF

PRO0142, Lance Corporal Leonard Clyde Bryant, 12th Battalion, AIF

PRO0316, W.H. McKenzie, 3rd Battalion, AIF

PRO0349, Captain W.M. Braithwaite, 22nd Battalion, AIF

PRO0717, Gunner Lewis Wilson, 102nd Battery, AIF

PRO0884, Major General C.H. Brand, AIF

PRO0917, Lieutenant Ronald Alison McInnis, 14th Brigade, AIF

PRO1020, Private C.G. Etherton, AIF

PRO1059, Lieutenant Garnet Veness, AIF

PRO1974, Brigadier General Robert Smith, 5th Brigade, AIF

PRO3232, Sapper Ernest Greenhill, AIF

PR82/015, Corporal W. H. Anderson, 4th Battalion, AIF

PR82/153, Lieutenant General Sir Talbot Hobbs, 5th Division, AIF

PR83/018, Private E.G. King, 5th Brigade, AIF

PR83/044, Private Percival Luke, 2nd Division, AIF.

PR84/336, Chaplain J.J. Booth, 8th Battalion, AIF

PR87/007, Mervyn Napier Waller, AIF

PR88/009, Major General J.M. Durrant, AIF

PR88/067, Lieutenant H.H. Leslie, 3rd Battalion, AIF

PR88/174, Lieutenant W.F.J. Hamilton, 26th Battalion, AIF

PR00276, Lieutenant George Stanley McDowell, 13th Battalion, AIF

1DRL343, Lieutenant R.G. Henderson, 18th Battalion, AIF

1DRL423, Lieutenant C. E, McCardel, 7th Battalion, AIF

1DRL526, Private E.C. Munro, 5th Field Ambulance, AIF

1DRL554, Captain L.C. Roth, 2nd Pioneer Battalion, AIF

1DRL625, Senior Chaplain Joseph Cue, 2nd Division, AIF

2DRL155, Captain F.B. Stanton, 14th Battalion, AIF

2DRL417, Captain Reginald Edwin Sanders, 14th Battalion, AIF

2DRL513, Brigadier General Harold 'Pompey' Elliott, 15th Brigade, AIF

2DRL589, Lieutenant Ernest William Harris, 3rd Machine Gun Company, AIF

2DRL786, Lieutenant T.J. Richards, 1st Battalion, AIF

2DRL792, Lieutenant William Shirtley, 13th Battalion, AIF

2DRL811, Sergeant H. Preston, 9th Battalion AIF

3DRL1473, Major General Sir John Gellibrand, AIF.

3DRL2715, Captain N.A. Nicolson, 114th Battery, AIF

3DRl3376, Field Marshal Lord William Birdwood, AIF

MSS1365, J.H. Case, AIF, Lest We Forget, unpublished manuscript

J.S. Battye Library of West Australian History, Perth
MN 1460, Papers of Lieutenant General Sir J.J.T. Hobbs

Mitchell Library, Sydney
ML MSS885, Corporal C.C. Benson, AIF

Chalk Collection, University of Tasmania
Published Material

Toft, P., 'Playing a Man's Game', *The Queensland Digger*, bound copies

Brand, C.H., 'Who Broke the Hindenburg Line?' *Reveille*, bound copies

Wiltshire, A.R., 'Liaison with the British at Bullecourt', *Reveille*, bound copies

Letters, diaries, unpublished manuscripts etc

Appleton, Fred, Personal papers

Chalk, E., Experiences as a Prisoner-of-War in Germany, unpublished manuscript

Chataway, T., Death Rides Abroad, unpublished manuscript

Davies, L., A Narrative of POW Experiences, unpublished manuscript

Fraser, D., Memoirs, unpublished manuscript

Guppy, CQMS A.L., Diary

Stewart, Campbell Nelson, Diary

Taylor, T., Peregrinations of an Australian Prisoner-of-War, unpublished manuscript

Miscellaneous items

Murdoch, K., 'The Australians at Bullecourt'

Interviews

Bland Percy, np, nd, AIF

Colmer, Reginald, np, nd, 13th Battalion, AIF

Etchell, Ernest, Melbourne Victoria, 26 February, 18 December 1985, 15th Battalion, AIF

Fitzpatrick, William, np, nd, AIF

Fraser, Donald, np, 13, 14 December 1985, 13th Battalion, AIF

Ganson, Horatio, Perth WA, 22, 23, 26 March 1986; 27, 28 March 1988, 16th Battalion, AIF

Groutsch, Victor, np, nd, 13th Battalion, AIF

James, Clarence, np, nd, 13th Battalion, AIF

McGinty, Frank, np, nd, 13th Battalion, AIF

Marshall, Albert, Ulverstone Tasmania, 23, 27 December 1985, 15th Battalion, AIF

Massey, Frank, np, nd, 13th Battalion, AIF

Norris, John, Perth, Western Australia, nd, 16th Battalion, AIF

Pooley, Len, Perth, Western Australia, 31 March; 4 April 1988, 16th Battalion, AIF

Rumble, Horace, Perth, Western Australia, 29 March 1986, AIF

Sharp, Lewis, Brisbane Queensland, nd, 13th Battalion, AIF

Spencer, Edmund, np, nd, 16th Battalion, AIF

Tamblyn, Keith, Renmark, South Australia, 30 September 1989, 50th Battalion, AIF

Wheeler, Jim, np, 15 September, 20 October, 3 November 1985; 22 March 1986, AIF

Whittington, Richard, np, 24, 31 March 1986, AIF

Imperial War Museum, London

275 Private Walter King

1665 Private A.P. Burke

2165 Private T.E. Crook

7266 Captain W. Maile

Liddell Hart Centre for Military Archives, Kings College, London

STERN, Papers of Lieutenant Colonel Sir Albert Stern

SPRS, Papers of Major General Sir Edward Spears

CLIVE, Papers of Lieutenant General Sir (George) Sidney Clive

LH, Papers of Sir Basil Liddell Hart

National Archives (United Kingdom) London

WO 45 War Office, Cabinet Papers

/116 Office of the Commander-in-Chief

WO 95 British Expeditionary Force War Diaries

/91 Tank Corps Headquarters, War Diary, April 1917

/97 1st Tank Brigade, War Diary, April 1917

/248 Fifth Army, Orders, April–May 1917

/519 Fifth Army, Headquarters, War Diary, May 1917

/748 Fifth Army, Intelligence, War Diary, May 1917

/982 1st ANZAC Corps, General Staff, War Diary, April 1917

/993 1st ANZAC Corps Heavy Artillery, War Diary, April 1917

/1632 7th Division, War Diary, May 1917

/3068 62nd Division, War Diary, April 1917

/3081 2/5th Infantry Battalion, War Diary, April 1917

/3082 185th Infantry Brigade, War Diary, April 1917

/3314 17th Battalion, AIF, War Diary, May 1917

/3443 4th Australian Division, GS War Diary, April 1917

WO 157 War Office, Intelligence Summaries, First World War

/ 209 Fifth Army Intelligence, War Diary, April 1917

/565 1st ANZAC Intelligence, War Diary, April 1917

National Library of Scotland, Edinburgh
Diary and Papers of Field Marshal Sir Douglas Haig

London Gazette, Issue No. 30462.

Books, Edited Chapters and Journal Articles
Andrews, E.M., 'Bean and Bullecourt: weaknesses and strengths of the Official History in the First World War,' *Revue Internationale d'Histoire Militaire*, No. 72, 1990.

——, *The ANZAC Illusion: Anglo-Australian Relations during World War I*, Cambridge University Press, Cambridge, 1993.

Atkinson, C.T., *The Seventh Division 1914-1918*, John Murray, London, 1927.

Austin, R., *As Tough as Bags: the History of the 60th Battalion 1st AIF 1914-1919*, R.J. & S.P. Austin, McCrae, Victoria, 1992.

Barrett, M., *Casualty Figures: How Five Men Survived the First World War*, Verso, London, 2008.

Bean, C.E.W., *ANZAC to Amiens*, Penguin, Ringwood, Victoria, 1993 (1946).

——, *Official History of Australia in the War of 1914–1918*, Vol. III, *The AIF in France 1916*, University of Queensland Press, St Lucia, 1982 (1929).

——, *Official History of Australia in the War of 1914–1918*, Vol. IV, *The AIF in France 1917*, University of Queensland Press, St Lucia, 1982 (1933).

Beckett, I. and Corvi, S. (eds), *Haig's Generals*, Pen & Sword, Barnsley, 2009.

Bond, B. and Cage, N. (eds), *Haig: A Reappraisal 70 Years On*, Pen & Sword, Barnsley, 1999.

Bourne, J.M., 'British Generals in the First World War,' in Sheffield, G. (ed) *Leadership and Command: Anglo-American Military Experience Since 1861*, Brasseys, London, 2002.

Burness, P., *Bapaume and Bullecourt 1917: Australians on the Western Front*, DVA, Canberra, 2007.

Butler, A.G., *The Official History of the Australian Medical Services in the War of 1914-1918*, Vol. II, *The Western Front*, Australian War Memorial, Canberra, 1930.

Campbell, C., *Band of Brigands: the First Men in Tanks*, Harper Press, London, 2007.

Carlyon, L., *The Great War*, Pan McMillan, Sydney, 2006.

Clark, A., *The Donkeys*, Pimlico, London, 1991.

Coombes, D., *The Lionheart: A Life of Lieutenant General Sir Talbot Hobbs*, Australian Military History Publications, Loftus, New South Wales, 2007.

Cutlack, F. (ed), *War Letters of General Monash*, Angus & Robertson, Sydney, 1935.

Davies, W., *In the Footsteps of Private Lynch*, Vintage Books, North Sydney, 2008.

Deayton, C., *Battle Scarred: the 47th Battalion in the First World War*, Big Sky, Newport, NSW, 2011.

De Groot, G., *Douglas Haig 1861-1928*, Unwin Hyman, London, 1988.

——, *The First World War*, Palgrave, Houndmills, Hampshire, 2001.

Dennis, P. and J. Grey (eds), *1917— Tactics, Training and Technology*, Australian Military History Publications, Loftus, New South Wales, 2007.

Dixon, N., *On the Psychology of Military Incompetence*, Jonathon Cape, London, 1976.

Bibliography

Doneley, B., *Black Over Blue: the 25th Battalion, AIF at war 1915-1918*, University of Southern Queensland Press, Toowoomba, 1997.

Downing, W.H., *To The Last Ridge: the First World War memoirs of W.H. Downing*, Duffy and Snellgrove, Sydney, 1998.

Ellis, A.D., *The Story of the Fifth Australian Division*, Hodder and Stoughton, London, 1920.

Evans, M., *Somme 1914-18: Lessons in War*, The History Press, Stroud, Gloucestershire, 2010.

Falls, C., *History of the Great War. Military Operations. France and Belgium, 1917:* [Vol. I] *The German Retreat to the Hindenburg Line and the Battle of Arras*, MacMillan, London, 1940.

——, *History of the Great War. Military Operations. France and Belgium, 1917:* [Vol. I] *The German Retreat to the Hindenburg Line and the Battle of Arras. Appendices*, Macmillan, London, 1940.

Farndale, M., *History of the Royal Regiment of Artillery: Western Front 1914-18*, Royal Artillery Institute, London, 1987.

Farrah-Hockley, A., *Goughie: the Life of General Sir Hubert Gough CGB GCMG KCVO*, HarperCollins, London, 1975.

Gammage, B., *The Broken Years: Australian Soldiers in the Great War*, Penguin, Ringwood, Victoria, 1987 (1974).

Gough, General H., *The Fifth Army*, Hodder and Stoughton, London, 1931.

——, *Soldiering On: Being the Memoirs of General Sir Hubert Gough GCB, GCMG, KCVO*, Arthur Barker Ltd, London, 1954.

Green, F., *The Fortieth: a record of the 40th Battalion AIF*, Government Printer, Hobart, 1922.

Grey, J., *A Military History of Australia*, Cambridge University Press, Oakleigh, Vic, 1990.

Griffith, P., *Battle Tactics of the Western Front: the British Army's Art of Attack 1916-18*, Yale University Press, New Haven, CT, 1994.

Hart, P., *The Somme*, Weidenfeld & Nicolson, London, 2005.

Hatwell, J.E., *No Ordinary Determination: Percy Black and Harry Murray of the First AIF*, Fremantle Arts Centre Press, Fremantle, 2005.

Herwig, H., *The First World War: Germany and Austria 1914-1918*, Arnold, London, 1997.

Hopkins, R.N.L., *Australian Armour: a history of the Royal Australian Armoured Corps 1927-1972*, Australian War Memorial, Canberra, 1978.

Hunter, D., *My Corps Cavalry: a History of the 13th Light Horse Regiment AIF*, Slouch Hat Publications, McRae, Victoria, 1999.

James, L., *Imperial Warrior: the Life and Times of Field-Marshal Viscount Allenby 1861-1936*, Weidenfeld & Nicolson, London, 1993.

Joynt, W., *Breaking the Road for the Rest*, Hyland House, Melbourne, 1979.

Keech, G., *Battleground Europe, Bullecourt: Arras*, Leo Cooper, South Barnsley, 1999.

Kelly, D., *Just Soldiers: Ordinary Australians Doing Extraordinary Things in Time of War*, ANZAC Day Commemoration Committee, Aspley, Queensland, 2004.

Kendall, P., *Bullecourt 1917: the Breaching of the Hindenburg Line*, Spellmount, The Mill, Gloucestershire, 2010.

Kershaw, R., *Tank Men: the Human Story of Tanks at War*, Hodder & Stoughton, London, 2008.

King, J., *The Western Front Diaries: the ANZACs' Own Stories*, Simon & Schuster, Pymble, New South Wales, 2008.

Longmore, C., *The Old Sixteenth: Being a Record of the 16th Battalion AIF During the Great War 1914-1918*, History Committee of the 16th Battalion Association, Perth, 1929.

McMullin, R., *Pompey Elliott*, Scribe Publications, Carlton, Victoria, 2002.

Mitchell, G.D., *Backs to the Wall*, Angus & Robertson, Sydney, 1937.

Neiberg, M., *Fighting the Great War: a Global History*, Harvard University Press, Cambridge, Massachusetts, 2005.

Neillands, R., *The Great War Generals on the Western Front 1914-18*, Robinson Publishing, London, 1999.

Newton, L., *The Story of the Twelfth: a Record of the 12th Battalion AIF During the Great War 1914-18*, John Burridge Military Antiques, Swanbourne, WA, 2010.

Nicholls, J., *Cheerful Sacrifice: The Battle of Arras 1917*, Leo Cooper, London, 1990.

Nicholson, G.W.L., *Canadian Expeditionary Force 1914-1919: the Official History of the Canadian Expeditionary Force in the First World War*, Queen's Printer, Ottawa, 1962.

Orchard, A. (ed), *Diary of an ANZAC: the front line diaries and stories of Albert Arthur 'Bert' Orchard M.C.*, Arthur Orchard, Otago, New Zealand, 2009.

Passingham, I., *All the Kaiser's Men: the life and death of the German Army on the Western Front 1914-1918*, Sutton Publishing, Stroud, Gloucestershire, 2003.

Pedersen, P., *Monash as Military Commander*, Melbourne University Press, Carlton, Victoria, 1985.

——, *The ANZACS: Gallipoli to the Western Front*, Viking, Camberwell, Vic, 2007.

Pemberton, M., 'How Bullecourt Was Won', *The War Illustrated*, 9 June 1917.

Philpott, W., *Bloody Victory: the Sacrifice of the Somme*, Little Brown, London, 2009.

Polanski, I.L., *We Were The 46th: the History of the 46th Battalion in the Great War of 1914-18*, Puttees and Puggarees, Townsville, Queensland, 1999.

Prior, R. and Wilson, T., *The Somme*, Yale University Press, New Haven, CT, 2005.

Ramsay, R. (ed), *Hell, Hope and Heroes: a Life in the Field Ambulance in World War I*, Rosenberg Publishing, Dural, New South Wales, 2005.

Reid, W., *Architect of Victory: Douglas Haig*, Birlinn, Edinburgh, 2006.

Robbins, S., *British Generalship on the Western Front 1914-18: Defeat Into Victory*, Routledge, London, 2006.

Sadler, P., *The Paladin: a Life of Major General Sir John Gellibrand*, Oxford University Press, South Melbourne, 2000.

Samuels, M., *Doctrine and Dogma: German and British Infantry Tactics in the First World War*, Greenwood Press, Westport, CT, 1992.

Sheffield, G. and Bourne, J. (eds), *Douglas Haig War Diaries and Letters 1914-1918*, Weidenfeld & Nicolson, London, 2005.

Sheffield, G. and Todman, D. (eds), *Command and Control on the Western Front: the British Army's Experience 1914-1918*, Spellmount, Staplehurst, Kent, 2004.

Sheffield, G., 'Haig and the British Expeditionary Force in 1917' in Dennis, P. and Grey, J. (eds), *1917 – Tactics Training and Technology*, Australian Military History Publications, Loftus, New South Wales, 2007.

——, *Forgotten Victory, The First World War: Myths and Realities*, Headline, London, 2001.

—— (ed), *Leadership and Command: Anglo-American Military Experience Since 1861*, Brasseys, London, 2002.

Sheldon, J., 'Bullecourt Day of Disaster: the Assault Seen From the German Side of the Wire', *Wartime*, Issue 63, Winter 2013, pp. 14–18.

Simkins, P., 'Building Blocks: Aspects of Command and Control at Brigade Level in the BEF's Offensive Operations, 1916-1918' in G. Sheffield and D. Todman (eds), *Command and Control on the Western Front: the British Army's Experience 1914-1918*, Spellmount, Staplehurst, Kent, 2004.

——, 'Haig and the Army Commanders' in Bond, B. and Cave, N. (eds), *Haig a Reappraisal 70 Years On*, Pen & Sword, Barnsley, 1999.

Smith, L., *Between Mutiny and Obedience: the Case of the French Fifth Infantry Division During World War One*, Princeton University Press, Princeton, NJ, 1994.

Stevenson, R., *To Win The Battle: the 1st Australian Division in the Great War, 1914-1918*, Cambridge University Press, Port Melbourne, 2013.

Strachan, H., *The First World War: an Illustrated History*, Simon & Schuster, London, 2003.

Travers, R., *Diggers in France: Australian Soldiers on the Western Front*, ABC Books, Sydney, 2008.

Travers, T., 'From Surafend to Gough', *Journal of the Australian War Memorial*, Issue 27 October 1995.

Walker, J., *The Blood Tub: General Gough and the Battle of Bullecourt 1917*, Spellmount, Staplehurst, 1998.

Wanliss, N., *The History of the Fourteenth Battalion AIF: Being the Vicissitudes of an Australian Unit During the Great War*, Arrow Printery, Melbourne, 1929.

White, T., *Diggers Abroad: Jottings by a Digger Officer*, Angus & Robertson, Sydney, 1920.

——, *The Fighting Thirteenth: The History of the Thirteenth Battalion AIF*, Tyrells Ltd, Sydney, 1924.

Williams, J., *Byng of Vimy: General and Governor General*, Leo Cooper, London, 1992 (1983).

——, *ANZACS, the Media and the Great War*, UNSW Press, Sydney, 1999.

Winter, D., *Haig's Command: a Reassessment*, Viking, London, 1991.

——, *Making the Legend: the War Writings of C.E.W. Bean*, University of Queensland Press, St Lucia, 1992.

Wrench, M.C., *Campaigning with the Fighting Ninth: In and Out of the Line with the 9th Bn AIF*, Boolarong Publications, Brisbane, 1985.

Wyrall, E., *The History of the 62nd (West Riding) Division*, Vol. I, John Lane The Bodley Head, London, 1924.

INDEX

Index

Index

Index